Is creativity a
Yes or no trait
OR a spectrum?

(13) developed, namurecek.

The Philosophy of Creativity

The Philosophy of Creativity

New Essays

EDITED BY ELLIOT SAMUEL PAUL
and
SCOTT BARRY KAUFMAN

OXFORD
UNIVERSITY PRESS

OXFORD
UNIVERSITY PRESS

Oxford University Press is a department of the University of
Oxford. It furthers the University's objective of excellence in research,
scholarship, and education by publishing worldwide.

Oxford   New York

Auckland   Cape Town   Dar es Salaam   Hong Kong   Karachi
Kuala Lumpur   Madrid   Melbourne   Mexico City   Nairobi
New Delhi   Shanghai   Taipei   Toronto

With offices in

Argentina   Austria   Brazil   Chile   Czech Republic   France   Greece
Guatemala   Hungary   Italy   Japan   Poland   Portugal   Singapore
South Korea   Switzerland   Thailand   Turkey   Ukraine   Vietnam

Oxford is a registered trademark of Oxford University Press
in the UK and certain other countries.

Published in the United States of America by
Oxford University Press
198 Madison Avenue, New York, NY 10016

Library of Congress Cataloging-in-Publication Data
The philosophy of creativity: new essays/edited by Elliot Samuel Paul and Scott Barry Kaufman.
pages cm
ISBN 978–0–19–983696–3 (hardcover: alk. paper)   1. Creative ability   2. Creation (Literary,
artistic, etc.)   3. Philosophy.   I. Paul, Elliot Samuel, editor of compilation.
B105.C74P53 2014
128'.3—dc23
2013026833

3 5 7 9 8 6 4 2
Printed in the United States of America
on acid-free paper

To my mother, Eugenia Jeanilia Paul, with the deepest gratitude for her wisdom and creativity—and for teaching me to read.

—ESP

To two of my best friends, Elliot Samuel Paul and Benjamin Irvine, who have deepened my appreciation for the value of philosophy.

—SBK

CONTENTS

LIST OF CONTRIBUTORS

Roy F. Baumeister Francis Eppes Eminent Scholar and Professor of Psychology (Florida State University)

Simon Blackburn Distinguished Research Professor (University of North Carolina, Chapel Hill) and Professor of Philosophy (Cambridge University)

Margaret A. Boden Research Professor of Cognitive Science (University of Sussex)

Noël Carroll Distinguished Professor of Philosophy (Graduate Center of the City University of New York)

Peter Carruthers Professor of Philosophy (University of Maryland)

Gregory Currie Professor of Philosophy (University of York)

C. Nathan DeWall Associate Professor of Psychology (University of Kentucky)

Owen Flanagan James B. Duke Professor and Professor of Neurobiology (Duke University)

Berys Gaut Professor of Philosophy (University of St. Andrews)

Alan Hájek Professor of Philosophy (Australian National University)

Scott Barry Kaufman Adjunct Assistant Professor of Psychology (New York University)

Matthew Kieran Professor of Philosophy and the Arts (University of Leeds)

Bence Nanay BOF Research Professor (University of Antwerp) and Senior Research Associate (Cambridge University)

Elliot Samuel Paul Assistant Professor of Philosophy (Barnard College, Columbia University)

Christopher Peacocke Johnsonian Professor of Philosophy (Columbia University) and Wollheim Professor of Philosophy (University College London)

Elizabeth Picciuto Adjunct Professor of Philosophy (University of Maryland, Baltimore County)

Dean Keith Simonton Distinguished Professor of Psychology (University of California, Davis)

Brandon J. Schmeichel Professor of Psychology (Texas A&M University)

Dustin Stokes Assistant Professor of Philosophy (University of Utah)

PART ONE

INTRODUCTION

Introducing *The Philosophy of Creativity*

ELLIOT SAMUEL PAUL AND SCOTT BARRY KAUFMAN

There is little that shapes the human experience as profoundly and pervasively as creativity. Creativity drives progress in every human endeavor, from the arts to the sciences, business, and technology. We celebrate and honor people for their creativity, identifying eminent individuals, as well as entire cultures and societies, in terms of their creative achievements. Creativity is the vehicle of self-expression and part of what makes us who we are. One might therefore expect creativity to be a major topic in philosophy, especially since it raises such a wealth of interesting philosophical questions, as we will soon see. Curiously, it isn't.

To be sure, some of the greatest philosophers in history have been taken with the wonder of creativity.[1] To name just few examples: Plato has Socrates say, in certain dialogues, that when poets produce truly great poetry, they do it not through knowledge or mastery, but rather by being divinely "inspired"—literally, breathed into—by the Muses, in a state of possession that exhibits a kind of madness.[2] Aristotle, in contrast, characterized the work of the poet as a rational, goal-directed activity of making (*poeisis*), in which the poet employs various means (such as sympathetic characters and plots involving twists of fate) to achieve an end (of eliciting various emotions in the audience).[3] Kant conceived of artistic genius as an innate capacity to produce

---

[1] Or what we now call "creativity." According to some scholars, that abstract noun did not exist in European languages until the 19th century—but the phenomenon, and interest in it, certainly did. (See, e.g. Władysław Tatarkiewicz, *A History of Six Ideas: An Essay in Aesthetics* (The Hague, NL: Martinus Nijhoff, 1980), esp. chapter 8.) For other discussions of the complex history of terms and concepts associated with creativity, see, e.g., Darrin M. McMahon, *Divine Fury: A History of Genius*. Perseus Books Group, 2013; Murray, Penelope, ed. *Genius: The history of an idea*. New York: Basil Blackwell, 1989; Milton Charles Nahm, *Genius and Creativity: An Essay in the History of Ideas*. Harper & Row, 1965.

[2] Plato, *Ion* and *Phaedrus*, in *The Complete Works of Plato*, eds. John M. Cooper and D. S. Hutchinson (Hackett Publishing, 1997). Cf. Elizabeth Asmis, "Plato on Poetic Creativity," in *The Cambridge Companion to Plato*, ed. Richard Kraut (Cambridge University Press, 1992).

[3] Aristotle, *Poetics*, in *The Complete Works of Aristotle: The Revised Oxford Trans- lation*, vol. II, ed. Jonathan Barnes (Princeton University Press, 1984). For a sophisticated defense of the Aristotelian

works of "exemplary originality" through the free play of the imagination, a process which does not consist in following rules, can neither be learned nor taught, and is mysterious even to geniuses themselves.[4] Schopenhauer stressed that the greatest artists are distinguished not only by the technical skill they employ in the production of art, but also by the capacity to "lose themselves" in the experience of what is beautiful and sublime.[5] Nietzsche saw the greatest feats of creativity, exemplified in the tragic poetry of ancient Greece, as being born out of a rare cooperation between the "Dionysian" spirit of ecstatic intoxication, which imbues the work with vitality and passion, and the "Apollonian" spirit of sober restraint, which tempers chaos with order and form.[6] This is just the barest glimpse of what each of these philosophers had to say about creativity, and many other figures could be added to their number.

Nevertheless, while some of the topics explored by earlier thinkers have come to occupy a central place in philosophy today—such as freedom, justice, consciousness, and knowledge—creativity is not among them. Philosophy has seen some very important work on creativity in the last few decades,[7] but not nearly at the rate that we see for subjects of comparable range and importance. Indeed, "the philosophy of creativity" is still a neologism in most quarters—just as, for example, "the philosophy of action" and "the philosophy of music" were not too long ago.

In contrast, psychology has seen a definite surge of interest in creativity. In 1950, J. P. Guilford gave a presidential address at the American Psychological Association calling for research on the topic.[8] And the field soon took off with waves of research investigating the traits and dispositions of creative personalities; the cognitive and neurological mechanisms at play in creative thought; the motivational determinants of creative achievement; the interplay between individual and collective creativity; the range of institutional, educational, and environmental factors that enhance or inhibit creativity; and more. Today, the blossoming of this field can be seen in the flurry of popular writing reporting on its results[9]; an official division of the American

---

idea that the creative process is fundamentally rational, see Berys Gaut. "Creativity and Rationality," *The Journal of Aesthetics and Art Criticism* 70, no. 3 (2012): 259-270.

[4] Immanuel Kant, *Critique of the Power of Judgment*, eds. Eric Matthew and Paul Guyer (New York: Cambridge University Press, 2001), pp. 43–50

[5] Arthur Schopenhauer, *The World as Will and Representation*, vols. I and II, trans. E. F. J. Payne (New York: Dover, 1969). See vol. I, pp. 184–194, and vol. II, pp. 376–402.

[6] Friedrich Nietzsche, *The Birth of Tragedy and Other Writings*, eds. Raymond Geuss and Ronald Speirs (Cambridge University Press, 1999).

[7] Samples of this work can be found in these collections: Michael Krausz, Denis Dutton, and Karen Bardsley (eds.), *The Idea of Creativity* (Boston: Brill, 2009); Berys Gaut and Paisley Livingston (eds.), *The Creation of Art: New Essays in Philosophical Aesthetics* (New York: Cambridge University Press, 2003); Margaret Boden (ed.), *Dimensions of Creativity* (Cambridge, MA: MIT Press, 2004); and Margaret Boden, *Creativity and Art: Three Roads to Surprise* (New York: Oxford University Press, 2010).

[8] J. P. Guilford, "Creativity," in *American Psychologist* 5 (1950), pp. 444–454.

[9] See, e.g., the psychology section of *The Creativity Post*: http://www.creativitypost.com/psychology.

Psychological Association on the psychology of aesthetics, creativity, and the arts (Division 10); numerous academic conferences; multiple peer-reviewed journals[10]; several textbooks[11]; and a growing number of undergraduate and graduate courses all devoted to the psychology of creativity. According to one historical overview, creativity has been studied by nearly all of the most eminent psychologists of the 20th century, and "the field can only be described as explosive."[12]

The swell of interest in the science of creativity is an inspiring example for the philosophy of creativity, but more importantly, it offers a resource that philosophers should be mindful of as they pursue this effort. Unfortunately, philosophers writing on creativity have sometimes tended to ignore the scientific literature. In some cases, they have gone so far as to claim—after citing just a few studies—that creativity is by its very nature unpredictable and therefore beyond the scope of science.[13] Although the question of whether creativity is explicable is a philosophical question, it is not one that is impervious to empirical work. After all, anyone who declares from the armchair that something cannot be explained is liable to be refuted in the event that researchers do find ways to uncover explanations. The question of whether creativity can be explained empirically is itself, at least partly, an empirical question.

In fact, a number of issues arise at the nexus between philosophy and psychology and are handled best with contributions from both. This interdisciplinary approach is embraced by a new school of creativity researchers who are part of much broader trend toward dialogue and collaboration between scientifically-minded

---

[10] *Psychology of Aesthetics; Creativity and the Arts; Creativity Research Journal; Journal of Creative Behavior; International Journal of Creativity and Problem Solving.*

[11] J. C. Kaufman, *Creativity 101* (New York: Springer, 2009). K. Sawyer, *Explaining Creativity: The Science of Human Innovation*, 2nd ed. (New York: Oxford University Press, 2012). R. W. Weisberg, *Creativity: Understanding Innovation in Problem Solving, Science, Invention, and the Arts* (New York: Wiley, 2006).

[12] Robert S. Albert and Mark A. Runco, "A History of Research on Creativity," in *Handbook of Creativity*, ed. Robert J. Sternberg (Cambridge, UK: Cambridge University Press, 1999), pp. 16–31 at p. 17.

[13] Paul Feyerabend, "Creativity—A Dangerous Myth," in *Critical Inquiry* 13, no. 4 (1987), pp. 700–711; Carl R. Hausman, "Criteria of Creativity," in *The Concept of Creativity in Science and Art*, eds. Denis Dutton and Michael Krausz (Amsterdam: Springer, 1985), pp. 75–89. Carl R. Hausman, *A Discourse On Novelty and Creation* (Albany, NY: SUNY Press, 1975). I. C. Jarvie, "The Rationality of Creativity," in *The Concept of Creativity in Science and Art*, eds. Denis Dutton and Michael Krausz (Amsterdam: Springer, 1985), pp. 109–128. John Hospers, "Artistic Creativity," in *The Journal of Aesthetics and Art Criticism* 43, no. 3 (1985), pp. 243–255. For more optimistic perspectives, see Dustin Stokes, "Incubated Cognition and Creativity," in *Journal of Consciousness Studies* 14, no. 3 (2007), pp. 83–100. Larry Briskman, "Creative Product and Creative Process in Science and Art," in *Inquiry* 23, no. 1 (1980), pp. 83–106; and Maria Kronfeldner, "Creativity Naturalized," in *The Philosophical Quarterly* 59, no. 237 (2009), pp. 577–592.

philosophers and philosophically-minded scientists.[14] And the essays in this volume illustrate numerous ways in which the exchange can be fruitful, as philosophers draw on scientific research and scientific work is informed by philosophical perspectives. Below, we present a bird's-eye view of these chapters and the themes and issues they explore.[15]

The Concept of Creativity

Perhaps the most fundamental question for any study of creativity, philosophical or otherwise, is *What is creativity?* The term "creative" is used to describe three kinds of things: a *person*, a *process or activity*, or a *product*, whether it is an idea in someone's mind or an observable performance or artifact. There is an emerging consensus that a product must meet two conditions in order to be creative. It must be *new*, of course, but since novelty can be worthless (as in a meaningless string of letters), it must also be *of value*. (Researchers sometimes express this second condition by saying a product must be "useful," "appropriate," or "effective.")[16] This definition is anticipated, in a way, by Immanuel Kant, who viewed artistic genius as an ability to

---

[14] For reflections on different trends in this movement, see Jesse Prinz, "Empirical Philosophy and Experimental Philosophy," in *Experimental Philosophy*, eds. Joshua Knobe and Shaun Nichols (New York: Oxford University Press, 2008); and "Introduction: Philosophy and Cognitive Science" in *The Oxford Handbook of Philosophy of Cognitive Science*, eds. Eric Margolis, Richard Samuels, and Stephen P. Stich (New York: Oxford University Press, 2012), pp. 3–18. The chapters of this handbook explore connections between philosophy and cognitive science on various topics. The integration is especially pronounced in research on such topics as color perception (e.g., Alex Byrne and David R. Hilbert, "Color Realism and Color Science," in *Behavioral and Brain Sciences* 26, no. 1 [2003], pp. 3–21) and causal cognition (e.g., Tania Lombrozo, "Causal-Explanatory Pluralism: How intentions, functions, and mechanisms influence causal ascriptions," in *Cognitive Psychology* 61, no. 4 [2010], pp. 303–332).

[15] For another survey of the field, see Berys Gaut, "The Philosophy of Creativity," in *Philosophy Compass* 5, no. 12 (2010), pp. 1034–1046.

[16] Notable exceptions to this view include Dustin Stokes, "Minimally Creative Thought," in *Metaphilosophy* 42, no. 5 (2011), pp. 658–681; and Mark A. Runco, "Parsimonious Creativity and its Measurement," in *Measuring Creativity: Proceedings of European Council Meeting On Creativity and Innovation*, ed. E. Villalba (Luxembourg: Publications Office of the European Union, 2010), pp. 393–405, who argue that (at least for certain purposes) it's best to work with a more minimal conception of creativity that involves novelty but doesn't require value. There may also be *additional* requirements. It has been argued, for example, that in order for a product to count as creative, it must also be surprising (e.g. Margaret Boden, *The Creative Mind: Myths and Mechanisms*, 2nd edition [New York: Routledge, 2004], pp. 1–10, 40–53; Margaret Boden, "What Is Creativity?" in *Dimensions of Creativity*, ed. Margaret Boden [Cambridge, MA: MIT Press, 2004], pp. 75–117; David Novitz, "Creativity and Constraint," in *Australasian Journal of Philosophy* 77, no. 1 [1999], pp. 67–82), or produced intentionally, or in a non-mechanical fashion with flair (e.g. Berys Gaut, "Creativity and Skill," in *The Idea of Creativity*, eds. Michael Krausz, Denis Dutton, and Karen Bardsley [Boston: Brill, 2009], pp. 83–103).

produce works that are not only original—"since there can be original nonsense"—but also "exemplary."[17] *I agree*

In chapter 1, Bence Nanay argues that creativity is primarily an attribute not of products, but of mental processes. Some have suggested that what makes a mental process creative is the use of a certain kind of functional or computational mechanism, such as the recombination of old ideas or the transformation of one's conceptual space. Against this view, Nanay offers what he calls an experiential account of creativity. He contends that what is distinctive about the creative mental process is not any functional/computational mechanism, but the way in which it is experienced. In particular, the process yields an idea that the creator experiences as one she hadn't taken to be possible before.

Aesthetics and Philosophy of Art

One might suppose that if creativity has been understudied in philosophy at large, this couldn't be so when philosophers are focused on art in particular. Art was long thought to have a monopoly on human creativity[18]; it is still the paradigm of a creative domain, as "creative" is sometimes used more or less as a synonym for "artistic" and, at least in modern times, artists are disparaged when seen as derivative and praised for originality. But while the philosophy of art has been concerned with such issues as the definition, interpretation, and ontology of art, it has tended not to reflect on the artist *as a creator*, or the artist's labors *as a creative process*, or the work of art *as an expression of creativity*. Thus Gaut and Livingston observe that "[a]lthough the creation of art is a topic that should be a central one for aesthetics, it has been comparatively neglected in recent philosophical writing about art."[19]

Gregory Currie brings the issue of creativity to the fore in chapter 2, where he examines the popular idea that eminently creative works of literature provide insight into the workings of the human mind. Many advocates of this view write as if its truth were self-evident. Currie suggests that it is not, that indeed there is little evidence in its favor, and he considers how the claim might be tested. Recent experimental studies by Oatley and colleagues look promising in this regard, but Currie suggests that their results so far provide very weak evidence at best. In the

---

[17] Immanuel Kant, *Critique of the Power of Judgment*, eds. Eric Matthew and Paul Guyer (New York: Cambridge University Press, 2001), pp. 43–50. See also Paul Guyer, "Exemplary Originality: Genius, Universality, and Individuality," in *The Creation of Art*, eds. Berys Gaut and Paisley Livingston (New York: Cambridge University Press, 2003), pp. 116–137.

[18] Władysław Tatarkiewicz, *A History of Six Ideas: An Essay in Aesthetics* (The Hague, NL: Martinus Nijhoff, 1980), esp. chapter 8.

[19] Berys Gaut and Paisley Livingston, "Introduction: The Creation of Art: Issues and Perspectives," in *The Creation of Art: Issues and Perspectives*, eds. Berys Gaut and Paisley Livingston (New York: Cambridge University Press, 2003), p. 1.

absence of better evidence, Currie puts a new spin on the debate by emphasizing the *creativity* that goes into producing such great works of fiction. Are there aspects of literary creativity that should reliably lead to insights about the mind? He considers two such aspects—the institutions of literary production and the psychology of literary creativity—and suggests that in both cases, there are some grounds for thinking that literary creativity is not reliably connected with the production of insight.

Noël Carroll brings another dimension of creativity into view in chapter 3. Although he agrees that we should attend to the creative activities of the artist, he suggests that we should also acknowledge the contribution of the *audience*. For in order for the artist to accomplish the effects to which she aspires, Carroll argues, the audience must creatively cooperate with what the artist has initiated. He explores how audiences co-create artworks through the play of imagination. Rather than treating the imagination as if it were a single monolithic phenomenon, however, he identifies and analyzes several different imaginative activities that are engaged in response to a variety of artworks, such as reasoning counterfactually, filling-in unspecified content, constructing story-worlds around fictional objects, mentally simulating characters' experiences and points of view, and freely devising and playing with different meanings, interpretations, and unifying themes. By means of these activities, Carroll suggests, it is ultimately the audience's contribution that makes a work of art "work."

In chapter 4, Christopher Peacocke raises interesting questions for aesthetics that bear upon the study of creativity. While philosophers have long debated the question of what makes something a work of art, Peacocke asks: What makes a work an example of a particular *artistic style*? He suggests that answering this question is a precondition for research on creativity in musical composition. Just as researchers who study perception understand that we cannot account for how the content of a perception is computed without specifying what the content is, Peacocke suggests that we cannot explain how a composer creates in his particular style unless we identify what is distinctive about that musical style. Using the example of the Romantic style of music, Peacocke's approach draws on the perception of expressive action in combination with an account of what is involved in hearing emotion and other mental states in music. The account can link the phenomenology of musical perception with the ideas and ideals of the Romantic movement. He notes that by changing various parameters in the account, we can explain what is variously distinctive about impressionist music, expressionist music, and some neoclassical composing in the style of Stravinsky.

Ethics and Value Theory

One thing that makes creativity such a gripping topic is that we cannot fully understand ourselves without taking it into account. Creativity seems to be linked to our very identity; it is part of what makes us who we are both as human beings and individuals. With regard to the latter, each of us can ask, "What makes me who I am (as an individual)?" and we might wonder whether the answer has something to do with creativity.

According to an ancient and still influential view, the self (one's life) is some kind of dramatic or artistic performance. Exploring this idea in chapter 5, Owen Flanagan notes that there are metaphysical and logical questions about whether and how self-creation and self-constitution are possible. But he points out that there are also normative questions associated with the idea that life is a performance and the self is something that both emerges in and is constituted by that performance. Are there norms or standards that apply to self-constituting performances, and if so, what are they? Flanagan examines three contemporary psychopoetic conceptions of person—"day-by-day persons," "ironic persons," and "strong poetic persons"—in order to explore potential normative constraints on "performing oneself." Flanagan's provocative paper has implications for a number of diverse views in philosophy and psychology, from Jerome Bruner's narrative theory of "self-making stories" to David Velleman's paradox of self-constitution.

In chapter 6, Matthew Kieran asks what it is to be a creative person, and whether it involves a kind of virtue or excellence of character. He notes that there is a minimal sense according to which being creative means nothing more than having the ability to produce novel and worthwhile artifacts. Yet, he argues, there is a richer sense of the term that presupposes agential insight, mastery, and sensitivity to reasons in bringing about what is aimed at. A stroke victim who reliably produces beautiful patterns as a byproduct of his actions is not creative in the richer sense in which an artist who aims to produce them and could have done so differently is. Is creativity in this richer sense ever more than just a skill? In the light of suggestive empirical work, Kieran argues that motivation is central to exemplary creativity. Exemplary creativity, he argues, involves intrinsic motivation and is a virtue or excellence of character. We not only praise and admire individuals whose creative activity is born from a passion for what they do but, other things being equal, we expect them to be more reliably creative across different situations than those who are extrinsically motivated. This is consistent with the recognition that intrinsic motivation is not required to be creative and people's creative potentials differ. Creativity in people will flourish when intrinsic motivation is foregrounded, with the relevant values and socioeconomic structures lining up appropriately. It tends to wither when they do not (unless a person's creativity, like Van Gogh's, is exceptionally virtuous).

Philosophy of Mind and Cognitive Science

In chapter 7, Simon Blackburn briefly remarks on the history of the idea—voiced by Plato, echoed by philosophers and artists in the Romantic tradition, and still present in the popular imagination—that creativity involves something mystical or supernatural. Against this notion, Blackburn draws on findings of modern psychology

I think interchangeable

a semantics → ethics v. morals

to offer a tamer view. He argues that even the most extraordinary creative achievements are the result of ordinary cognitive processes.

In chapter 8, Dustin Stokes ventures to clarify exactly what the relation is between creativity and imagination. In his view, imagination is important for even the most minimally creative thought processes. This would be a pointless tautology if "imagination" just means (the capacity for) creativity. The key, then, is to identify what imagination is such that it is *not* the same thing as creativity but still essential for it nonetheless. As Stokes notes, few philosophers have thought through the distinction between imagination and creativity, and few psychologists have directly tested the difference between the two constructs. While grounding his paper in contemporary philosophy, Stokes also draws on cognitive and developmental psychology to identify the architectural features common to genius-level creativity, as well as more everyday forms of creativity. He starts by making a distinction between "truth-boundedness"—cognitive states that function to accurately represent the world—and "non truth-bound" states that do not function to accurately represent the world, but instead facilitate the manipulation of the information they represent. He argues that richly creative achievements in the arts and sciences, as well as more everyday breakthroughs, draw on cognitive manipulation processes. Stokes concludes that imagination serves the cognitive manipulation role and is typified by four features: It is non truth-bound, under immediate voluntary control, engages with affective and motivational systems, and drives inference and decision-making. Stokes's essay has implications for a number of philosophical problems relating to imagination and fiction, as well as psychological issues relating to the role of conscious, deliberate thought in creativity.

On the latter question, there is a tendency that appears in various forms throughout intellectual and artistic history to regard conscious thought as irrelevant or even inimical to creativity. In the classical story where creative inspiration comes to an artist from an external muse, the artist's consciousness is not the source, but rather the recipient, of creative work. The same is true when an insight is said to emerge from the unconscious mind, showing up in consciousness as a kind of pleasant surprise (Eureka!). There is also the popular perception that conscious thought *impedes* creativity; thus the familiar accounts of artists using drugs, alcohol, or other trance-inducing practices as a means of surrendering conscious control and giving free rein to the creative unconscious. *agree*

In chapter 9, however, psychologists Roy Baumeister, Brandon Schmeichel, and C. Nathan DeWall suggest that consciousness deserves more creative credit. They present evidence to support the notion that creativity requires an interactive collaboration of conscious and unconscious processes. In their view, creative impulses originate in the unconscious but require conscious processing to edit and integrate them into a creative product. They review psychological experiments showing that creativity declines sharply when consciousness is preoccupied (for example, improvising jazz guitar while counting backward by six, or drawing with colored pencils while listening closely to music). They conclude that the research contradicts the popular view in both psychology and philosophy that consciousness is irrelevant or an impediment to the creative process. Instead, they believe that the research fits well with recently emerging understandings of the special capabilities of conscious thought.

Earlier, when we discussed the potential connection between creativity and self-understanding, we were concerned with what makes each of us who we are as individuals. But we can also ask, more generally, what makes us who we are *as a species*, and there is a long tradition of Western thought that seeks to understand what makes us human in terms of what makes us *distinctively* human, and set apart from other animals in particular. Whatever we think of the existing proposals that highlight our allegedly unique possession of reason, language, and metacognition, creativity seems as good a candidate as any. The tricky question, of course, is how did creativity evolve in humans?

In chapter 10, Elizabeth Picciuto and Peter Carruthers provide an integrated evolutionary and developmental account of the emergence of distinctively human creative capacities. Their main thesis is that childhood pretend play (e.g., imagining battling spaceship invaders) is a uniquely human adaptation that functions in part to enhance adult forms of creativity. In support of their view, they draw on a wide literature spanning evolutionary, cognitive, and developmental psychology. They begin by reviewing evolutionary accounts of what makes humans unique, including our language, enhanced working memory, culture, and convergent and divergent thinking. They consider pretend play as a distinctively human ability, noting its universality, and showing that nearly all children, cross-culturally, engage in it. They review existing views of the functional roles of pretend play, including the facilitation of social schemata and theory of mind. Unconvinced by these accounts, they argue instead that pretend play facilitates creative thought—a process that involves both defocused attention and cognitive control. They review a number of common capacities of both pretend play and creativity, including generativity, supposing, bypassing the obvious, and selection of valuable but less obvious ideas. They conclude that childhood pretense paves the way for creativity in adulthood. This chapter is a fine example of how philosophers can contribute to our understanding of issues that are also pursued by scientists, in this case concerning the emergence of the capacities we have as human beings to pretend and create.

In our technologically driven age, it is not uncommon to think of what makes us human in contrast not only to other animals but also to machines, computers, and robots. Artificial intelligence is becoming ever more sophisticated, and some programs already display certain marks of creativity, appearing in major art galleries and garnering patents. These are machines whose products are both valuable and new. In addition to these two standard conditions, Margaret Boden maintains in chapter 11 that a creative product is one that is surprising as a result of the combination, exploration, or transformation involved in producing it. She gives examples of artificial intelligence systems that fit all of these criteria, and raises this intriguing question: Could a computer-based system ever "really" be creative? This leads to interesting philosophical issues about what constitutes "real" creativity. With some qualification, she argues that real creativity involves autonomy, intentionality, valuation, emotion, and consciousness. But as she points out, the problem is that each one of these elements is controversial in itself, even if we don't consider it in relation to creativity and/or artificial intelligence. Boden concludes that we will not be able to understand whether creativity and artificial intelligence is a contradiction in terms until we have clear and credible accounts of all these matters. Her chapter thus highlights the important role that philosophy can play in both psychology and artificial intelligence by further clarifying the constructs involved.

Philosophy of Science

Today, it's understood that creativity can be at work in virtually every human pursuit. In the past, however, thinking about creativity tended to be much less inclusive. Once again, Kant is a telling example. Having defined genius as the capacity to produce ideas that are both original and exemplary (i.e., "creative" in our terms), he asserted that genius could only be manifested in the fine arts.[20] Scientists were not geniuses because they follow the set procedures of the scientific method rather than giving free rein to their imaginations. Even Isaac Newton, whom Kant called the "great man of science," was not deemed to be a creative genius. Nor, for that matter, was Kant himself!

Despite the much broader scope that we now accord to creativity, there is still a remnant of the Kantian intuition in popular stereotypes of the creative person that are more strongly associated with the artist than with anyone else. In chapter 12, psychologist Dean Keith Simonton argues, in effect, that there is something right about this Kantian tendency, as he explores the question: How does creativity differ between domains? In so doing, he integrates two philosophical traditions. The first tradition, stemming back to Auguste Comte, is concerned with whether the sciences can be arrayed into a hierarchy. The second tradition, which includes Alexander Bain and William James, concerns whether creativity and discovery involve a process of blind-variation and selective-retention (BVSR). The key part for this issue is blind-variation. Roughly, a process is "blind" to the extent that the probability of it's generating a certain idea is not a function of that idea's utility or value. A completely random procedure would be an example, though not the only example, of a blind process. Drawing on psychological research, Simonton shows that a valid hierarchy can be formed based on objective criteria regarding creative ideas, products, and persons. In place of Kant's stark dichotomy between the sciences and the fine

[20] Kant (ibid.).

arts, Simonton's hierarchy comprises a wide range of disciplines in the sciences, the humanities, and the arts. Where a discipline falls in the hierarchy depends on the extent to which practitioners need to engage in BVSR processes in order to make contributions that are creative (new and useful). Domains at the top of the hierarchy (i.e., sciences) rely more on sighted variations, whereas domains at the bottom (i.e., arts) depend more on blind variations. Simonton also shows that a discipline's position in the hierarchy depends on the characteristics and developmental experiences of the creator. Simonton's chapter is an intriguing synthesis of issues in both psychology and philosophy regarding the classification of creativity across domains.

Philosophy of Education (and Education of Philosophy)

developed or educated

Our final two chapters deal with the teaching and learning of creativity. It is not unusual to find people who assume that creativity is an innate capacity that cannot be taught or learned. Edward Young and Immanuel Kant were part of a long tradition of thinkers who held such a view, and in arguing for it, they did us the service of exposing the kinds of assumptions that make it seem compelling. In chapter 13, Berys Gaut identifies two key arguments: The first is that learning requires imitation, which is incompatible with creativity; the second is that learning consists in following rules, which is incompatible with creativity. After criticizing these arguments, Gaut develops a positive case for the teachability of creativity, based on the teachability of the kinds of abilities and motivations that are involved in creativity. There is a sense in which Gaut's question can be settled empirically: We can show that creativity *can be* taught simply by pointing to cases where it *has been* taught. Gaut himself discusses such examples as they occur in mathematics and fiction writing, noting in particular how heuristics or rules of thumb are used in these domains. But while such cases may suffice to show that creativity can be taught, Gaut further enriches our understanding by explaining *how this is possible* despite the common misconceptions that may seem to rule it out. Having given a philosophical account of how creativity can be taught, he ends by applying his analysis to the teaching of creativity within philosophy itself.

With this last theme, Gaut has a kindred spirit in Alan Hájek, the author of our final chapter. In fact, between the two of them, we have an instance of "multiples" in creativity research, cases where people working independently arrive at the same discoveries at about the same time.[21] Although Gaut and Hájek were unaware of each other's essays before submitting them for this volume, they converged on an interesting proposal—that by using various heuristics, philosophers can enhance

---

[21] Dean Keith Simonton, *Creativity in Science: Chance, Logic, Genius, and Zeitgeist* (New York: Cambridge University Press, 2004).

their abilities to make valuable contributions to their field, including ideas that are distinctively creative.

As Hájek notes, it is said that anyone of average talent can become a strong chess player by learning and internalizing certain *chess heuristics*—"castle early," "avoid isolated pawns," and so on. Analogously, Hájek suggests, philosophy has a wealth of heuristics—*philosophical heuristics*—although they have not been nearly so well documented and studied. Sometimes these take the form of useful heuristics for generating counterexamples, such as "check extreme cases." Sometimes they suggest ways of generating new arguments out of old ones, as in "arguments involving possibility can often be recast as arguments involving time, or space." Sometimes they provide templates for positive arguments (e.g., ways of showing that something is possible). Hájek offers this chapter partly as an introduction to a larger project of identifying and evaluating philosophical heuristics, illustrating them with numerous examples from the philosophical literature. This work is a creative contribution to the philosophy of education. And it offers insights for the philosophy of creativity too, as it shows in fine detail how, contrary to a common assumption, creativity can be compatible with and even enhanced by the following of rules.

We are thankful for the input, encouragement, and support of Taylor Carmen, Kephun Chazotsang, Tamara Day, Hamutal Dotan, Michael Della Rocca, Milena Fisher, Eugene Ford, Nancy France, Don Garrett, Tamar Szabó Gendler, Lydia Goehr, Joy Hanson, Benjamin Irvine, Markus Labude, Karen Lewis, Rebecca McMillan, John Morrison, Emily Downing Muller, Fred Neuhouser, Eugenia Jeanilia Paul, Carol Rovane, Michael Taylor, and our wonderful colleagues and students at Barnard College, Columbia University, and New York University. Special thanks to Liz Boylan, former provost of Barnard College, for generously sponsoring the conference we held on the philosophy of creativity in preparation for this volume. We thank film director Tao Ruspoli for making a video of the event, artists Jill Sigman and Paul D. Miller (a.k.a. "D.J. Spooky") for their participation as special guests, and Geovanna Carrasco, Melissa Flores, and Emily Neil for their excellent work as research assistants. We thank Peter Ohlin, Lucy Randall, Stacey Victor, and their colleagues at Oxford University Press for helping us see this book to print. Last but not least, we are very grateful to our contributors for illustrating the value of interdisciplinary exchange, the intellectual richness of the philosophy of creativity, and the exciting possibilities for how this field can grow. We hope this volume helps to stimulate new insights, questions, and collaborations—new ways to illuminate (and perhaps even to exemplify) this magnificent facet of human life.

PART TWO

THE CONCEPT OF CREATIVITY

An Experiential Account of Creativity

BENCE NANAY

1. Introduction

The aim of this essay is to shift the focus of thinking about creativity from functional/computational accounts to experiential ones. My main claim is that what is distinctive about creative mental processes is not a functional/computational mechanism, be it the recombination of old ideas or the transformation of one's conceptual space, but the way in which this mental process is experienced.

I start with a clarification of what the *explanandum* of theories of creativity is supposed to be, and contrast creativity, an attribute of mental processes, with originality, an attribute of the products of mental processes, and limit the discussion to creativity (section 2). After arguing that creativity is not a functional/computational natural kind, I sketch an experiential account of creativity and argue that it comes closer to capturing what is distinctive about creativity than functional/computational accounts (sections 3 and 4). Finally, I argue that although experiential and functional/computational accounts of creativity are not exclusive of one another, the experiential account I propose has significant explanatory advantage over any functional/computational accounts in explaining some of the most important and historically most influential features of creativity (section 5).

2. Creativity and Originality

First, we have to be clear about what we are trying to explicate. What is creativity an attribute of? We often talk about the creativity of acts, (mental) processes, ideas, people, and artifacts. The connection among these notions is intricate. A further important question is which one of these notions, if any, is explanatorily basic. If we manage to explain, say, what constitutes the creativity of ideas, will all the other notions of creativity come for free? Can we reduce the creativity of artifacts to the creativity of the acts that produce it? These are thorny questions, and there is no clear agreement in the literature as to how to proceed (see Briskman 1980).

Many philosophers of art seem to assume that the explanatorily basic notion is that of the creativity of artifacts (e.g., Carroll 2003, Halper 1989, but see Gaut 2003, p. 151 for a dissenting view), and that all the other notions of creativity can be defined with the help of this notion. This also seems to be the strategy of those who argue about whether computers are capable of producing something creative (Finke 1995, Schooler and Melcher 1995). Psychologists, in contrast, seem to think that it is the creativity of ideas or of mental processes that we should first and foremost explain (Boden 1990, 1994a, Simonton 1999, Harré 1981, Polanyi 1981; see Taylor 1988 for a good summary).

The difference between these two explanatory projects has been made explicit by a number of distinctions in the creativity literature. Fred D'Agostino, for example, distinguishes between subjective and inter-subjective creativity (D'Agostino 1986, pp. 174–175). Inter-subjective creativity is an attribute of artifacts, whereas subjective creativity is an attribute of acts (D'Agostino 1986, p. 175). Similarly, Ian Jarvie talks about subjective and objective creativity: Subjective creativity, as he puts it, is "a property of persons or their minds," whereas objective creativity is "a property...of created works" (Jarvie 1981, p. 117). Francis Sparshott also talks about two different uses of the term "creative process." It can refer to "all processes, whatever they may be, whose outcome meets some appropriate criteria for originality" (Sparshott 1981, p. 61). In other words, it can refer to a process that leads to objective/inter-subjective creativity. And it can refer to a specific process that is itself held to be (subjectively) creative.

Yet another distinction comes from Margaret Boden, who distinguishes between psychological or P-creativity and historical or H-creativity (Boden 1992, pp. 32–25, Boden 1994a, p. 77). An idea is H-creative if and only if it is P-creative and it has never occurred before.[1]

It follows from Boden's definition that P-creativity is necessary but not sufficient for H-creativity. If Bill has a P-creative idea on Monday, and Jane, independently of Bill, has the same P-creative idea a day after, then Jane's idea is not H-creative, because Bill has already had the idea. But Jane's idea is just as P-creative as Bill's. I think that it is important to draw a distinction between something like subjective/P-creativity

---

[1] It is important to note the difference between the subjective versus objective/inter-subjective distinction and Boden's contrast between P-creativity and H-creativity. While subjective and objective/inter-subjective creativity are attributes of different entities, mental processes and products respectively, Boden's distinction is supposed to be neutral about the entity to which we are attributing creativity. A product can be P-creative if it is created by a P-creative thought process. And a mental process or idea can be H-creative if it has not occurred before. On the differences between Boden's and D'Agostino's distinctions, see also Novitz 1999, p. 70, fn. 6.

on the one hand and objective/H-creativity on the other. But I will draw this distinction somewhat differently.

Creativity and originality are often used as synonyms. I think this is a mistake. Being original is usually contrasted with being derivative: An idea, for example, is original if it is not derived from someone else's idea. A scientific discovery or an artwork is original if it is not derivative.[2] Whether a scientific discovery or artwork is original tells us relatively little about the nature of the mental process of the person who produced it. Originality is a property of normally publicly observable entities (not just of physical objects, but also of styles, utterances, and behaviors).

Creativity, in contrast, is not normally publicly observable. It is a feature of our mental processes. Being creative is not contrasted with being derivative, but rather with being mechanical (see, e.g., Gaut 2003, pp. 150–151).[3] Whether a mental process is creative tells us nothing about what kind of entities (if any) it produces. Some artists' and scientists' mental processes are creative, but so are the mental processes of many who are solving crosswords or killing time at the airport with a difficult sudoku puzzle.

There is no simple connection between these two notions. Creativity is neither necessary nor sufficient for originality.[4] A scientific discovery can be original and still be the product of a purely mechanical mental process that is, by definition, not creative. Goodyear's often quoted discovery of vulcanization is a possible example (but see section 4 for further wrinkles). Here is another example: If I write a letter of recommendation for a student of mine and I emphasize how original her work is, I do not thereby also comment on her mental processes. I don't know much about the functional/computational structure of her mental processes, but I know their outcome: that her research is very original.

Conversely, the products of a creative mental process can be completely banal and derivative. Suppose that I am in high school and I am trying to solve a math problem. There is a mechanical way to solve it: I have to try out all the natural numbers between 1 and 999 one by one, and one of them will be the solution. But there is also a creative way of solving it. If I manage to solve it in the creative manner, my mental process is creative (it is not mechanical), but the product of this mental

---

[2] In the case of artworks, originality is also used in another sense: We talk about an original Vermeer as opposed to a fake Vermeer. I am interested in the concept of originality per se (and not of being an original Vermeer, Cézanne, etc).

[3] This is not meant as a necessary and sufficient condition. If a mental process is creative, it is not mechanical. But a mental process can be non-mechanical and still fail to count as creative.

[4] It is often claimed that novelty is a necessary feature of creativity. My contrast between creativity and originality is supposed to highlight that we may not need to accept this as an unquestionable assumption. As we shall see, the concept of novelty will be very important for characterizing creativity, but in a less straightforward way than it is normally assumed. In contrast, novelty is clearly necessary for originality.

process is not original at all; all the other students in my class solve the very same math problem, after all.

The distinction between creativity and originality could be thought to be a version of Ian Jarvie's distinction between subjective and objective creativity (Jarvie 1981, p. 117). But it is important to note that while Jarvie claims that subjective creativity is "of no interest" in and of itself (Jarvie 1981, p. 117), the aim of this chapter is to understand the difference between (subjectively) creative and noncreative mental processes.

Creativity, as I understand it, is quite a banal phenomenon. It is not to be restricted to the mental processes of a select few: Beethoven, Einstein, and the like. It is something much more common and much less mysterious. Originality, in contrast, is much rarer. There are many fascinating questions about originality that are usually discussed as questions about creativity (Carroll 2003, Olsen 2003), but I will leave all of them aside.

I am interested in creativity and aim to give an account of the difference between mental processes that are creative and mental processes that are not. It is important that the account I propose is an account of creative *mental processes*.[5] As we have seen, the concept of creativity is also often used as an attribute of other entities, such as persons. I do not claim that these uses of the concept will reduce to the creativity of mental processes (whether a person is creative, for example, probably depends on whether she creates something original and not just on whether her mental processes tend to be creative).

The explanation of the creativity of mental processes does not presuppose an account of originality, as whether a creative act has occurred before should not matter when describing how the mind works when one is thinking creatively. One could, however, argue that an account of creativity should give at least some guidance about the attribution of originality. I return to this question briefly in the last section.

3. The Experiential Account of Creativity

We have an *explanandum*: how the mind works when one is thinking creatively. To put it differently, the account I give here aims to explain the difference between creative and noncreative mental processes.

There are two influential strategies for talking about the difference between creative and noncreative mental processes. The first one is to claim that this difference is a functional/computational difference. Say, creative mental processes are those

---

[5] I will also talk about "creative ideas," by which I merely mean "ideas that are the outcome of creative mental processes." These, as we have seen, are very different from "original ideas."

types of mental processes that transform one's conceptual space, whereas noncreative ones are the ones that don't (Boden 1992, 1994a—note that this is Boden's account of radical creativity, not of creativity per se). Or, only creative mental processes are bisociative ones (Koestler 1975, 1981). It is important to note that these explanations analyze a mental process type (creative mental processes) in terms of a functional/computational process type (bisociation, transformation of conceptual space, recombination, etc.), and this functional/computational process is supposed to be the one that is causally responsible for the emergence of the creative idea/thought.

The second strategy is to deny that any psychological explanation is possible. There are many versions of this claim (Feyerabend 1987, Jarvie 1981, Hausman 1981, 1984, Hospers 1985; and see Stokes 2007 for criticism). It has been argued that the difference between creativity and noncreative mental processes cannot be explained at all, perhaps because creativity is a one-off phenomenon in which every token of creativity is different, and therefore no mental process type that would be responsible for creativity can be identified (Jarvie 1981). Another old and influential version of this view is that, although we can explain this difference, it is not a psychological difference: It is not our doing, but rather a result of either divine intervention (as Plato claims) or our mysterious subconscious (as Freud claims). In other words, even if there is an explanation for creativity (say, divine intervention), this explanation is not a psychological one.

An advantage of, and the main inspiration for, the functional/computational account is that it would make it possible to build creative computers. If creativity is a matter of instantiating a functional/computational process, then computers can do it as much as we can. And, conversely, some of the claims about the impossibility of a psychological account of creativity are fueled by doubts about computer creativity. I return to the question of computer creativity at the end of the chapter.

My claim is that the difference between creative and noncreative mental processes is a psychological difference, but not a functional/computational one. In short, this difference is constituted by the way our mental processes are experienced.

Thus, I am making a negative and a positive claim. The negative claim is that what is distinctive about creativity is unlikely to be a functional/computational process type. I argue for this claim in this section. My positive claim is that what is distinctive about creativity is still something psychological: the way our mental processes are experienced. I explicate this claim in the next section.

As I have said, what is distinctive about creativity is unlikely to be a functional/computational process type (Weisberg 1993 argues for a version of this claim). A simple fact to notice is that no functional/computational account proposed so far is without counterexamples. I will mention only two of the most influential of such theories. Margaret Boden's account, according to which (radical) creativity implies the transformation of our conceptual space, has been criticized for not covering some clear cases of creativity (Novitz 1999, pp. 68–70). Novitz's account, according to which creativity implies the mere recombination of old ideas (Novitz 1999), also fails to cover all cases of creativity (including the ones Boden was focusing on; see Boden 2001).[6]

I would favor a more pluralist approach. Creative mental processes can be implemented by more than one functional/computational process. Boden is (partly) right: Her functional/computational explanation for the emergence of creative ideas is the right kind of explanation in some cases of creative mental processes. But Novitz is also (partly) right: His account gives us the right way to explain some *other* cases of creative mental processes. But neither account is satisfactory as a general account of the difference between creative and noncreative mental processes.

Not all mental phenomena form a functional/computational natural kind. Being in love, for example, is unlikely to be a functional/computational natural kind. The same goes for being happy. My claim is that creativity is also unlikely to be a functional/computational natural kind (see also Bundy 1994, who makes a similar point). What is in common between the diverse mental processes that we take to be creative is not something functional/computational, but rather something experiential.

It is important that I am not denying that for each token creative process, there is (or at least can be) a functional/computational process that implements it. What I deny is that there is anything interesting in common between these token processes (besides the fact that they all implement creative processes). Creativity comes in different (functional/computational) forms: Some creative mental processes involve a mere recombination of old ideas. Some others involve a radical transformation of our conceptual space.[7] The functional/computational level is not the right level of analysis if we want to explain the difference between creative and noncreative processes.

Does this make creativity miraculous? Definitely not. Each token creative mental process is realized by a token series of neuron firings. So are token instances of happiness or being in love. The point is that what is in common between these neural events is unlikely to be captured in functional/computational terms. But, as in the case of happiness and being in love, it can be captured in experiential terms.

A functional/computational and an experiential explanation of a creative mental process are not exclusive of one another. I believe that a full explanation of creative mental processes would require both. But I do think that the experiential description captures something about creative processes in general, whereas the functional/computational description does not. And I also think that many important

[6] One could, of course, defend one of these functional/computational accounts against the alleged counterexamples (Novitz 2003 attempted to do exactly this).

[7] Note that Boden would probably agree with these last two claims (see also Stokes 2007, 2008 for a similar pluralist approach). She would nonetheless pitch her account of creativity on the functional/computational level.

features of creativity can be explained by the experiential explanations (rather than the functional/computational ones).

In the next section, I outline an experiential account of creativity. In section 5, I argue that much of what needs to be explained about creativity can be explained by these experiential characteristics rather than functional/computational ones.

4. The Experience of Creativity

Margaret Boden argues that an idea is (radically) creative only if "the person in whose mind it arises could not (in the relevant sense of 'could not') have had it before" (Boden 1994a, p. 76). There are notable difficulties spelling out just what is meant by the "relevant sense of 'could not'" and there may be some questions about whether this account could apply in the case of all instances of (radical) creativity (see Novitz 1999, pp. 68–70). But Boden is almost right; we could rephrase her definition in the following manner: An idea is creative only if the person in whose mind it arises *experiences it* as something she *has* not taken to be possible before.

So the claim is that it is a necessary feature for creative mental processes that their outcome is experienced in a certain way: that we experience the outcome of the mental process as something we have not taken to be possible before. But what does it mean to say that an experience represents a mental process as something the agent has not taken to be possible before? My answer is simple. At time t, the agent considered a number of possibilities. Later, at time t*, she comes up with a possibility that she experiences as something that is different from all the possibilities she considered at time t.

So far, I only set a necessary condition for creative mental processes. My claim was that the most we can say about the necessary condition for creative mental processes is that they are experienced as something we have not taken to be possible before. It is important that this is a necessary and not a sufficient condition. But if we add a couple of further conditions, we may be in the position to give (or at least come close to giving) a necessary and sufficient condition for creativity.

It is important to note that the aim of this chapter is not to give a necessary and sufficient condition for creativity—creativity is an ordinary language concept, and it may be difficult to capture its meaning with strict necessary and sufficient conditions. Rather, the aim is to argue that the right kind of analysis for the concept of creativity should be about our experiences (rather than functional/computational mechanisms). I will suggest a rudimentary way of thinking about the necessary and sufficient conditions of creativity, but the main point is not to defend the details of this account, but to argue that this is the *kind* of account we should be looking for if we want to understand creativity.

Further, even if we find a necessary and sufficient condition for creativity in terms of our experiences, this does not mean that these experiences are causally responsible for the emergence of our creative ideas. It is neural processes that are causally responsible for the emergence of our creative ideas. My claim is that in order to capture some of the crucial features of creative processes, we need to analyze them on the experiential level.

I can experience an idea as something I have not taken to be possible before, but I may be wrong: Experiences can misrepresent. I may experience an idea as creative, as something I have not taken to be possible before, but perhaps I had taken it to be possible before, but I forgot that I had. Thus, if we want to give a (close to) sufficient condition for creativity, we need to add that the experience that defines creative mental processes needs to be veridical: The idea in question really needs to be something I have not taken to be possible before—it is not enough if I experience it as such.[8]

There is a further wrinkle: We also need to rule out cases where we do experience something as a possibility we haven't considered before, and this experience is even veridical, but we know for sure that we didn't come up with this novel possibility ourselves: We know that our friend Bill told us about it. Hearing Bill suggesting a thus-far unexplored possibility is clearly not a creative mental process. We need to add to our characterization of creativity that the novel idea is not only experienced as something we have not considered to be possible before, but it is not experienced as something we have learned from someone else. We may experience it as something we come up with or as something that "just popped into my head," but we don't experience it as something we know to come from someone else. So a rudimentary necessary and sufficient condition for creativity is that a mental process is creative if and only if it produces an idea that is veridically experienced as something we have not thought to be possible before and as something we have not learned from someone else.

There may be some further conditions we need to add in order to arrive at a genuine necessary and sufficient condition for creativity. But again, the aim of this chapter is not to argue for some strict necessary and sufficient condition for creativity, but rather to argue that the right level for the characterization of (and for giving a necessary and sufficient condition for) creativity is not the functional/computational level but the experiential one.

Finally, an important example for a noncreative mental process is Charles Goodyear's discovery of vulcanization. He apparently dropped random substances, including cream cheese, into liquid rubber until he stumbled upon sulfur, which is capable of vulcanizing rubber. Was this a creative act? Most theories of creativity

---

[8] Note that this additional veridicality condition does not make my account fall back to Boden's original necessary condition for (radical) creativity. My condition is that I experience an idea as something I have not taken to be possible before. If we add the veridicality condition, what we get is that this idea is something I have not taken to be possible before. Contrast this with Boden's condition, according to which this idea is something I could not have had before. The scope of the modal operator is very different in these two claims.

assume that it was not (Novitz 1999, p. 75, Novitz 2003, p. 190, n. 14, Gaut 2003, p. 171, n. 6). I am not so sure. I think that we do not have enough information to judge. If Goodyear put all the substances found in his lab, including cream cheese and sulfur, in a row and then dropped them into liquid rubber one after another to see what happens, then I agree with the mainstream view that his act was not creative; it was a prime example of a mechanical act. When he discovered that putting sulfur in liquid rubber led to its vulcanization, it is unlikely that he experienced this idea as something he had not thought to be possible before. He clearly had, as sulfur was one of the substances he was going to try out.

But perhaps he did not proceed this way. Maybe he tried all kinds of substances, including cream cheese, without success and then got stuck. He thought that he had tried everything that had a chance of succeeding in vulcanizing rubber. If cream cheese didn't do it, what could? And then maybe it occurred to him that he hadn't thought of sulfur. Thus, in this scenario, he experienced the idea of trying sulfur as something that he had not thought of as a possibility before. Thus, according to my definition, he was indeed creative.

My conclusion is that we don't have enough information to judge whether Goodyear was creative. It is also important to note that what is interesting about Goodyear's example has little to do with creativity. What is striking about it is that he was incredibly lucky. He did not know that to achieve vulcanization, rubber, a macromolecular chain (polyisoprene), needs to be mixed with a substance that is capable of forming cross-links between two points of the chain, which would make it form a dense and flexible network. If he had known that, the range of possibilities would have been quite limited, and finding sulfur in it would have been quite easy. The point is that he had no idea. So, for him, the range of possibilities for what to use for vulcanizing was vast—it included cream cheese, after all. Yet he did manage to find one of the very few substances that can be used for vulcanization. That he picked out sulfur from a very vast set in itself says nothing about whether his thought process was creative. In order to determine that, we would need to know more about how the idea of mixing sulfur with rubber came about in his mind.

A couple of potential objections need to be addressed. First, it may seem that my account over-intellectualizes the creative process. Small children are capable of creativity, but it may seem dubious that they even possess concepts like possibility. Note, however, that experiencing an idea as something I have not taken to be possible before does not necessarily imply possessing the concept of possibility. Take the following analogy: Animals can experience objects as edible, that is, as things that are possible to eat, but that does not imply that they master the concept of possibility (see Rodriguez-Pereyra 2002, p. 94, Peacocke 2001, Nanay 2011).

Second, take Billy, the not particularly bright student. He is trying to solve a math problem, but it's just not happening. All the other students have already solved the same problem, but Billy is still trying. Finally, he manages to solve it; further, he does experience the solution as something he had not taken to be possible before.

So, in my account, he was creative. But was he? It seems though that few would call him creative. Note that Billy's case is a counterexample to the sufficiency claim, not the necessary one I defended here. This case does not show that my account is incorrect, only that there may be additional conditions to add to the necessary condition I have been defending, besides the ones I have already added above, in order to get a necessary and sufficient condition for creativity. But, again, I am not sure that finding a necessary and sufficient condition for a concept like creativity is possible or in fact desirable. My aim is to show that if we were to look for one, we should be looking at experiential factors.

Finally, I want to be clear what the experiential account of creativity does not give us: It will never give us a recipe for how to be creative. My claim is that the difference between creative and noncreative mental processes is that the former (but not the latter) are experienced in a certain distinctive way. This claim is utterly useless if we want to find out how to be creative. Functional/computational accounts, in contrast, would give at least some hint as to what thought processes to follow if one wants to be creative—transforming one's conceptual space or recombining one's existing thoughts, for example. But I am not sure that the inability to give a recipe for creativity is a disadvantage of my account. An important and historically influential question about creativity is whether it can be learned or taught (see Boden 2001 and Lucas 2001 for summaries, and Gaut, this volume). But this is a different question from whether there is a recipe for being creative. If we accept the experiential account, we need to say that there is no privileged recipe for creativity; there are many ways of being creative. It may be taught and learned, but there is no royal road to creativity.

5. Functional/Computational Accounts versus Experiential Accounts of Creativity

In this section, I argue that experiential accounts have greater power in explaining some of the crucial features of creativity than the functional/computational ones. Given that the most salient features of creativity are experiential ones, this claim should not come as a surprise.

I consider three features of creativity that are taken to be important enough so that any comprehensive theory of creativity must be able to explain (or at least say something about) them. There may, of course, be many more such features. But I focus on these three as they have played an important role in shaping our conception of creativity.

(1) A theory of creativity needs to be able to explain why it is tempting to intuitively think that creativity is something that happens to us, rather than something we do.

(2) A theory of creativity needs to be able to explain why the experience of appreciating other people's creativity can seem similar to the experience of one's own creativity.

(3) A theory of creativity needs to be able to explain why we take creative actions to be genuine actions and not mere bodily movements.

I will take these three features in turn and elaborate on them.

5.1. Explaining why it is tempting to think that creativity is something that happens to us, rather than something we do

This is maybe the most important intuition we seem to have about creative mental processes. It is unlikely to be correct (I see no reason why creativity would, by definition, be something that happens to us), but that is not important for our purposes: The question is why it is tempting to hold this intuition, which smoothly leads to attributing creativity to divine intervention or to the subconscious and also fuels claims about the impossibility of explaining creativity. Because this intuition that creativity seems to happen to us feeds into claims that creativity is inexplicable or that it is to be attributed to something supernatural or subconscious, it is important to differentiate the intuition to be explained here and the stronger claims to which this intuition can give rise.

The intuition we are trying to capture is neatly summarized by Mozart in a letter that is probably a forgery by Friedrich Rochlitz (see Solomon 1991, Stafford 1991, pp. 243–248). But as it had a significant influence on the perception of Mozart's creativity and creativity in general, even if it is not original, it is worth analyzing:

> When I am... entirely alone, and of good cheer—say, traveling in a carriage or walking after a good meal, or during the night when I cannot sleep; it is often on such occasions that my ideas flow best and most abundantly. Whence and how they come, I know not, nor can I force them. (Quoted in Holmes 1845, p. 255.)

Or, as Dostoyevsky put it, "a creative work comes suddenly, as a complete whole, finished and ready, out of the soul of a poet" (quoted in Miller 1981, p. 49). The same intuition seems to be very powerful not just in the case of artistic creativity, but also in scientific creativity. As the mathematician Morris Kline writes:

> The creative act owes little to logic or reason. In their accounts of the circumstances under which big ideas occurred to them, mathematicians have often mentioned that the inspiration had no relation to the work they happened to be doing. Sometimes it came while they were traveling, shaving or thinking about other matters. The creative process cannot be summoned at will.
>
> (Kline 1955, p. 82; see also Schooler and Melcher 1995)

It is important to note that the intuition captured in these quotes is that it *seems to us* that creativity is not something we do but something that happens to us (see, e.g., Poincaré 1952). This is a claim about our experience of our own creativity, and it needs to be distinguished from a stronger claim about the nature of creativity itself: that creativity is in fact not something we do but something that happens to us. If we accept this stronger claim, then we can definitely explain why it seems to us that creativity is not something we do but something that happens to us, but this is not the only way to do so. And accepting the stronger claim moves us closer to attributing creativity either to divine intervention or mysterious unconscious forces. The main point is that an account of creativity needs to be able to explain why it *seems to us* that creativity is not something we do but something that happens to us, even if we deny that it in fact is.

Functional/computational accounts have no simple explanation for this intuition: If creativity is a functional/computational mental phenomenon, why would it seem to us that it is not something we do but something that happens to us? Functional/computational accounts do not exclude the possibility of such explanation, but they do not provide one.

The experiential account explains this intuition in a straightforward manner. If creative mental processes are accompanied by the experience of an idea as something we have not considered to be possible before, then it sounds plausible that the emergence of this idea that we have not considered to be possible before strikes us as something that happens to us and not as something we ourselves do; after all, a second ago we didn't think it possible and now here it is.

5.2. Explaining why the experience of appreciating other people's creativity can seem similar to the experience of one's own creativity

A notable feature of creativity is that our experience of our own creativity can seem similar to the appreciation of someone else's creativity. If I am struggling to solve a math problem and I finally come up with a creative solution, what I experience is similar to my experience if, after much thinking, I give up and my friend gives me the creative solution. In both cases, what I experience is something like an "aha" experience (see Koestler 1975, 1981), something like the experience of a solution I have not thought of before, regardless of whether it comes from me or from my friend.

I take this to be a relatively uncontroversial feature of creativity, but it needs to be distinguished from some influential and much stronger claims in the vicinity. It has been argued that appreciating someone else's creativity and being creative share some important features, in both the cases of scientific and artistic creativity. As the mathematician Jacob Bronowski writes:

> The appreciation of... any creative acts is an act of re-creation. When the man makes *you* see the unexpected likeness, makes you feel it to be natural

that this likeness exists, then you in your modest way are re-creating. You re-live the act of creation and that is why (in my view) appreciation is… an activity of the same kind as the original act of creation, even though it is lower in intensity.

(Bronowski 1985, p. 248; see also Carroll, this volume)

And here is a famous quote by Marcel Duchamp, who undoubtedly knew a thing or two about creativity:

The creative act is not performed by the artist alone; the spectator brings the work in contact with the external world by deciphering and interpreting its inner qualification and thus adds his contribution to the creative act.

(Duchamp 1957/1959, p. 78)

Both Bronowski and Duchamp seem to suggest something stronger than what I take to be a notable feature of creativity. Bronowski assumes that genuine creativity and the appreciation of someone else's creativity are processes "of the same kind." Duchamp goes even further and seems to argue that the appreciation of someone else's creativity is necessary for fully finishing the creative act. These are both stronger claims than the one I am making.

All I claim is that the *experience* of one's own creativity is similar to the *experience* of appreciating someone else's creativity. This experiential similarity can be explained if we assume, with Bronowski, that the actual processes are also similar, but this is not the only way of doing so. Our experience of our own creativity may, after all, be similar to our experience of appreciating someone else's creativity, but the underlying processes may be very different. In short, an account of creativity must be able to explain why the *experience* of one's own creativity is similar to the *experience* of appreciating someone else's creativity.

Functional/computational accounts face some difficulties explaining the apparent similarity between the experience of one's own creativity and the appreciation of other people's creativity. For the functional/computational account, if a mental process has certain functional/computational features, it is creative. If it doesn't, it isn't. Appreciating other people's creativity is not being creative. Hence, our mental processes when appreciating other people's creativity do not have the functional/computational features that make creative mental processes creative. But then, how can we explain the similarity between our experience of our own creativity and our appreciation of other people's creativity?

A functional/computational account of creativity can, of course, be supplemented with an account of why the experience of appreciating other people's creativity is similar to the experience the functional/computational process in question gives rise to. But such explanation is not provided by the functional/computational accounts themselves.

According to the experiential account, what is distinctive about creative mental processes is that they are accompanied by the experience of creativity: the experience of something that we have not thought to be possible before. And when we are appreciating someone else's creativity, our mental processes are likely to be accompanied by an experience that is similar to this: I experience the idea that I just learned from Bill as something I have not thought to be possible before. In the "creativity" case, I came up with the idea; in the "appreciating creativity" case, someone else did. But in both cases, I experience this idea as something I have not thought to be possible before. The experiential account of creativity can explain both the similarities and the differences between being creative and appreciating other people's creativity.

5.1. Explaining why we take creative actions to be genuine actions and not mere bodily movements

Creative actions are genuine actions. They are not mere bodily movements. Hence, our theory of action, whatever it is, must apply to them. More precisely, we must be able to find whatever makes actions genuine actions, that is, more than mere bodily movements, in both the cases of noncreative and creative actions.

But what makes actions more than just bodily movements? Whatever it is that makes the difference, it must be a mental state that triggers, or perhaps accompanies, the bodily movements. If bodily movements are triggered (or accompanied) by mental states of a certain kind, they qualify as actions. If they are not, they are mere bodily movements.

The big question is, of course, what mental states are the ones that trigger (or accompany) actions. The most popular candidate is intention. The standard way of explaining the difference between actions and mere bodily movements is that while the former are triggered by intentions, the latter are not. If I form an intention to raise my arm and this intention triggers the bodily movement of my arm going up, this makes it a genuine action. If the same bodily movement is triggered by a neuroscientist fiddling with my brain and not by my intention, then it is a mere bodily movement.

Without getting lost in the jungle of philosophy of action, it is important to point out that, at least on the face of it, this account does not fit well with creative actions. In the case of creative actions, we do not have an intention to do Q before we do Q. If we did, the action would not be creative: It would be the mechanical execution of an already existing plan. As John Hospers says:

> In creative activity you do not know when you begin the activity what the end-product will be like.
>
> (Hospers 1985, p. 244; see also Hintz 1958, Tomas 1964, 1993)

There are (at least) three ways of modifying the account of what makes creative actions genuine actions in a way that would avoid this problem. The first one is to point out that the content of the intention that triggers an action is normally more coarse-grained than the content of the action, in both creative and noncreative actions. It has been argued that before we begin performing an action, we have only a vague idea about how to perform it (Bach 1978, Brand 1984, Pacherie 2001). When I am scratching an itch, for example, I only have a very vague idea as to where exactly I should scratch, but as I am performing the action and receiving a lot of feedback about my scratching attempts, my representation of the whereabouts of the itch becomes more and more determinate. One could argue that creative actions work the same way. When I am trying to solve a math problem, I do have some kind of intention with some vague content (of solving the problem). I do not have any more specific intention about how to do so. So the asymmetry between the less determinate content of intention and the more determinate content of action is there in both the cases of noncreative and creative actions.

A problem with this solution is that it only works in the case of one kind of creative action, one that Berys Gaut calls "active creativity," when we are "consciously trying out different approaches" in order to perform a creative action (Gaut 2003, p. 156). If our action is "passively creative," then there is no intention that would trigger our creative action, as in these cases, we are not trying to do anything, the creative idea or action just "pops into our head" (Gaut 2003, p. 156). Actions that are passively creative do not seem to be preceded and triggered by any intention, regardless of the individuation of the content of this intention.

The second way of accounting for the fact that creative actions are genuine actions is to abandon the idea that the mental state that makes actions genuine actions is a *prior* intention. There are many ways of doing this. John Searle famously differentiated prior intentions from "intentions in action" (Searle 1983, pp. 83–98; see esp. p. 93). The former is not necessary for actions, whereas the latter is. In the case of some actions, the bodily movement is not caused by any prior intention, but it is caused by an intention in action. When I suddenly stand up from my desk and start pacing around my office, I have not formed a prior intention to do so. Nevertheless it is a genuine action as my bodily movement is caused by my intention in action. Perhaps we should analyze creative actions in a similar way.

Even if we have doubts about Searle's concept of intention in action (see O'Shaughnessy 1991), this way of explaining what makes creative actions genuine actions may be the most fruitful one. The idea is that the mental state that makes actions genuine actions and not mere bodily movement is not a state that occurs before the action is performed, but something that occurs at the same time as when the action is performed (Nanay 2013). Some possible candidates besides Searle's intention in action include Kent Bach's "executive representation" (Bach 1978), Myles Brand's "immediate intentions" (Brand 1984), John Perry's "belief-how" (Israel et al. 1993), and dynamic action schemas (Jeannerod 1997; see also the discussion of Carruthers 2002, 2008 in the context of creativity).

The third way of resisting the problem in hand would be to deny that actions can be genuinely creative. Maybe creative actions are ones that are triggered by creative intentions. There is nothing creative about the execution of the intention. The locus of creativity is not the action itself, but the mental process that precedes the action. Some support for this way out could be drawn from Mozart's famous (but, again, probably misattributed) self-report:

> The committing to paper is done quickly enough, for everything is already finished; and it rarely differs on paper from what it was in my imagination.
> (letter to Baron von P... quoted in Holmes 1845, p. 255)

What is creative here is not the "committing to paper," but the idea that was there in his mind before he started committing it to paper. Although some creative actions are undoubtedly just boring executions of genuinely creative ideas, it does not seem likely that this is true of all creative actions. Notable examples include the creativity of improvisations in jazz and modern dance. When one is improvising, one does not seem to have a creative idea that then one executes (Berliner 1994, Johnson-Laird 1991; see Carruthers 2008, pp. 257–258 for an excellent summary). The creativity seems to be part of the improvised act itself.

To sum up, there seems to be some tension between the very idea of creative actions and the mainstream accounts of what makes actions genuine actions and not mere bodily movements. This tension may be interesting to explore from a philosophy-of-action point of view and examine in what ways the possibility of genuinely creative actions puts constraints on our theories of action. I will not do this here, as this essay is about creativity and not the theory of action. What I am interested in is which accounts of creativity make the least dubious assumptions about philosophy of action.

What can the functional/computational accounts of creativity say about this problem? The mental state that is supposed to make an action a genuine action and not a mere bodily movement is supposed to be a functional/computational state, like intention (whether it is prior intention or intention in action). It is individuated in functional terms. Thus, the functional/computational accounts of creativity hold that what makes creative actions creative is a functional/computational state and what makes creative actions genuine actions is also a functional/computational state.

In other words, according to the functional/computational account, whatever mental state makes our creative actions creative must also make our creative actions genuine actions. There is no contradiction here: A certain kind of mental state makes our actions genuine actions, and some of these mental states also make our creative actions creative. But although there is nothing contradictory here, this picture does put constraints on what a functional/computational account can say about the set of mental (functional/computational) states that make creative actions genuine actions and not mere bodily movements, as at least some of these mental states must also be able to make our creative actions creative. And the most plausible candidates for mental states that make our creative actions genuine actions are very different from the most plausible candidates for mental states that make our creative actions creative.

According to the experiential account, what is distinctive about creative actions is the way they are experienced, so there are no such constraints. What makes actions genuine actions is something functional/computational, but what is distinctive about creative actions is something experiential: The two questions are orthogonal to one another.

In other words, if we accept the experiential account of creativity, no assumptions are made about the grand question in philosophy of action about what makes actions genuine actions. If we accept a functional/computational account, the moves to explain how creative actions qualify as genuine actions will be limited.

6. Conclusion: Creativity and Originality Reconsidered

It is time to return to the relation between creativity and originality. I argued in section 2 that creativity and originality are very different concepts: Creativity is a feature of our mental processes, whereas originality is a feature of the product of our mental processes. I also argued that creativity is neither necessary nor sufficient for originality. The account I outlined here is an account of creativity. But what, if anything, does it tell us about originality?

Suppose that I am fully informed about the state of my field: I know exactly what ideas have been explored. And now I have a creative idea. According to my account, this idea is experienced as something I have not thought to be possible before, and this experience is veridical. But if I am really fully informed about my field, then it follows that this idea is not only creative; it is also original. Thus, my account of creativity helps us to understand how the concepts of creativity and originality are related to one another (and why they are so easily confused).

Finally, my account gives a straightforward answer to the question of whether computers can be creative: They can, but only if they can have experiences. However, I suspect that what really worries computer and cognitive scientists is not whether some processes of a computer could be considered to be creative, but whether computers are capable of producing something genuinely original. The experiential account of creativity would definitely not exclude this possibility.[9]

⁹ This work was supported by the EU FP7 CIG grant PCIG09-GA-2011-293818 and the FWO Odysseus grant G.0020.12N. I am grateful for comments from Peter Carruthers, Jordan Dodd, Laura Franklin-Hall, Scott Barry Kaufman, Matthew Kieran, Philip Kitcher, Dustin Stokes, Achille Varzi, and especially Elliot Samuel Paul.

References

Bach, Kent. 1978. A representational theory of action. *Philosophical Studies* 34: pp. 361–379.

Berliner, Paul F. 1994. *Thinking in jazz. The infinite art of improvisation.* Chicago: University of Chicago Press.

Boden, Margaret. 1992. *The creative mind: Myths and mechanisms.* Reading, PA: Cardinal.

Boden, Margaret. 1994a. What is creativity? Margaret Boden, ed., *Dimensions of Creativity.* Cambridge, MA: MIT Press, pp. 75–118.

Boden, Margaret. 1994b. Author's response. *Behavioral and Brain Sciences* 17: pp. 558–567.

Boden, Margaret. 2001 Creativity and knowledge. Anna Craft, Bob Jeffrey, and Mike Leibling, eds., *Creativity in Education.* London: Continuum, pp. 95–102.

Brand, Myles. 1984. *Intending and Acting.* Cambridge, MA: MIT Press.

Briskman, L. 1980. Creative product and creative process in science and art. *Inquiry* 23: pp. 83–106.

Bronowski, Jacob. 1985. The creative process. *Leonardo* 18: pp. 245–248.

Bundy, Alan. 1994. What is the difference between real creativity and mere novelty? *Behavioral and Brain Sciences* 17: pp. 533–534.

Carroll, Noël. 2003. Art, creativity, and tradition. Berys Gaut and Paisley Livingstone, eds., *The creation of art. New essays in philosophical aesthetics.* Cambridge, UK: Cambridge University Press, pp. 208–234.

Carruthers, Peter. 2002. Human creativity: Its cognitive basis, its evolution and its connections with childhood pretence. *British Journal for the Philosophy of Science* 53: pp. 225–249.

Carruthers, Peter. 2008. The creative action theory of creativity. Peter Carruthers, Stephen Laurence, and Stephen Stich, eds., *The Innate Mind, Vol. 3.* Oxford, UK: Oxford University Press, pp. 254–272.

D'Agostino, F. 1986. *Chomsky's system of ideas.* Oxford, UK: Clarendon.

Duchamp, Marcel. 1957. The creative act. Transcript of Duchamp's talk at the Session on the Creative Act, Convention of the American Federation of Arts, Houston, TX, April 1957, in Robert Lebel. 1959. *Marcel Duchamp.* New York: Grove Press, pp. 77–78.

Feyerabend, Paul. 1987. Creativity—A dangerous myth. *Critical Inquiry* 13: pp. 700–711.

Finke, R. 1995. Creative realism. Steven M. Smith, Thomas B. Ward, and Ronald A. Finke, eds., *The creative cognition approach.* Cambridge, MA: MIT Press, pp. 301–326.

Gaut, Berys. 2003. Creativity and imagination. Berys Gaut and Paisley Livingstone, eds., *The creation of art. New essays in philosophical aesthetics.* Cambridge, UK: Cambridge University Press, pp. 148–173.

Halper, Edward. 1989. Is creativity good? *British Journal of Aesthetics* 29: pp. 47–56.

Harré, R. 1981. Creativity in science. D. Dutton and M. Krausz, eds., *The concept of creativity in science and art.* Dordrecht, NL: Martinus Nijhoff, pp. 19–46.

Hausman, Carl R. 1981. Criteria of creativity. D. Dutton and M. Krausz, eds., *The concept of creativity in science and art.* Dordrecht, NL: Martinus Nijhoff, pp. 75–90.

Hausman, Carl R. 1984. *A discourse on novelty and creation.* Albany, NY: SUNY Press.

Hintz, Howard W. 1958. Causation, will, and creativity. *Journal of Philosophy* 55: pp. 514–520.

Holmes, Edward. 1845. *Life of Mozart.* London: J. M. Dent and Sons.

Hospers, John. 1985. Artistic creativity. *Journal of Aesthetics and Art Criticism* 43: pp. 243–255.

Israel, David, John Perry, and Syun Tutiya. 1993. Executions, Motivations and Accomplishments. *Philosophical Review* 102: pp. 515–540.

Jarvie, I. C. 1981. The rationality of creativity. D. Dutton and M. Krausz, eds., *The concept of creativity in science and art.* Dordrecht, NL: Martinus Nijhoff, pp. 109–128.

Jeannerod, M. 1997. *The Cognitive Neuroscience of Action.* Oxford, UK: Blackwell.

Johnson-Laird, P. N. 1991. Jazz improvisation: A theory at the computational level. P. Howell, R. West, and I. Cross, eds., *Representing musical structure.* London: Academic Press, pp. 291–266.

Kline, Morris. 1955. Projective geometry. *Scientific American* 192 (1): pp. 80–85.

Koestler, A. 1975. *The act of creation.* London: Picador.

Koestler, A. 1981. The three domains of creativity. D. Dutton and M. Krausz, eds., *The concept of creativity in science and art*. Dordrecht, NL: Martinus Nijhoff, pp. 1–18.

Lucas, Bill. 2001. Creative teaching, teaching creativity and creative learning. Anna Craft, Bob Jeffrey, and Mike Leibling, eds., *Creativity in Education*. London: Continuum, pp. 35–44.

Miller, R. F. 1981. *Dostoyevsky and the Idiot: Author, narrator and reader*. Cambridge, MA: Harvard University Press.

Nanay, Bence. 2011. Do we sense modalities with our sense modalities? *Ratio* 24: 299–310.

Nanay, Bence. 2013. *Between Perception and Action*. Oxford: Oxford University Press.

Novitz, David. 2003. Explanations of creativity. Berys Gaut and Paisley Livingstone, eds., *The creation of art. New essays in philosophical aesthetics*. Cambridge, UK: Cambridge University Press, pp. 174–191.

Olsen, Stein Haugom. 2003. Culture, convention, and creativity. Berys Gaut and Paisley Livingstone, eds., *The creation of art. New essays in philosophical aesthetics*. Cambridge, UK: Cambridge University Press, pp. 192–207.

O'Shaughnessy, Brian. 1991. Searle's Theory of Action. E. Lepore and R. Van Gulick, eds., *John Searle and His Critics*. Cambridge, MA: Blackwell, pp. 271–287.

Pacherie, Elisabeth. 2001. The content of intentions. *Mind & Language* 15: pp. 400–432.

Peacocke, Christopher. 2001. Does Perception have a Nonconceptual Content? *Journal of Philosophy* 98: pp. 239–264.

Poincaré, Henri. 1952. Mathematical creation. Brewster Ghiselin, ed., *The creative process: A Symposium*. New York: Mentor, pp. 34–42.

Polanyi, M. 1981. The creative imagination. D. Dutton and M. Krausz, eds., *The concept of creativity in science and art*. Dordrecht, NL: Martinus Nijhoff, pp. 91–108.

Rodriguez-Pereyra, Gonzalo. 2002. *Resemblance Nominalism*. Oxford, UK: Clarendon.

Schooler, Jonathan W., and Joseph Melcher. 1995. The ineffability of insight. Steven M. Smith, Thomas B. Ward, and Ronald A. Finke, eds., *The creative cognition approach*. Cambridge, MA: MIT Press, pp. 97–134.

Searle, John. 1983. *Intentionality*. Cambridge, UK: Cambridge University Press.

Simonton, Dean Keith. 1999. *Origins of genius: Darwinian perspectives on creativity*. New York: Oxford University Press.

Sparshott, P. E. 1981. Every horse has a mouth: A personal poetics. D. Dutton and M. Krausz, eds., *The concept of creativity in science and art*. Dordrecht, NL: Martinus Nijhoff, pp. 47–74.

Stafford, William. 1991. *Mozart's death. A corrective survey of the legends*. London: Macmillan.

Stokes, Dustin. 2007. Incubated Cognition and Creativity. *Journal of Consciousness Studies* 14: pp. 83–100.

Stokes, Dustin. 2008. A metaphysics of creativity. K. Stock and K. Thomson Jones, eds., *New Waves in Aesthetics*. London: Palgrave Macmillan.

Taylor, C. W. 1988. Various approaches to and definitions of creativity. R. J. Sternberg, ed., *The nature of creativity: Contemporary psychological perspectives*. Cambridge, UK: Cambridge University Press, pp. 99–121.

Tomas, Vincent. 1958. Creativity in art. *Philosophical Review* 67: pp. 1–15.

Tomas, Vincent. 1964. *Creativity in the arts*. Englewood Cliffs, NJ: Prentice-Hall.

Weisberg, R. 1993. *Creativity: Beyond the myth of genius*. New York: Freeman.

PART THREE

AESTHETICS AND PHILOSOPHY OF ART

2

Creativity and the Insight That Literature Brings

GREGORY CURRIE

"You have never dipped into the Greek pastoral poets, nor sampled the Elizabethan sonneteers?"

"No never. You will think me lamentably crude: my experience of life has been drawn from life itself."

—Max Beerbohm, *Zuleika Dobson, ch. VII*

1. Literature, Creativity, and the Positive View

Calling an artist, poet, or novelist creative is faint praise, like saying a mathematician is numerate. We expect artists to be creative and wonder only *how* creative they are. It is difficult, on the other hand, to hear a judge or an accountant described as creative without sensing an implication of dishonest practice or incompetence. Their jobs are sober ones of getting at the truth, and creativity is easily thought of as getting in the way. What about scientists? Here, attributions of creativity need carry no suspicion of irony, though our next question will be whether their creativity is balanced by respect for evidence and argument. A reflective assessment may focus as well on institutional constraints; the characters of individual scientists matter less if the reward system of science punishes cheats and rewards those who show that the latest speculations don't stand up to experimental tests. But whether we emphasize personal or institutional factors or both, creativity is regarded as something that needs to be constrained if it's to be directed at truth. A creative person—or an uncreative one for that matter—may stumble on truth by accident, but one does not reliably arrive at truth *merely* by being creative.

What constrains literary creativity in the direction of truth? There is no obligation to answer this unless we think that truth is a goal of literature: truth by implication, suggestion, or illustration more often than by direct assertion, though instances of assertion can be found. And many people have thought that truth is a goal, or at least a desirable outcome, of literature. Like Emerson, who said that Shakespeare was inconceivably wise, they think that works of great literature are the expressions of exceptional minds, sensitive to aspects of the real world, especially the human world of decision, thought, and feeling. The deconstructive turn has muted advocacy of this view in literary circles. But it remains a serious option in philosophy, with Martha Nussbaum's defense strikingly reminiscent of Lionel Trilling half a century earlier. Robert Pippin and Jenefer Robinson take the philosophical arm of the tradition into the new century.[1] And the current literary world is not uniformly hostile: Jonathan Bate notes a "welcome return...to the Johnsonian idea that [Shakespeare's] plays illuminate not just the mentalities of their own age but rather...'the human condition'"; David Bevington tells us that *Hamlet* is "able to speak to persons and societies of all nations and all ages who have turned to it for a better understanding of themselves."[2]

Call that the *Positive View*: the view that literature may give us insight into the mind and its workings. As well as those who argue in its favor, I include among advocates of the Positive View those who assume it in their philosophical practices. Wollheim, for example, is notable for his reliance on fictional characters to illustrate theses in moral psychology, appealing to incidents in Proust, and content on one occasion to treat Bertrand Russell and Anna Karenina as evidential equals.[3]

Friends of the Positive View typically combine an interest in the psychological and the moral dimensions of narrative, holding that the best kinds of fictions are those that focus on the ways characters negotiate or fail to negotiate moral problems and dilemmas. Works such as Conrad's *Lord Jim* are valued partly for their vivid portrayal of the stresses that produce moral failure, and such failure's psychological aftermath. They focus on representations of decision and action, and the roles of emotion, weakness of will, ignorance, self-deception, and partiality of view in complicating (and occasionally enabling) such action. There is also a special emphasis in the novel on the long-term effects of choices and their tendency to produce unpredicted and ironic consequences for the agents concerned, something that Shakespeare, so much more confined, gives us in a great rush at the end of *Measure for Measure*.

Part of my aim here is to muster some opposition to the Positive View by thinking about the psychology of creativity, but a couple of points will help orient the project. First, I don't claim that the Positive View, or at any rate some reasonable version of it, is false; surely there is important truth in it somewhere. But too often, its advocates are allowed a free pass, perhaps because of their civilized tone, and in consequence are given to vague and inflated formulations—some of which I illustrate

---

[1] Nussbaum 1994, Trilling 1951, Pippin (2001), Robinson 2005, esp. ch. 6.
[2] Bate 2011, Bevington 2011, p. vii.
[3] See, e.g., Wollheim 1984, pp. 82–83, 170.

further on. Advocates are also typically unclear about what they would regard as evidence for it other than their own intuitive convictions. Indeed, the idea that the view might be systematically tested is rarely considered. This is an issue I would like to see given more attention. Being confronted with a case to answer strikes me as good for the Positive View, and that is what I am starting to construct.

Second, much recent opposition to the Positive View within literary theory and criticism derives from a suspicion about the use of truth as a critical, normative device. There is enough reasoned opposition to this suspicion to justify my ignoring it.[4] Besides, denying a role to truth would make it impossible for an advocate of the Positive View to argue that truth is a value in literary representations, cutting off much of the debate at the start. Wanting to give my opponents a fighting chance, I avoid the nuclear option and accuse no one of incoherence when friends of the Positive View claim that literary representations sometimes convey important truths to us. I'm doubtful about this claim, but my doubts are not based on philosophical scruples; I think, rather boringly, that we need better evidence for it.

A final clarification: By "literature," I mean fictional narratives of high quality in written or dramatic form. To some extent, this is stipulative, but it suits my purpose. We could, for example, include film and other media outside the domains I specify, but I am responding here to a tradition that takes its examples mostly from drama and the novel; besides, it would be unwise to extend the debate, given the present limitations of space. The restriction to fictional cases is in place because we would need a quite different debate about, say, history, journalism, or biography.[5] And the reference to quality is there only because I focus on works of the kind that advocates of the Positive View have claimed to be the best illustrations of their arguments: the products of the great tragedians; the landmark novels and novelists from Austen to James; Woolf, Joyce, and the modernist turn. Exactly what this canon includes I don't presume to say: I simply agree that the works typically brought forward on behalf of the Positive View *do* represent very high levels of creative achievement; *do* repay serious, sustained, and repeated attention; and *do* convey the impression of illuminating dark and puzzling aspects of human motivation. My question is whether this impression is one we should endorse.

These preliminaries out of the way, let's have some more preliminaries—unfortunately, they are necessary.

---

[4] See, e.g., Devitt and Sterelny 1999, Williams 2002, Bogossian 2006; for the literary case, see esp. Lamarque and Olsen 1994.

[5] I happen to believe that some of the arguments presented below would carry over, perhaps in modified form, to these genres.

2. Kinds of Knowledge and How to Test for Them

Constraints on literary creativity take many forms, from the rules of genre to extrinsic and apparently stultifying requirements such as those imposed by the Hayes Code, which turned out to provoke some artistically interesting responses.[6] What constraints push the literary creator in the direction of truth? We do talk about truth in art and literature, but often in rhetorical tones and with no suggestion that anything is in place that would make truth a more likely outcome than it would be if left to the unconstrained exuberance of the creator. "Literature is where I go to...find not absolute truth but the truth of the tale," says Salman Rushdie, without hinting at any interpersonally valid standard for such truth.

If literature is to give us genuine insight rather than merely captivating images, it needs to be constrained in two different ways. We need some independent standard of success, something other than the mere garnering of acclaim. For it cannot count as the generation of genuine insight merely that people have the feeling that insight has been generated; being insightful is not like being funny or creepy. And we need some concept of evidence for the relevant kind of success. We cannot say that literary insight is attained when we arrive at truth, or at something that enhances the reader's moral and interpersonal capacities, and leave it at that. We must offer some means, no doubt fallible, to gauge success, however success is understood. I will say something about the possibility of such standards in the next section. Following that, I turn to the principle question: If literature, or some literature, aims to teach, how does the apparently very high value that we place on literary creativity contribute to that aim? Might it, instead, compromise it? Overall, I find that to be a difficult question, and I don't attempt a comprehensive answer to it here. I simply outline some reasons to unsettle the opinion that literary creativity and the search for insight are good companions.

So far I have spoken as if the independent standard that an advocate of the Positive View must acknowledge is truth. Things are more complicated. What is central to the creed of the Positive View is the idea that we may learn from literature. But it is a mistake, some say, to think that literature gives us truths, for truth ties us to knowing-that or propositional knowledge, and the kind of knowing that ought to be in question is knowing-how. Nussbaum emphasizes the extent to which literature tunes us to the exquisite particularity of ethical judgment, helping us to become those people on whom, in Henry James's words, "nothing is lost."[7] Coming from a

---

[6] See Elster 2000.

[7] From his preface to *The Princess Casamassima*. See esp. Nussbaum's discussion of the scene in *The Golden Bowl* between Adam and Maggie Verver where Adam's formation of an image of her as a "sea creature" helps him endorse, and not merely permit, her womanly independence (1994, ch. 5). But see also her endnote to "Literature and the Moral Imagination" (ch. 5) where she grants that the moral lesson of a literary work may have a propositional expression (though it would be "very long and probably open-ended").

different and more empirically focused perspective, psychologist Keith Oatley and his colleagues at the University of Toronto have recently argued that fictions educate, not by standing in for lectures, but by providing simulations not unlike those we run on computers to predict the weather.[8]

It's not clear how far such an approach will take us away from truth and truthfulness. A radical response to the know-how challenge argues that knowing how is, after all, a form of propositional knowledge.[9] I agree that there are cases where knowing how reduces to knowing the truth of some proposition, but as a general reductive strategy, this does not strike me as plausible.[10] Still, the case for basing knowing how on some sort of representational correspondence is not yet lost. Consider artificial grammar learning (AGL):

> In a typical AGL study, participants are first exposed to a set of strings, derived from an artificial grammar, under the pretext of a memory or pattern learning experiment. Participants are then told of the rule-based nature of the strings and asked to classify a new set of strings—some of which are generated by the same grammar and some of which are not— according to whether these novel strings follow the same rules as the ones they saw earlier. Classification performance on such AGL tasks is typically above chance, despite participants' general lack of overt knowledge of the underlying regularities.[11]

Subjects in these experiments pick up a degree of practical knowledge, being able, after a time, to distinguish grammatical strings from non-grammatical ones. They know nothing, apparently, of the rules that determine whether a string is grammatical. But we may think of the source of their knowing how to be, if not propositional knowledge of their own, then some representational structure—an internalized grammar—possessed sub-personally. In that case, their competency is explained in terms of correspondence (or lack of it) between the inner representation and the rule of the grammar.

Could all know-how be accounted for in this way? I don't need an opinion on this. One may accept that much knowing how is not explicable as representational

---

[8] See, e.g., Oatley 1999, Mar et al. 2006, 2008, Maja et al. 2009. Some of this material is reviewed further on in the text. One difficulty not considered by Oatley in appealing to the simulation model is that, while computers don't need imagination in order to run weather simulations, novels provide simulations only with the help of the subject's imagination. One would then need to consider the reliability of the imagination. There is some evidence that, in ways relevant to the simulation analogy, imagination is rather unreliable. See, e.g., Kahneman et al. 2006.

[9] See Stanley and Williamson 2001, Snowdon 2003.

[10] See Devitt 2011.

[11] Christiansen et al. 2010. For philosophical reflection on the idea of sub-personal representational states and their role in the explanation of behavior, see Davies 2000.

correspondence and still want the friends of the Positive View to suggest a standard of success when they speak of learning from literature. And we are good at creating and implementing such standards for various forms of practical knowledge: Plumbing apprenticeships aim to produce good plumbers, and we check their effectiveness by seeing how well the apprentices fix plumbing problems. There is such a thing as getting it right in plumbing, lion-taming, and other respectable practical skills, and such a thing as confirmation that the learner has gotten it right. The sensitivity training purportedly offered by literature cannot be treated as a mysterious exception to this.

One other form that the Positive View may take needs to be reviewed; it is the oft-heard assertion that literature teaches us what it would be like to be in certain kinds of situations.[12] When Robert Pippin speaks of "[Henry] James' brilliant treatment [in *The Wings of the Dove*] of what such an experience would mean for a man like [Merton Densher], and why, under what psychological conditions, it would take place," the subjunctive form indicates a carryover from the literary to the real world.[13] In the person of Densher, James, it is said, provides us with a substitute for a certain kind of experience, a substitute that acquaints us with the experience; I will call knowledge of this kind "acquaintance" from now on. What constitutes acquaintance is disputed. Frank Jackson argued that it is factual knowledge: There are facts about what experiences are like that are not physical facts, and we come to know these facts only by having the relevant experience.[14] David Lewis and others have argued that acquaintance is a kind of ability: Someone who knows what seeing the blue of the sky is like is someone who has the ability to recall the color, to identify other objects as having the same or similar colors, and so on.[15] It remains a possibility, however, that acquaintance is not reducible to either knowing that or knowing how, raising the question of how to validate a claim that this or that work shows us what such and such an experience is like.[16]

Perhaps this metaphysical issue need not detain us. Even if acquaintance is not itself a kind of knowing how or knowing that, we would naturally expect that changes in a person's know-how and/or propositional knowledge would be consequent on increments of acquaintance. And the extent to which provision of acquaintance is a value is surely dependent on its capacity to induce these other changes; those who admire literature's tendency to provide acquaintance emphasize the humanizing effects of such acquaintance, its capacity to make us more sympathetic judges,

---

[12] I'm grateful here to comments from Elliot Samuel Paul.

[13] Pippin 2001, p. 3.

[14] See Jackson 1982.

[15] See Lewis 1988. Lewis develops a thesis first put forward by Nemirow 1980. See Jackson 1986 for a reply, and for a recent defense of the abilities hypothesis, see Nemirow 2006.

[16] Another possibility is that acquaintance, as we ordinarily conceive it, does not exist and that the closest reality gets to this notion is some form of knowing-how or propositional knowledge.

more willing and effective providers of assistance, and more insightful resolvers of conflict.[17] So even an advocate of the Positive View who thinks that acquaintance is an irreducible aspect of what literature provides should be happy to say that, when it comes to testing such a claim, tests designed to elicit practical and propositional knowledge will do very well. At least they will do as a start, whether or not they are capable of settling all the questions we might have about the kind and degree of acquaintance a person has.

This conclusion returns us to an earlier worry: the fact that those who insist on literature's capacity to make us more sensitive, interpersonally attuned beings don't feel called on to provide the most obvious form of evidence for their claim, namely evidence that people who read literature do become more sensitive and interpersonally attuned. Nussbaum's advocacy of the moral and psychological benefits of literature is not accompanied by any such evidence, or any suggestion that such evidence would be a good thing to have. Perhaps Nussbaum would appeal here to her own experience as evidence. But much experimental work in the last 50 years suggests that self-evaluation in this area, as in others, is highly unreliable.[18] Self-understanding is governed by such irrational and self-serving principles as the Fundamental Attribution Error, whereby people explain their own failings as due to circumstance and those of others as due to defects of character. The training of an intellectual discipline does not seem to help much; in a university study, 68 percent of academics believed that their teaching was in the top 25 percent.[19] People also rate themselves as less biased than others, perhaps because biases are, contrary to expectation, relatively inaccessible to introspection; we judge the biases of others by their behaviors, and our own by introspection, which fails to find it.[20] Certainly, people who like literature often claim it is educative. Smokers sometimes claim that their habit is good for them; I suggest we ask for evidence in both cases. Certainly, no one would take seriously the idea that a nation's school system is in good shape based on the fact that the students *thought* they had learned a lot; only some objective test of learning would bear the claim out.

Are objective tests of any kind available when it comes to literature? An attempt to find and implement some was recently launched by Keith Oatley and his colleagues. Admittedly at an early stage, this work has not so far produced evidence significantly in support of the thesis I am considering here.[21] In one of their experiments, subjects were assessed on an author recognition test as to their relative commitments to fiction and nonfiction reading.[22] Various measures of empathy were

[17] See, e.g., Nussbaum 1997.
[18] Some of the evidence and argument is summarized in Wilson 2002.
[19] See Cross 1977.
[20] See Pronin and Kugler 2007.
[21] This, of course, is not a reason to find the results uninteresting from other points of view, or to reject them as pointers to future work that may be of just such a kind as to engage with the Positive View.
[22] Mar et al. 2006.

then found to be correlated positively with an interest in fiction reading and nega-tively with an interest in nonfiction. As the authors note, it is not possible to say on the basis of these results what is the direction of causation; it may be that greater levels of empathy orient people toward fiction reading, without the fiction reading affecting empathy levels much or at all.

But I do not need to take up arms against the idea that there is a generally positive effect of fiction reading on empathy or other aspects of interpersonal understand-ing. As I have said, the Positive View is one that concerns the specially insightful and educative potential of fictional works of unusual quality: works of very great literary merit, marked by their emphasis on the detailed examination of motive and feeling, often employing innovative and demanding tropes of narration, voice, and point of view. These are among the works we regard as indicative of very high attain-ment in creativity. Fictions considered more generally, including ones we would rate as not especially creative, may well have played a significant role in enhancing interpersonal understanding by, say, dramatizing the moral abuses of slavery, sexual discrimination, or homophobia. Such exercises often don't employ and might not benefit from the kind of exploratory and finely tuned approach to the mind I want to focus on here, working instead by eliciting from an audience such "ground-floor" responses as the recognition of the basic personhood of the relevant agents, and a sympathetic response to their manifest suffering. We do not need to understand anything much about the details of thinking and feeling to come to see, from such a fiction, how unpleasant it would be to be in a concentration camp or to be abused for the color of one's skin. It may also be that children's moral and psychological development is helped by their exposure to simple moral tales; perhaps stories at this level assist the development of their folk psychological/moral understanding. Whether it is so or not, I am not questioning the idea here.[23]

This is of some relevance to the empirical results offered by the Toronto group, because they did not, in the study referred to above, attempt to distinguish the effects of fiction at different levels of quality. The author recognition test they employed named a range of fictional authors from Thomas Mann through Umberto Eco and Ken Follett to Jackie Collins and Sydney Sheldon. Finding a sample group selec-tively responsive to the names of highly canonical literary figures would be difficult,

---

[23] See, e.g., Peskin and Astington 2004. For somewhat contrary views, see Narvaez 2002 and Nash 1997. A useful introduction to this debate from a position at least hospitable to the Positive View is Mar and Oatley (2008). While I'm at it, I'll also admit that there is a sense in which we *do* learn a lot that is important about the mind—especially the creative mind—from great literature. We learn from it more about what the mind is capable of producing, and we learn of the ideas about the mind that inhabit some (real) minds. Both these kinds of knowledge are important data that may help us develop better theories of the mind and of creativity; perhaps the best way to understand creativity is by reference to its products. But the existence of neither kind of knowledge is relevant to the claim I am considering here, which concerns the truthfulness or truth-likeness of the representations of mind that we find in great narrative art.

and we might require very sensitive measures of empathy for the reactions of such a group to be instructive. Still, those are the sorts of studies one must look to if one is serious about finding evidence for the Positive View.[24]

All this suggests that serious adjudication of the Positive View will be a messy and difficult business. It gets worse, for no advocate of that view claims that *all* literature of high quality gets it right. And a wise opponent of it will never argue that *no* work of literature ever does. The field of literature, even when defined rather narrowly as it is here, is vast and varied; it would be absurd to claim that no diligent reader ever gained a true belief or an improved capacity from literature. The argument ought to be about the *aptness* of literature, or certain kinds of literature, to convey insight. Fortunetellers are surely right some of the time, and the advice they offer may occasionally change people for the better. That does not make them useful resources for those who want to know how to plan their futures. The methods, institutions, and goals of fortunetellers are not apt to convey insight. Can we say something about the educative potential of literature? In the absence of detailed studies of individual learning relevant to the Positive View, we are thrown back onto general arguments, some of which do bring empirical considerations to bear on the issue, if only indirectly.

Recall that here we are concerned with the relation between literary insight and creativity. I want to focus on two issues: the already highlighted issue of institutional support for truth-aptness in creative endeavor, and the psychology of creative people. Is there anything we can say about the capacities of creative writers to provide the kind of insight that Emerson and others credit them with?

---

[24] In another study, the same group did use a distinctively literary example—a short story by Chekov—to test for the effects of reading on personality. They found that, relative to controls, "the experimental group experienced significantly greater change in self-reported experience of personality traits." It is, however, hard to believe that one reading of a short story could have a significant effect on personality rather than, say, mood; if that were so, one would expect dedicated long-term readers to have startlingly unstable personalities. There was no indication given of how long-lasting the change was. The authors at one point claim that "fiction can produce *fluctuations* in one's own traits.... It is not our argument that art necessarily causes strong personality changes in those who encounter it" (p. 28, my emphasis), or whether a less literary example would have produced comparable results. Further, personality changes, even real ones, are not in themselves evidence of learning, though some such changes would reasonably be regarded as associated with learning. And the authors of the study noted that there was no general direction of self-reported change: "each individual had unique changes across all five [personality] traits" (p. 27). Certainly, it is hard to know what to make of their claim that "Reading Chekhov induced changes in [subjects'] sense of self—perhaps temporary—such that they experienced themselves not as different in some way prescribed by the story, but as different in a direction toward discovering their own selves" (Mar et al. 2008).

3. Literature, Science, and the Search for Truth

Think first about constraints in science. There, one aim (not the only one) is explanatory success: We want theories with high degrees of confirmation. Accordingly, the institutions of science constrain the behavior of scientists in ways that make it more likely that they will come up with highly confirmed theories. We expect them to put forward highly testable theories and to conduct carefully designed experiments that will test them, and to find their theories confirmed (to some degree) in the process. We reward scientists well if they do that, and less well or not at all if they don't. If there are indications, as there sometimes are, that people have tried to avoid the constraints by cheating, professional ruin is likely to follow.

It is the existence of very real constraints of these kinds that makes it sensible to talk about science as an institution, as opposed to, say, an edifice of theories and experiments. Can we speak in the same way of literature as an institution? There are patterns of association, influence, and antagonism in literature, but these do not really amount to institutional structures.[25] Funding, other than via sales of the literary works themselves, is negligible, and organizations like PEN have virtually no influence on the activities of their members or the upshot of those activities. Indeed, the goal is to free writers from constraints on the content of their work. Were it ever suggested, PEN would surely oppose the introduction of formal assessments of the psychological insights that literary works provide. There are no literary institutions that set or constrain epistemic goals, and the idea of introducing them strikes everyone as absurd—partly because this would be an unreasonable constraint on creativity.

We do, it is true, possess institutions of criticism: literature departments, prizes, journals, reviews, and newspaper columns.[26] But they are not designed to promote, nor are they connected in any systematic way with, epistemic reliability. Indeed, it is noticeable that the last 40 years of criticism have seen a great deal of enthusiasm for the rejection of such ideas as truth, knowledge, and objectivity; no comparable movement has gotten far in the sciences. And when truthfulness is invoked in criticism, it often seems to mark the achievement of some vivid effect, with no very obvious connection to the idea of being right about something. To look no further than a recent issue of the *Times Literary Supplement*: It is said of Thackeray's *Barry Lyndon* that "the narrowing of the gap between voice and ventriloquist allows Thackeray to achieve a profound truthfulness about his protagonist's inner life."[27] It

---

[25] Peter Lamarque (2009) suggests that there is explanatory mileage in the idea of literature as an institution, but I am puzzled why (as he says in his response to Blackburn's doubts about this) the idea that reading literature as literature requires a distinctive kind of attention means that there are "conventions" of literary reading (see Blackburn 2010 and Lamarque 2010, p. 102).

[26] Though this does not make criticism an institutional phenomenon; criticism can exist without them.

[27] Taylor 2011.

would be odd and probably unprofessional for a reviewer within academic psychology to declare a piece of research as profound truth with no further specification or argument. This same ideology of truthfulness is found in such things as Nobel Prize citations, describing an oeuvre wherein "beauty and truth are closely allied or completely fused together."[28]

This outlook is not new. Johnson said of Shakespeare that "he has not only shewn human nature as it acts in real exigences, but as it would be found in trials, to which it cannot be exposed."[29] Perhaps Johnson knew from experience how human nature acts in real exigencies; it is less clear how he could be confident that people would act this or that way in circumstances he admits no one, including himself, has experienced—or even could experience. And should Johnson have been confident that Shakespeare has shown how human nature acts in real exigencies, when he, Johnson, carried out no surveys or carefully structured experiments to find out whether it really was so? When Leavis says, rather grudgingly, that *Hard Times* does not give "a misleading representation of human nature,"[30] it is tempting to ask how he could possibly know something that not even the greatest psychologist would think of claiming: what human nature is. This tendency of critics to imagine themselves able to survey human nature, as well as its literary representation, may help to make understandable the postmodern revulsion against humanistic criticism.

Communities that aim to increase knowledge or merely spread it around have audiences, and the responses of an audience can be institutionalized to make them significant determinants of truth-aptness. Here, once again, the contrast between literature and science is stark. The relevant audience in the case of science is the scientific community itself: highly trained, highly critical, and with a professional interest in showing up a proposal's weaknesses or elaborating on it if it shows promise. In contrast, the audience for a piece of narrative art, however knowledgeable and well versed in the conventions and techniques of the genre, is simply not tuned to the issue of truthfulness, and is likely to be swayed by powerful emotional forces unleashed by the work itself. It's worth underlining these points with some recent ideas in psychology about the emotions and belief formation.

Emotions affect beliefs in somewhat the way perceptions do. When things are observed to be inconsistent with what we believe, our beliefs tend to shift accordingly. And when our emotions are in conflict with what we believe, there is at least some tendency to bring the two into harmony by adjusting belief, at least when emotion does not easily give way.[31] That is often to the good; neurological patients in Damasio's gambling experiments did badly because they failed to get the right kind of aversive emotional cues from high-risk strategies and did not rethink the

---

[28] Nobel Prize for Literature citation speech in honor of Patrick White, 1973.
[29] Johnson 1765.
[30] Leavis 1948, p. 233.
[31] See Clore and Gasper 2000.

options for their play; people with intact orbitofrontal cortexes were guided by their emotions, adopted more sensible strategies, and avoided big loses.[32] But emotion is course-grained and provoked by representations of events as easily as by events themselves; the emotions aroused by manifestly fictional representations of events may have quite strong effects on beliefs, although there is no guarantee or even much indication of a correlation between the fictional representation and the real events themselves. Even well-educated viewers of Oliver Stone's rather unreliable *JFK* turn out to have been highly influenced by the film in their beliefs about the likelihood of a wide-ranging conspiracy behind the Kennedy assassination.[33] And we are strongly affected in our beliefs about a represented situation by emotionally arousing aesthetic features of the representational vehicle that have no bearing on the question of whether what is represented is true; we see this in the care taken to aestheticize religious practices and state ceremonies.[34]

Belief formation is susceptible to other influences that blunt the receiver's critical faculties. Note first a theory due to Dan Gilbert that makes the problem seem particularly acute.[35] In one of Gilbert's experiments, subjects read an account of a crime; at the end, they were asked to recommend an appropriate sentence for the crime. Within the narrative were certain false embellishments to the descriptions of the crime that, if taken seriously, would make the crime seem worse. These "fictional" passages were not disguised; they were clearly indicated as false. Indeed, they were printed in red, while the rest was in black. Nonetheless, the results indicated that subjects who were distracted while reading the account by a digit-search task (and hence less vigilant) were influenced in their decisions by the material in red, tending to give longer sentences than were given by people who were not exposed to the false material.

Gilbert's explanation is that anything we are told goes straight into the belief system; it then requires effort, which is not always available or exercised, to remove

---

[32] See Bechara et al. 1994. For criticism of the experiment and the conclusions drawn, see Barnaby et al. 2006.

[33] See Butler et al. 1995.

[34] I note some convergence with a claim made by David Velleman (2003). He argues that narrative fails as a vehicle for knowledge because it imposes on us emotional transitions and a sense of closure that make us think we have caught on to a causal-explanatory process when all we have is our own "sense of an ending." Velleman has in mind the emotional "cadence" of a narrative's overall structure; but the same idea could apply at the micro-level, where we consider, as we do in the case of Adam Verver in *The Golden Bowl*, a character's transition from thought to action. A writer can create an emotionally powerful effect that takes us across this mysterious divide, making us conclude that thinking that way really can help us act well—or equally, that thoughts with a certain quasi-aesthetic defect (the wrong image, maybe) will send us astray (see Nussbaum 1994[AQ: Please provide complete details of "Nussbaum 1990" in the reference list love's knowledge; date was my error.], ch. 5). But these ideas need better support than they get from our merely finding them emotionally or aesthetically satisfying.

[35] Gilbert et al. 1993.

it. So the distraction task had the effect of allowing the false material to stay in the belief box. Dan Sperber and Hugo Mercier have what seems to me a better idea: It's not that everything we hear is initially believed; we possess a mechanism of vigilance that keeps things out of the belief box, but operating it involves costs.[36] So the mechanism is likely to be activated in situations of perceived risk and not in others. In particular, when the information is of no great personal relevance—as it was not in Gilbert's sentencing experiments—we would not expect there to be much vigilance displayed. Fictions that suggest or implicate real-world claims are not likely to have much vigilance lavished on them, unless they unusually display relevance to our personal circumstances.[37] If material is not very personally relevant—and so not likely to call our epistemic defenses into play—*and* is emotionally charged through the use of expressive language or artfully arranged episodes of conflict and resolution, the chances of it getting through the defenses of our belief system are quite high. And fictional material of superior quality often has both of these characteristics.

I said that Gilbert's subjects were influenced by the avowedly false material because they were distracted; this may lead us to question the relevance of his experiment to conclusions about the gullibility of fiction readers. It's true that fiction readers are not generally expected to do a task while they are reading and are not thusly distracted. But there are often other distractions present in attending to the kinds of fictions we are focusing on here. Consider the tendency in high-end literature and drama to render language and other representational devices harder to process than they would be in less self-conscious projects, with complex sentences, strange tropes of narration, and so on. These are elements of what we call style, and Sperber and Wilson have claimed that the function of style is to facilitate the discovery of relevance in communication. With epizeuxis, as in

There's a fox, a fox in my garden,

we understand that the speaker was surprised or excited by the presence of the fox; the extra processing cost imposed by the repetition indicates that relevant information is available that would not be accessible otherwise.[38] But style may serve purposes that are the opposite of knowledge-enhancing. I suggest that one of the reasons we enjoy complexity in fiction—and hence one reason we find complexity in successful fiction—is that it provides the kind of distraction that lowers vigilance, helping thereby to generate an illusion of learning. Paradoxically, the sheer

[36] Sperber and Mercier 2010.

[37] The implicatures are likely to be weak, in the sense of Sperber and Wilson (1995, pp. 217–224). For more on the mechanisms whereby fiction encourages changes in a reader's perspective on real-world matters, see, e.g., Gendler 2010, ch. 12.

[38] See Sperber and Wilson 1994, p. 219.

complexity of great narrative art, so often taken as a sign of cognitive richness and subtlety, may increase its power to spread ignorance and error.

Why does style count for so little in science when it counts for so much in literature? In science (please indulge my realism), truth is what matters, and so we do not burden the scientist with the responsibility for providing us with anything other than truth; we don't demand that it be truth-in-meter or truth-with-a-strong-emotional-effect; if we did, we'd expect to get less truth. But the demands of literature are quite the reverse. Pasternak said of Shakespeare that "Half his thought, and the words that verbalised them, were prompted by metre." That sounds right—perhaps in a way that Pasternak did not intend. What poets write is metrically constrained, and so is the thought they express. More than that, the demands of conformity to meter—or, if you are a novelist, the need to lay a trail of temporarily unanswered interesting questions—make everything more difficult, leaving fewer cognitive resources to think about truth. When you make it more difficult for people to do something, they are likely to do it less well.

There is another way in which the organizations of science and literature differ dramatically that is relevant to assessing literature's capacity for insight. Epistemic goals in science are met not simply by imposing rewards and punishments on the activity of creative individuals, but by facilitating *arguments* among them. One quite surprising result of the recent psychological study of rationality is the discovery of how fragile human reasoning seems to be; we are prone to errors of logic and statistical inference that, from a formal point of view, are simple and obvious, but which specialist training does little to insulate us against. When we are thinking about epistemic goals, it is sensible to ask whether an institution—science, literature, or anything else—supports and enhances reasoning, helping to overcome its weaknesses. I suggest that there is something about the situation of the literary creator that militates against the effectiveness of their reasoning and that contrasts dramatically with the situation in science.

I have in mind the extreme *individuality* of creativity in the narrative arts. Occasionally, we find jointly authored fictions, but usually there are only two authors involved, and in those cases, it is often true that the work was largely divided between them. Certainly, the celebrated values of literature are those usually associated with an individual and highly idiosyncratic vision of the human situation. But there is some reason to think that the cognitive capacities necessary for the effective use of reason are best exercised *interactively*. When people try to perform reasoning tasks alone, their performance is surprisingly poor; as indicated above, even highly educated people are prone to fallacies that defeat their purposes time and time again. When the same tasks are undertaken by groups of about eight people working together, success is much higher. This apparently isn't because the group defers to someone who is obviously good at the task; rather, it is because the argumentative context, in which people listen to a proposed way of solving a problem and then criticize and improve on it, aids them in overcoming their individual tendencies toward error.[39] And studies do show that people reason well in argumentative contexts and respond well to reasoning directed at them—much better than in isolation. Sperber and Mercier (2011) note that "when people want to attack alternative views, they are very good at making use of *modus tollens* arguments.... On the other hand, half of the people tested in standard reasoning tasks lacking an argumentative context fail on *modus tollens* tasks." Even preschoolers do well in groups at spotting fallacies in argument, while late adolescents outside of an argumentative context perform not much better than chance.[40]

Science helps to protect the creator from fallacies of reasoning by providing a richly argumentative environment. There are notable instances of great scientific breakthroughs by individuals working in personal isolation. But they did not lack an *argumentative* context. Einstein, far from the center of the physical universe (Berlin) was working in an intense intellectual environment characterized by Newton's absolutism about space and time, the null result of the Michelson-Morley experiment, Maxwell's electrodynamics, and the theories of Lorentz and Poincaré. Newton, isolated at Woolsthorpe, discovered the theory of gravitation and much else besides—but against the background of competing theories from Descartes, Huygens, Wren and Hooke, and against which he was constantly testing his own theories. Newton's and Einstein's *argumentative* contexts were richly social ones.

Once again, the contrast with literature is stark. I don't say writers never argue; sometimes they argue about their work. But argument is not to them the professional necessity it is to the scientist. And while writers may argue about aspects of style, plot, and theme, it is much less usual for them to debate the facts of human psychology, or the best way to make readers more empathic or otherwise better understanders of other people. In such matters, writers are more inclined to follow their own vision, often considered to be an essential feature of what differentiates them from other writers and hence not something where convergence to a common view would be welcomed.

While we await serious empirical studies of the social epistemology of literature, my tentative conclusion is that literature has no significant institutional constraints that push its creative activity in the direct of truthfulness or impose practical tests for truth on its outcomes. It has instead, and rather paradoxically, a set of institutional structures—prizes, critical commentary—whose representatives are given to making large and untested (perhaps untestable) claims about literature's capacity for insight. Literary creativity is strongly constrained in various ways, but not toward truthfulness. The real constraints on literary creativity are keyed to the development

---

[39] Sperber and Mercier hazard that this is because reasoning (inference at the personal level, generally accessible to consciousness) arose as a tool of social cognition; communicated information is highly likely to be deceptive, and so we developed a capacity to check for consistency between what is communicated and what we know or believe—that is our capacity to reason.

[40] Sperber and Mercier 2011.

of arresting, emotionally engaging characters and plot, the artful creation of uncertainty, suspense, and the feeling that we, the audience, are being stretched and challenged by the work. All this may go along with the *promise* of psychological insight, and indeed with a genuine ambition on the author's part to be psychologically insightful. But the shared desire for psychological insight is not *constrained* by the practices of fiction. Would science produce highly explanatory theories if it was constrained merely to produce theories that people *felt* were explanatory? That is the way of magic and astrology.

4. The Creative Personality

So far, I have put the problem in terms a social psychologist would find agreeable, emphasizing the situational constraints on creativity in the arts versus those that prevail in the sciences. Might personal factors also play a part? Here we enter especially difficult territory. There is a mass of work on the psychology of creativity, and some on personality differences between creative people in the arts and elsewhere, not all of it tending in the same direction. Conclusions at this stage must be tentative, but what follows seems to me a reasonable view to take in light of current evidence.[41]

Highly creative people are unusual simply by being highly creative, but they are often unusual in other ways. Some of these seem to be enabling conditions for the possession or development of extreme creativity. Extreme levels of creativity in any discipline are said to be accompanied by a significant capacity to be galvanized by one's own imaginings, rather than being dependent on external stimulus; a high level of responsiveness to one's own inner conceptions, projects, and standards of success, rather than being driven by the prospect of external reward; a high degree of immersion in and obsessive concern with one's own work; and a corresponding unwillingness to respond to personal and domestic responsibilities—a theme I will return to.

Not all creative people are unusual in the same way. Individual differences aside, there are differences according to the form that creativity takes. While it is said that creative writers share with scientists a degree of introversion and a tendency toward hostility and arrogance, they are less conforming and less socialized and more prone to intense affective experience than scientists are—bringing to mind a traditional picture of the literary artist as difficult, self-absorbed, and unstable.

---

[41] It is not agreed among psychologists of creativity whether there is a unified ability manifested in different degrees and ways according to the task demands in place or disparate groupings of capacities and inclinations we happen to lump together under one term. An example of the unifying stance is Claridge (1993), and my exposition is broadly in keeping with his proposal. But much of what I claim here could be reformulated, with some complications, within a pluralistic theory.

Other research gives some support to this last idea: Simonton (2000) distinguishes creative endeavor by degrees of unconventionality, drawing rough distinctions between "normal" and "revolutionary" scientific activity and between academic and avant-garde art; the less conventional the creative activity, the more proneness to psychopathology.[42] Additionally, artistic creativity at any level tends to go with greater proneness to psychopathology than does scientific creativity. Thus we get a scale of increasing psychopathology along which we can progressively place normal science, revolutionary science, academic art, and avant-garde art. The creative people I am focusing on here would appear in the two most at-risk categories. Retrospective studies of notable creators—a genre with methodological problems that make its results very questionable—tend to support this.[43] In Post's study of 50 great writers, only one was considered free of psychopathology (Maupassant, a suicide), and this group contained the highest proportion of individuals with severe psychopathology (nearly 50 percent) compared with the other groups of creative people considered: scientists, statesmen, thinkers, artists, and composers.[44]

What kinds of psychopathology are in question here? Recent research into creativity has focused on two things: schizophrenia and affective or emotional disorders, notably bipolar disorder (BD). The relation between them is disputed, but some evidence supports the idea that they are aspects of a single underlying pathology.[45] However connected, there is evidence that both kinds of traits are disproportionately represented in highly creative groups.[46] Severe forms of both are too disabling to sustain creative work; creativity is promoted not by the disorders themselves but by possession of the "underlying cognitive styles and personality traits" for these disorders.[47] This sometimes involves a life history in which psychotic episodes are interwoven with normal or relatively normal functioning.

---

[42] Simonton discusses related issues in ch. 12 of this volume.

[43] The few studies there are of eminent writers—e.g., Claridge, Pryor, and Watkins 1998, and Jamison 1993—are often avowedly speculative, and it is hard to draw definite conclusions from them. In particular, their conclusions about the relation between creativity and madness (a favored theme) may be confounded by temporary cultural factors like romanticism that shift the boundaries of acceptable behavior; see Sass 2001.

[44] Post 1994. Another study looked at 30 creative writers and found "a substantially higher [than normal] rate of mental illness, predominantly affective disorder, with a tendency toward the bipolar subtype" (Andreasen 1987).

[45] See, e.g., Claridge 1998, Claridge and Blakey 2009; see also Ludwig 1995.

[46] For opposing views about the relative importance of these two for creativity, see Sass 2000–2001 and Jamison 2000–2001.

[47] Glazer 2009. "The relationship is not between actual psychosis and creativity, but rather between 'schizotypy' or 'psychoticism' and creativity....The putative link is with non-clinical expressions of schizotypal temperament and information processing style, along a personality dimension that leads from 'normality' at one end, through differently weighted combinations of schizotypal traits, towards full-blown psychosis at the other end" (Brod 1997, p. 276).

What does this suggest about the credentials of creative writers when it comes to insight into the mind? Individual differences make generalizations hard, but I note emerging evidence that both schizophrenia and bipolar disorder are marked by difficulties in the area of understanding other people's minds—the area where we are apt to credit great literary artists with especially penetrative powers.[48] There are by now well-developed tests in this area. Sometimes called "theory of mind tests," many were developed in order to help us understand aspects of child development. It has subsequently been shown that these tests can reveal individual differences later in life, as well as point to situations in which people's normal ability to track the mental states of others is, with surprising ease, compromised.[49] A large number of studies have now found impaired understanding of mental states in patients with schizophrenia. In the meta-analysis of Sprong et al. (2007), this correlation was shown to be strong, with patients on average one standard deviation below normal performance; the correlation held for patients currently without symptoms.[50] Understanding of mental states is also impaired in people genetically at risk for schizophrenia.[51] Thus the effect does not seem to be explicable wholly as a result of other symptoms such as thought disorganization; Sprong and colleagues hazard that "mentalising impairment is a susceptibility indicator for schizophrenia and hence may be trait-dependent."[52]

What about bipolar disorder? There is also evidence here of a connection with theory of mind deficits. One study found impaired performance on theory of mind tests for both depressed and manic patients, but not for patients in remission.[53] Another study examined bipolar patients currently in a normal mood state and found that they performed poorly when compared with controls on verbal theory of mind tests, but at a level comparable to controls on nonverbal tasks, though they were slower to respond.[54] A third study of patients with unipolar or bipolar depression currently in remission concluded that they were impaired on a relatively complex theory of mind test, the second-order false belief test.[55] Finally, a very recent report indicates that "the bipolar patient group as a whole, as well as all three clinical subgroups [manic, depressed and remitted], were impaired on all measures of ToM [theory of mind] relative to controls, but did not differ from each other in most ToM scores."[56] So here, as with schizophrenia, there is some evidence that problems

[48] See Brüne 2005, Harrington et al. 2005a, Sprong et al. 2007. I'm grateful to Peter Carruthers for drawing my attention to the last and most comprehensive of these studies.

[49] Isaacs et al. 1996.

[50] See also Herold et al. 2002.

[51] See Langdon and Coltheart 2001, 2004, Irani et al. 2006, Marjoram et al. 2006, Meyer and Shean 2006, Pickup 2006, Schiffman et al. 2004, Wykes et al. 2001.

[52] Sprong et al. 2007, p.11. See also Bora et al. 2009. But see Pousa and Ruiz 2008.

[53] Kerr et al. 2003.

[54] Olley et al. 2005.

[55] Inoue et al. 2004.

[56] Assion et al. 2011.

with mentalizing are connected to the underlying traits of the disorder and are not merely a product of the emotionally disturbed states that it manifests.

The conclusion is that traits strongly associated with literary creativity include impairments in understanding mental states—contradicting our intuitive picture of the creative writer as an insightful observer of the human scene. Add to this the thought that creative writers often seem to be rather distanced from the reality of their subject—interpersonal relations: "... the creator rarely cares much for others" is the brutal summary of a survey in this area.[57] It is striking, isn't it, that we tend to credit a certain group of individuals, who are apparently highly prone to mental disturbance, with a deep insight into human nature and conduct because of their imaginative depictions, and that we are not discouraged by the fact that many of them seem to have little experience of or even interest in the corresponding reality.

5. How We Think, and How We Ought to Think

I conclude with an objection. All this is irrelevant to the value of literary representations of moral thinking; the value they have is in their showing us how we *ought* to think, feel, and act, not how we often do these things when we are in the grip of debilitating forces. Henry James himself noted the objection that some of his characters seem too far above the level of real human moral achievement for their activities to be of any help to the rest of us; his reply that they are "in essence an observed reality" is not one I have found easy to accept. This, along with Nussbaum's endorsement—"there is no better way to show one's commitment to the fine possibilities of the actual than to create, in imagination, their actualization"—simply begs the question. What, after all, *counts as* a possibility "of the actual" or as an "essence" of observed reality? Both writers seem to assume that we have some agreed standard. I am suggesting that we don't. Any claim about what is ideal or merely valuable in thinking has to take into account the real difficulties that face us in trying. The best advice about how to get to Paris from here is not to take the geodesic route that joins them, though that will always be the shortest path on the surface of Earth; we take account of the fact that there is an ocean to cross, restricted points of entry, a train service that runs only along certain pathways, and so on. My suggestion is that novelists, like the rest of us, have not much idea what the corresponding difficulties are that confront our attempts at moral thinking, their magnitudes, and the kinds of circumstances in which they show themselves most powerfully. Suppose someone argued for the virtues of formal logic in education on the grounds that the laying out of sound inferences is the "essence" of human thinking; after all, they say, we are rational animals. There certainly are times when it is good to check for validity,

[57] Policastro and Gardner 1999, p. 222, n. X.

but the fact is that the human mind is not built for logic. It is designed to operate via shortcuts and rules of thumb—something we know the details of only because of systematic experimental work. This makes nonsense of the idea that we would do better overall by putting our pedagogic efforts into teaching formal logic. What might be helpful would be to find out where people actually do go systematically wrong in reasoning—ignoring base rates, observing the law of "small numbers," and the rest—and devising ways to guard against these errors when it matters. We cannot do that on the basis of a novelist's conception of how the mind works.

We must not take any of this too far. Not all authors, even great ones, are mad; fewer write effectively in a state of madness; and some are no more socially incompetent than the rest of us. We certainly need better studies of the psychology of outstandingly creative people in all walks of life, a better understanding of how competence in mind- reading is distributed throughout normal and compromised populations, and good studies of the social epistemology of literature. And we must retain a critical attitude toward what psychologists tell us. My aim here is to simply suggest the merits of a very moderate skepticism in dealing with claims about the insightful nature of literary creativity.[58]

References

Andreasen, N. C. 1987. Creativity and mental illness: Prevalence rates in writers and their first-degree relatives. *American Journal of Psychiatry* 144: pp. 1288–1292.

Assion, H.-J., F. Wolf, and Martin Brüne. 2011. Theory of mind and neurocognitive functioning in patients with bipolar disorder. *European Psychiatry* 26: p. 191.

Bate, Jonathan. 2011. Review of Lupton, Thinking with Shakespeare. *Times Higher Education Supplement*, June 16.

Barnaby D. Dunn, Tim Dalgleish, and Andrew D. Lawrence. 2006. The somatic marker hypothesis: A critical evaluation. *Neuroscience and Biobehavioral Reviews* 30: pp. 239–271.

[58] An earlier version of this essay was read at the Philosophy of Creativity Conference, Barnard College, Columbia University, in November 2010; I'm grateful to the organisers of the conference and editors of this volume, Elliot Samuel Paul and Scott Barry Kaufman, for their comments and their encouragement. Other versions were delivered at Manchester, CUNY, MIT, Nottingham, Tartu, and Tufts. A great many people on all these occasions and in correspondence were extremely helpful with comments and suggestions, though sometimes visibly repelled by the scientism of my outlook. Among them are Cathy Abell, Nancy Bauer, Brian Boyd, Noel Carroll, Peter Carruthers, Julian Dodd, Owen Flanagan, Jonathan Gilmore, James Helgeson, Richard Holton, Matthew Kieran, Rae Langton, Aaron Meskin, Margaret Moore, Elizabeth Picciuto, Jessie Prinz, Jon Robson, Natallia Schabner, Joel Smith, and Molly Wilder. I'm particularly grateful to Steve Ross who (literally) went out of his way to argue about this, and to Terence Cave, whose project "Literature as an Object of Knowledge" gives me an ideal group of people to discuss this with, including Terence himself. I am grateful, finally, to the U.K.'s Art and Humanities Research Council for generous financial support for the research project "Method in Philosophical Aesthetics" during which this paper was conceived and written.

Bechara, A., A. Damasio, H. Damasio, and S. Anderson. 1994. Insensitivity to future consequences following damage to human prefrontal cortex. *Cognition* 50, pp. 7–15.

Bevington, David. 2011. *Murder Most Foul: Hamlet Through the Ages*. Oxford, UK: Oxford University Press.

Blackburn, Simon. 2010. Some remarks about value as a work of literature. *British Journal of Aesthetics* 50: pp. 85–88.

Bogossian, P. 2006. *Fear of Knowledge: Against Relativism and Constructivism*. Oxford, UK: Clarendon Press, 2006.

Bora, Emre, Murat Yucel, and Christos Pantelis. 2009. Theory of mind impairment in schizophrenia: Meta-analysis. *Schizophrenia Research* 109: pp. 1–9.

Brod, J. 1997. Creativity and schizotypy. G. Claridge, ed., *Schizotypy: Implications for Illness and Health*, pp. 276–298. Oxford, UK: Oxford University Press.

Brüne, M. 2005. "Theory of mind" in schizophrenia: A review of the literature. *Schizophrenia Bulletin* 31: pp. 21–42;

Butler, L., C. Koopman, and P. G. Zimbardo. 1995. The psychological impact of viewing the film "JFK": Emotions, beliefs, and political behavioral intentions. *Political Psychology* 16: pp. 237–257.

Christiansen, Morten H., et al. 2010. Impaired artificial grammar learning in agrammatism. *Cognition* 116: pp. 382–393.

Claridge, Gordon. 1993. When is psychoticism? And how does it really relate to creativity? *Psychological Inquiry* 4: pp. 184–188.

Claridge, Gordon. 1998. *Genius and the mind*. Oxford, UK: Oxford University Press.

Claridge, Gordon, R. Pryor, and G. Watkins. 1998. *Sounds from the Bell Jar: Ten psychotic authors*. Cambridge, MA: Malor Books.

Claridge, Gordon, and Sarah Blakey. 2009. Schizotypy and affective temperament: Relationships with divergent thinking and creativity styles. *Personality and Individual Differences* 46: pp. 820–826.

Clore, G. L., and K. Gasper. 2000. Feeling is believing. Frijda et al., eds., *Emotions and Beliefs: How feelings influence thought*. Cambridge, UK: Cambridge University Press.

Cross, P. 1977. Not can but will college teachers be improved? *New Directions for Higher Education* 17: pp. 1–15.

Davies, Martin. 2000. Interaction without Reduction: The Relationship between Personal and Sub-personal Levels of Description. *Mind and Society* 2: pp. 87–105.

Devitt, Michael. 2011. Methodology and the nature of knowing how. *Journal of Philosophy* CVIII: pp. 205–218.

Devitt, Michael, and Kim Sterelny. 1999. *Language and Reality*. Oxford, UK: Blackwell.

Elster, Jon. 2000. *Ulysses Unbound: Studies in Rationality, Precommitment, and Constraints*. Cambridge, UK: Cambridge University Press.

Gendler, Tamar Szabo. 2010. *Intuition, Imagination, and Philosophical Methodology*. Oxford, UK: Oxford University Press.

Gilbert, Daniel T., Romin W. Tafarodi, and Patrick S. Malone. 1993. You Can't Not Believe Everything You Read. *Journal of Personality and Social Psychology* 65: pp. 221–233.

Glazer, Emilie. 2009. Rephrasing the madness and creativity debate: What is the nature of the creativity construct? *Personality and Individual Differences* 46: pp. 755–764.

Harrington, L., R. J. Siegert, and J. McClure. 2005a. Theory of mind in schizophrenia: A critical review. *Cognitive Neuropsychiatry* 10: pp. 249–286.

Herold, R., T. Tenyi, and K. Lenard et al. (2002) Theory of mind deficit in people with schizophrenia during remission. *Psychological Medicine* 32: pp. 1125–1129.

Inoue, Yumiko, Yuji Tonooka, Kazuo Yamada, and Shigenobu Kanba. 2004. Deficiency of theory of mind in patients with remitted mood disorder. *Journal of Affective Disorders* 82: pp. 403–409.

Irani, F., S. M. Platek, I. S. Panyavin et al. 2006. Self-face recognition and theory of mind in patients with schizophrenia and first-degree relatives. *Schizophrenia Research* 88: pp. 151–160.

Isaacs, J., et al. 1996. Contamination in reasoning about false belief: An instance of realist bias in adults but not children. *Cognition* 59(1): pp. 1–21.

Jackson, F. 1982. Epiphenomenal Qualia. *Philosophical Quarterly* 32: pp. 127–136.

Jackson, F. 1986. What Mary Didn't Know. *Journal of Philosophy* 83: pp. 291–295.

Jamison, K. R. 2000–2001. Reply to Louis A. Sass: Schizophrenia, Modernism, and the "Creative Imagination." *Creativity Research Journal* 13 (1): pp. 75–76.

——. 1993. *Touched with fire: Manic-depressive illness and the artistic temperament.* New York: Free Press.

Johnson, Samuel. 1765. *The Plays of William Shakespeare.*

Kahneman, D., A. B. Krueger, D. Schkade, N. Schwarz, and A. A. Stone. 2006. Would you be happier if you were richer? A focusing illusion. *Science* 312: pp. 1908–1910.

Kerr, N., R. Dunbar, and R. Bentall. 2003. Theory of mind deficits in bipolar affective disorder. *Journal of Affective Disorders* 73: pp. 253–259.

Lamarque, Peter, and Stein Olsen. 1994. *Truth, Fiction and Literature.* Oxford, UK: Oxford University Press.

Lamarque, Peter. 2009. *The Philosophy of Literature.* Oxford, UK: Blackwell.

Lamarque, Peter. 2010. Replies to Attridge, Blackburn, Feagin, and Harcourt. *British Journal of Aesthetics* 50: pp. 99–106.

Langdon, R., and M. Coltheart. 2001. Mentalising, executive planning and disengagement in schizophrenia. *Cognitive Neuropsychiatry* 6: pp. 81–108.

Langdon, R., and M. Coltheart. 2004. Recognition of metaphor and irony in young adults: The impact of schizotypal personality traits. *Psychiatry Research* 125: p. 125.

Leavis, F. R. 1948. *The Great Tradition.* London: Chatto & Windus.

Lewis, D. 1988. What Experience Teaches. G. W. Lycan, ed., *Mind and Cognition.* Oxford, UK: Blackwell.

Ludwig, A. M. 1995. *The price of greatness: Resolving the creativity and madness controversy.* New York: Guilford Press.

Mar, Raymond A., et al. 2006. Bookworms versus nerds: Exposure to fiction versus non-fiction, divergent associations with social ability, and the simulation of fictional social worlds. *Journal of Research in Personality* 40: pp. 694–712.

Mar, Raymond A., et al. 2008. Effects of reading on knowledge, social abilities, and selfhood. S. Zyngier, M. Bortolussi, A. Chesnokova, and J. Auracher, eds., *Directions in empirical studies in literature: In honor of Willie van Peer.* Amsterdam: Benjamins, pp. 127–137.

Mar, Raymond A., and Keith Oatley. 2008. The Function of Fiction is the Abstraction and Simulation of Social Experience. *Perspectives on Psychological Science* 3: pp. 173–192.

Marjoram, D., P. Miller, A. M. McIntosh et al. 2006. A neuropsychological investigation into "Theory of Mind" and enhanced risk of schizophrenia. *Psychiatry Research* 144: pp. 29–37.

Meyer, J., and G. Shean. 2006. Social-cognitive functioning and schizotypal characteristics. *Journal of Psychology* 140: pp. 199–207.

Narvaez, D. 2002. Does reading moral stories build character? *Educational Psychology Review* 14: pp. 155–171.

Nash, R. J. 1997. *Answering the Virtuecrats: A moral conversation on character education.* New York: Teachers College Press.

Nemirow, Laurence. 1980. Review of Thomas Nagel, *Mortal Questions. Philosophical Review* 89: pp. 473–477.

Nemirow, Laurence. 2006. So This Is What It's Like: A Defense of the Ability Hypothesis. Torin Alter and Sven Walter, eds., *Phenomenal Concepts and Phenomenal Knowledge: New Essays on Consciousness and Physicalism.* Oxford, UK: Oxford University Press.

Nussbaum, Martha. 1994. *Love's Knowledge.* Oxford, UK: Oxford University Press.

Nussbaum, Martha. 1997. *Poetic Justice: The Literary Imagination and Public Life.* Boston: Beacon Press.

Oatley, Keith. 1999. Why fiction may be twice as true as fact: Fiction as cognitive and emotional simulation. *Review of General Psychology* 3: pp. 101–117.

Olley A. L., G. S. Malhi, J. Bachelor, C. M. Cahill, P. B. Mitchell, and M. Berk. 2005. Executive functioning and theory of mind in euthymic bipolar disorder. *Bipolar Disorders* 7, Supp. 5: pp. 43–52.

Peskin, J., and Janet Astington. 2004. The effects of adding metacognitive language to story texts. *Cognitive Development* 19: pp. 253–273.

Pickup, G. J. 2006. Theory of mind and its relation to schizotypy. *Cognitive Neuropsychiatry* 11: pp. 177–192.

Pippin, R. 2001. *Henry James and Modern Moral Life*. New York: Cambridge University Press.

Policastro, Emma, and Howard Gardner. 1999. From case studies to robust generalizations: An approach to the study of creativity. Sternberg, ed., *Handbook of Creativity*. New York: Cambridge University Press.

Post, F. 1994. Creativity and psychopathology. A study of 291 world-famous men. *British Journal of Psychiatry* 165: pp. 22–34.

Pousa, Esther, and Ada I. Ruiz. 2008. Mentalising impairment as a trait marker of schizophrenia? *British Journal of Psychiatry* 192: p. 312.

Pronin, Emily, and Matthew B. Kugler. 2007. Valuing thoughts, ignoring behavior: The introspection illusion as a source of the bias blind spot. *Journal of Experimental Social Psychology* 43: pp. 565–578.

Robinson, Jenefer. 2005. *Deeper than Reason: Emotion and Its Role in Literature, Music, and Art*. Oxford, UK: Oxford University Press.

Sass, Louis. 2001. Schizophrenia, modernism, and the "creative imagination": On creativity and psychopathology. *Creativity Research Journal* 13: pp. 55–74.

Schiffman, J., C. W. Lam, T. Jiwatram et al. 2004. Perspective-taking deficits in people with schizophrenia spectrum disorders: A prospective investigation. *Psychological Medicine* 34: pp. 1581–1586.

Sperber, Dan, and Deirdre Wilson. 1995. *Relevance: Communication and Cognition*, 2nd edition. Oxford, UK: Blackwell.

Sperber, Dan, and Hugo Mercier. 2011. Reasoning as a Social Competence. H. Landemore and J. Elste, eds., *Collective Wisdom: Principles and Mechanisms*. New York: Cambridge University Press.

Sprong, M., P. Schothorst, E. Vos, J. Hox, and, H. Van Engeland. 2007. Theory of mind in schizophrenia: Meta-analysis. *British Journal of Psychiatry* 191: pp. 5–13.

Stanley, Jason, and Timothy Williamson. 2001. Knowing How. *Journal of Philosophy* 98: pp. 411–444.

Snowdon, Paul. 2003. Knowing how and knowing that: A distinction reconsidered. *Proceedings of the Aristotelian Society* 104: pp. 1–29.

Taylor, J. D. 2011. *Times Literary Supplement*, July 15: p. 15.

Trilling, Lionel. 1951. *The Liberal Imagination*. New York: Harcourt.

Velleman, David. 2003. Narrative explanation. *The Philosophical Review* 112: pp. 1–25.

Williams, B. 2002. *Truth and Truthfulness: An Essay in Genealogy*. Princeton, NJ: Princeton University Press.

Wilson, Timothy. 2002. *Strangers to Ourselves: Discovering the Adaptive Unconscious*. Cambridge, MA: Harvard University Press.

Wollheim, Richard. 1984. *The Thread of Life*. Cambridge, MA: Harvard University Press.

Wykes, T., S. Hamid, and K. Wagstaff. 2001. Theory of mind and executive functions in the non-psychotic siblings of patients with schizophrenia. *Schizophrenia Research* 49: p. 148.

3

The Creative Audience

Some Ways in which Readers, Viewers, and/or Listeners Use Their Imaginations to Engage Fictional Artworks

NOËL CARROLL

> The creative act is not performed by the artist alone; the spectator brings the work in contact with the external world by deciphering and interpreting its inner qualification and thus adds his contribution to the creative act.
>
> —Marcel Duchamp[1]

> To be a great artist, there must be a great audience.
>
> —Walt Whitman

1. Introduction

When discussing the relation between fictional art and creativity, the customary tendency is to focus on the artist. This, however, encourages neglect of the audience's creative share in making the fictional artwork function. Indeed, this neglect can sometimes escalate into obliviousness, as when some commentators write, with respect to at least some artworks, that the audience is utterly passive. Undoubtedly, this is especially the case with popular fictions. Yet it is difficult to conceive of any fiction (including popular fiction) that does not require some active, productive, or creative input from readers, viewers, and listeners in order to achieve its intended output.[2]

---

[1] Marcel Duchamp in a talk at the Creative Act Convention, Houston, in April 1957, cited in Robert Lebel, *Marcel Duchamp* (New York: Grove Press, 1959), pp. 77–78.

[2] This article restricts its purview to fictional artworks across the various media. However, this is not to say that some of the operations of the audience's imagination with respect to fiction do not also obtain in nonfictional art forms, such as orchestral music.

The artist designs her fiction to elicit a response from the audience. But the audience does not register the impact of the artwork in the way in which a mechanical device might automatically record a sound. Audiences mobilize their imaginations in order to negotiate the artistic stimulus. Of course, the artist guides the audience's deployment of their imaginations, mandating certain forms of engagement and not others. However, being guided by the author does not render us passive. True, we may be so absorbed in the artwork that we find it difficult to break away from it, as in the case of "page turners." But in such cases, our absorption is in large measure a function of our active and imaginative engagement with the work. Absorption, that is, need not signal passivity. It can be a sign that our creative juices are flowing.

In this essay, I would like to substantiate the claim that the audience's response to fictional artworks is typically creative. I attempt to do this by canvassing a number of the recurring types of imaginative engagements that audiences recruit in order to make fictional artworks of various sorts work. It is true that such artworks demand imaginative contributions from creators in the first instance; but in order to work as they are designed to, such artworks also standardly call for various kinds of imaginative responses from their readers, viewers, or listeners. I will chart a preliminary list of some of the pertinent types of imaginative activities that fictional artworks ask of audiences. The list does not pretend to exhaustiveness, nor are the categories examined necessarily exclusive. In some cases, they grow out of each other.

Moreover, although all of these creative activities have some claim to being slotted under the label of *the imagination*, it is not clear that exercising the imagination is one and only one kind of mental activity. Rather it seems to be something more like a genus with several species vaguely united in that these species each go beyond what is given or has been given to the perception as fact in either the past or in the here and now. In this regard, it may be more accurate to speak of different kinds of imaginations. In any event, that is the policy that I will adopt in what follows.

2. Kant, the Imagination, and Aesthetic Ideas

As noted by R. G. Collingwood, there is an enduring theory of art in the Western tradition—which he calls *the technical theory of art*—that treats the audience's response to art as passive and uncreative.[3] Plato, for example, represents the work of poetry as if it simply pushed our buttons, eliciting virtually automatically a preordained series of emotional responses. This approach is still very common with respect to discussions of popular fictions, like movies, which are conceived of as working on audiences, as Collingwood would put it, like a drug. Kant, in contrast,

---

[3] R. G. Collingwood, *The Priniciples of Art* (Oxford, UK: Oxford University Press, 1958), pp. 17–20.

pictures aesthetic engagement as active and creative, due in large measure to the way in which the imagination is mobilized in the course of aesthetic experience.

Referring to the judgment of free beauty, Kant writes of a sensation

> ...whose universal communicability a judgment of taste postulates, as the quickening of the two powers (imagination and the understanding) to an activity that is indeterminate but, as a result of the prompting of the given presentation nonetheless accordant... the facilitated play of the two mental powers (imagination and understanding) quickened by their reciprocal harmony.[4]

This is admittedly a dense passage. What Kant appears to have in mind here is that when one encounters the kind of stimulus that we are wont to call beautiful, our mental powers—those of imagination and understanding—*play* with it, rather than, as is the way of ordinary cognition, subsuming it under a determinate concept. Typically, in everyday experience, the imagination synthesizes various perspectives of, for instance, a horse (say the front and the left side) and fills in what is unseen, and the understanding files this under the determinate concept *horse*. But the aesthetic encounter is quite different.

When aesthetically engaging with clouds, for example, we do not subsume the stimulus under the determinate concept *cloud*. Rather, we let our minds play with it. Our imagination synthesizes it first as a face, perhaps a familiar one, and then as a puff of cotton, and maybe then as a mountain, or vanilla ice cream, and so on, with no determinate point of closure. The imagination and the understanding conspire in a game of seeing-as. There is no determinate concept—such as *mountain*—under which the stimulus must be subsumed. This is not to say that we do not realize that we are looking at a cloud, but only that in the process of experiencing it aesthetically, our minds explore its aspects freely, that is, not constrained to see it under just one defining concept. Instead, we are free to allow our imaginations to roam over it, organizing it in accordance with various patterns with no necessary end in view. The limit of the experience is the limit of our imagination.

This example is one of experiencing the beautiful in nature. As is often remarked, Kant's theory of free beauty is best exemplified by responses to natural beauty. Nevertheless, a similar story can be told about aesthetic experiences of art. In order to see how this may be done, we need to consider Kant's notion of aesthetic ideas.

According to Kant, an aesthetic idea is "... a presentation of the imagination which prompts much thought but to which no determinate thought whatsoever, i.e., no determinate concept, can be adequate."[5] Again, this is a dense passage. But

---

[4] Immanuel Kant, *Critique of Judgment*, trans. Werner Pluhar (Indianapolis, IN: Hackett, 1987), p. 63.

[5] Kant, 182.

what I think Kant is getting at can be illuminated by Shakespeare's metaphor of "Juliet is the sun." Here, we do not subsume *Juliet* under the determinate concept of the *sun*. Rather, we are meant to treat the *sun* as the source of associations that can be seen to *fit* Juliet or, to enlist a more technical mode of speech, that can be seen to map onto her.

For example, we may gloss the metaphor as "Juliet is the center of my universe," as "Juliet gives me life," as "Juliet warms me," as "Juliet is the light of my life," and so on without any preordained point of closure. That is, one may go on discovering associations wherever and whenever the imagination locates a fitting correspondence between Juliet and the sun. The metaphor invites much thought, but there is no fixed limit or stopping point to that thinking—no determinate concept that is *the* thought upon which one's musings must arrive.

Of course, not every association that the determinate concept the *sun* affords is applicable to Juliet. It will not do to interpret the metaphor as suggesting that Juliet is a gaseous body. Rather, the imagination is free to pick and choose between the various associations that belong to the concept of the *sun* on the basis of whether or not they supply a good heuristic for capturing Romeo's feelings toward Juliet. Again, we are not intended to subsume Juliet under the determinate concept *sun* by applying every defining feature of it to Juliet. In contrast, the imagination is playing with the concept of the *sun*, selecting certain aspects for contemplation and explaining them in a way analogous to our previous example of cloud-gazing.

One way of understanding Kant's conception of artworks—or, at least, the ones that are the product of genius—is that they are aesthetic ideas. Perhaps we may attribute the view to Kant that ideally artworks are just aesthetic ideas, affording the unbounded interplay of our imagination and understanding. An example that Kant offers is that of a representation of the god Jupiter figured as an eagle in whose talons lightning bolts are clutched. Here, the imagination is free to play with the concept of *eagle*, matching associations from the source domain (the source concept) to its target, Jupiter, in a way that is unlimited in the sense that there is no antecedently fixed set of associations that must be applied to Jupiter; at the same time, Jupiter cannot be subsumed under the determinate concept *eagle* in terms of every defining feature of eagles applying to Jupiter. That is, we may take the aesthetic idea of Jupiter-as-eagle-plus-lightning-bolts to suggest that "Jupiter is powerful," "Jupiter is master of the sky," Jupiter commands the elements," and "Jupiter is lofty," but (probably not) "Jupiter is a chicken thief."

Likewise the fictional description by Shakespeare of Hamlet's Denmark as rotten is an aesthetic idea. Nor are aesthetic ideas absent from popular art; recall the '60s rock song "My Love is Like a Red, Rubber Ball."

Perhaps needless to say, the exploratory imagination is not only provoked by metaphors and symbols. Christian Marclay's video installation *The Clock* invites viewers to construct myriad narratives of all sorts out of shots that have been culled from hundreds of disparate motion pictures.

Now Kant is certainly correct that this sort of imaginative activity is often engaged by artworks, including fictional ones. Let us label this sort of creativity on the part of readers, viewers, and listeners an exercise of the *exploratory imagination*. However, the exploratory imagination does not exhaust the range of imaginative functions that audiences are called upon to discharge. In what follows, I chart some of these.

3. The Fictive Imagination

Over the course of history, the imagination has been invoked as the name of a number of different psychological phenomena, including mental imagery, counterfactual thinking, mental simulation, the filling-out and synthesizing of perceptions, fantasy, daydreaming, and eidetic imagery, among other things. Often it seems that when we are at a loss about what to call some mental phenomenon, we resort to the notion of *the imagination*. Whether there is just one mental process here with numerous functions or there are several different kinds of imaginations is not now a matter of our concern. The lesson that we want to draw from this recognition of a multiplicity of imaginations (or of functions of the imagination) is the implication that this has for the way in which audiences engage artworks. For, just as we find several disparate applications of the notion of the imagination in general, there is likewise a range of different audience activities involved in responding to fiction that employ different functions or faculties of imagination.

Kant specified what we have characterized as the exploratory imagination—the contemplative play with the artwork, searching out and testing the fitness of the various associations the work suggests. But perhaps a far more pervasive exercise of the imagination today in a culture in which we are surrounded on every side by narratives is the *fictive imagination*. This imaginative power is rooted in our capacity to think counterfactually. Children exemplify it at a very early age. And it is the fictive imagination that makes possible everything from mass-market movies, comic books, and triple-decker novels to modernist plays, noveaux romains, and portraits of Ophelia.

A fruitful way in which to understand the fictive imagination is to contrast it with belief. Let us think of a belief as a propositional content that is held in the mind as asserted. To believe that it is raining outside is to hold in the mind the thought (that it is raining outside) as asserted. To imagine, on the other hand, is to hold a propositional content in the mind as unasserted. To imagine, as I might in a daydream, is to entertain the thought that I am the world's greatest dancer without really believing it. The imagination is key to planning. I can imagine how to escape my home should it catch fire without believing that it is now or ever was on fire.

The institution of fiction is founded upon our ability to engage in contrary-to-fact thinking. A fiction is a structure of sense-bearing signs toward which the producer intends that readers, listeners, and viewers adopt the fictive stance—that is, that they entertain the propositional content conveyed by the structure of sense-bearing signs as unasserted.[6] The creator of the play does not intend viewers to believe that what they are seeing is a woman really being threatened with a fate worse than death. That would flirt with the inconvenience of rubes rushing onstage to the rescue. Instead, the playwright means us to entertain the thought that a maiden is in distress without taking the representation to be assertoric. Likewise, when I read that a man named Fagan deceives a boy called Oliver Twist, I neither believe that these people ever existed nor that anyone was actually deceived. I merely imagine it.

When reading a history book, I regard the contents as asserted facts. I take an assertoric stance toward them. In the typical course of events, I usually believe what I read in history books, unless I suspect that the author is untrustworthy; ordinarily, I take the assertions that I find in history books onboard. I do this because I recognize that that is what I am supposed to do; the author of a history book intends me to regard the propositional content of his treatise as asserted, and I realize that, in consequence, its assertions are to be evaluated in terms of truth and plausibility, and falsity and improbability. That is, when I read that an atomic bomb was dropped on Nagasaki in 1945, I hold it in my mind as asserted—I believe it—because I recognize that that is what the author intends me to do.

However, the authorial mandate is different when it comes to fiction. Here we are intended to imagine the propositional content of the sense-bearing signs. We recognize that the author means us to adopt the fictive stance and only to entertain the thought as unasserted that, for example, Dracula travels to London from Transylvania. We do not believe that Dracula exists or that the author intends us to take him as making an assertion. We realize that he wants us to imagine Dracula and his properties. Although there is no Dracula, we do not take the author to be lying. His novel is not false; it is fictive. As Sir Philip Sydney observed, such stories neither affirm nor deny. We do not believe them but simply entertain them. Moreover, the very possibility of fiction depends upon the audience's exercise of its fictive imagination on the basis of the author's mandate to do so.

Although so far we have been contrasting believing and imagining in terms of the stances they mandate toward their propositional content, they are also functionally similar inasmuch as they interact with many, but not all, of the same mental mechanisms.[7] Shaun Nichols expresses this idea by saying that imaginative states and belief states are in a single code; he writes: "On the single code hypothesis, if a mechanism takes pretense representations as inputs, that mechanism will process the pretense representation in much the same way it would process an isomorphic

---

[6] I use the locution "sense-bearing signs" because fictions can be visual, as well as verbal.

[7] See Jonathan Weinberg and Aaron Meskin, "Puzzling over the Imagination: Philosophical Problems, Architectural Solutions," in *The Architecture of the Imagination: New Essays on Pretence, Possibility, and Fiction*, edited by Shaun Nichols (Oxford, UK: Oxford University Press, 2006), p. 178.

belief."[8] One of the mechanisms that Nichols has in mind here is our emotions. His hypothesis is that imagining, under the guidance of the author, that the apocalypse is in the offing will elicit the same kind of palpitations of fear that a comparable belief state would.

Undoubtedly, the fact that imaginings can engender emotional states is one of the leading factors contributing to the popularity of the institution of fiction. It is enjoyable to be in emotional states, especially when one does not have to pay the price that many of the emotions exact (as sadness typically requires loss). Via the activation of the fictive imagination, readers, viewers, and listeners are able to undergo a range of emotions of varying intensity without incurring the risks that such emotions usually entail.

Of course, the fictive imagination did not evolve in order to make novels and movies possible. Yet art forms such as the novel, the movies, and many others are the beneficiaries of our ability to imagine contrary-to-fact situations which imaginings, in turn, move us emotionally. Surely, many a youngster survived and reproduced because the elders of the tribe spun scary stories about what would happen if children got too close to the swamp where the crocodile ruled. This is not to say that the practice of fiction is not also adaptive, since by instilling converging imaginings and emotings among groups of people, it can encourage bonding and fellow feelings of the sort that encourage cooperative behavior. Undoubtedly, that is why we find the practice of fiction so widely distributed across humanity.

However, if fiction is a product of evolution such that it may have some claim to being nearly universal, then some readers may question my presumption that the audience's exercise of the fictive imagination is genuinely creative. For if nearly everyone has the capacity to fictively imagine that a gigantic shark is marauding off the coastline (and nearly everyone who is exposed to the movie does so), does that still warrant being called creative?

This worry is underwritten by the likelihood that there are probably at least two senses of *creative* in tension here. One is the descriptive sense and the other is honorific. On the descriptive sense of creative, a creative activity is an act of human intelligence that produces something or that brings something off or about, notably something appropriate to the situation. On the honorific sense of creativity, a creative act is one that is strikingly original or virtually unprecedented and of great value. For Kant, geniuses are creative in this sense. But this sense of creative seems to me to be primarily commendatory and overlooks the fact that much of ordinary human life is creative in a descriptive sense. When I figure out how to balance my grocery bags so that I can hold them up and open the trunk of my car at the same time, I have done something creative. I have exercised human intelligence to bring

---

    [8] Shaun Nichols, "Imagining and Believing: The Promise of a Single Code," in *The Journal of Aesthetics and Art Criticism* 62 (2004), p. 131.

something about—in this case, transporting my groceries in a way that is apposite, is what the situation calls for..

Although a great deal of attention has been spent examining creativity of the sort exemplified by the DaVincis, Mozarts, and Einsteins, various commentators have stressed the need to examine creativity of the more modest variety that is exercised by ordinary folks in mundane circumstances.[9]

Exercising the fictive imagination may not in the usual course of events be creative in the honorific sense (except perhaps in cases of avant-garde fictions that are challenging to imagine). Nevertheless, mobilizing the fictive imagination is creative in the descriptive sense, since it brings something off—the activation of the novel in virtue of the way in which the fictive imagination is connected to the pertinent mental mechanisms, such as the emotions. Patently, fictions are typically designed to bring about emotional states. Obviously, those emotional states are not in the novel. They are events the novel aspires to bring about. The novel achieves this by kick-starting the fictive imagination. Thus the fictive imagination is instrumental in bringing off a new, particular state of affairs, through the enlistment of human intelligence, and is creative—additive—at least in the descriptive sense of *creative*.[10]

4. Filling in the Fiction

Confronted by a fiction, we fictively imagine the explicit propositional content of the relevant sense-bearing signs. But we do not solely imagine what we are told or shown. We fill in the fiction. We may never be told that the protagonist has a left foot and a right foot. But we presume that he does. No fictioneer can describe fully everything presupposed by her fiction. The fictioneer needs the audience to supply creatively what is missing in order for the fiction to be intelligible. The audience meets this task by inducting what we may call the elaborative imagination.

Every fiction is perforce incomplete and indeterminate. All manner of things are left out of the fiction. These include details of the character's physical biology, such

---

[9] Ronald Beghetto and James C. Kaufman, "Toward a Broader Conception of Creativity: A Case for 'mini-c' Creativity," in *Psychology of Aesthetic Creativity and the Arts*, vol. 1, no. 2 (2007), pp. 73–79. Although the kind of creativity I am invoking here is not what they call 'mini-c' creativity, it resembles it insofar as it calls forth a response that is creative—that goes beyond the given—*from the perspective of the individual*, rather than something that interpersonally novel.

[10] In this section, I have been talking about the fictive imagination with respect to the narrative arts. Some theorists might extend it to pure music as well, although this is highly controversial. See, e.g., Jerrold Levinson, "Music and Negative Emotion," in his *Music, Art and Metaphysics* (Ithaca, NY: Cornell University Press, 1990), pp. 306–335; and Saam Trivedi, "Imagination, Music, and the Emotion," *Revue Internationale de Philosophie*, vol. 60, no. 238 (12/2006), pp. 415–436. For comment, see Margaret Moore, *The Mind's Ear* (Philadephia: Temple University [unpublished doctoral thesis in philosophy], 2008).

as that the character will die if the villain fires a pistol at point-blank range into her heart. We also fill in what is missing about the geography, the history, the physics, psychology, and so forth that the fiction presupposes but about which it remains silent. In a way of speaking, we creatively construct vast stretches of the world of the fiction. The author tells us that the protagonist boards a plane. We not only fictively imagine that, but also that the plane has an engine and a pilot and that it is larger than a breadbox. In this special sense, the audience is a co-creator of the fiction.

Nor is the elaborative imagination only in operation with respect to literary fictions. Plays and movies, though they present a massive amount of detail, don't show and/or tell everything. We never see Hamlet's appendix nor is it mentioned, yet we presume that he was born with one. When a scene opens with Tony Soprano knocking on his mother's front door, we suppose he got there by means of some kind of vehicle or on foot, and not by means of one of those transporters featured on *Star Trek*. Some audiences may go too far in their imaginings, as when they entertain the thought of a determinate number of Lady Macbeth's children. But no fiction can do without the audience's exercise of the elaborative imagination for the purpose of filling in what has been left out of the story but which nevertheless must be presupposed if the story is to remain coherent.

A major factor that enables the elaborative imagination to fill in the fiction can be explained in terms of Nichols's suggestion that imagination and belief are connected to many of the same mental mechanisms. These include such things as domain-specific conceptions of folk psychology, folk physics, folk biology, and so on. Just as when we come to believe that the man standing at the bar desires a drink in virtue of folk psychology, so we imagine that the man standing at the bar in a movie desires a drink in virtue of the application of the same folk psychological schemas. We believe that death is likely when my neighbor is beheaded; likewise in virtue of the same folk biology, I entertain the thought that the character will die when he is beheaded in the fiction. That is, to a great extent, we fill in the missing background in fiction by accessing the same sorts of information that we use to render the real world intelligible. For this reason, we can call the heuristic that we employ in this way in order to fill in the fiction the "realistic heuristic."

When consuming a fiction, the realistic heuristic is generally our default assumption. And it works a great deal of the time. But it is not always reliable, since fictions may deviate from the operation of the actual world. This is very obvious when it comes to science fiction and horror fiction. In the former, spaceships can enter black holes and come out intact; in horror fictions, the dead can rise. Applying the realistic heuristic in cases like these will render the fiction unintelligible. If you suppose that there are no such things as zombies in the world of the fiction, *Night of the Living Dead* will not make any sense to you. In cases like this, the realistic heuristic needs to be suspended and replaced with something else. But what?

One alternative is what can be labeled the "genre heuristic." Different fictional genres play by different rules. Very often, we are informed of deviations from the realistic heuristic in the course of a fiction's unfolding. For example, we may be told that certain things can go faster than the speed of light. But sometimes, we know the rules of the genre without being explicitly alerted to them by the fiction. All horror fans are aware of the premise that vampires live on blood and, even if it is not explained in the fiction, we use our knowledge of the genre to make sense of why the man in the cape is biting all those virgins. Similarly, when the vampire follows the young woman into the dark alleyway, we conjecture that he desires to drain her.

So if application of the realistic heuristic produces anomalies and we have not been told to ignore them because that's just the way the pertinent fictional world is, we might try out a genre heuristic to alleviate the discrepancies. Of course, sometimes we don't wait for the realistic heuristic to falter. When we settle into a viewing of *Son of Dracula*, we enlist the genre heuristic from the get-go. Likewise, we go along with the supposition that animals can converse in English because that's a given feature of the fairytale world.

Of course, sometimes neither the realistic heuristic nor the genre heuristic will render the fiction intelligible. This may occur when the fiction comes from a time and a place that do not share our conceptions of how the world works. In that case, we need to fill in the fiction in accordance with the relevant convictions of the culture in which the fiction originated. If a ghost appears in a fiction that is not a ghost story, we may explain this deviation from the realistic heuristic in terms of the supposition that the reality of ghosts was accepted in the fiction's culture of origin. Let us label this the "culture heuristic."

The realistic heuristic, the genre heuristic, and the culture heuristic are three tools that the elaborative imagination employs in order to fill in fictions. There are no algorithms governing the application of these heuristics. Readers, viewers, and listeners must experiment to discover which assumptions jibe best or which promote the greatest intelligibility with respect to what appears to be presented as true in the fiction—that is, as what we are mandated to imagine is thus and so in accordance with the relevant fiction.[11]

Furthermore, in some cases, the audience must not only fill in what is presupposed by the fictional discourse, but also the context in which it is uttered. This is especially true of much contemporary lyric poetry. For example, consider this section of John Ashbery's "A Worldly Country":

---

[11] For some, this category of the elaborative imagination may once again raise the question of whether this deserves to be called creativity, since virtually every viewer does this, usually in ways that at least broadly converge. That is, is it creative if everyone does it? As already indicated, I don't think that this should be a problem; there is creativity in the everyday course of events. Moreover, the exercise of this imaginative function, I suspect, probably enhances intrapersonally our capacity to follow and to construct stories. And, if that is the case, then it contributes to *enlarging* our powers in ways that may lead to more distinctive manifestations of creativity. Thus, as Beghetto and Kaufman (op. cit.) argue, it is not helpful to treat the activities that make the more impressive creative achievements possible as categorically different from creativity.

Not the smoothness, not the insane clocks on the square,
the scent of manure in the municipal parterre,
Nor the fabrics, the sullen mockery of Tweety Bird,
Not the fresh troops that needed freshening up. If it occurred in
in real time, that was OK, and if it was time in a novel,
that was okay, too. From palace and hovel
the great parade flooded avenue and by way
and turnip fields became just another highway.

Here, in order to render the poem intelligible, the reader needs to elaborate a context in which this string of observations makes sense. One way to do so is to imagine
a context in which the speaker (who, if Ashberry, is a transplant to New York) is trying to convey the clashing images one experiences upon encountering Manhattan—
where the country aroma of the manure that trails the horse-drawn carriages floats
by the enormous billboards in Times Square, and palaces jostle against hovels.[12]
Of course, this need to elaborate the context of the enunciation of a fiction is not
restricted to contemporary modernist poem. The contemporary popular song
"Time to Say Good-bye" makes a similar demand upon the listener.

The exercise of the elaborative imagination on the part of readers, viewers, and
listeners is indispensable to securing the intelligibility of fictions, both prose and
poetry, whether verbal, oral, or visual. The artwork needs the audience to elaborate
upon it. This elaboration may require varying degrees of effort. But it is all creative;
by means of the imagination, the audience adds to what is explicitly given to them
by the author.

5. Mindreading

Mindreading in the philosophy of mind refers to our never-ending attempts to glean
the thoughts, intentions, desires, emotions and so on of other people (a.k.a. our
conspecifics). Humans, of course, could not survive if we were unable to discern
what is on other people's minds. We mindread in order to predict how others will
behave and to explain that behavior. We weave our own plans around what we
anticipate on the basis of our assessments of the mental states of those whose lives
impinge upon our own. We are typically obsessed with what others are thinking.
This is strategic, but such curiosity is also something that we find to be naturally

---

[12] I owe this insightful interpretation of the Ashberry poem, as well as the idea that lyric poems
often call upon readers to imaginatively elaborate the context of enunciation, to John Gibson's pen-
etrating essay "The Question of Poetic Meaning." This was a talk at the third annual Wittgenstein
Conference at the University of Southampton in 2010.

absorbing. And it is the possibility of this sort of intense absorption that is one of the major calling cards of fiction.

We are often drawn to fiction by the opportunity to scrutinize characters, which, it is perhaps needless to say, involves mindreading. Through mindreading, we fill in the mental states of characters. That is, we imagine their psychologies—predicting what they intend, desire, believe, and so forth. From one perspective, mindreading with respect to fiction is a special case of the elaborative imagination inasmuch as we use it to flesh out the characters. But some, as we shall see, argue that because mindreading primarily involves the mental simulation of characters, it deserves its own category.

In the classic western *The Searchers*, a prime focus of our attention is what the leading character Ethan intends to do to his niece should he ever find her. We are pretty sure that he means to kill her. Also, we surmise in an earlier scene, prior to the Indian attack, that Ethan loves his brother's wife, his niece's mother, and that the mother loves Ethan. Part of the pleasure we derive from the movie, like the pleasure we derive from everyday gossip, has to do with tracking the inner lives of such characters. Mindreading is not only a necessity of human life; it is one of our pleasures as well, a pleasure that fiction promises to reward big-time.

How does mindreading in fiction proceed? In many ways, just as mindreading is typically pursued in the flow of daily life. Despite critical admonitions designed to break our addiction to treating fictional characters much in the way we scope out our conspecifics, in large measure, we size up or mindread fictional characters by using the same heuristics, schemas, cues, etc. that we employ to survey the mindscapes of the flesh-and-blood folks with whom we interact in the quotidian. We read the way that Ethan and his sister-in-law look at each other as we might observe longing glances outside the cinema. And we imagine that they love each other.

In this, the audience goes beyond what they are shown onscreen. They make a contribution of something that has gone unsaid to the narrative. And through their imaginative attribution of an unstated bond here, they creatively enlarge the story, albeit in ways guided by the director John Ford and his actors.

As in the case of the application of folk biology to the bodies of fictional characters, something akin to the realistic heuristic is generally our default mode for filling in the mental states of the denizens of fiction. However, it doesn't always work. Sometimes we need to resort to genre heuristics in order to render the intentional states of fictional characters intelligible. Why is it that when the characters in thrillers are accused of crimes they did not commit, they break away from the police in order to find the real culprits, while being simultaneously stalked by the bad guys and the cops? In everyday life, we would imagine that a more realistic line of thinking would decide that consigning oneself to the police and hoping that they would sort it out would be the way to negotiate the situation. But if characters were made to think realistically, think of how many fewer thriller stories we would have. The protagonists in thrillers have to think a certain way in order for the story to take off.

So, when mindreading such characters, we mold our imaginations to the dictates of the genre. Likewise, romance stories come with their own psychological heuristics, and so on.[13]

So far I have treated mindreading as a special instance of the elaborative imagination; mindreading elaborates on the mental states of characters much as folk physics is used to elaborate on the operation of gravity in a mountaineering fiction. But some theorists maintain that because of the way in which mindreading elaborates on the inner states of characters, it should be marked off as a separate kind of imaginative engagement. What these philosophers contend is that the way in which we mindread our conspecifics in general and our fictional conspecifics in particular is by means of simulation.

Simulation is a matter of imaginatively putting oneself in the place of a character in a fiction and then asking what I would intend, desire, believe, and so on from that vantage point. To state the idea of simulation more technically, I use my own psychological constitution to track the thoughts of characters. I do this, as simulationists say, by taking my action-engaging system offline and inputting into my own mental processing system the beliefs and desires of the characters, as given in the story, in order to determine what they are likely to be thinking, planning, intending and so forth. Thus the simulationist slogan: Folk psychology is simulation.

Admittedly, my psychological constitution may be something of a black box. But inasmuch as it is isomorphic to other people's black boxes, once decoupled from my particular beliefs, desires, interests, etc. and supplemented with the relevant information from the other, my psychological processing system should, so it is alleged, serve up a reliable approximation of what is going on in the character's mind. Thus, on this view, the reader, viewer, and/or listener fleshes out the mental states of characters by imagining herself in the situation.

Whether the mindreading of others in ordinary life is primarily a matter of simulation is a debate we can put aside. Our question is whether the mindreading of fictional characters is primarily a matter of simulation. My own inclination is to say that it is not, at least when we are consuming fictions. Clearly, movies and plays usually unfold too quickly for us to indulge in simulations. Nor do we need to, since most often the characters tell us outright what they intend, desire, plan, believe, fear and so forth. We have no call to simulate in those cases. And even in cases when we are not directly informed about the mental states of characters, visual narratives are usually so constructed that we know without simulating what the characters are thinking because of the director's salient and emphatically foregrounded exploitation of the kinds of schemas, heuristics, cues and so on that we employ in everyday life for the purpose of mindreading.

---

[13] Of course, sometimes neither the realistic heuristic nor the genre heuristic will do the trick. In those cases, it pays to explore the culture heuristic.

Literature, of course, proceeds at the reader's pace, whereas motion pictures and theater proceed with the velocity the director determines. So, the reader is better positioned to take time out to simulate with respect to, say, a novel than with respect to a movie. However, even though there is time for simulation with novels, I still do not think that the mindreading to which we subject fictional characters is primarily simulative. For, once again, we do not really need to simulate in order to understand literary characters most of the time. Often we are privy to the minds of the characters. We may be told directly by the author what they are thinking, feeling, intending, believing, and desiring. Who needs to simulate in order to get into Holden Caufield's head or into the mind of the murderer in Poe's *The Telltale Heart*. In addition, we may be shown the world from the character's viewpoint, either directly or indirectly. Moreover, when describing the behavior of characters, authors, like movie and theater directors, may emphasize the schemas, heuristics, and cues etc. that we use in everyday life in order to mindread. I cannot demonstrate that simulation *never* comes into play when we imagine the mental states of characters, but I think there are ample grounds for being skeptical about the claim that simulation is the primary way in which we grok the mental states of characters, especially *during* our consumption of fiction.

I have added the qualification "during our consumption of a fiction" to allow for the possibility that simulation may occur with greater frequency *after* we have seen, heard, or read a fiction. Having just read or seen *Captain Horatio Hornblower*, I might try to simulate what it might feel like to be the master of a warship in the Napoleonic era. Perhaps some consumers of stories use the adventures of fictional characters as stimulants to their imaginative engagement with the narrative in what we might call the creative afterlife of the fiction in which the reader, listener, or viewer explores the fiction through the mind's eye.

So although much mindreading in fiction is a matter of the deployment of the elaborative imagination, there is also room for thinking that, particularly with reference to the creative afterlife of the fiction, there can be another species of mindreading, namely simulation. Whereas the elaborative imagination operates on propositions (imagining that…), simulation takes as its domain that of acquaintance, that is, learning what it would be like (to be Captain Horatio Hornblower, e.g.).

6. The Constructive Imagination

Narrative fictions, as we have seen, need to be filled in by the spectator. The reader, listener, and/or viewer must supply, among other things, the historical, geographical, biological, psychological, physical, and moral background that the author has left off the page, stage, or screen, but which information is requisite for the story to be intelligible. We have attributed much of this work to the elaborative imagination. But that information itself requires a spatiotemporal-causal structure in which it can be organized. We can call the imaginative capacity to accomplish this "constructive imagination."

Narrative fictions typically come with spatial, temporal, and/or causal ellipses. At one point, the novel *Frankenstein* is set in Switzerland, but later the action transpires in the Arctic. The time of the telling of the story, which is sometimes labeled the "discourse," can vary from the linear progression of time in the story world (whose temporal ordering is often simply called the "story"). There can be flashbacks, as in the novel *Brideshead Revisited*. And there can be flash-forwards, as in the movie *Easy Rider*. Jean-Luc Godard famously once remarked that films have beginnings, middles, and ends, but not necessarily in that order. Discourse and story—or *syuzhet* and *fabula*, as the Russian Formalists referred to them—can diverge, and it is up to the audience to construct the story out of the discourse.

Since temporality and causality are related, and present and past can be reversed in the discourse, causes and effects can similarly be reversed, as when the cause of the murder that opens the tale is not represented until the penultimate scene. Moreover, on occasion, pertinent causes and effects of events in the tale may pass unannounced in such a way that the audience needs to supply them.

Typically the reader, viewer, and/or listener is required to use the discourse or telling of the tale in order to assemble an intelligible story world—one that is spatially, temporally, and causally interconnected and unified. The audience meets this task by dint of the constructive imagination. The constructive imagination formats, so to speak, the explicit and implicit information imparted by the discourse and/or supplied by the elaborative imagination and unifies it spatially, temporally, and causally into a coherent whole.

Although the elaborative imagination and the constructive imagination are both engaged in filling in the story world, it seems useful to mark a distinction between them. The elaborative imagination is local or piecemeal. It fills in such details as the unmentioned presupposition that the railroad train has an engineer on a detail-by-detail basis. As items are added to the story, the elaborative imagination fleshes them out. The constructive imagination functions more globally. It takes all of the objects, events, places, persons, and actions in the story world and organizes them into an interconnected spatiotemporal-causal order. It is the armature upon which the discourse is arrayed. It operates on the information supplied by the discourse in a way roughly analogous to the way Kantian reproductive imagination operates on perception.

The constructive imagination works both retrospectively and prospectively on the fictional input. As each new detail is added to the story, the creative imagination hooks it up with the spatial, temporal, and causal information that has preceded it. Thus the arrival of the fire trucks in the second chapter is connected to the outbreak of fire in the same house in the first chapter. The constructive imagination puts together a spatiotemporally-causally unified fictional world piece by piece as each new detail is added to the discourse. Sometimes this happens seamlessly. However, on other occasions, putting the fiction world together in this way can command discernible effort on the part of the audience, as in the case of mystery novels. In such cases, a piece of the causal puzzle is missing, and it is up to us to try to find it.

The constructive imagination sews together the incoming information at a steady pace while processing the narrative. But often, it also stands back and retrospectively reviews the fiction as a whole once the story has terminated, because information that is added at the end frequently forces us to reconfigure what we had thought was going on in a new way, as when we learn that what we have been told so far has been reported to us by a madman or is a dream).

The constructive imagination not only connects the present of the story with the past, keeping track of what is happening by means of a unifying spatiotemporal-causal framework; the constructive imagination also operates prospectively, anticipating the events and states of affairs that may emerge from the story so far. In some cases, this may involve precisely predicting what will happen next. For example: The duelists agree to meet at dawn, and we predict that they will do so. But, more often than not, we do not anticipate exactly that some specific thing is about to go down; rather, we construct a range of possible outcomes. For example, when we learn that the heroine has been tied down to the train tracks by the villain, we entertain the thought that she may or may not be demolished by the oncoming locomotive).

Since the possibilities about what might happen next in the story are most often somehow causally related to what has already transpired in the story, anticipating the kinds of things that can happen next falls into the domain of the constructive imagination. Without the constructive imagination's maintenance of causal order in the fictional world, we would be in a constant state of surprise as the story unfolds. That we are not is a function of the constructive imagination keeping us apprised of the range of kinds of things that are likely to happen next. This, of course, is an important factor in what makes narrative suspense possible. We are riveted in our seats because we recognize that the heroine will be either run over or saved.

In virtue of the constructive imagination, successive episodes of the narrative seem to fall into place. That is because the constructive imagination is, as Husserl would say, protentive, as well as retentive. It carves out a space of possibilities regarding what is likely to emerge from what has preceded it. This is not to say that we are not sometimes taken aback or surprised by a narrative turn of events. But in those cases, we realize in retrospect that there was a possibility hidden in the story that was somehow camouflaged or otherwise rendered recessive. For the most part, most fictions deliver up events that fall within the range of the kinds of things we expect to happen. This is what the constructive imagination tracks prospectively. Yet there are standard deviations when that range of expectations is upset and we are surprised. In those cases, the constructive imagination reconstructs the chain of events retrospectively and thereby recovers the intelligibility of the fiction as a whole.

7. The Thematizing Imagination

A lot is happening toward the end of Fritz Lang's *Metropolis*. The workers' quarters in the deepest stratum of the city are flooding, and the children who live there are being rescued while their parents (the workers and their wives) are destroying the great machines that power the metropolis; at the same time, elite revelers are being egged on in their debaucheries by the robot Maria. These scenes of intense activity then give way to Rotwang pursuing the saintly Maria and the workers fighting with revelers and burning the robot Maria at the stake, while young Frederson rushes to the rescue of the Good Maria and his father searches for him. Lang crosscuts furiously between these streams of hyperactivity, and it is up to the constructive imagination to keep track of it all, locating the relation of each sequence of events to the others spatially, temporally, and causally (i.e., the constructive imagination is what holds the action together as a spatial, temporal, and causal unity).

Yet *Metropolis* is also unified as a whole in another respect: It is unified by an idea. The film does not hide this idea, but rather broadcasts it openly. It is the notion, stated figuratively, that the head and the hands must be mediated by the heart. Here the hands stand for the workers and the head stands for the designers of the city of Metropolis. Between them, the film avows that there needs to arise a compassionate mediator who can promote peace and understanding on both sides of the divide. That person, of course, is the so-called heart, young Federson.

Granted, this idea would seem to have little to recommend it. Nevertheless, the work it is supposed to do in the film is fairly straightforward. It is meant to unify the film by providing a conceptualization under which many of the film's disparate elements can be subsumed or colligated. These include the conflict between the workers and the designers and the emergence of the mediator, who is linked to both sides by his love relationships—on the one hand, with the saintly Maria, a member of the working class, and on the other hand, by the love for his father, the master designer of Metropolis. That is, a large number of the dramatic elements—elements of character, plot, and incident—can be collected under the notion that the mind and the hand need to be supplemented by the addition of a heart.

We can call this kind of unity "thematic unity". Although the unifying theme that organizes *Metropolis* is explicitly given, many (probably most) narrative fictions leave it up to readers, viewers, and/or listeners to discover them. Contemplating Shakespeare's *A Midsummer's Night Dream*, one might be struck with the repetition of the motif of love as a result of, shall we say, chemical inducement through the machinations of Puck. This suggests an overarching theme to the play—that love is some kind of brute biological process rather than something romantic and spiritual. The attribution of such a theme to the play connects key narrative elements like Titania's enchantment with Bottom and the fickle wavering of the affections of the humans in the forest. Moreover, Puck, the agent of all this mischief, is a forest spirit—a force of nature, in other words—and not an airy ideal.

This sort of interrogation of a narrative for its overarching significance is one of the central constituents of what is involved in the creative understanding and appreciation of a fiction. It is the work of what we may call the "thematizing imagination"—the imaginative activity of going beyond what is given in the narrative and finding a conceptual unity among its various parts.

The kinds of concepts that the imagination uses to organize a fiction come in at least three forms. The first is what we may regard as a simple theme. A simple theme might be something like courage in a narrative that compares and contrasts a range of different examples of acts of bravery and cowardice. But fictions may also be organized around theses, not only exploring the relation between the head and the hands, but recommending the best way for that relation to obtain. *Lord of the Flies* is plotted in accordance with the thesis that basic humanity—as manifested in children separated from society—is savage. The fallen nature of human nature is the conceptualization that drives the narrative arc of *Lord of the Flies*.

Finally, the concept that the imagination discovers to be organizing a fiction might be an idea about the purpose of the work. The opera *Satyagraha*, for example, taxed many viewers because of its apparent lack of psychological development or, indeed, of any psychological dimension whatsoever. It struck viewers as nothing more than a collection of episodes. In this, they misconstrued the purpose of the piece, which was to celebrate nodal moments in Gandhi's career in the fashion of a pageant. And of course, seen that way, the spectacle stands as a unified piece. Often the purpose of a fiction is not obvious and requires insight to discover. Indeed, conceiving of what makes a fictional artwork hang together conceptually is generally considered to be one of the pinnacles of creative reading, listening, and viewing.

The thematizing imagination ranges over not only elements of plot, but also elements of style, searching for concepts that not only reveal the significance of the reasons for weaving various events together, but also embody those events by means of certain modes of presentation. For example, Hemingway not only organized his characters and events around a certain conception of manliness, but also reinforced that conception by means of the muscular, laconic style of his sentences. In contrast, the repeated use of linguistic condensations in Joyce's *Finnegan's Wake* stylistically advanced the sense of the narrative as a fitful dream state.

In responding to such fictions, the thematizing imagination takes notice of the way in which the narrative content and style operate in concert via a presiding concept, theme, or purpose. The best appreciation of a work is typically the one that is able to thematically organize the most elements of narrative content and style under its rubric.[14]

---

[14] Of course, the thematizing imagination can also be aimed at discovering the unity of a segment of a larger narrative, as when one grasps that the prelude to *Das Rheingold* sustains 135 measures with a key change in order to project the untroubled depths of the Rhine at the commencement of the opera.

In some ways, the thematizing imagination reminds us of the exploratory imagination. Both try out frameworks for organizing a work. But they differ in this respect: There is no closure with respect to the exploratory imagination, whereas the thematizing imagination aims to find a definite concept that will reveal the relation of the parts to the whole in terms of the significance, meaning, or purpose of the fiction. The thematizing imagination is like the constructive imagination insofar as it aims at discovering the interrelation of the narrative elements of the work. But while the constructive imagination does this with respect to space, time, and causality, the thematizing imagination operates at the level of significance and artistic intent.

The critics nowadays that we find to be most impressive and creative ones are generally experts in the exercise of the thematizing imagination. But the thematizing imagination is not the province of critics alone. Most of us find ourselves mobilizing it when we ask each other why this or that belongs in the fiction in our informal discussions about artworks that we've shared. In this regard, ordinary readers, listeners, and viewers are no less creative than esteemed critics.

8. Concluding Remarks

Discussions of creativity and the arts usually dedicate most of their energy to examining the creative activities of the artist. There is no doubt that this is a worthy subject. But when focusing on the creativity of the artist, the audience's creativity should not be dismissed, because it is ultimately the audience's contribution that makes any work of art work. For the artist to accomplish the effects to which she aspires, the audience must creatively cooperate with what the artist has initiated. With respect to fiction, the reader or viewer must exert imagination in various ways if the work in question is to achieve its maximum intelligibility, completeness, unity, and significance.

This chapter has explored some functions of the imagination that audiences enlist to process creatively fictional artworks. They include the exploratory imagination, the fictive imagination, the elaborative imagination, various kinds of mindreading, the constructive imagination, and the thematizing imagination. I do not claim that this list is exhaustive, nor would I want to deny that some of these imaginations may be combined in interesting and overlapping ways. My more modest claim is that the creative activities of these imaginations are elicited by the vast majority of narrative artworks, and that, as a result of this, the success of most narrative artworks depends on the creative contribution of readers, listeners, and/or viewers.

One sort of imagination that has not been discussed here is the sensory imagination—the notion, for instance, that when processing a fiction, we envision it in the mind's eye, perhaps after the fashion of an inner movie. With a number of narrative art forms, positing an inward visual representation of the story would seem redundant. Standing before Delacroix's *Arab Horseman Attacked by a Lion,* there seems little justification for the idea that one replicates the image in one's mind's eye. Indeed, the claim that we might need to do so would probably invite an infinite regress of homunculi.

On the other hand, similar problems would not beset the suggestion that when reading fictions, we produce something like an inner movie in our minds. Yet this is a controversial issue. Even though this is the way in which some people claim that they read, others deny visualizing when reading. Thus, even if we allow that some creative reading involves visualizing imagery,[15] it is not as ubiquitous as the other exercises of imagination that we have seen are typically mandated when reading or otherwise consuming fictions. And for that reason, it is not on my list of some of the central creative activities that audiences contribute to making fictional artworks work through the activation of their imaginations.

---

[15] Sometimes, listeners describe their response to music in terms of visual imagery. Indeed, people have even been encouraged to indulge in visualizing as a form of music appreciation. However, this is not a generally reported experience with regard to pure music; and musical formalists would argue that it is an inappropriate way to engage with absolute music.

4

Musical Style and the Philosophy of Mind

CHRISTOPHER PEACOCKE

The philosophy of mind has in important ways not done justice to the range of phenomena presented by music. This sin of omission is all the more striking in that contemporary philosophy of mind already contains resources that, when properly deployed, can be used to address the rich range of phenomena presented by music. Current aesthetics and philosophy of mind have certainly continued to address some traditional and important questions in the philosophy of music. They have offered more or less plausible answers to such longstanding questions as what is required for music to have some kind of meaning and emotional significance. It seems to me, however, that there are musical issues that are also distinctively philosophical in that they concern the very nature of certain phenomena, as opposed to the empirical psychological origins of those phenomena or their historical and social context. These issues have hardly been raised by philosophers.

The issues I have in mind also have a bearing on music criticism, music theory, the right way of conceiving of performance practice theories, and the right way to formulate issues in the history of music. Resolution of the issues will also provide a starting point for empirical theories of creativity in the specific domain of musical composition. A theory of why a composer is creative in a particular way cannot get off the ground without a proper characterization of the particular way in which her compositions are creative. We cannot give an explanation without a proper description of what is to be explained. If a work of art (or anything else) is creative by virtue of its possession of a particular property, a correct account of what is involved in having that property is a precondition for constructing a good theory of how its creator achieved a work with that property. In the theory of vision, it is widely accepted (and is a working constraint in much empirical research) that it makes no sense to address the question of how the content of a perception is computed without a specification of what it is that is computed (Marr 1980). An empirical theory that explains why a composer, scientist, poet, or mathematician is creative in just the ways he is will be a complex thing. We are certainly very far off from having any such theory, in any rich or interesting area. But we know now that we should not be satisfied with a theory that fails to explain the distinctive aspects of the products of creative activity. If a set theorist (Cantor, for example) is creative in introducing a completely new method of proof, then a good, full explanation of his creative activity must explain why it is that method of proof he discovered. In that case, we have no difficulty in articulating the distinctive novelty in his products (such as diagonalization). But in the arts, matters are not so simple. We can often recognize that a poem, or novel, or composition is of some new kind that involves creative activity, without our being able to characterize in any explicit and articulated way necessary for a psychological theory precisely what that new kind is. We may and often do have a word for a new kind of art. But unless we can say more about what that kind is, we will not have a sufficiently structured characterization of it to be suitable as the explanatory goal of a computational, or any other, psychological theory. The goal of this essay is to supply a characterization in the particular case of a range of musical kinds, a characterization that, among other things, is sufficiently explicit and articulated to be a resource for a theory of creativity in musical composition.

As a piece of autobiography here, what brought home to me this issue and the unrealized opportunities it presents to the philosophy of mind was a task in my teaching. My main appointment is at Columbia University, which shares with the University of Chicago and with almost no other major Anglophone research university a strict core curriculum. "Music Humanities" is one of the courses in the core curriculum at Columbia. It is a course that presents some basic music theory together with a tour of Western music from the Middle Ages to the present. A few years ago, I agreed to teach it. I thought that it would occasionally include some interesting questions about the perception of music, even though some sessions would not have any philosophical dimension.

I could not have been more wrong—about the "occasionally" part. There was no session at all in which some essentially philosophical, constitutive issue did not leap from even the most straightforward presentation of the subject matter. I initially thought that a session on medieval church music would certainly be philosophy-free. Yet this is the period when notation emerged. Does acquiring a system of musical notation enhance or reduce the expressive power of a musical tradition? It is very obvious that the answer must be positive in some respects and negative in others, and that the task of saying which respects, and why, is as interesting and as intrinsically philosophical as the partly, but only partly, parallel task of explaining the relations between thought and language.

The kind of questions on which I think the philosophy of mind has hitherto failed in relation to music, and on which there are real opportunities for doing better, can be introduced by discussing in more detail one of the constitutive questions that arose from teaching such a course as Music Humanities. It quickly became apparent that the parts of philosophy on which one needs to draw concern not only perception, but also the emotions, the explanation of action, and the expression of mental states.

What makes a piece of music Romantic in style? (I use the capitalized "Romantic" when speaking of styles of music as something to be distinguished not only from the ordinary meaning of "romantic," but also as a term intended to be neutral on the historical or geographical origins the work, on which more later.) The Romantic style of a piece of music is a specifically perceptual phenomenon. Someone who is familiar with the concept of Romantic style in music can tell by listening to only a few bars whether a work is Romantic in style. A listener needs to hear no more than a second or two of example 4.1 to recognize it as Romantic in style.

So, whatever the correct answer is to the question of what makes a piece of music Romantic in style, it must draw on resources in the theory of perception.[1] But there are also two further challenges in giving a perceptual characterization of musical style.

The first is that of developing an account that draws on resources of sufficient generality that various parameters of the account can be altered to generate accounts of other perceptible musical styles, such as expressionism, impressionism, and neoclassicism (as in Stravinsky in the years 1920–45). These various styles are each immediately perceptually identifiable too. We ought to be able to say what perceptual features make the styles so recognizable.

The second challenge is more specific to Romantic style. Romanticism has a rich and very extensively discussed cultural relation to poetry, literature, other art forms, and to moral and political thought. Any account of Romantic style in music must adequately explain the connection between the apparently perceptual phenomenon and this broad current of thought and values. What can possibly be the connection between the rich brew of cultural ideas that involves the mix of the Schlegel brothers, Rousseau, Keats, Byron, and revolutions in Europe on the one hand, and a specifically perceptual auditory phenomenon on the other? We intuitively feel that there is a connection between the ideas and ideals and Romantic music as perceived, but what is it? I will try to do something to overcome the skepticism expressed by O. Baensch, who placed the Classic-Romantic polarity in the category of

> basically nothing but vague collective terms for feelings we find qualitatively related, though we cannot further demonstrate this relationship by anything in the feelings themselves, and cannot reduce it to distinct characteristics.
>
> (Baensch 1961, p. 33)[2]

---

[1] Leonard Meyer recognized the datum that suggests that Romantic style in music is a perceptual phenomenon: "we know that competent listeners can usually recognize that a work is Romantic after hearing only a few measures" (1989, p. 218). But I think Meyer's characterization of Romantic style does not capture the perceptual phenomenon in question: see below.

[2] Quoted also by Maynard Solomon (2003).

Im wunderschönen Monat Mai

Robert Alexander Schumann (1810 - 1856)

Example 4.1   Opening of R. Schumann, 'Im wunderschönen Monat Mai,' from *Dichterliebe* Op. 48.

I will be searching for some distinct characteristics that respect both the perceptual character of a Romantic style in music and the links with the history of ideas and the development of romantic ideals.

The distinctive characteristic of the Romantic style in music is not intensity of expression alone. Great intensity is sometimes present on occasion in pre-classical

Miserere my Maker

Thomas Campion

Example 4.2 Thomas Campion, 'Miserere my Maker.'

music. Consider Thomas Campion's song "Miserere my Maker," and particularly its last line, "Miserere, miserere, Miserere I am dying," in example 4.2.

Leonard Meyer writes at one point of "the shift from the eighteenth-century idea that music *represented emotions* (affects) to the nineteenth-century belief that music *expressed the feeling* of the composer" (1989, p. 221, Meyer's italics). Whatever shift there may be in ideas about music, when we are concerned with the characterization of the perceived music itself, as opposed to ideas about it, it seems an impossible position to hold that the last line in the Campion excerpt is merely representing emotions, and not expressing feelings. The same could be said about some high points of 18th-century music. Mozart's B minor *Fantasia* K.540 for piano also involves the expression of emotions, and not merely their representation.

In the case of literature, Walter Pater, writing in 1910, offered this characterization of Romanticism: "in the classical literature of Greece and Rome, as in the classics of the last century, the essentially classical element is that quality of order in beauty, which they possess, indeed, in a pre-eminent degree" (1910, pp. 245–246). He continued: "The desire of beauty being a fixed element in every artistic organization, it is the addition of curiosity to this desire of beauty, that constitutes the romantic temper" (1910, p. 246). Later in the same essay, he adds the property of "strangeness" to that of curiosity in his attempt to define Romanticism. Certainly in the musical case, strangeness and curiosity are far from sufficient to make a work in Romantic style. Erik Satie's piano works are both strange and curious, but they are not Romantic in style. I doubt that the characterization works for literature either (the characterization would also include literature of the absurd, for instance).

An alternative proposal is that what distinguishes Romantic style is that it involves the expression of a distinctively Romantic emotion or state of mind. The states of mind that have been suggested as belonging to this category include "terror, longing, ecstasy and awe."[3] There are certainly some distinctively Romantic attitudes and emotions. A deep kind of alienation is among them, the kind expressed in the last song "Der Leiermann" of Schubert's *Die Winterreise*. It is indeed not clear how a work in classical style could ever express that or do it so successfully. Nevertheless, some emotions expressed in Romantic music are identical to those expressed in classical style. They include romantic love, a sense of triumph, despair, and much more. I think the fundamental and fully general distinction between the Romantic and the classical must be a matter of how the emotion is expressed, rather than which emotion is expressed. It is the "how" that we need to investigate. Moreover, if there are some emotions more appropriately or satisfactorily expressed in Romantic style, there is presumably some property of that style that explains why that is so. We still have the task of identifying what that characteristic is.

There is some limited illumination to be gained from considering accounts of Romantic style in music that do not work, but I now turn from that to trying to build a positive treatment. The account I offer is built using three elements, each of which involves a particular distinction in the realm of the psychological, a distinction drawn and discussed in contemporary philosophy of mind and psychology.

The first element is drawn from the philosophy of action. Some actions are expressive actions. You may slump with your face resting on your hands and your elbows on your desk after hearing bad news. You may skip with delight at good news. In both cases, you may be careful not to damage nearby objects. In neither case is your action explained by means-end reasoning. There need not be anything you are aiming to achieve by these actions, but they are actions nonetheless; they are intentional, even though there may not have been any prior intention, conditional upon the quality of the news, to act one way or another. In both cases, the action is explained by the emotion that the action also expresses. Such actions were unsurprisingly neglected when belief-desire models of action explanation were dominant. In the past two decades, there has been more philosophical discussion of the characteristics of these expressive actions.[4]

The second element in the account brings the first element into the content of perception. Humans perceive some events as actions—as runnings, assertions, pushings, wavings, and so forth. An action may be perceived as aimed at attaining some goal—reaching for the elevator button, removing something from one's

---

[3] See the discussion in Solomon (2003, p. 38).

[4] See Hursthouse 1991 as a fine starting point for these discussions.

pocket, running for the bus. But some events are perceived specifically as expressive actions. I may perceive you as slumping from disappointment, raising your arms in joy, banging the table in anger, etc.

Musical performances are actions, and those who listen to performances perceive them as actions. Casey O'Callaghan (2009) has argued convincingly that sounds are events in which a moving object disturbs a surrounding medium and sets it moving. I further add that the sounds in musical performances are both heard as events in the objective world and experienced as actions of the musical performers. I will argue that these points have an aesthetic significance.

The third element concerns our human capacity to represent one thing metaphorically-as something else, an important phenomenon in cognition generally. This is not primarily or fundamentally a linguistic phenomenon. It occurs in imagination, thought, and perception. The linguistic phenomenon of metaphor exists only because there are mental states in which one thing is thought of, imagined as, or perceived as something else. In metaphorically representing one thing as something else, as when you think of a network of freeways as a nervous system, there is a relevant mapping from one domain (freeways and their properties and relations) to another (nerves and their properties and relations). The metaphorical mapping is not thought about in such mental states, and it need not be explicitly represented. The metaphor is rather exploited. The subcase in which one experiences one thing metaphorically-as something else is especially important in characterizing the content and nature of musical experience (Peacocke 2009).

When listening to Schubert's "Auf dem See" (example 4.3), one hears the syncopated notes metaphorically as the lapping of water on a boat. Much more remarkably, in bars seven and onward, one hears the lower notes of the piano as the mountains passing by as the boat travels along. These are examples in which certain types of events in the physical world are in the metaphorical content.

Metaphorical content can also concern mental states. One can experience the changing features of a piece of music metaphorically as the gradual change in affect involved in the transition from despair to serenity. One can experience some features of a piece of music metaphorically-as characteristics of a mood of determination without triumphalism (a state of mind that should not be classified as an emotion).

We need to take some care in formulating more precisely what it is that we are trying to characterize. Our target should not be taken as the experience of hearing something as Romantic in style, under one natural reading of that phrase. It seems clear that someone can hear and appreciate a piece of Romantic music without having the concept *Romantic*. I would say too that, even for a non-conceptual notion of the Romantic, a person can hear and appreciate a Romantic work without hearing it as falling under that notion. It is one thing for a piece of music to have Romantic characteristics that are appreciated in the hearing of the music. It is a further thing for those characteristics to be grouped under the general classification *Romantic*,

Example 4.3 From F. Schubert, 'Auf dem See' D. 543.

whether conceptually or at some more primitive non-conceptual level. So what I propose to do is to give an account of what it is to hear a piece of music in a way that is Romantic. The way in which the piece is heard will have something in common with ways in which other works may also be heard, and which are Romantic ways. The task I am setting myself is that of saying what it is that these ways have in common, without thereby or necessarily putting any notion of what that common feature is into the content of the experience of the listener.

So much for identifying the target of this investigation. The central claim of this chapter is then that to hear a piece of music in a way that is Romantic is

(a) to perceive the action of performing the music as an expressive action;
(b) to perceive the action as expressive of some emotion or mental state E, where the music is heard metaphorically as E; and
(c) to perceive it as an action in which the emotion or mental state E is controlling action in such a way that the classical musical forms or conventions are over-stepped in one or more respects, and this overstepping expresses the strength of the emotion or mental state E.

"Perceiving as" is not to be understood factively here. The action of performing the music need not be expressive of some actual state of despair that the performer is suffering. I will call this positive account "the expressive-perceptual account," or "the perceptual account" for short.

Though I have not written out the condition formally to make it obvious, some of the same points apply pari passu to the reference to "classical musical forms or conventions" in clause (c) of this account as I made in formulating the target of this account. A listener does not have to have any notion or concept of the classical forms and conventions, let alone be able to say what they are, to meet this condition. The listener has only to possess a capacity to hear the music in a certain way, regard-less of whether he classifies such music under the notion or concept "in classical style." What the listener who appreciates a piece of music in Romantic style does have to have is an ability to hear certain features of the music as standing in distinc-tive relations to certain different properties of music that is in fact in classical style. The relations need not be conceptualized as the relations they are, either.

The account is structured with complex embeddings in both the specification of the way the performance action is perceived and in the specification of the way the music produced in the action is perceived, in particular in respect of its perceived metaphorical content in the sense given above. So this characterization is doubly perceptual. The performance action must be perceived in a certain way. The music that is performed must be heard in a certain way. There must also be a certain rela-tion between these two perceptions, the relation stated in clauses (a) through (c).

You may perceive the performance action as expressive of emotion as described in these conditions while also knowing that the performance action is entirely carefully calibrated by the performer and not in fact an expression of his actual emotion at all. The emotion may be one that he does not feel at all (though it may be important to the performer to imagine it from the inside). These points just reflect the general distinction between knowing something to be the case and how one perceives some state of affairs. Your completely confident knowledge that what you are seeing is a trompe l'oeil painted on a flat surface is entirely consistent with your vivid visual experience of it as a three-dimensional object. However much you know about how the performer operates, if the performer is successful in affecting your perceptions, you will perceive his performance action as expressive of the emotion or mental state that is in the metaphorical content of the music. This independence of the perceptual state from knowledge is present in the theatre too. When we perceive a good actor in the theatre, we can perceive his actions as expressive of certain emotions and states of mind, even if we know the person who is acting does not really experience those emotions and states of mind.

On this account, your ability to hear the expressed state E in the metaphorical content of the music is essential to, and constitutively explanatory of, your perceiving the performance action as expressive of E. Gestures that would be expressive of an emotion in a nonmusical context, however exaggerated or obvious, will not by themselves suffice to place that emotion within the metaphorical content of the music. (It is the stuff of comedy to imagine cases in which someone tries to achieve that end by that means.) This is an important difference between perceiving a good actor on the stage and perceiving an expressive musical performance. The capacity to appreciate the actor's performance draws on the ability to perceive any human action successfully. It does not, except per accidens, draw on the ability to relate the content of some world of a specific metaphor to give the right kind of meaning to the actor's performance. But appreciation of an expressive musical performance does draw on the content of a world of metaphor. The performance action, to be perceived as musically expressive, must be perceived in a way determined by the metaphorical content of the music. To perceive the performance action as expressive of, say, resolute determination, resolute determination must be heard in the music. As we might say, the content that is heard in the music crosses a boundary to contribute to the perception of the performance action in the real world.

For the same reason, perceiving the action of performing the music as having a certain property is not the same as perceiving that property in the music. There is such a thing as hearing anger in the music itself. The "Rondo-Burlesque" of Mahler's Ninth Symphony is an example. But a person might perform a piece of music angrily, without there being any anger in the metaphorical content of the music. A pupil, irritated with his teacher, might perform a Haydn piano sonata angrily by emphasizing in an extreme way the features his teacher says were lacking in his previous performances. That would not result in there being any anger in the music as heard, in the way in which we hear anger in Mahler's "Rondo-Burlesque."

There is a wide range of classical forms and styles to which a Romantic composition may not conform. It may involve any of the following non-classical features: unusual inner accenting patterns and use of *rubato* (Chopin); chromaticism (Chopin); more distant key relationships than in highly classical music (Schubert); orchestral means not balanced in the way classical works are (doubled strings in unison, as in Tchaikovsky); unresolved chords and passages (as in the Schumann song previously discussed); the use of non-classical forms and structures within movements and across movements of a given work; and so forth. In short, it may involve anything outside the target area of Berlioz's remarks when he said that "the deadliest enemies of genius are those lost souls who worship in the *temple of Routine*" and wrote of those who succumb to "the *lure of conventional* sonorities" (1969, pp. 218, 241). The conventions and styles that Romantic expression ignores are, more specifically, those found in Haydn and much of Mozart, in whom, as Hegel says in one of his more pleasing formulations, "the luminous sense of proportion never breaks down in extremes; everything finds its due place knit together in the whole" (1920). What is heard as Romantic music must in some respect or other *not* be heard as being there because of its "due place."

Earlier, I acknowledged that there are some distinctively Romantic attitudes and emotions. A distinctively Romantic attitude may be expressed in a work whose musical style is classical. One example is the mysterious poem by Salis-Seewis, "Ins stille Land, wer leitet uns hinüber?," as composed by Schubert in the first of his four settings of the poem (example 4.4).

The musical setting is classical in form and its key changes. The chromaticism it contains is no more than in many of Mozart's minor key works. The sense of Romantic mystery is already present before there is much chromaticism in the setting. So the distinction between Romantic attitudes and attitudes that are not distinctively Romantic cuts across the distinction between works that are in Romantic musical style and those that are not.[5]

On the account I have offered, the classification of music as Romantic makes sense only against a presupposed classical background. By Romantic musical style, we usually mean something that takes the first Viennese school as the classicism with respect to which Romanticism is defined. One could correspondingly define a style as standing in a Romantic-like relation to any given style, with a range of forms and conventions taken as the corresponding "classical" paradigm. This basis for a classical/Romantic distinction in style also permits some finer-grained distinctions with broad categories of style. Some of Mozart's contemporaries commented on (and sometimes complained about) his overstepping the boundaries of an earlier sub-variety of classical style. They commented on the way he used wind instruments in the accompaniment to operatic arias (Deutsch 1966, p. 328); his difficulty and ingenuity (Deutsch 1966, pp. 334–335, 383); and the "lack of that sense of unity, that clarity of presentation, which we rightly admire in Jos. Haydn's symphonies" (Deutsch 1966, pp. 472–473, a quotation from *Teutschlands Annalen des Jahres* for 1794). That is, these contemporaries heard Mozart's music in ways that are Romantic relative to Haydn's and other earlier styles, something that makes sense on the present account of Romantic style. What we call "the" classical style has many subdivisions and an interesting historical development, within which we should distinguish (at least) the Mannheim composers, the several periods of

---

[5] I thank Joseph Dubiel for questions that have altered my thinking on this.

Example 4.4 From F. Schubert, 'Ins stille Land' D. 403, first setting.

work in Haydn's long life, and Mozart—as just the first step toward the distinctions we ought to make. Some of the transitions within the historical development of this classical style are movements toward the more Romantic, in the sense I have been trying to characterize. The chromaticism and the minor ninth leaps in the first movement of Mozart's great G minor String Quintet (K.516) are elements of Romantic style relative to what preceded Mozart in the classical tradition. What distinguishes the composers traditionally classified as Romantic in their style of music is a range of broadly classical musical features with respect to one or more of which they expressively overstep classical boundaries, in the way specified in clause (c) of the expressive-perceptual account.

As is implied by the examples we have already given, music can be very highly expressive without there being any form of classicism to which it stands in the same relation as I have identified the Romantic as standing to the classical music of Haydn and Mozart. We have the Campion example; the more expressive parts of Monteverdi operas also provide many such examples.

F. Blume writes of "the many intermediate positions in the continuing development of this antinomy" between the classical and the Romantic (1970). Hearing something as Romantic is not, however, fundamentally a matter of degree on the perceptual account. There may be more or fewer classical features that a Romantic work ignores, and that is indeed a matter of degree. It is also a matter of degree, for any one of those features, how much the work departs from the classical paradigm. But it is not a matter of degree whether there is some classical feature such that the performance action is heard as an expressive action in which the agent's controlling emotion or state of mind produces an overstepping of that classical feature in the manner of clause (c) of the account. That is an all-or-nothing matter. The all-or-nothing conditions may of course be met in some parts of the piece and not in others.

This account of Romanticism helps to explain the extreme difficulty scholars have had in deciding whether to classify Beethoven, especially late Beethoven, as Romantic or as classical. Beethoven invented new forms beyond the classically recognized ones. The new forms are often specific to a single work. But he also conformed to these forms as the work progressed, and the hearer can perceive the particular work as conforming to these new forms. This is part of the significance of Maynard Solomon's point about Beethoven: "his will to form—his classicism, if you like—enabled him to set boundaries on the infinite, to portray disorder in the process of its metamorphosis into order" (2003, p. 40).

I want to claim more than just that Romantic music is to be characterized in terms of this expressive-perceptual account. It also seems to me that the expressive-perceptual account is explanatorily and teleologically fundamental. It is possible, and obviously of importance to music theory, to characterize the various compositional techniques involved in the change from classical to Romantic style. There has been much highly illuminating writing on precisely that in the past two decades. I would mention particularly Charles Rosen's chapter "Formal Interlude" in *The Romantic Generation* (1996) and the discussion of Schubert's key relationships by Richard Taruskin in his *Music in the Nineteenth Century* (2005). These compositional developments are characterizable in broadly syntactic terms, independent of their emotional and expressive significance. But the compositional developments are at the service of a goal that can be characterized fully only by saying that this music is meant to be heard in ways that are Romantic, as characterized in the expressive-perceptual account. From the point of view of the theory of creativity, the achievement of Romantic composers is not just a set of compositional techniques, but the appreciation that these techniques could result in works of a distinctive kind of expressive power so appropriate to the more general romantic movement in thought and culture. This is the property that constitutes the explanandum of an empirical theory of creativity in a composer in the Romantic style.

So how does this characterization of Romanticism in music meet the desideratum I mentioned at the outset, that it should dovetail with the ideas and ideals of the Romantic movement more generally, with ideals that can apply across the various art forms and even in the moral and political realm too? Here is a well-known passage from Wimsatt and Brooks attempting to formulate these general ideas and ideals:

> Classic art was conceived by the German critics as "beauty"; romantic art
> as "energy." Classic was universal and ideal; romantic was individual and

"characteristic." Classic was plastic (like sculpture), finite, closed, pure in genre. Romantic was picturesque (like painting), infinite, open, mixed. (1962, p. 368)

Friedrich von Schlegel wrote:

Romantic poetry is constantly developing. That in fact is its true nature: it can forever only *become*, it can never achieve definitive form.... It alone is infinite. Its overriding principle is that the poet's fantasy is subject to no agreed principles.... (Letturay and Day 1981, pp. 246–247)

Many of these ideas find reflection in Romantic music that meets the expressive-perceptual criterion. Such music is heard as expressive action not wholly constrained by classical forms and conventions specified in advance. It is correspondingly open-ended. Perhaps one can even understand, if not endorse, the use of the term "infinite" on one reading—since the Romantic work is not always constrained by classical forms, there is no form to be completed. (Perhaps this is more like Aristotelian infinity, something to be explained in terms of possibility, rather than as an actual infinity.) Since Romantic music is heard as music expressive of emotion or attitudes that are so forceful that the music breaks classical boundaries, it is correspondingly authentic. It is a less constrained expression of the self. One can also connect the lack of constraint by form with the Romantics' emphasis on organicism, in which the music is supposed to grow out of some seed motif or idea. Similarly, the "axial" melodies favored by some composers in the Romantic style, such as the second theme in the first movement of Schubert's *String Quintet in C*, revolve and wander around a note to which they keep returning, without apparent formal constraint.

This characterization of what makes a piece of music Romantic in style differs at significant points from the description given by Richard Taruskin in the chapter "The Music Trance" in his book *Music in the Nineteenth Century* (2005). Taruskin discusses the effect of certain kinds of modulations on "the audience's experience of time" and writes that it "is comparable to the effect of an operatic scene in which static 'aria time' supervenes on the action time of recitative. To evoke such an introspective effect in instrumental music is precisely the act whereby instrumental music becomes romantic" (p. 69). A few sentences later, he writes, "Faust will lose his soul to the devil Mephistopheles, the latter warns, as soon as he calls out to the passing moment, 'Stop, stay awhile, thou art so fair!' [Weile doch, du bist so schön.] That moment, the moment in which *ethos* (responsible action) is sacrificed to *pathos* (passive experience, surrender to feeling), will be the moment of damnation. This is the moment romanticism celebrates" (pp. 69–71). Taruskin says of the representation of the child's apparent consciousness of the Elf King in Schubert's son *Erlkönig*, "The representation of 'inwardness' as it interacts with and triumphs over the perception of external reality is the true romantic dimension here" (p. 152).

Taruskin's remarks do correspond to a streak in a certain sub-variety of romanticism. But it is natural to wonder how they can be of general applicability to a romanticism of which Friedrich von Schlegel said, "Romantic poetry is a progressive, universal poetry" (an *Athaneum* fragment of 1798, quoted by Solomon 2003, p. 38); of the romantic tendencies of Beethoven who, as Maynard Solomon wrote, "was proud of his adherence to the central tenets of this so-called Josephinian Enlightenment... its idealization of reason, furtherance of reform, critique of superstition, and altruistic commitment to virtue" (2003, p. 28). Such a romantic figure as Byron was hardly free of strongly held political views, and he fought for some of them.

I think what is missing in Taruskin's description is that the trancelike states he talks about are often ones that involve "feelings," and more specifically emotions. Emotions have a normative content. They represent states of affairs as good or bad in quite specific respects. An emphasis on the emotion involved in a certain situation may be an emphasis on the value that is an essential component of that emotion. Sometimes the value may lie in the nature of some personal relationship itself, either lost as in Schubert's song setting of Claudius's poem "Am Grabe Anselmos" (D.504), or celebrated as current in the middle songs of Schumann's *Frauenliebe und Leben*. Similarly, in act III, scene 3 of *Die Walküre*, Brünnhilde is expressing a moral demand, that she not be humiliated, when she asks to be protected by fire surrounding the rock on which she is to be placed. There certainly is such a thing as wallowing in an emotion for its own sake, not an attractive thing. But a piece of music that is perceived in a Romantic way may equally succeed in highlighting and bringing home to the hearer aspects of the values involved in the emotions of which the performance action is heard metaphorically as an expression. Music that succeeds in doing this need not have any commitment to some kind of relativism or subjectivity about truth.[6]

Not just any departure from classical forms amounts to Romanticism. Romanticism involves the specific kind of departure in the expressive-perceptual account, having to do with the performance action being heard as expressive in

---

[6] Taruskin's fine book contains a few very puzzling pages (2005, pp. 61–63) at the start of the second chapter, where he seems to associate romanticism with some form of relativism about truth. "Truth is therefore relative, at least to a degree, to the individual vantage point and therefore to some degree subjective" he writes, in reporting Romantic thought (p. 62). He does not consider the possibility of combining the idea that the individual with a conscience can reason to a conclusion or a moral view or attitude with the proposition that truth in the relevant domain is not relative at all. Rejection of implausible institutional authorities, which is indeed a romantic idea, does not at all require relativism about truth.

relation to the metaphorical content of music, with departures from the classical forms being heard as a result of the power of emotion or mental state expressed.

I would sharply contrast the expressive-perceptual account of the Romantic style with the characterization it receives in Leonard Meyer's *Style and Music*. Since I am about to criticize his writing on one particular topic, I would like first to express my admiration for this book. Meyer majored in philosophy as an undergraduate, and the deeply philosophical, constitutive nature of the questions he asks about music shine through on almost every page of that book (as indeed they do in his other writings). Meyer does not, as far as I can tell, formulate any particular restrictions for the music to be Romantic in style. He does observe that many, if not all, of the conventions of classical style are broadly syntactic in character, rather than involving what he calls "secondary parameters," which he says, "establish continuums of relative, not stipulative, states of tense and repose—that is, louder/softer, faster/slower, thicker/thinner, higher/lower" (p. 209). Meyer notes that departures from classical paradigms involve a de-emphasis on syntactic relations. But Meyer's account does not involve the notions of expressive action, perception of action, and hearing something metaphorically as something else.

There are at least four broad kinds of musical style that we ought to try to characterize in perceptual terms, and that are departures from the classical, even if we restrict our attention to broadly tonal Western music in postclassical times. We should aim to say what is perceptually distinctive of each of the Romantic, expressionist, impressionist, and neoclassical styles. I suggest that each of these styles can and should be given a distinct characterization in the framework I have been using.

Let us take an impressionist example first (example 4.5).

In this music, we hear the wind pick up and flutter through sails or veils (Debussy does not tell us which). Now this is not an example of classical style, but it is certainly not music in the Romantic style either. Meyer says that three things distinguish Debussy's impressionistic music. He says that it emphasizes the "sensuous qualities of sound." The sensuous qualities of sound can be emphasized in music of many different styles and cannot be uniquely distinctive of impressionist music. The "sensuous qualities of sound" are emphasized in some of Berlioz's orchestral music and certainly in some of his songs, particularly some of those in *Les Nuits d'Été*. Of Debussy's "suggestive symbolism," he writes the following sentence:

> Rather, it arises from the form and processes of the sound patterns and their juxtaposition as they interact with the cultural environment and psychological dispositions of listeners. (p. 270)

This sentence formulates a condition that is true of a huge range of interesting musical features and again can hardly uniquely fix what is distinctive of an impressionist work. I think these first two criteria do not contribute even partially to explaining what is distinctive of an impressionist work.

Example 4.5   From C. Debussy, 'Voiles,' from *Préludes*, Vol. 1.

I suggest that what is distinctive about an impressionist piece of music is that the performance action is not heard as the action expression of any emotion or mental state at all. The music itself is still heard metaphorically as, for instance, the flapping of sails (or veils) in the wind, or as the movement of the dancers at Delphi, or as the floodwaters gradually submerging a cathedral. The music can be heard in any of those ways without the action of performing the music being heard as an expression of an emotion or other mental state. In this respect, the music has a certain objectivity. If we use the apparatus of philosophy, we could say that in Romantic music, there is an intentional object, which we can call "the expressing subject," an object generated by the expressive content of the Romantic music. According to the account I outlined, in Romantic music what the expressing subject expresses is the emotional or mental state that is distinctively in the content of Romantic music. By contrast we can say using this apparatus, that what is distinctive of Debussy's impressionistic music is that it generates no expressing subject.

This criterion explains the third feature of Debussy's impressionist music, rightly noted by Meyer, that it does not contain the syntactically goal-directed movements of classical music—in returning to a tonic, or to a local tonal center, or to some syntactically determined rhythmic structure. In Debussy's impressionist music, one characteristic purpose is that the notes are placed as they are so that they can be heard metaphorically-as some objective event or state of affairs, rather than metaphorically as some mental state experienced from the inside. In Schubert's song "Auf dem See," it is indeed true that the metaphorical content of the music is of mountains passing by as a boat travels, but that content is embedded in a context in which the journey is also an emotional one and has an emotional coloring (liberation from an old love, as the poem later reveals). The metaphorical content of the music is not emotionally neutral as it is in *Voiles*.

Expressionist music departs from music in the classical style in a different way from Romantic music. The performance action in expressionist music is perceived as intentionally exaggerating or taking to extremes the violation of the classical constraints and forms. Sometimes this can be done in combination with the non-classical features of the music being perceived as expressive of emotions and the violation being there in part because the emotion is so strong. This aspect of the distinction between the Romantic and certain kinds of expressionism exploits a distinction that we apply to expressive actions entirely outside music. We draw a distinction between one person who slams his hand on a surface in anger without any thought of how hard he is slamming it, and another person who is also slamming his hand down as a genuine expression of anger but who intentionally slams it particularly hard.

In both expressionism and neoclassicism, there is an intention with respect to the classical constraints, but they are completely different intentions. In neoclassical music, the work is heard as intentionally conforming to some but not all of the classical constraints (not all, otherwise it would be classical). But in neoclassical music, the departures from the classical constraints are experienced as controlled departures. They are not experienced as departures purely because of the intensity of the expressed emotion. The departures may have a playful character, as in Stravinsky's *Pulcinella*; they may be expressive of serious emotion (Jocasta's anxiety in Stravinsky's *Oedipus Rex*); they may sometimes be extremely funny, as in the partially Mozartean parody in Anne's aria "I go, I go to him" in *The Rake's Progress* (example 4.6), which almost always seems to get a laugh from audiences.

In all these examples, the neoclassical music has a second-order character. Such music is, and is intended to be, heard as standing in certain relations to classical paradigms. The classical paradigms have become part of the heard content of the music, rather than first-order means.

There are various issues for which the distinctions I have been trying to articulate may prove helpful. The distinctions may help in articulating the character of the music of some specific composers more sharply. Despite where Mendelssohn falls

Example 4.6   From I. Stravinsky, *The Rake's Progress*, opening of Anne's 'Cabaletta.'

in the chronology, I suspect many thinkers about music would have some hesitation in classifying him straightforwardly as a Romantic composer. This hesitation
would be vindicated by the expressive-perceptual account. Very few, if any, passages
of Mendelssohn's music are ones the performance of which is perceived as expressive action that breaks classical conventions because of the intensity of the emotions
or states of which the music is heard metaphorically as an expression.

The character of some of the music of other composers can also receive a somewhat more precise description using the distinctions I have been marshaling. There
is irony in some passages of Mahler. Such passages are not the extreme of expressionism, and they are certainly not the playful kind of neoclassicism in Stravinsky.
I suggest that they should be described as passages in which the performance action
is perceived as one that is expressed in partly classical ways because the composer
has chosen to, rather than as an unquestioned default, and is making a point in having chosen to conform, a point sometimes shown up by other less classical features
of the passage. Appreciation of irony in music involves the hearer perceiving the

performance action as one involving the expression of a second-order attitude to the conformity to the conventions.

Another domain in which these distinctions have some application is that of the description of performance practice. The performer may not be experiencing grief, or euphoria, or a change of mood, but it will be a weaker performer whose actions are not informed by his knowledge from the inside of what it is like to be in these states, and possibly from his imagining them from the inside in performing successfully. The ways that imagination of the mental state can affect performance and how the performance action is perceived, and the empirical conditions for the presence of more or less expressive power in the perceived action—all these are surely worthy questions of investigation. The proper framing of the questions requires the notions of the perception of expressive action and of the states E of which the music is heard metaphorically-as involving E.

If this discussion has been going in the right general direction, in the sense that it is at least drawing on the right kind of notions needed to characterize musical style, I would be inclined to draw three general lessons. The first lesson is always to address the constitutive issues from the start. We can no doubt find many features distinctive of each of the styles I have been characterizing in this framework. If, however, we want to say why those features are there, we need to allude to the fundamental features of the style—the ones that make the style what it is. Second, in music as elsewhere, we should always be alive to the possibility that adjacent fields—in this case, the philosophy of action and the perception of action—may be able to supply materials for the construction of constitutive theories of the very nature of the subject matter. Finally, we should always think very hard about what is in our actual heard phenomenology of musical experience. It may sometimes be (perhaps it is always) very hard to articulate precisely what it is that we experience. If what I have been saying is right, however, many crucial distinctions were already there, at some unarticulated level, in our very consciousness in listening to music.[7]

[7] This is a revised text of a public lecture given at the University of Chicago on March 7, 2011. The lecture provoked a rich interdisciplinary discussion from which I hope the revised version has benefited. I am grateful to members of three departments in the University of Chicago—the Committee on Social Thought, the Philosophy Department, and the Music Department—for their intellectual contributions to that occasion. I was particularly helped by the comments of Jason Bridges, Martha Feldman, David Finkelstein, Gabriel Richardson Lear, Jonathan Lear, Josef Stern, and Robert Pippin. At an earlier meeting at Columbia, I learned from the remarks of Lydia Goehr, Felix Koch, and the participants in Lydia Goehr's aesthetics discussion group. More recently, I received illuminating comments from the editors and from Joseph Dubiel and Ian Rumfitt. I am conscious of the many points at which my approach can be, and needs to be, extended. An extension to the perception of joint action, joint attitudes, and joint emotion is evidently possible and necessary to account for our perception of some performances by groups of musicians.

References

Baensch, O. 1961. "Art and Feeling," in *Reflections on Art*, ed. S. Langer. New York: Oxford University Press

Berlioz, H. 1969. *Memoirs*, trans. D. Cairns. New York: Norton.

Blume, F. 1970. *Classic and Romantic Music: A Comprehensive Survey*, trans. M. Herter. New York: Norton.

Deutsch, O. 1966. *Mozart: A Documentary Biography*. London: A. & C. Black.

Hegel, G. 1920. *The Philosophy of Fine Art*, trans. F. Osmaston. London: Bell.

Hursthouse, R. 1991. "Arational Actions," *Journal of Philosophy*, vol. 88, pp. 57–68.

Letturay, P., and Day, J. 1981. *Music and Aesthetics in the 18th and Early 19th Century*. Cambridge, UK: Cambridge University Press.

Marr, D. 1980. *Vision*. San Francisco: Freeman.

Meyer, L. 1989. *Style and Music: Theory, History, and Ideology*. Philadelphia: Pennsylvania University Press.

O'Callaghan, C. 2009. "Sounds and Events," in *Sounds and Perception: New Philosophical Essays*, eds. M. Nudds and C. O'Callaghan. Oxford, UK: Oxford University Press.

Pater, W. 1910. *Appreciations, with an Essay on Style*. London: Macmillan.

Peacocke, C. 2009. "The Perception of Music: Sources of Significance," *British Journal of Aesthetics*, vol. 49, pp. 257–275.

Rosen, C. 1996. *The Romantic Generation*. London: HarperCollins.

Solomon, M. 2003. *Late Beethoven: Music, Thought, Imagination*. Berkeley, CA, and Los Angeles: University of California Press.

Taruskin, R. 2005. *Music in the Nineteenth Century*. Oxford, UK: Oxford University Press.

Wimsatt, W., and C. Brooks. 1962. *Literary Criticism: A Short History*. New York: Knopf.

PART FOUR

ETHICS AND VALUE THEORY

5

Performing Oneself

OWEN FLANAGAN

Essentially the person exists only in the performance of intentional acts, and is therefore essentially *not* an object.... A person is in any case given as a performer of intentional acts which are bound together by the unity of a meaning.... What, however, is the ontological meaning of "performance"?

—Heidegger, *Being and Time I, p. 1*

1. "All the World's a Stage"

So begins the famous monologue in act II, scene 7 of Shakespeare's comic *As You Like It*. The speech continues:

And all the men and women merely players;
They have their exits and their entrances,
And one man in his time plays many parts.

Shakespeare speaks here as the lifespan developmental psychologist with a script and staging largely determined by the natural psychobiology of *Homo sapiens*. The acts of the play of life involve the "seven ages of man," which start with "the infant/ Mewling and puking in the nurse's arms," work through adolescence, mature adulthood, and culminate full circle in "second childishness and mere oblivion,/Sans teeth, sans eyes, sans taste, sans everything."

Shakespeare's idea, and that of Greek playwrights and the Roman philosopher Seneca long before him, was that there is an analogy between living and the performance of an actor who follows a script, with the stages of life analogous to the different acts of a play and the performance structured by the age, range, and skill of the actor and the audience's response, which, taken together, determine whether the life was comic, tragic, a little bit of both, or something in between. Charlie Chaplin, the great comic silent film actor, channeled Shakespeare this way: "Life is a play that does not allow testing. So, sing, cry, dance, laugh and live intensely, before the curtain is closed and the piece ends with no applause."

There are weak and strong versions of the idea that life is a performance: Some lives are like performances in certain respects; all lives are like performances in certain respects; modern lives and/or lives of the well-off have more performative possibilities than ancient and/or poor lives; human life is just a performance, and so on. And there are descriptive and normative views: Lives are like performances; it would be good if lives were less or more matters of performance, self-creation, originality, and so on.

If the staged play was the preferred analogy in the West for the performative conception until the 17th century, contemporary analogies of life with art forms include poetry, painting, autobiography, and the novel. Jerome Bruner explicitly compares the self to an artistic production, specifically an autobiography or a set of autobiographical sketches:

> A self is probably the most impressive work of art we ever produce, surely the most intricate. For we create not just one self-making story but many of them, rather like T. S. Eliot's rhyme "We prepare a face to meet/the faces that we meet." The job is to get them all into one identity, and to get them lined up over time.
>
> (Jerome Bruner 2002, p. 14)

In autobiography, unlike biography, the protagonist and the author are the same individual, and thus the protagonist retains authorial control over how his story is spun for others and possibly for himself.[1]

Then there is the analogy of life, of personhood, with fiction, with a self-enacted, self-told, self-authorized novel, and, depending on how much self-serving spin and self-deception are thought to be normal, of the self as the fictional character in the novel. Daniel Dennett, who endorses the picture of the self as a fictional construct, marries the fiction and autobiography analogies this way:

> We are virtuoso novelists, who find ourselves engaged
> in all sorts of behavior, more or less unified, but
> sometimes disunified, and we always put the best
> "faces" on we can… that story is our autobiography, the
> chief fictional character at the center of the story is one's
> self.
>
> (D. C. Dennett 1988).

---

[1] Bruner, like many narrative theorists, faces the objection that beneath, below, or behind any narrative self are the facts about what a person or self is really like, what she actually did, and so on. This is the distinction between the self and the self as represented, between "self-represented identity" (SRI) and "actual full identity" (AFI) (Flanagan 1991, 1995, 2011, Jopling 2000, Kristjansson 2010).

In both the autobiography and novel analogies, as well as in admixtures of them, the self is the protagonist (as Dennett explicitly says), as well as involved in writing the story and creating the appearance of unity—"we are all virtuoso novelists." One task, one normative demand, on autobiography or fiction—at least classically conceived, although perhaps not postmodernly conceived—is, as Bruner puts it, to get the different "self-making stories" into some sort narrative unity: "the job is to get them all into one identity, and to get them lined up over time."[2]

One question is: How is it possible—scripting, producing, directing, acting,—all at the same time? How does one write a piece of fiction about an existing person, a "real protagonist," who is, at the same time, at least partly, a creation of the work of fiction in which he is embedded? How could autobiography work such that it both tracks and makes its chief character?

Velleman neatly states the puzzle—the paradox of self-constitution—that affects all three analogies, of a life (a person) to a play, to an autobiography, and to a piece of fiction:

> Many philosophers have thought that human autonomy includes, or perhaps even consists in, a capacity for self-constitution—a capacity, that is, to define or invent or create oneself. Unfortunately, self-constitution sounds not just magical but paradoxical, as if the rabbit could go solo and pull himself out of the hat.
>
> (2006, p. 203)

The paradox of self-constitution is the most obvious metaphysical or logical puzzle faced by any very strong performative conception. There are also a host of normative questions faced by all performative conceptions, weak or strong. What are the standards—epistemic, aesthetic, and moral—if any, by which performances ought to abide?

One way to provide standards and to constrain a performative conception is to mate it to a normative theory. My own favorite is what I call "platonic unification," which says that it is best to live at the interstices of what is true, beautiful, and good.[3] Then the claim that life is what I call a "psychopoetic performance (2007)" is to be understood this way: To whatever degree the idea of performative persons makes sense, there are defensible first and third personal standards for judging the quality of performances, namely, how well the life is keyed to what is true, beautiful, and

---

[2] There have always been the outbursts of the Kafkas and Dostoevskys of the world, and the more good-natured Whitmans who recognize and relish the fact that they "contain multitudes."

[3] One might call the view I dub "platonic unification" "sub-platonic," since the triumvirate of the true, the good, and the beautiful is conceived as less than platonic forms, but as names for three zones of human life, three spaces of meaning and significance, that have some recognizable autonomy.

good, and, especially, to where they intersect.[4] First, "platonic unification" recommends that we aim to be virtuosos of knowledge, especially self-knowledge, to fashion a life that is an artistic success, and to be a morally excellent or at least a good person. The main question for a psychopoetic conception constrained by the ideal platonic unification concerns the warrant for platonic unification itself, as opposed to some other normative theory or no normative theory at all.[5] From hereon, I set the logical/metaphysical issues about performative persons aside and focus on the normative issues.

2. Classical Norms of Personhood

The idea that human life is a performance or that it at least has interesting performative aspects is ancient. Classical performative persons are called upon to abide these norms:

- Know thyself.
- Speak truthfully about yourself.
- Be true to yourself.
- Take responsibility for yourself.
- Make something interesting/worthwhile of/with yourself.

Each norm involves doing something to oneself, and this, it seems, requires some kind of reflexivity, the self conceiving of itself as object and doing something to itself so conceived. The last norm especially, "Make something interesting/worthwhile of/ with yourself," which is also the most modern, might seem to require something like diachronic attention, scripting, directing, playing protagonist, keeping one's eye on the prize, on one's plans, and adjusting, reorienting, repairing, even changing course. I say "might" because if the familiar picture of Neurath's boat, which one must repair at sea while afloat, fits both epistemology and the psychopoetics of personhood, then one might not think that too much deliberate attention, planning,

---

[4] I use the concepts of psychopoetic persons and performative persons interchangeably as convenient names for any performative conception.

[5] The argument for platonic unification might go this way: Some lives that are aesthetic successes are morally suspect or involve self-deception or failure to pay attention to the way the world is, in which case, they fail epistemically. Elijah Millgram (unpublished manuscript) gives Oscar Wilde's life as an example. Other lives (say, Tolstoy's peasants) are morally good but neither aesthetic nor epistemic successes, and so on. So a good life might seem best characterized as a life above some threshold on all three markers: good or good enough, beautiful or, if not, attractive enough, and truthful or at least attentive to certain available facts about oneself, others, and the external world. Such a life would aim at platonic unification and literally be sub-platonic.

and cognitive reflexivity need be involved. Just keeping one's eye on the prize, accomplishing what one intends/wishes to accomplish, getting to shore, to the end of the day, to graduation, and the like involve keeping track only of how one is doing relative to the goal right now, and doing improvisational things to correct course, if necessary, in order to get back ontrack.

An additional norm, possibly recently added and analyzed in depth by philosophers like Alasdair MacIntyre and Paul Ricoeur and psychologists like Jerome Bruner, is that one be able to tell a story, a truthful, coherent, and interesting story about one's life. Call this the demand of narrativity:

• Know and be prepared to tell the story of your life.

The demand of narrativity is itself a superordinate norm and is governed by sub-norms of a more detailed sort. The standard sub-norms governing the demand of narrativity are that one's narrative be

• Pinned on culturally available/endorsed narrative hooks.

Normally, we are not sensitive to how much we do this because most of us choose narrative hooks from among the familiar forms of our everyday worlds that are worn, like eyeglasses, and not really seen.[6] In *Lolita*, Nabakov gives this powerful example when Humbert Humbert explains why he and Charlotte are on the outs:

> Never in my life had I confessed so much or received so many confessions. The sincerity and artlessness with which she discussed her "love-life," from first necking to connubial catch-as-catch-can, were, ethically, in stark contrast with my glib compositions, but technically the two sets were congeneric since both were affected by the same stuff (soap operas, psychoanalysis, and cheap novelettes) upon which I drew for my characters and she for her mode of expression. [S]he showed a fierce insatiable curiosity for my past. She made me tell her all about my marriage to Valeria, who was of course a scream; but I also had to invent, or to pad atrociously, a long series of mistresses for Charlotte's morbid delectation. To keep her happy I had to present her with an illustrated catalogue of them, all nicely differentiated. [S]o I presented my women, and had them smile and sway— the langorous blonde, the fiery brunette, the sensual copperhead—as if on

---

[6] "Narrative hooking" is normative and not simply descriptive, because one learns that one ought to deliver stories and the like on such hooks, and that one's audiences rely on the massive amounts of background information contained in these shorthand schemata to place an individual and judge whether he is normal, reliable, honest, clever, or odd—overall to figure out where one is "coming from."

parade in a bordello. The more popular and platitudinous I made them, the more Mrs. Humbert was pleased with the show.

(Nabokov 1955, pp. 79–80)

Other demands on narratives, on the psychopoetics of self-expression, include these:

- The narrative is responsive to/tracks the important facts, "what really matters."
- The narrative is open-ended (epistemically)—one doesn't know how things will turn out. ("I planned for a career in architecture, but then I was drafted, worked as a medic, decided to go to med school....")
- But the direction of the narrative, the future, is structured/constrained by antecedent intentions, plans, and projects. ("I will always be there for my children." "I promise to have and to hold....")
- The narrative is filled with post facto revising, reinterpretation. ("I never loved her anyway." "She was important in my life, but not as important as I once thought.")
- The narrative is complete up 'til now: I can (barring dementia) tell/write it as it is from the beginning to the present (the standard is "what really matters," not everything that I did, experienced, or that happened to me).

It is normal, at least in the North Atlantic, to meld the classical norms of personhood with their close cousin, *the demand of narrativity*, or its doppelganger, *the demand of dramativity*,[7] and thus to gainsay the idea that life is a psychopoetic performance or at least that a life has significant aspects that are performative (e.g., it is spun in a self-serving manner; bad things I did are edited out and/or discounted; good things are highlighted). Minimally, the self-representation of the life has performative aspects; maximally, it (both the life itself and whichever genre is chosen to script or represent it) is just a performance. The "just" in the strong thesis that life or personhood is "just a performance" could be cashed out to mean a false/dishonest counterfeit that doesn't reflect or copy or reveal who the person really is. But the more credible interpretation is that the "just" in "just a performance" is intended to deny that there really is any person to copy independent of the performance, which, once again, includes the script, novel, or autobiography.

---

[7] *Dramativity*: A narrative is demanded by the picture that says life is (or is like) a fiction or autobiography. If, on the other hand, one thinks life is (or is like) a play or a poem, then the norms that demand a narrative require that you provide something more like the script or the written or spoken poem that was enacted or is in the process of being enacted by you. The actual autobiographical, dramatic, or poetic enactment, and whatever representation you offer of it or about it, constitute, taken together, your life. One rationale for the demand of representations in the form of fictional, autobiographical, dramatic, or poetic sketches is to help those who missed the original performance catch up.

In sum, among performative theorists, there is a consensus that personhood is best understood descriptively and normatively in these terms:

- It involves knowing and being able to tell a story that is one's autobiography.
- The self, the person, is produced in its own enactment, which the autobiography/fiction/drama tracks, although possibly the self is not reducible or equivalent to its enactment.
- The enactment and the story that tracks the enactment are, in some important sense, constitutive of identity.
- There are audience pressures to conceive and tell a unified story about oneself, despite the disunities.
- This guarantees that the story that (at least partly) constitutes the self is (partly) fictive (insofar as it denies, flattens, or glosses over disunities).
- We are called upon, to some degree, to create our own self by playing author/scriptwriter, more likely co-author; or, if we conceive life as more like a play than a novel or autobiography, by being the scriptwriter, director, and producer—or again, most likely co-scriptwriter, co-director, and co-producer—of the very life that is being performed or enacted.

3. Narrative-Forensic Persons and the Metaphysical-Teleological Structure of the Universe

An obvious and pressing question for one who favors the performative conception of personhood, the idea that life is a psychopoetic performance is: What, if anything, constrains the performance? In artistic performance, there are genres and there are audiences that have a say in whether the show gets out of previews, sells tickets, lasts a long time, or gets a big venue. There are genres and audiences that have expectations about genres, as well as elaborate standards for judging quality within genres.

Inside the Abrahamic traditions or their secular counterparts in the Enlightenment, there are some objective standards that constrain the performance of personhood. These standards mark the acceptable genre or, if there are several, the acceptable genres.

To see this, start with the modern conception of narrative-forensic personhood, which is of course most famously articulated by Locke, when he writes:

> Person, as I take it, is the name for this self.... It is a forensic term, appropriating actions and their merit.... The personality extends itself beyond present existence to what is past, only by consciousness, whereby it becomes concerned and accountable, owns and imputes to itself past actions, just

upon the same ground and for the same reason that it does the present....
And therefore whatever past actions it cannot reconcile or appropriate to
that present self by consciousness, it can be no more concerned in than if
they had never been done.

(*Essay*, Section 26: Person is a Forensic Term)

No sooner has Locke articulated and endorsed the autobiographical
narrative-forensic conception of a person than he raises this objection about how
the quality of lives is judged first by men and ultimately by God:

[F]or supposing a man punished now for what he had done in another
life, whereof he could be made to have no consciousness at all, what difference is there between that punishment, and being created miserable?
And, therefore, conformable to this, the apostle tells us, that, at the great
day, when every one shall "receive according to his doings, the secrets of
all hearts shall be laid open." The sentence shall be justified by the consciousness all persons shall have, that they themselves, in what bodies
soever they appear, or what substances soever that consciousness adheres
to, are the same that committed those actions, and deserve the punishment for them.

Here is the objection and the reply in a nutshell: A person, according to the autobiographical memory or consciousness criterion, is whomever he represents himself as being subjectively. This is self-represented identity (SRI) (Flanagan 1991,
1995, Jopling 2000, Kristjansson 2010). Even if the individual abides by the classical norms of personhood and works to know himself and to speak truthfully,
we expect forgetfulness, self-serving spin, and so on. The narrative revealed in
SRI will at best only approximate actual full identity, (AFI), which is the true
and complete story of who a person was, how he lived, what he did, and why.
God knows each person's AFI, and insofar as SRI does not converge with AFI,
God will restore memories, necessary insight into what actions one actually performed (not the ones described from a self-serving point of view), and whatever
else needs to be restored so that the individual sees himself as truthfully and completely as necessary to justify his reward or punishment. Only when SRI is aligned
with AFI can reward or punishment be legitimately doled out in the "soever."

The question arises: What justifies the norms by which a life ought to abide?
The answer for Locke is this: Insofar as a human life involves authorship, scripting,
ownership, and enactment, some kind of psychopoetic performance, the structure
is constrained by what is allowed and, more importantly, what is endorsed by God.
God knows the norms; he possibly invented them, presumably with perfect reason.

What I want to say is this: On the Lockean picture, which still informs how
we conceive of personhood even in secular contexts, the performance of a life is

constrained by the virtues, practices, forms of life, and genres that permit living a good life by in light of the norms for these things as endorsed and/or invented by an all-knowing, all-good, and all-loving God.

The project of the Enlightenment is of course the project of trying to vindicate these very same norms and constraints without the theological props. But the persistent worry expressed not only in the hearts and minds of many ordinary people, but also in the works of great thinkers as diverse as Dostoevsky, Nietzsche, Alasdair MacIntyre, and Charles Taylor, is that secular foundations are just not strong enough to warrant claims of objectivity.

4. Deconstruction

Saying what I have just said is tantamount to saying this: If living has been conceived as a kind of performance, or at least partly as such since classical times, it was also conceived, at least inside the Abrahamic traditions, as a radically constrained performance in the following sense. You could in principle perform your life whatever way you wish because you are an agent with free will. But you should not perform or do your life in any way you wish. There are reliable, well-established guidelines or norms for good living, and if your performance does not abide by these guidelines, there will be payback.

But what happens when the metaphysical-teleological structure of the Lockean universe breaks down, and thus the form of the performance is no longer conceived as grounded and legitimated by the authoritative voice of an omnipotent being who knows what is best? Or even when it is no longer legitimated by a secular social order that is sure of itself? What happens when Nietzsche meets Locke?

In recent philosophical literature, there are three conceptions of personhood that have a Nietzschean edge to them and that will therefore serve well to represent versions of the idea that personhood is best conceptualized as a psychopoetic performance, but now one without clear genre guidance in many places in the West. For ease of expression, I call these characters:

1. Day-by-day persons
2. Ironic persons
3. Strong poetic persons

Day-by-day persons (= person[Galen Strawson]) show that there is/can be a disconnect between a person's historical self and her inner phenomenological self that undermines some of the normative scripting and genre constraints on lives framed by the Lockean picture. Day-by-day personhood marks a different type of disconnect than the classical one between a person's SRI and AFI. The disconnect between SRI and

AFI is largely a disconnect in two ways of representing one's historical (diachronic) self. Day-by-day personhood marks the fact that one's phenomenal self, the way it seems to be me now, today, is (or at least can be) entirely separate and distinct from the historical person I am or any representation (by me, you, or God) of that historical person. Once the space of performance is opened up, I discuss *ironic persons* and *strong poetic persons* in order to push the idea that a person can be conceived as a psychopoetic performance without normative constraints to (something like) the limit. Pushing an idea to its limit is almost always a good thing in philosophy. It positions us to think more clearly about whether recommending or enacting the extreme idea is smart or worthy, a good idea, as we say.

5. "Day-by-day" Persons

Galen Strawson (2004) draws attention to phenomenology (and metaphysics) in order to question several of the classical norms of personhood. One norm that is called into question has to do with reliability, consistency, and what I will call constancy. It is an elaboration, possibly a consequence, of the norm above that says, "Take responsibility for yourself." Another norm that Strawson questions is this: "Keep the narrative on track; keep the direction of the narrative structured/constrained by antecedent intentions, plans, and projects." ("I will always be there for my children." "I promise to have and to hold....")

To see how the deconstruction works, consider this two-part elaboration of the Lockean narrative-forensic picture of persons. These conditions hold necessarily for any Lockean person (I use myself, OJF, as the example):

α: If I—OJF—did ϕ 10 years ago, then I, OJF, am the same person now who did ϕ then.

β: If α, then I, OJF, am the proper object of reward or punishment for having done ϕ 10 years ago.

A consequence of Strawson's excavation of the existence, or at least the possibility of what I call day-by-day persons[8] is (so I say) that if α and β are true, it is because they are normatively endorsed, not because they are descriptively true. They are true, if they are, because they are stipulated as public rules for accountability, not because they are true or necessary as a matter of philosophical psychology or

---

[8] Strawson recommends calling day-by-day persons "transient persons." I originally called them "divided persons," but Strawson rightly pointed out that "the trouble with 'divided' is that it suggests synchronic dividedness = conflict, as well as diachronic inconsistency, neither of which is any necessary part of being 'Episodic'/'Transientist'" (personal correspondence). I now prefer day-by-day persons because transient suggests to me greater phenomenal ephemerality than is required. Day-by-day allows the possibility that I qua phenomenal self might reliably show up/wake up as the same fellowfellow each, or most, days. Maybe, maybe not.

metaphysics. They are sensible norms in a world with the metaphysical-teleological structure of the Lockean universe, but not necessarily in worlds with a different metaphysical-teleological structure. And this fact has big consequences for the structure of scripting a life, for "storying" a life, and most importantly for the norms governing the performance, the living itself. Let me explain.

Start with this distinction that one might think is not allowed according to the standard narrative-forensic conception of persons. The distinction is between "One's experience of oneself when one is considering oneself principally as a human being taken as a whole, and one's experience of oneself when one is considering oneself as an inner mental entity or 'self' of some sort" (2004, 429).

Suppose I, OJF, did do φ 10 years ago (e.g., wrote a love letter to A declaring my undying love). If so, then according to α, I, OJF, now did φ then. And this seems true if I am talking about OJF "considered principally as a human being taken as a whole." But what if I consider myself "as an inner mental entity or 'self' of some sort"? I shall call myself considered this way (in terms of something like "my personal being *now*") OJF*, where the asterisk* is used to distinguish myself considered in this inner way (asterisked*) from my self considered as the historical being, the guy, that I am, OJF (no asterisk). The question is: Can OJF and OJF* come apart? Do they come apart for ordinary people? And if so, is there something amiss, or can their coming apart be okay, even desirable?

If OJF and OJF* can come apart, then α, conceived descriptively, needs to be rewritten this way as α':

> α': If I—OJF—did φ 10 years ago, then I, OJF, am the same "historical" person now who did φ then. But I, OJF, may or may not be (or contain or be correlated with) the same subject of experience or the same inner self or same person*, OJF*, as I was then [where 'person*' has an asterisk to distinguish it from the standard use of 'person,' which more or less equates with the historical guy]. For example, my character, my major values, my major beliefs, major relationships, my career, my life plan may have all changed a lot, and thus my experience of myself may have changed too. How I have done my life in the intervening time, as well as how fate has formed me in those years, may have changed my inner self OJF* significantly, even if my self considered as the historical being OJF is the same—and it is, as long as philosophers' fantasies of fission of bicameral brains are not actual, since OJF is always the closest continuer of OJF in this actual world. If once I was a guy who loved money and no longer do or was the kind of guy who declared to A that she was the love of my life, but am no longer the same fellow, then I, OJF*, now is different from both the guy and the fellow I was then. Indeed, although my historical self is accretive (but always the same accretion), I am always OJF. My inner self is really a set OJF* {ojf*, ojf*****, ojf**, ojf*******...} for as many distinctive inner selves as

I experience myself being. Some inner selves, say where ojf* is secure and happy versus where ojf*** is anxious and filled with fear, are, all else being equal, more desirable. Multiple ways of being internally *, ***, **, ****** can, in principle, accompany any unasterisked life (any historical self).

There are various options concerning β at this point once α is modified to be α'. One could decide that all moral and legal practices related to reward and punishment for past sins, crimes, and misdemeanors accrue to the closest continuer of each historical self, in my case, OJF, now for what OJF (but possibly not OJF*) did then, or not. So my loved ones, even the law, as it does with statutes of limitations, might decide that I am different now than I was then in the * sense and decide to forgive and forget, or in the case of the really swell things I did in the past, stop giving me credit.

This distinction between the self as historical subject and the self* as subject of experience allows Strawson to wonder whether perceived self-sameness in the inner sense is an illusion fostered by our normative expectations as opposed to a reality.

Strawson distinguishes between *diachronic self-experience* and *episodic self-experience*:

> (**D**): The basic form of Diachronic self-experience is that (**D**) one naturally figures oneself, considered as a self, as something that was there in the (further) past and will be there in the (further) future.
>
> If one is Episodic, by contrast, (**E**) one does not figure oneself, considered as a self, as something that was there in the (further) past and will be there in the (further) future (2004, 430).

D and **E**, as characterized, are outlooks or expectations. One question is this: If you do not expect **D**, but take something like a neutral phenomenological pose, can or does experience of oneself ever seem to be actually of the **E** sort? Does who I am historically ever (regularly, over certain swaths of time, in different kinds of situations) diverge from who I am and what I am like as a subject of experience. Does the guy I am, OJF, ever/regularly, etc. diverge from the fellow, OJF*, I am?

Strawson thinks that the answer is yes for some people who are constitutionally (**E**). Another possibility is that we are all (**E**)-ish some of the time, possibly often, but don't see it or admit it because of normative pressures to see the self and the self* as aligned. Either way, the disconnect is consequential. If I don't think, and thus don't expect or require, that OJF*t1 is the same fellow as OJF*t100, even though OJFt1 = OJFt100 qua historical being, then, if and when I seek to tell you who I am or when you try to predict, explain, or story my life, we need to be wary of confidence that the guy OJF and the fellow OJF* (more specifically, the fellows ojf*, ojf****, ojf******, and ojf**) are the same. The story of who I am may be easily tractable; the story of who I* am may not be; and the story of how I and I* inter-relate is likely to be extremely complicated. This might mean that narrative and/or theatrical expectations for lives change and are adjusted, and with them, the foren-sic practices, which in the Lockean picture of persons are wedded to them. Strawson writes:

> Self-understanding does not have to take narrative form, even implicitly. I am a product of my past, including my very early past, in many profoundly important respects. But it simply does not follow that self-understanding, or the best kind of self-understanding, must take a narrative form, or indeed a historical form. If I were charged to make my self-understanding explicit, I might well illustrate my view of myself by reference to things I have done, but it certainly would not follow that I had a Diachronic out-look, still less a Narrative one (448–449).

If the possibility of a divided self—where the self (no asterisk) and self* are divided, and selves* vary over time and possibly proliferate—seems disturbing, then it is made less so by the following facts: Persons do (thanks to their psychobiology, the persistence of social structures, as well as norms that say we ought to maintain and make consistent and reliable our fellowhood*) normally experience a certain simi-larity in the person inside* each of us, and thus we maintain without trying a certain degree of phenomenological unity over time.

One obvious objection to day-by-day persons, especially if they relish or pro-mote the proliferation of selves*, is that this makes for irresponsible and unreliable people. Sure, I, OJF, did that then, but I am not the same fellow now as I was then (I was ojf***, but now I am ojf**), so "fuck it," or some such. But there are three responses: First, most everyone is divided sometimes in exactly the way the analysis suggests; second, a day-by-day person can take responsibility for his historical self, even as he drops the expectation that he now is the same "fellow" phenomenologi-cally, in the inner sense*, as he was before, when he did that, and will be the same fellow* in the future.

Whether a life can *really* be any kind of performance depends on metaphys-ics, on whether genuine creativity is possible. Even if ex nihilo creativity is out of the question—and it is—it seems pretty safe to assume that the normal powers of intelligent agents in complex social ecologies are sufficient to permit creativity in self-construction and self-constitution. But whether effort should be expended to create novel, interesting, artistic ways, means, and ends depends on certain facts about ethics and epistemology, specifically whether the norms governing the ways, means, and ends of good lives are already established as "best practices." If there is still controversy or if there is renewed controversy because of such things as the death of God or multiculturalism or cosmopolitanism about genres and norms and ends and means, then the possibility space for how one might be or make oneself (both one's historical self and one's inner self*) opens up. If the metaphysical-teleological structure of the universe doesn't display or reveal the norms, genre, or blueprint for living a good life, if I must do more, or better, or something entirely different than copy or conform to what is known to be right and good, then the question of "how shall I live" takes on a new cast and perhaps a kind of vertiginous urgency.

6. Newer Kinds of Persons: Ironic Persons and Strong Poetic Persons

The disconnect in day-by-day persons between one's historical self and one's inner, phenomenological self (or more likely, one's inner phenomenological selves) when considered in the light of a breakdown in the metaphysical-teleological structure of the Lockean universe suggests conceiving of human life as both more complex and more normatively open, filled with more options for style, genre, and substance than it has in a fixed Abrahamic universe. In this final section, I explore briefly two kinds of vertiginous agency that are endorsed by some, *ironic persons* and *strong poetic persons*, which are made possible by the breakdown of the normative order of the sort that preexisted Locke, and that his widely accepted view of personhood depends on.

Richard Rorty describes a certain familiar contemporary kind of person that he calls a "liberal ironist."[9] The liberal ironist has lost confidence in his ability to detect and discern the metaphysical-teleological structure of the universe or, more likely, has lost confidence that there is a determinate set of norms that he ought to aim at because they are God's norms or the right ones as determined by some secular methods. Rorty writes:

I shall define an "ironist" as someone who fulfills three conditions:

(1) She has radical and continuing doubts about the final vocabulary she currently uses, because she has been impressed by other vocabularies taken as final by people or books she has encountered;
(2) She realizes that argument phrased in her present vocabulary can neither underwrite nor dissolve those doubts;
(3) Insofar as she philosophizes about her situation, she does not think her vocabulary is closer to reality than others, that it is in touch with a power not herself.

The ironist has the sensibilities more of an anthropologist than the first philosopher who seeks certainty and believes that there are arguments with self-evidently

[9] Rorty (1989)

true premises that justify her form of life *sub specie aeternitatis*. This much, being impressed by the contingency of her form of life, any form of life, is part of what makes her an ironist. A "liberal ironist"—always a "she" for Rorty (for liberal reasons)—hates cruelty. She "puts cruelty first," as Judith Shklar used to say. And she is concerned with justice and equality. She is an heiress to a set of values that emerge from the European and American Enlightenment—liberté, egalité, fraternité—and these values structure her ends, goals, and public aspirations. She is impressed by the contingency of the language she speaks and the way it names and categorizes things. And she is impressed by the contingency of her self, actually any and all selves, and of human communities. She understands that she might have been a Confucian or a Hindu or an aboriginal in Ecuador or Australia. She happens to be a North Atlantic liberal. Perhaps by now—two decades after Rorty's seminal description—she is a cosmopolitan liberal, a multiculturalist, a fusion philosopher, or insofar as the ironism has taken on a more skeptical edge, a hipster, a sort of liberal cynic.

The liberal ironist is anti-metaphysical. This is part of what it means to be an ironist. She lacks confidence that there is a detectible metaphysical-teleological structure of the universe. She is epistemically skeptical (ironism), but she behaves in a practically confident manner in accord with Enlightenment values (liberalism). Liberal values are good in the sense that they provide workable practical solutions to problems of living that arise in complex, crowded, democratic communities of morally diverse people. The confidence reflected in her public behavior, her public performance, belies her nagging knowledge that her final vocabulary, the one that emerged in the democratic movements of the 18th century, could have been otherwise. Her private life is another story. In the public other-regarding sphere, she abides by conventional moral values. Her private self-regarding life is pretty much as she (contingently) wishes it to be. How she does that part of her life, the self-regarding part, is entirely up to her, as long, that is, as there is no leakage into the public sphere of private values, or behavior that undermines the glue of public liberal morality. For example, sadomasochism inside consenting adult relationships is at most "weird," and if it violates the no-cruelty and no-inequality values of the liberal, it is tolerated and tolerable as long as it does not leak into and pollute the shape of public values. Sadomasochism might be weird, but if engaged in privately, it is not wrong. "Wrong" is an old-fashioned word, best suited to non-ironic times and worlds.

This way of conceiving of the constraints and demands of public life, which demands and constraints are largely justified pragmatically (they work; they are efficient; they are the ones we have), and the demands of private life, which are largely free-form and up to the individual, has important implications for the way our psychopoetic performances are conceived, and it permits the metamorphoses of a liberal ironist into a performative person. The ironist is divided, or has the option of being divided, both in the Strawsonian way, which is already open to everyone and actualized by most of us although not seen, and in another way. She walls off her public self-performance, her civic self and self-presentation, from her private self, her personal self-regarding life.

The difference between an ironist and a strong poetic person is that a strong poetic person is more anxious, or clearer, or both about the fact that she is an heiress to a certain contingent form of life. And thus she sees no deep reason, perhaps no shallow reason even, to take its givenness as important, as final even in the epistemically provisional, ambivalent way that the liberal ironist takes the values of liberalism as "final." In addition, a strong poetic person is something of an aesthete, perhaps a dandy.[10] He values play, being artful, creative, surprising, daring, and edgy. A strong poetic person can be described in two not incompatible ways: He is skeptical of both the foundationalist justification of the Enlightenment form of public life, as is the liberal ironist, but he is also skeptical of the pragmatic justification of that public life form. He gets that prudence (social, moral, legal punishment), which could be considered the most thin or superficial sort of pragmatic reason, might warrant public conformity to a set of genres, norms, and ends. But really there is no deep reason for the values that guide these practices other than that they are familiar, normal, regular, and usual—the standard values in his vicinity and of the group to which he finds himself belonging. In a situation in which the ways, means, and ends of successful lives are multiple, he puts a premium on the aesthetics of living in a different way and on not being a mere copy.

Harold Bloom called this fear of mere copying, of being *Homo Xerox*, the "anxiety of Influence." (Bloom considers it a widespread but largely unnoticed modern malaise.)[11] A strong poetic person has Nietzsche's spirit, if not his talent, and works to be a "strong poet" to create new ways of being and doing himself that make him, as it were, a total original, one of a kind. Why?

(a) [B]ecause there just are no required norms, no way of being either created or endorsed by God, and thus there are no deep reasons to be one way rather than another either publically or privately;

(b) given (a), it is interesting, clever, and fun to do one's own thing and to surprise oneself and others.

---

[10] It is a bit polemical to say that the strong poetic person is an aesthete or a dandy. Alexander Nehamas's work on Nietzsche (1985) is sometimes read as supporting a purely aesthetic self-fashioning view (see Millgram, unpublished manuscript), but Nietzsche is—at least Nehamas's Nietzsche is—extraordinarily self- and world- scrutinizing and also morally serious; at least he is twisted up about morality. Whether he therefore satisfies the standards of platonic unification or sub-platonism is a more difficult question than it might initially seem. Anderson and Landy (2001) have a deep discussion of the self-fashioning trope in Nehamas's work and what self-fashioning means and how well it works for some of his favorite characters: Socrates, Montaigne, and Nietzsche.

[11] Bloom (1973)

Euthyphro's problem of whether God *creates* the norms that are good or *endorses* the ones that are antecedently good is not one that troubles a person who aspires to be a strong poet. There are no deep puzzles about the warrant of norms. There are historical, sociological, and genealogical stories about norms, values, genres, and the like, but that's it: utter contingency.

One way a strong poetic person responds to the angst that she is just copying others in character, morals, career, etc. is to "do it a new way, mix it up, improvise." For any role, activity *phi* (e.g., gender, class, race, temperament, linguistic practices, job), do *phi* differently by doing *alpha, beta…zeta*. Or do *not phi* (the opposite of *phi*). If you are gay, do straight. Or do blue or fish instead of *phi*. Or do phi^2, etc.

Some advocates of strong poetic personhood—Judith Butler, for example—think, and rightly so, that it is hard to know what is fixed by nature and what is not until one refuses to assume what is already assumed about the divide. The case of gender is the possibility proof that what seems fixed, not subject to playfulness, innovation, invention, creativity, and artfulness, is malleable and not so fixed (Einstein and Flanagan 2003). But sex and gender and Shakespeare's seven ages of man (maybe, 60 is the new 50, but 60 just isn't the new 20) are also used as examples where one confronts relatively non-contingent facts about oneself, and possibly about persons generally.

In any case, the imperative to "do it a new way, mix it up, improvise" is itself a norm, simply one suggested by the community of souls who suffer the anxiety of influence. The norm is infinitely regressive in the sense that if you try to "do it a new way, mix it up, improvise," and do "it"—the norm itself—in a new way, you are still in a web of normativity since you have just followed a norm. Furthermore, one's creative options are limited metaphysically. That is, even if creative acts can come as psychological or epistemic surprises, they are limited as true novelties by the mathematics of permutation and combination. Finally, advocates of strong poetic personhood are predictably young, hip, urban, and urbane—citizens of communities that value doing it a new way, mixing it up, improvising, which should make one worry, first, that the catchment of influence is inescapable (they are hip because they live among hipsters); and second, that "doing it a new way" is just another fad—and if it is new now, it will become old, predictable, and boring fast; and finally, that unlike either the Lockean way or the ironic way of being a person, performative personhood is frivolous for its own sake, which is to say frivolous for no reason at all. Absurd.

7. Conclusion

So where does this leave us? I started with the suggestion that standard Lockean persons might conceive of life, even of their personhood, in terms of narrative, a story, a standard autobiography, or possibly as a play, a dramatic performance.

Even if, or insofar as, Lockean lives and Shakespearean lives involve creativity on the part of the author/protagonist or playwright/actor, it is only creativity within the bounds of normative constraints on how the narrative or drama is supposed to go. The protagonist and the acceptable genres are classical, not what, in literary theory, we'd call "modernist" ("modern" in literature is James Joyce and Virginia Wolf, not, as in philosophy, Descartes). The reason is that there is confidence about the metaphysical-teleological structure of the universe and thus about the wisdom, indeed the necessity, of conformity to it. A protagonist/actor might enact a disaster precisely because on the classical model, there really are objective disasters, real happy or sad endings, genuinely bad people and good people. Abrahamic standards, secularized but not eliminated in the Enlightenment, reign as constraints on protagonists/actors, genres, scripts, and direction.

The three contemporary ideas of persons I have glossed, "day-by-day persons," "ironic persons," and "strong poetic persons" are all possible, normatively possible, because of the breakdown of classical metaphysical-teleological structure. It is hard to know whether, if one has a nostalgia for classical personhood, personhood done the Lockean way, this nostalgia can be vindicated as anything more than a nostalgia for a certain old-fashioned way of doing a self, which, if it is seen that way, can be done or performed, but only as an affectation, as a way of having or revealing a possibly short-lived taste for a certain classical style, like a taste for classic cars or vintage clothing.

One worry that one might have about post-Lockean persons is that they elevate artfulness and give priority to the form of beauty because they have a certain skepticism about the determinateness of the forms of the good and the true (all now forms with a small "f"). But one might point out that skepticism about standards of artfulness—beauty, novelty, creativity, and the like—are older and deeper (*de gustibus non est disputandum*), and for good reason, than skepticism about the good and the true.

A wise ironist or advocate of the concept of strong poetic persons could and should just accept this. Standards of artfulness in doing, performing, and describing one's life (as drama, fiction, autobiography, or poetry) come and go. For reasons that are perhaps hard to explain, what is considered creative, interesting, and artful changes, sometimes comes back, and so on. That's just the way things go.

This chapter began as meditation on the ideas that the self is a work of art, that a person is a performance, somehow enacted and described or at least describable in a drama, autobiography, or fiction. Perhaps a poem, painting, or musical score, where they are both enacted by and about the person himself, could also work as useful analogies or models of persons and their lives. If the standards and thus the modes of doing lives are variable as just suggested, we might expect this.

One worry I have tried to motivate is that the pictures of day-by-day, ironic, and strong poetic persons are all born of various kinds of skepticism that there is a person behind or beyond the life enacted, performed, and described in some optional art form; that instead the person and his life are in some sense the performance and its description, however that is executed. The next observation, which leads, I think, to vertigo, is that there are no external, transcendental norms that govern how the life qua psychopoetic performance is supposed to be executed. This is the result of the breakdown of the metaphysical-teleological structure of the Lockean universe.

That said, the thought that life is some kind of psychopoetic performance has often, post-Nietzsche, been a way of thinking of a good life as one where meaning is associated and aligned with and measured by such things as how in charge of one's life one is, how heartfelt the performance of one's life is, how much reflective identification there is with oneself as the protagonist, and how successful one is at living at the interstices of goodness, truth, and beauty, what I call platonic unification. One worry, of course, is that such norms (like other norms) can't really be justified, but are nonetheless sweet, dear, cute, and adorable remnants of *temps perdu*.

I will leave things at that. I am not sure how to go on. I conclude with this observation and a couple of hopes or guesses: Our world is a postmodern one in exactly the philosophical sense that foundationalism and thus cocky confidence in any particular form of life, and any associated way of being or doing a life lacks any kind of deep warrant. Can persons, philosophical persons and reflective souls, go on to find their lives meaningful while accepting only contingent, immanent warrants for how they choose to live? I think so. Will there being any discoveries about these contingent, immanent norms that will reliably warrant performances that are not frivolous or selfish? I doubt it. What will continue to happen though will be that the rest of us, the audiences, will continue to call some people "self-indulgent," "selfish creeps," and "immature," and that may be—it will have to be—enough.

Acknowledgments

I am grateful to Elliot Samuel Paul, Scott Barry Kaufman, and Galen Strawson for extremely helpful comments on the first version of this essay. Conversations with Alison Gopnik, Joshua Landy, Alexander Nehamas, Thomas Pavel, Elijah Milgram, and Lanier Anderson were helpful at the penultimate stage.

References

Anderson, R. Lanier, and Joshua Landy. 2001. "Philosophy as Self-Fashioning: Alexander Nehamas's Art of Living," Review: *The Art of Living: Socratic Reflections from Plato to Foucault*, by Alexander Nehamas, *Diacritics*, vol. 31, no. 1 (Spring), pp. 25–54.

Bloom, H. 1973. *The Anxiety of Influence: A Theory of Poetry*. Oxford, UK: Oxford University Press.

Bruner, Jerome. 2002. *Making Stories: Law, Literature, Life*. New York. Farrar, Straus, and Giroux.

Butler, J. 1990. *Gender Trouble: Feminism and the Subversion of Identity*. London: Routledge.

Dennett, Daniel C. 1988. "Why Everyone is a Novelist." *TLS*, no. 4, p. 459.

Einstein, Gillian, and Owen Flanagan. 2003. "Sexual Identities and Narratives of Self," in *Narrative and Consciousness*. Gary Fireman, Ted McVay, and Owen Flanagan, eds. Oxford, UK: Oxford University Press.

Flanagan, O. 1991. *Varieties of Moral Personality: Ethics and Psychological Realism*. Cambridge, MA: Harvard University Press.

Flanagan, O. 1995. *Self-Expressions: Mind, Morals, and the Meaning of Life*. Oxford, UK: Oxford University Press.

Flanagan, O. 2011a. "My Non-Narrative, Non-Forensic Dasein," in JeeLoo Liu and J. Perry, eds., *Consciousness and the Self: New Essays*. Cambridge, UK: Cambridge University Press.

Flanagan, O. 2011b. "Phenomenal and Historical Selves," in Katja Crone, Kristina Musholt, and Anna Strasser, eds., *Grazer Philosophische Studien*, special issue on "Facets of self-consciousness."

Jopling, D. A. 2000. *Self-Knowledge and the Self*. London. Routledge.

Kristjansson, K. 2010. *The Self and Its Emotions*. Cambridge, UK: Cambridge University Press.

Locke, John. 1690. *Essay Concerning Human Understanding*, http://oregonstate.edu/instruct/phl302/texts/locke/locke1/Essay_contents.html.

Millgram, Elijah. "The Life as Artwork and Paradoxes of Narcissism," unpublished manuscript.

Nabokov, Vladimir. 1955. *Lolita*. New York: Vintage.

Nehamas, Alexander. 1985. *Nietzsche: Life as Literature*. Cambridge, MA: Harvard University Press.

Rorty, Richard. 1989. *Contingency, Irony, and Solidarity*. Cambridge, UK: Cambridge University Press.

Strawson, Galen. 2004. "Against Narrativity," *Ratio* XVII 4: pp. 428–452.

Velleman, David. 2006. *Self to Self: Selected Essays*. Cambridge, UK: Cambridge University Press.

6

Creativity as a Virtue of Character

MATTHEW KIERAN

1. Introduction

What is it to be a creative person? How can we best cultivate creativity? When, where, and why does creativity underwrite judgments of esteem and praise? These questions are of fundamental practical and philosophical significance.

Creativity is responsible for the most valuable advances of humankind from the natural and human sciences to engineering, technology, business, and the arts. Furthermore, we are often told that it is crucial for economic growth (BIAC 2004), individual fulfillment (Maslow 1968), or associated with well-being (Park, Peterson, and Seligman 2004). Hence, for example, the constant worries about how school education stifles creativity through the pressures and failings of "teaching to test" (Lim 2010, Rosenthal 2010). At the same time, disciplines taken to foster creativity, such as art or music, are often cut from curricula (Burton 2011), and public provision is slashed in times of austerity (Jacobs 2011). What we should think and do about such matters depends upon how we think of creativity.

The philosophical interest in creativity ranges over a host of issues from the acquisition of concepts, the construction of representational resources, generative knowledge, and conceptual changes in science to creating works of art. It is a philosophical commonplace that creativity is highly valued. Yet just what kind of achievement it is to be a creative person has been much neglected. Is it most fundamentally to possess some kind of amazing capacity or skill? Or is there more to it than that? In what follows, it is argued that exemplary creativity should be thought of as a virtue of character rather than just a mere skill or capacity. Indeed, paying attention to the neglected role of motivation will show us what exemplary creativity consists in, why this makes best sense of our evaluative practices, and how it is that creativity may best be cultivated.[1]

---

[1] It is sometimes assumed that creativity is an intellectual or artistic virtue in the literature (see, e.g., Zagzebski 1996, p. 167). Arguments put forward for the claim often focus on psychic health or emotional well-being (Swanton 2003, pp. 161–173, Goldie 2008). The argumentative route taken here

2. Reliability in Virtue of What?

Creative acts are commonly held to be ones that produce something novel and valuable through the use of skills, abilities, or aptitudes. An influential characterization of creativity in this vein is given by Boden (2004, p. 1) as "an ability to come up with ideas or artifacts that are new, surprising and valuable." Although this captures the sense in which someone qualifies as creative just in virtue of the capacity to produce in specific and many instances artifacts or ideas that are novel and worthwhile, it is not particularly helpful in getting at the kind of relationship among character, thought, and action required for an agent to be praiseworthy as a creative person (Stokes 2008, pp. 116-7).

In order to bring this out, consider the following case. A stroke victim is in recovery and striving to learn to write again. In writing therapy classes, he can only produce marked patterns that are hopeless as linguistic notation but are both novel (at least relative to some previous performance efforts) and aesthetically valuable as abstract art. The sessions with the therapist require intense concentration, and a huge amount of perseverance is required. The sessions are also immensely frustrating and humiliating. He knows he should be able to write, envisages the marks on the page as they should be, and yet systematically lacks the control over his hand that is required to produce the words on the page. The continual failure to write makes the stroke victim feel angry and ashamed. Although this would be enough to make some people give up, it only strengthens his resolve to master writing once more.

Let us assume that it is amazing that the stroke victim can produce what he does given the nature of the stroke. Despite a problem with the visual system sub-serving motor guidance, his exceptional visual ability explains how he is able to do what he does. Nonetheless, the ability to produce beautiful abstract patterns and the inability to render words on the page are the result of a mismatch between the damaged motor-guiding vision system (information passing through the dorsal stream) as contrasted with the exceptionally attuned descriptive vision (ventral stream). Note that the systems can dissociate either way, explaining why visual agnosics, after damage, can fail to recognize familiar objects and yet manipulate and even draw them perfectly accurately (Matthen 2005, Milner and Goodale 1995). Furthermore, the nature of the systematic mismatch is such that were he to attempt to produce valuable abstract patterns, he would fail (i.e., the results would be a mess).

In a sense, the stroke victim is creative. He possesses both the visual aptitudes and personal traits that dispose him toward engaging in acts producing novel and valuable artifacts. It is partly in virtue of the strength and combination of courage,

---

is rather different, focusing as it does on motivation (though it has affinities with Woodruff 2001). This is particularly significant given the neglect of the role of motivation in the philosophical literature on creativity (as noted by Gaut 2010).

perseverance, and self-control of emotions that the stroke victim engages in the writing activity each day with its concomitant results. Yet the marks made are neither a result of any aesthetic insight nor willed (i.e., aesthetically motivated). Indeed, the marks are not really the result of intention since he is attempting to make linguistic symbols and failing. He has no aesthetic sensibility or interest, fails to see the patterns on the page as aesthetically valuable, and is wholly unmotivated to attempt to produce them for aesthetic reasons. What he does produce is aesthetically novel and valuable only as a systematic byproduct, albeit one that is a function of personal traits and aptitudes, of something else that he is striving to do. In an aesthetic sense then, what we have is a lucky accident of a particularly reliable and systematic kind within an extremely narrow range (i.e., the capacity to produce novel and appreciable simple abstract patterns on paper).

What does this show? The stroke victim is aesthetically creative in a minimal sense, insofar as what is meant is just the creation of novel and valuable artifacts. He is also admirable and praiseworthy insofar as he shows courage, determination, and some flair in what he does. Nonetheless, given that he does not aim at, in any way respond to, do anything with, elaborate, or develop the initial aesthetically valuable marks on the page, we should think of this as merely novel behavior that accidentally though systematically leads to the production of novel and worthwhile products. This is to be distinguished from novel, valuable behavior that is agential in being guided by and directed toward fulfilling the agent's intention or purpose. Creativity in the more robust sense involves something like "a relevant purpose (in not being purely accidental), some degree of understanding (not using merely mechanical search procedures), a degree of judgment (in how to apply a rule, if a rule is involved) and an evaluative ability directed to the task at hand" (Gaut 2010, p. 1040).[2]

Creative people experiment with what they do, for example by trying out different ways of elaborating initial attempts (sometimes obsessively so if we consider the nature of models and preparatory sketches), in ways that enable them to refine or transform what they do in the service of the goals and values of the relevant domains. Indeed being able to recognize the good in a "lucky accident" and going on to use it to advantage depends upon the kind of insight and mastery tied up with being a creative individual. The creative person is sensitive to and acts in the light of reasons. It is her responsiveness to reasons that grounds her judgments and actions in recognizing what is new and valuable in the relevant domain. Thus, for example, an artist standing in the right kinds of creative relations to such abstract patterns would tend to explain choices in terms of what it is for a pattern to sit right, what

---

[2] Gaut uses the word "flair" to capture these features in recognition of the idea that creative acts have to come about a certain way (2003, pp. 150–151). What matters here, irrespective of particular details, is that we should recognize something like a sensitivity- to-reasons account of creativity that is stronger than the minimal sense proffered by Boden (2004, p. 1).

this particular color tone achieves, and so on (Kieran 2007). The stroke victim, in contrast, has no idea about such matters.

This explains why we would expect an artist who made the patterns to be creative in the aesthetic domain, whereas we would not expect the stroke victim to be able to do anything more. We would presume that an artist who made the patterns would be able to do things differently, be able to make other patterns that would be aesthetically appealing or elaborate and develop them in appreciable ways. The stroke victim's aptitudes, abilities, and character traits are causally responsible, and reliably so, for the production of aesthetically novel and valuable artifacts. Nonetheless, he is not praiseworthy in the same kind of way as an artist would be in bringing insight and mastery to bear on the imaginative production of something that is similarly aesthetically appreciable.

What is the upshot thus far? There is a minimal sense of creativity that is tied to agents just producing novel and valuable artifacts. However, there is a further sense of creativity that is tied to presuppositions of mastery, control, and sensitivity to reasons in guiding how agents bring about what they aim to do. It is creativity in this sense that attracts a certain kind of praise for agents in being responsible in the right kinds of ways for the imaginative realization of ideas or artifacts.

3. Motivation and Creativity as a Virtue

It is one thing to show that praising someone as a creative person rests on assumptions about agents acting in light of the appropriate kinds of reasons. It is quite another, however, to show that this is a matter of virtue. Creativity is a virtue only if part of what is praiseworthy and admirable concerns excellence of character. According to Aristotle, "virtuous acts are not done in a just or temperate way merely because they have a certain quality, but only if the agent acts in a certain state, viz. (1) if he knows what he is doing, (2) if he chooses it, and chooses it for its own sake, and (3) if he does it from a fixed and permanent disposition of character" (1976, II.4, pp. 1105a28–1105a33).

Let us consider the second condition. Interest in the relevant task or domain of activity for its own sake seems central to creativity. Indeed, there is a wealth of studies in experimental psychology that are highly suggestive in this respect. In one classic study (Amabile 1985), 72 creative writing students were given the task of writing poetry. A control group was given the task of writing poetry with a snow theme, reading a short story, and then writing another poem on the theme of laughter. The other two groups were given the same tasks, except that after the short story, they were told to read and rank-order lists of reasons for writing. One group was given a list of previously established intrinsic motivating reasons for writing (e.g., self expression, the joy of wordplay, insight). A second group was asked to read and order a list of extrinsic reasons for writing (e.g., making money, social status, graduate prospects). As judged by 12 independently successful poets, the group primed with extrinsic motivating reasons produced the least creative work of the three groups.

The undermining effect of extrinsic motivation is hardly specific to artistic cases. Even further back, Garbarino (1975) conducted an experiment where 24 fifth and sixth grade (i.e., 12-year-old) schoolgirls were given the task of tutoring 24 first and second grade (i.e., 6-year-old) girls in a simple poker chip game. The subjects were randomly assigned into pairs and one of two conditions: a no-reward condition and an extrinsic- reward condition (a movie ticket). Those primed for the extrinsic reward performed the task less well. They grew more impatient more quickly with their charges, were less interested if their charges really understood the task at hand, and tended to be more negative in emotional tone when compared to the no-reward group. Those devoid of any extrinsic reward were more careful, patient, and positive in emotional tone and used their time more efficiently. As a result, the 6-years-olds tutored by those in the no-reward condition learned more and made fewer errors. What might we make of such studies?

Intrinsic motivation seems to be understood in terms of aiming at the values internal to the relevant domain. Thus, for example, self-expression, delight in wordplay, and cultivating understanding are taken to be intrinsic motivations in the respective studies. Extrinsic motivation, in contrast, is taken to aim at ends or goals that are not themselves part of the values internal to literature or teaching but, rather, ones that can be instrumentally realized through performing the relevant task or kind of activity. This might be brought out in the following way: Intrinsic motivation involves acting out of a desire to realize what makes something valuable under the relevant description in the given domain. In the literary case, this involves being motivated to produce something that is expressive, imaginative, or beautiful. It is a desideratum of any adequate account of artistic values that it precludes certain attributes, ranging from price to social cachet, as counting toward a work's value as art. Hence in creating a literary work, to be motivated to write something in order to get financial reward or attract social prestige is to be extrinsically motivated. It is, we might say, to treat the creation of an artistic work as a mere means to the realization of ends and values that are external to the domain of artistic values.

In the scenarios presented, whether a task is framed in terms of intrinsic or extrinsic motivations makes a significant difference as to how creatively or otherwise the subjects performed. Why might that be? There are several possible explanations. One possibility is that subjects primed by extrinsic motivations suffered from divided attention in a way that those primed by intrinsic motivations did not. Perhaps thinking about a prize or social benefits led subjects to devote less attention to the respective tasks. An alternative explanation is that those primed with intrinsic motivations were more sensitive to and motivated by reasons bound up with the goods internal to the activity in question.

In this light, consider someone whose governing motivation in making music, say, is just to gain social credence. Whatever else is true, social status is hardly something that is internal to the values of art, though of course art is often used to achieve or bolster it. Imagine, in this case, that the person's extrinsic motivation explains the kind of jazz or dance music chosen and how playing it is approached. While being driven to play the music as he does may attract the sought-after social cachet, it also explains exactly why the playing is formulaic and unimaginative. It explains, for example, why the person is less likely to take risks or experiment. Experimenting would not only involve paying greater attention to and seeking to understand the music at some deeper level, but put at risk the very extrinsic goods so easily attained without that much hard work or thought. After all, what matters to this person is less that the music is as good or interesting as it could be and more that the extrinsic goods of social recognition are realized. Indeed, the person is less likely to have the patience, honesty, and courage required to be as creative as possible if the motivating goals governing what he does are really just the extrinsic social ones. He is much more likely to be satisfied with any resultant popularity and acclaim when he plays than someone who is motivated by the relevant goals and values pertinent to music. The extrinsically motivated agent is keying into certain social dynamics and goods, where the aesthetic quality and value is coincidental to such, whereas the situation is exactly the reverse for someone who is intrinsically motivated. Intrinsically motivated musicians strive to get noticed, build up a following, and get paid in order to be able to make their music; the purely extrinsically motivated desire social success or money and use display in the musical activity in order to try and get it.

In some given domain, extrinsic motivation often explains why someone identifies the easiest aims and goals to lead most directly to the desired outcome. Thus, when creativity is governed by extrinsic rather than intrinsic motivation, someone is far less likely to be creative. Why? When the governing motivation is not directed toward intrinsic values but contingent extrinsic ones, and when extrinsic values pull away from the internal ones, extrinsic motivation will be inimical to creativity.

Consider two students at the same level in some domain who are both equally motivated to pass a test. Bullish Boris cares little for his subject but wants good grades for his job prospects. He strives to internalize the relevant knowledge, capacities, and perceptual, cognitive, and affective routines as quickly as possible. Careful Cara cares passionately for her subject and hence works in a different way. She works at breaking down the components of the general routines, capacities, and knowledge required. This enables her to analyze and work at them in ways that block easy and automatic internalization. Bullish Boris's progress at a superficial level will be a lot quicker than Careful Cara's. Boris may well, for example, be in a position to pass the test much sooner than Cara. Nonetheless, Cara will have much greater understanding and control concerning what sub-serves the general capacities, routines, and expertise called for. While Cara may well have covered far less ground for the test than Boris over the same time frame, she will nonetheless be in a position to realize far greater understanding and mastery over what she has studied. Cara can attend to, critically explicate, and make use of a far greater number of perceptual, cognitive, and affective variables than Boris can. Cara is thus in a position to be creative, with respect to what she has learned, in ways that Boris is not.

Motivation shapes attentiveness, the envisaging of possibilities and openness to revision of ends as a work proceeds. If motivation is intrinsic, a subject is more likely to take risks, more likely to attend in an open-minded way to what she's done, envisage different possibilities, and be directed by thought in action toward realizing the inherent values of a given domain. When the motivation is extrinsic, someone is more likely to take the easiest and most unimaginative, formulaic, and glib way of creating something. Why? Work in the service of extrinsic goals often only coincidentally tracks and typically pulls away from the intrinsic values of the given domain. Hence, creative excellence in a given domain depends upon being motivated by the values intrinsic to it. Furthermore, the motivation to be sensitive to, respond in the light of, and act for the sake of the relevant reasons and values internal to some given domain can be more or less deeply embedded in someone's character. The more deeply embedded the intrinsic motivation, the more creative someone will be in a given domain across different situations, and the more we admire and praise them as a creative person.

It is worth pausing to address a particular challenge and in so doing bring out the argument structure. It might be objected that all that has been shown is that intrinsic motivation is instrumentally valuable in leading to the production of more creative results. What matters here, the challenge states, is surely the creative results rather than how they were arrived at. To the extent that people are intrinsically motivated, they will tend to produce more creative work. All that has been shown is how to arrive at the best results. This is a good deal short of showing that exemplary creativity is a virtue of character (at least as virtue is traditionally understood).

What it is to be intrinsically motivated with respect to some domain, say, art, philosophy, or science, is for one's activity to be guided by the values internal to that domain. In structuring our attention, judgments, responses, and actions toward what it is that is valuable in the relevant domain, intrinsic motivation enables us to be creative across different times, situations, and challenges. In contrast, when someone is purely extrinsically motivated, say, by the drive for social recognition or distinction, domain- irrelevant features will tend to play a causal role in their activity and figure in the wrong sorts of roles in judgments and actions. This explains why, lucky circumstances aside, what it is to be a robustly reliable creative person tends to depend upon intrinsic motivation. Furthermore, staying true to intrinsic motivations in the face of difficulties and temptations is an achievement of character.

Consider Van Gogh. After his failure as a pastor and missionary, Van Gogh decided to take up art in 1880. He had some natural talent (though no more so than many). His pen and ink drawing *A Marsh (near Etten at Passievart)* (1881) demonstrates a flair for the use of intricate cross-hatching to achieve texture and depth in landscape depiction. Nonetheless, for the first five years or so, his paintings tended to be clumsy, flat, and poorly composed. Even as late as 1885, Van Gogh struggled with depicting movement and the persuasive rendering of figures. His first major painting *The Potato Eaters* (1885) was fiercely criticized, at least as perceived by Van Gogh, for the ineptitude of its figures, and this spurred him on to work obsessively at depicting the figure in motion. He dedicated the entire summer of that year to persevering with figuration over and over again. The noticeable resulting improvement in figuration came together with his discovery of Japanese Ukiyo-e prints and neo-impressionist color experiments. Thus Van Gogh came to develop his geometric, almost calligraphic notations in paint to mark out figures and landscapes. This enabled him to render features with immense variation in visual density, openness, and texture. In doing so, he was able to convey a great sense of rhythm, flow, and movement. What explains why Van Gogh developed as he did? The explanation concerns, at least in part, Van Gogh's motivation.

Van Gogh modified motifs for the sake of pictorial order and emotional significance. Many painters who have such goals do not worry about the lack of realistic delineation or movement. Yet this was a particularly significant problem for Van Gogh given that he desired his painting to be a visually expressive exploration of landscape forms and the people in them while also being verisimilar. Van Gogh's motivation was directly concerned with realizing some of the values internal to art in new ways, in contrast to what he saw as the tired academicism of his day. The motivation explains why something was a particular artistic problem for Van Gogh, in ways it would not be for other painters, and indeed how and why he came to the innovative solution he did. However, Van Gogh's intrinsic motivation is neither just a causal factor enabling his achievement nor just an explanatory one that makes sense of the artistic problems apprehended by him and the solutions he arrived at. The strength and depth of his intrinsic motivation over time are praiseworthy given his extreme perseverance, courage, and honest self-criticism. After all, this is a man who persevered despite the lack of recognition, who sold only one picture in his lifetime, to his brother Theo, and who lived in extreme poverty in order to create his art.

Van Gogh is an extreme case. There are, after all, many creative people who attain recognition, social status, and material wealth. But Van Gogh is especially praiseworthy because of the extremities involved in staying true to his intrinsic motivation. Nonetheless, the point is that someone's intrinsic motivation in a domain as a basic disposition across time and situations is itself a praiseworthy achievement of character.

It matters not whether we are talking about creativity in art, philosophy, or science. It takes honesty to evaluate the nature and value of what one is doing properly; it takes courage to be prepared to fail; it takes humility and open-mindedness to recognize when one has gone wrong; and it takes perseverance and fortitude to continue to work at something for its own sake or in seeking to do justice to an idea. This is in part because creativity typically pushes the limits of what has already been done and is thus often difficult to achieve. It is, however, also because the drives and biases that are part of the human condition tend to pull us toward compromise, self-deception, and over-inflated estimations of the nature and value of what we do. It is tempting for those who achieve success or status to allow extrinsic motivations to intrude. When a person starts to worry about social status or wealth, for example, rather than striving to do what is worthwhile, it is all too easy for judgment to become corrupted by considerations of popularity, recognition, and belonging. Even in circumstances of relative comfort and after previous successes, people can be motivated by extrinsic concerns, such as the flattery of others or the drive to appear superior (Kieran 2010). Creativity requires, after all, a kind of independence from conventionality and freedom from just these kinds of drives and biases.

This is not to claim that creative action as such requires intrinsic motivation and not all creativity is virtuous. Nonetheless, there is good reason to conceive of creativity as a virtue when agents' creative successes are driven by deep-seated intrinsic motivations. Why? Deep-seated intrinsic motivation is an aspect of character that guides and explains why a person is creative across different times, situations, and external pressures. It is, moreover, partly constitutive of excellence of character and, as such, is to be praised and esteemed.

4. Motivational Complexities

A crucial point to note is that the contrast between intrinsic and extrinsic motivations as adduced in the psychological literature requires nuance. There are, after all, domains and practices in which social recognition or wealth, for example, are values internal to the relevant activities. A socialite, a particular kind of pop star, or a hedge fund manager all aim in virtue of their vocations at realizing the very things that are usually characterized in the literature as extrinsic motivations. Yet in such cases, financial and/or social recognition are criteria of success (i.e., to be motivated by such things in these kinds of cases is to be intrinsically motivated when this just means to be motivated by the values internal to the relevant domain). Exemplary creativity clearly can be manifested in those domains in ways that are admirable, praiseworthy, and enable us to distinguish those who excel from those who do not. So, matters are complicated, but for present purposes, we need only recognize that the values realized in creative acts can take different forms. Creative achievements might concern values that are intrinsic (truth), extrinsic (making people happy), inherent (expressive of feeling), purely instrumental (achieving huge financial returns), or relational (one vacuum cleans better than another). Intrinsic motivation conceived as it is here, as motivation by the values and goals internal to some relevant domain, does not straightforwardly equate with the direct realization of intrinsic values.[3]

We also need to recognize that extrinsic motivation sometimes reinforces rather than undermines creativity. William Blake was surely overstating matters in claiming that "where any view of money exists, art cannot be carried on" (Blake 1826). Indeed, Dr. Johnson is not only more worldly but surely truer to the mark in observing that "no man but a blockhead ever wrote except for money" (Boswell 1776, p. 731) or, we might add, recognition, status, and esteem (and usually some combination thereof). In any given domain where creativity is prized, people are often spurred on by motivations that are extrinsic to the values internal to the domain. These run the whole gamut of human motivations from the desire for financial gain, prestige, social conformity, adulation, or rebellion to revenge. Moreover, as the evidence suggests, such extrinsic motivations can sometimes enhance rather than undermine creativity.

Recent psychology studies have shown significant enhancement effects on creativity due to extrinsic rewards. In one experiment (Eisenberger and Rhoades 2001), 115 college psychology students were asked to read a short story about popcorn popping in a pan and asked to provide five titles. Every second student was given, as part of the printed instructions, the promise of a financial reward if the titles were judged to be among the most creative (e.g., "The Little Kernel that Could," "The Golden Years," and "Growing Pains"). Those students promised a reward produced titles of significantly greater creativity than those in the no-reward incentive condition ($Ms = 2.75$ and 2.56, respectively), $t(114) = 1.72, p < .05$. This should come as no surprise to anyone versed in the history of domains where creativity is at a premium.

How can we explain the apparent tension? It seems that on conceptual and psychological grounds, we have good reason to hold that when intrinsic motivation is embedded in character and drives creativity, it both underwrites creative achievement and is praiseworthy. Yet extrinsic motivation clearly sometimes can and does enhance creativity. Collins and Amabile (1999) claim that we should distinguish between synergistic extrinsic motivation, which can enhance creativity under limited circumstances by providing information or enabling intrinsic motivation, and non-synergistic extrinsic motivations, which diminish a subject's feeling of self control and undermine creative activity. Even so, extrinsic motivation is assumed in general to interfere with creativity and "when individuals are attempting to solve a problem or generate possible solutions, being intrinsically involved in the task and not distracted by extrinsic concerns will help them to produce more original

---

[3] The natures of intrinsic, extrinsic, final, non-final, conditional, and relational values are complex and a subject of philosophical controversy. See, e.g., Korsgaard 1983, Rabinowicz and Rønnow-Rasmussen 1999, and Rønnow-Rasmussen 2002.

ideas" (Collins and Amabile 1999, p. 305). What explains why extrinsic motivation in some circumstances enables or reinforces creativity and in others undermines it?

Creative excellence does not require that the motivation involved be direct in the sense of consciously aiming at being creative, nor does it require that the motivation be *solely* for the sake of the internal ends of the relevant domain (i.e., for its own sake). We often just see and respond to certain kinds of considerations as appropriate and are motivated to act accordingly without thinking in terms of what the creative thing to do is. What matters is how an agent's motivational set enters into and guides judgment and activity. Creative excellence involves being motivated by the appropriate kinds of reasons, figuring in appropriate roles in guiding deliberation and activity toward the values internal to the relevant domain. This can be reinforced or undermined by extrinsic motivation depending upon how it enters into the thought processes, apprehensions, responses, and judgments arrived at in the carrying out of the particular activity in question. When extrinsic rewards are seen as being positively related to the pursuit of the values internal to the relevant domain, then extrinsic motivation can enhance intrinsic motivation (e.g., by reinforcing attention to the very same features and kinds of reasons). Hence, we can recognize the importance of bootstrapping and reinforcement effects of extrinsic motivations (Goldie 2011) when they feed into the cultivation of intrinsic motivation. It also explains why creative environments tend to be ones where pursuing the values internal to the domain in question line up with recognition, achievement, and advancement. When extrinsic motivations are in tension with the pursuit of the values internal to a domain, an agent's creativity will tend to be diminished. In such cases, extrinsic motivation tends to distract from attention to the features and reasons that intrinsic motivation would be directed toward. What matters is what the agent's hierarchy of motivating ends is and how the various interrelations thereby shape the responses and judgments as the agent engages in the activity.

Exemplary creativity is not just mere skill since it involves more than some level of insight and mastery to bring about desired ends. It involves excellence of motivation. First, it is typically involved in acquiring the relevant mastery and insight to bring about the desired ends. Indeed, agents whose capabilities and dispositions are not governed at the appropriate level by the relevant intrinsic motivations will typically fail to live up to the requisite excellence required to be reliably creative (or at least as creative as they could be). Second, our attributions of praise vary accordingly. We esteem and admire those whose creativity is born out of a love for and intrinsic motivation concerning the values of a relevant domain in ways in which we do not praise or admire those who are extrinsically motivated.

The argument does not deny that those who are extrinsically motivated can be creative in the sense of producing novel and worthwhile thoughts or artifacts. It is just that, given the embedded motivational structure, the extrinsically motivated will tend to certain kinds of errors or compromises that the intrinsically motivated would not (at least when the environment's extrinsic rewards do not line up with the relevant values). Hence Faulkner was no doubt creative when hacking out screenplays for Hollywood, but not as creative as when he was simultaneously writing Nobel Prize-winning novels.

Conceiving of exemplary creativity in virtue-theoretic terms captures central aspects of our evaluative practices. We not only praise and admire individuals whose creative activity is born from a passion for what they do but, other things being equal, we expect them to be more creative than those who are purely extrinsically motivated. Those lacking intrinsic motivation, other things being equal, will tend to produce work that is not as creative because they have goals and values that are at best accidentally and tangentially connected to the intrinsic values of the relevant domain. Hence, among other things, the intrinsically motivated will not only work in different ways from the extrinsically motivated but will tend to be more courageous, perfectionist, patient, and work harder in more intensive ways and display fortitude in the face of public disdain. Furthermore, it makes sense to cultivate intrinsic motivation in order to cultivate creativity. If we value and reinforce intrinsic motivation, it will make people more robustly and reliably creative in the face of contingent and unreliable extrinsic pressures. Exemplary creativity is a virtue of character.

5. Art Star

Despite the argument already given, it might be objected that surely someone could be purely extrinsically motivated and non-accidentally hook up to the appropriate values internal to a given domain. When this is the case, the objection runs, surely someone could come to be as creative, other things being equal, as she would have been had she been intrinsically motivated. If this is so, the objection goes on to say, exemplary creativity cannot be a virtue of character since it need not involve excellence of motivation.

To make the point in concrete terms, consider an artist like Jeff Koons, who was a commodities broker on Wall Street when he sought to move into the art world. Rather than misattribute motivations to Koons, let us imagine a fictional but closely related person Koons*. Assume that Koons* thinks it would be easier for him to make money and gain celebrity status in the art world than by pursuing a career in trading. Thus Koons*'s move into the art world is solely motivated by the desire for things like commercial gain and celebrity status that are external to the values of art.

Koons* moves from trading into the art world by entering high-profile art exhibitions; this makes sense given the external rewards that are targeted. In deliberating about what kind of works to make, how to go about doing so, and how to present them, Koons* does not consider the values internal to art as such. Rather, he carefully looks at and researches the background, track record, and aesthetic preferences of the art prize panels. The judges, let us assume, are all good aesthetic evaluators and closely approximate the relevant criteria for being excellent critics (i.e., possess the refinements of sentiments, capacities, and broad range of comparative experiences required to be good aesthetic judges) (Hume 1757). Thanks to thorough research and a certain natural felicity, Koons* wins the art prizes and is reliably creative. Thus, the objection goes, to be as creative as possible does not require intrinsic motivation. If that is so, then exemplary creativity cannot be a virtue.

The response to the objection is twofold. First, notice that Koons* is as creative as he is in virtue of non-accidentally, systematically, and reliably tracking the values internal to art, albeit tangentially and indirectly.[4] We might think that as a socio-psychological matter, this is highly implausible. After all, even when extrinsic rewards are related to the values and goods internal to a given domain, the interrelationships are typically extremely complex and indirect. Nonetheless, the objection only requires that this is a conceptual possibility (and moreover, as noted earlier, we might hope or strive to ensure that external rewards line up with the creative realization of values internal to the relevant domain). What enables Koons* to track the relevant values is the subservience of his own responses, judgments, and creative actions to the character and judgments of the good critics on the art prize panels. Thus, whatever else is true, the nature of Koons*'s creativity is heteronomous rather than autonomous. It is one thing to defer to and follow the judgments of others; it is quite another to exercise your own judgment in arriving at what you do. While the value of what is created may be the same, creating something just by following the path laid out by others is not the same kind of praiseworthy achievement as creating something by exercising your own judgment. Koons*'s creativity constitutes a failing or lack of the kind of autonomy we expect and praise in exemplary creativity.

Picasso, Einstein, or the student who achieves an outstanding first in philosophy is praised because of the presumed relation to the nature of the creative achievement involved. We take it that, at least in part, creative insights are an upshot of the individual's own critical understanding and appreciation of the relevant domain, rather than a heteronomous transposition or application of the insights of others. This is not to deny that individuals can and do arrive at creative insights via

---

[4] The assumption is that Koons* is fairly well protected modally in virtue of tracking the art prize judges who track the appropriate art standards. Nonetheless, in the real world, one might think that, following Hume, given that good critics are rare, the chances of Koons* picking the right judges to track are going to be pretty low. Thus it is likely that he will be susceptible to error in a way that the intrinsically motivated agent would not be (i.e., by pandering to the dictates of contemporary artistic fashion). Nonetheless, it remains a conceptual possibility, however unlikely, and that is all that the objection requires. Exactly how creative Koons* is will depend upon how reliable he is in tracking the art panel judges and how one is supposed to determine the relevantly close possible worlds. This is tricky assuming that many possible worlds vary along every conceivable dimension. Nonetheless, whatever the relevant conditions (see, e.g., Lewis 1973, 1986), the intuition here is that someone can be reliably creative in a given domain for the wrong sort of motivating reasons.

epistemic deference to others. Indeed, this is exactly what Koons* does. It is just that exemplary creativity involves arriving at creative insights autonomously through the appropriate exercise of the agent's own judgment, skills, and dispositions. Autonomous creativity is more valuable and a greater achievement. Heteronomous creativity, in contrast, is either blameworthy (when, e.g., the heteronomy involved is to be explained by the possession of a vice; Kieran 2010) or constitutes a failing in lacking the praiseworthy relation that someone who is creative on his own possesses. It is one thing to be creative via heteronomous deference to others; it is quite another to be autonomously creative. The achievement in the latter case is more valuable and greater.

Note, furthermore, that the way in which Koons*'s artistic activity is heteronomous and yet highly creative depends upon the motivations and character of the art prize judges (Kieran 2011). It is only because the art judges are well motivated (i.e., motivated to make their judgments as they do based on the values internal to art) that Koons* is in a position to track and create valuable works. If the judges were principally extrinsically motivated, and the prizes were awarded on the basis of financial gain or nepotism, then Koons* would not be tracking good standards and would not be that creative or successful.

Koons* is rather like the agential equivalent of the system used by Epagogix. It is a proprietary expert system utilizing neural network-based algorithms to predict success for movie studios, producers, and investors. Indeed, the predictions and advice proffered include what particular changes to locations, stars, scripts, and plots will do for a movie's chances of success and likely financial return. In essence, it works by looking for patterns among previous hits and making predictions based on those patterns. It is big business. Now perhaps Epagogix is really good at these predictions. This is not much different from Koons* being good at creating works by taking on the criteria inferred from the judgments of good critics. Thus, as a conceptual matter, it is clear that an agent could be extremely creative by being purely extrinsically motivated and non-accidentally tracking the appropriate judgments and values internal to a given domain. However, this is only so when the structuring of the relevant external rewards follows from and is tied up in some indirect and systematic way to access the judgments of relevant people who are intrinsically motivated. Indeed, the way in which this is so manifests a lack or blameworthy failing insofar as it manifests a heteronomous rather than autonomous relation to the creative insights involved. Thus Koons*'s extrinsically motivated creativity is parasitic on the judgments of those who are intrinsically motivated (i.e., the virtuous case).

Nonetheless, the objector might further press, Koons* *could come* to acquire creative autonomy (unlike Epagogix). The pure extrinsic motivation gives rise to his tracking of the art panel judges. In so doing, Koons* comes to acquire justification for and understanding of aesthetic judgments, acquires the capacity to deliberate critically about such for himself, and thereby comes to acquire creative autonomy. What this shows is that the distinction is not to be carved simply in terms of whether someone is extrinsically motivated or intrinsically motivated. Rather, what matters is whether or not someone's extrinsic motivation feeds into judgments and actions in a way that considerations inappropriate or irrelevant to the realization of the relevant internal values come to play the wrong kind of role.

Let us characterize a judgment extrinsicalist as someone whose creative activity in some task is guided by judgments driven by goals and considerations external to the domain in question (e.g., in art—money, social status, etc.). A motivation extrinsicalist, in contrast, is motivated by such considerations and goals but does not allow them to enter into or inappropriately drive her judgments in what is created. The former acts the way he does because it will enhance financial reward or social status. The latter is motivated by the appropriate ways of realizing the values internal to the relevant domain. Now it could in principle be that someone who is purely extrinsically motivated may thus be driven to create *only* those kinds of artworks that have features that, she believes, will enhance or maintain her income or social status. The judgment extrinsicalist, in contrast, may deem that transgression in making contemporary art is good because it is the kind of thing that gets you noticed; so he is likely to go wrong in creating what he does on the basis of an aesthetically irrelevant reason. In contrast, the motivation extrinsicalist makes aesthetic judgments for the right sorts of reasons. The purely extrinsically motivated agent can be as creative as his talent and expertise allow him to be, given that his thought in action is nonetheless driven and shaped by being motivated by values intrinsic to the relevant domain (in this case, aesthetic ones).

As a psychological matter, an agent's insulation of judgment from motivation in the manner just sketched above seems difficult to achieve. Notice that the motivation extrinsicalist can only realize creative excellence when the extrinsic motivation itself hooks up with and either creates or reinforces motivation to attend and respond to appreciative judgments in appropriate ways for the right sorts of aesthetic reasons. A different way of making the point is that, unless an agent is intrinsically motivated in the activity in question, however conditional upon some further end and whatever the higher order explanation for being such, then extrinsic motivation will feed into and lead to judgment extrinsicalism. Hence, we tend to be wary of those whose goals concerning an activity are stated in purely extrinsic terms. Intrinsic motivation in the activity of creation must come to be the governing motivation if the creative activity is to be as excellent as possible. This is compatible with the motivational spring for engaging in the activity itself being something other than the internal values and ends, whether it is from a desire to alleviate boredom, improve the mind, pass an exam, socially conform, or gain financial reward. The recognition that this is so enables us to acknowledge the many mixed motives from which creativity may spring and the bootstrapping effect they may have, while nonetheless respecting the crucial role that intrinsic motivation plays.

Virtue as an achievement of character involves in part excellence of motivation. It does not follow from this that intrinsic motivation is constitutive of or required to individuate any creative action. In the case of some virtues, it seems to be a conceptual matter that what it is for something to count as an action of the relevant kind requires individuation partly in terms of the relevant excellence of motivation. Thus, for example, for an action to count as kind, it may necessarily be the case that the agent must be motivated by the welfare of others. I may give money to a beggar because I want him to stop bothering me, or because I want to impress my girlfriend, or because I am moved by his plight. The action may only qualify as kind if it is performed under the last of those motivations. However, this is not the case for other kinds of cases. Creativity as such does not require intrinsic motivation. It is, in this respect, akin to honesty (when we mean something like just telling the truth). We can tell the truth or make new and worthwhile artifacts while being purely extrinsically motivated. However, what it is to possess the virtue of honesty or exemplary creativity is to be motivated to tell the truth or produce new and worthwhile things for the right sort of reasons. A deep-seated intrinsic motivation is a disposition that explains why, other things being equal, the virtuously honest person will reliably tell the truth or why someone will be creative across a range of situations even in the face of variance in extrinsic reasons. Furthermore, excellence of motivation is itself an admirable and praiseworthy achievement. Still, agents can in principle be creative in the sense of imaginatively doing something or coming up with new and worthwhile ideas while being purely extrinsically motivated. This is non-virtuous creativity.

Virtuous creativity involves excellence of motivation, and this in turn helps to insulate agents against drives and temptations that undermine or diminish the realization of creative potential. This is stronger than a purely consequentialist conception of virtue, according to which, virtue is just the possession of dispositions of character that systematically produce good (in this case) creative consequences (Driver 2007). There is a sense in which the view articulated incorporates something like the consequentialist claim. If you want to be as creative as possible, then, at least typically, it will be better to be intrinsically motivated. However, ingrained intrinsic motivation is also an achievement of character that is in and of itself praiseworthy and admirable. We do not and should not praise the extrinsically motivated person as we would praise the intrinsically motivated one.

6. Shaffer's Mozart Phenomenon

A distinct objection zeroes in on the apparent recognition that many extremely creative people have achieved what they have as a side-effect of peculiarities of character and natural talent. The possession of creative excellence sometimes seems to be bound up with aspects of personality that ordinary people cannot meaningfully aim at. Given that virtue is considered to be an excellence or disposition of character that we can normally meaningfully aim at, exemplary creativity, the objection goes, cannot be a virtue.

Consider Mozart as portrayed in Peter Shaffer's play *Amadeus*. Mozart is a kind of semi-autistic childlike fool who is gifted with a supreme talent. In contrast, Salieri's intrinsic motivation drives him to work exceedingly hard. Nonetheless, Salieri's mediocrity as a composer stands in striking contrast to the brilliance of Mozart's eccentric brilliance. Salieri's envy causes him to rage against what he takes to be a divine cosmic joke, motivating the Machiavellian plotting and rivalry around which the play revolves. There is nothing that Salieri can do to outshine Mozart. Take, for example, the scene where Mozart is introduced to the court at Vienna. Salieri plays the "March of Welcome" he has worked on so painstakingly.

> Bewildered, Mozart does so [halts and listens], becoming aware of Salieri playing his "March of Welcome." It is an extremely banal piece, vaguely— only vaguely—reminiscent of another march to become famous later on.
> (Shaffer 2007)

Mozart mockingly proceeds to play Salieri's piece in front of the court, making cruel fun of its comparative mediocrity and reshaping the music into what would become the march from the *Marriage of Figaro*. The love of art and cultivation of intrinsic motivation cannot compensate for either Salieri's lack of natural gifts or the peculiarities of personality upon which Mozart's creative genius seems to rest. Creative excellence, the objection runs, is often a byproduct of fundamental talents and oddities of character that we cannot meaningfully aim at. Furthermore, given that creativity depends on natural talent, which varies immensely, it is not open to all of us to be a creative genius no matter how well motivated we might be. Thus, the objection goes, even exemplary creativity cannot be a matter of virtue.

It might be tempting to dismiss the objection as being based upon a falsely romanticized fiction. This would be a mistake. There are numerous biographies that suggest creative excellence often depends on a combination of natural talent with idiosyncratic character traits or clinical conditions (Jamison 1993). John Nash achieved far more than the Princeton colleagues who outclassed him at complex chess games. Einstein, famously, was not the brightest person in his class. Francis Bacon and Van Gogh were greater painters than some of their more naturally talented peers. Although it is true that in at least some such cases, part of the explanation must advert to the role of intrinsic motivation, this is not always the case. Nasar's (1994) highly acclaimed biography of John Nash suggests that his creative achievements issued partly out of oddities of condition and character, specifically the nature of his social ineptitude and his paranoid schizophrenia. If Nash had been divested of such, we are led to believe, then he would not have been as creative as he was. In a similar light, recent biographers have suggested that the realization of

Caravaggio's genius was tied to his explosively violent temperament or a borderline antisocial personality disorder (Graham-Dixon 2010, Robb 2000).

We cannot aim to suffer from certain mental conditions or possess certain temperaments or particular idiosyncratic personality traits. Yet, the objection suggests, many highly creative people are creative in part as a byproduct of such. Indeed, in at least some cases, it would seem that cultivating intrinsic motivation would have led to less, rather than more, creative results. This shows, the objector will insist, that exemplary creativity is not a virtue.

It seems commonsensical to accept that the creativity of many individuals is intimately bound up with idiosyncrasies of health, psychology, and motivation. Nonetheless, this does not tell against conceiving of exemplary creativity as a virtue. Creativity, like other intellectual or practical virtues, involves intricate skills, the basis and workings of which may depend upon and be enhanced or diminished by certain natural talents, temperaments, and idiosyncrasies of character. To take one example, the virtue of temperance requires skills bound up with the self-governance, regulation, and expression of emotion. How difficult it is to achieve such states may vary from individual to individual according to natural differences in temperament and talent. We should think of virtue in terms of possessing and typically manifesting at a minimal threshold level certain characteristics in action along the relevant dimensions. All that is required to answer the objection is to point out that creativity is multidimensional and admits of degree. It is no part of the argument that intrinsic motivation ensures creativity or even creative excellence in achievement. As we saw earlier in Aristotle's characterization of virtue, the reasons one is motivated to act are only part of the story. Why? Creative virtue also depends on judgment, talent, and opportunity (among other things). Nonetheless, the extent to which an agent is intrinsically motivated is the degree to which she is excellent in a respect that is central. It is a praiseworthy achievement and explains why the agent will be less susceptible to certain kinds of creative errors or temptations than those who are extrinsically motivated.

7. Conclusion

An exemplary creative person is someone who has acquired a certain degree of mastery and knows what she is doing in coming up with novel and worthwhile ideas or artifacts. In doing so, she is motivated by the values internal to the relevant domain and chooses what she does for reasons that hook up with those values in the right kind of ways. The exemplary creative person does this not as a matter of happenstance, but rather out of an ingrained disposition of character. This is admirable and praiseworthy. To remain true to the right kind of motivations in some domain while avoiding the myriad biases and temptations to which we are naturally subject is an achievement of character. This is not to claim that creative action or even being reliably creative in some domain necessarily requires intrinsic motivation. However, it does explain why the exemplary person is praiseworthy in a way that the extrinsically motivated person is not and why it is that, other things being equal, the intrinsically motivated person will often be more reliably creative than the extrinsically motivated person. Intrinsic motivation insulates agents from pressures against and inhibitors of creativity and thus helps to ensure robustness across different situations and influences.

It follows, as a practical matter, that if we desire to cultivate creativity or design an education system geared toward doing so, it is ill conceived to emphasize purely extrinsic motivations. A much better way forward is to emphasize intrinsic motivations while designing organizational structures, systems, and rewards in such a way that they are perceived to be related to and arise from a domain's relevant internal values. Creativity flourishes when intrinsic motivation, values, and socioeconomic structures line up appropriately. It tends to wither when they do not (unless, like Van Gogh, a person's creativity is exceptionally virtuous).[5]

References

Amabile, Teresa M. 1985. "Motivation and Creativity: Effects of Motivational Orientation on Creative Writers," *Journal of Personality and Social Psychology*, 48 (2): pp. 393–399.
Aristotle. [367–322 B.C.] 1976. *Nicomachean Ethics*, rev. ed., trans. J. A. K. Thomson and H. Tredennick. Harmondsworth, UK: Penguin.
Blake, William. 1826. *Laocoön* (drawing and engraving).
Boden, Margaret. 2004. *The Creative Mind: Myths and Mechanisms*, 2nd ed. London Routledge.
Boswell, James. [1776] 1953. *Life of Johnson*. Oxford, UK: Oxford University Press.
Burton, Christina. 2011. "Decreased Arts Education Affecting Minority Students," *The Atlanta Post*, March 29.
Business and Industry Advisory Committee to the Organization for Economic Cooperation and Development. 2004. *Creativity, Innovation and Economic Growth in the 21st Century*. Paris: BIAC.
Collins, Mary Ann, and Teresa M. Amabile. 1999. "Motivation and Creativity," in R. Sternberg, ed., *Handbook of Creativity*. Cambridge, UK: Cambridge University Press, pp. 297–312.
Driver, Julia. 2007. *Uneasy Virtue*. Cambridge, UK: Cambridge University Press.
Eisenberger, Robert, and Linda Rhoades. 2001. "Incremental Effects of Reward on Creativity," *Journal of Personality and Social Psychology*, 81 (4), 2001: pp. 728–741.
Garbarino, J. 1975. "The Impact of Anticipated Reward Upon Cross-Age Tutoring," *Journal of Personality and Social Psychology*, 32 (3): pp. 421–428.

[5] I would like to thank the editors of this volume, my colleagues at Leeds, Berys Gaut, Dominic Lopes, Alison Niedbalski, Dustin Stokes, and audiences at New York University, Seoul National University, Manchester University, and the Society for Philosophy and Psychology annual conference, 2010, for helpful discussion of versions of the essay. Grateful acknowledgment is also made to the U.K. Arts and Humanities Research Council for funding this work as part of the "Method in Philosophical Aesthetics: The Challenge from the Sciences" project.

Gaut, Berys. 2003. "Creativity and Imagination," in B. Gaut and P. Livingston, eds., *The Creation of Art*. Cambridge, UK: Cambridge University Press, pp. 148–173.

Gaut, Berys. 2010. "The Philosophy of Creativity," *Philosophy Compass*, 5 (12): pp. 1034–1046.

Goldie, Peter. 2008. "Virtues of Art and Human Well-Being," *Aristotelian Society Supplementary Volume* 82 (1): pp. 179–195.

Goldie, Peter. 2011. "The Ethics of Aesthetic Bootstrapping," in P. Goldie and E. Schellekens, eds., *The Aesthetic Mind: Philosophy and Psychology*. Oxford, UK: Oxford University Press.

Graham-Dixon, Andrew. 2010. *Caravaggio*. London: Allen Lane.

Hume, David. [1757]1993. "Of the Standard of Taste," in *Selected Essays*. Oxford, UK: Oxford University Press, pp. 133–153.

Jacobs, Emma. 2011. "Cuts Will Widen Arts Divide," *Financial Times*, February 14.

Jamison, Kay Redfield. 1993. *Touched with Fire*. New York: Free Press.

Kieran, Matthew. 2007. "Artistic Character, Creativity and the Appreciation of Conceptual Art," in P. Goldie and E. Schellekens, eds., *Philosophy and Conceptual Art*. Oxford, UK: Oxford University Press, pp. 197–215.

Kieran, Matthew. 2010. "The Vice of Snobbery: Aesthetic Knowledge, Justification and Virtue in Art Appreciation," *Philosophical Quarterly*, 60: pp. 243–263.

Kieran, Matthew. 2011. "The Fragility of Aesthetic Knowledge: Aesthetic Psychology and Appreciative Virtues," in P. Goldie and E. Schellekens, eds., *The Aesthetic Mind: Philosophy and Psychology*. Oxford, UK: Oxford University Press, pp. 32–43.

Korsgaard, Christine. 1983. "Two Distinctions in Goodness," *Philosophical Review*, 92: pp. 169–195.

Lewis, David. 1973. *Counterfactuals*. Oxford, UK: Blackwell.

———. 1986. "Counterfactual Dependence and Time's Arrow and Postscripts," in *Philosophical Papers: Volume II*. Oxford, UK: Oxford University Press, pp. 32–66.

Lim, William K. 2010. "Asian Test-Score Culture Thwarts Creativity," *Science* 26: pp. 1576–1577.

Maslow, Abraham H. 1968. *Toward a Psychology of Being*. New York: D. Van Nostrand.

Matthen, Mohan P. 2005. *Seeing, Doing, and Knowing: A Philosophical Theory of Sense Perception*. Oxford, UK: Oxford University Press.

Milner, A. D., and M. A. Goodale. 1995. *The Visual Brain in Action*. Oxford, UK: Oxford University Press.

Nasar, Sylvia. 1994. *A Beautiful Mind*. New York: Pocket Books.

Park, Nansook, Christopher Peterson, and Martin E. P. Seligman. 2004. "Strengths of Character and Well-Being," *Journal of Social and Clinical Psychology* 23 (5): pp. 603–619.

Rabinowicz, Wlodek, and Toni Rønnow-Rasmussen. 1999. "A Distinction in Value: Intrinsic and For Its Own Sake," *Proceedings of the Aristotelian Society*, 100: pp. 33–52.

Robb, Peter. 2000. *M: The Man Who Became Caravaggio*. New York: Henry Holt.

Rønnow-Rasmussen, Toni. 2002. "Instrumental Values: Strong and Weak," *Ethical Theory and Moral Practice*, 5: pp. 23–43.

Rosenthal, Elizabeth. 2010. "Testing, the Chinese Way," *New York Times*, September 11, Week in Review Section.

Shaffer, Peter. 2007. *Amadeus*. London: Penguin.

Stokes, Dustin. 2008. "A Metaphysics of Creativity," in K. Stock and K. Thomson-Jones, eds., *New Waves in Aesthetics*. Basingstoke, UK: Palgrave Macmillan, pp. 105–124.

Swanton, Christine. 2003. *Virtue Ethics*. Oxford, UK: Oxford University Press.

Woodruff, David M. 2001. "A Virtue Theory of Aesthetics," *Journal of Aesthetic Education*, 35 (3): pp. 22–36.

Zagzebski, Linda. 1996. *Virtues of the Mind: An Inquiry into the Nature of Virtue and the Ethical Foundations of Knowledge*. Cambridge, UK: Cambridge University Press.

PART FIVE

PHILOSOPHY OF MIND AND COGNITIVE SCIENCE

7

Creativity and Not-So-Dumb Luck

SIMON BLACKBURN

1

The Greeks had no doubt about the divine origin of creative inspiration. Homer begins the *Iliad* by invoking the goddess to sing his story; Plato, at least through the mouth of Socrates in the *Phaedrus*, is even more explicit: The creative poet needs divine madness:

> the madness of those who are possessed by the Muses; which taking hold of a delicate and virgin soul, and there inspiring frenzy, awakens lyrical and all other numbers; with these adorning the myriad actions of ancient heroes for the instruction of posterity. But he who, having no touch of the Muses' madness in his soul, comes to the door and thinks that he will get into the temple by the help of art—he, I say, and his poetry are not admitted; the sane man disappears and is nowhere when he enters into rivalry with the madman.

The same view is presented in the *Ion*: "the poet is a light and winged and holy thing, and there is no invention in him until he has been inspired and is out of his senses, and the mind is no longer in him: when he has not attained to this state, he is powerless and is unable to utter his oracles." Shakespeare voices the same association between the poet and madness, comparing the poet's frenzy to that of the lunatic and the lover:

> The poet's eye, in fine frenzy rolling,
> Doth glance from heaven to Earth, from Earth to heaven.
> And as imagination bodies forth
> The forms of things unknown, the poet's pen
> Turns them to shapes and gives to airy nothing
> A local habitation and a name.

A slightly more sober version of the Plato-Shakespeare view arrives with the Romantics. Presenting his famous distinction between fancy and imagination, Coleridge wrote:

> The primary IMAGINATION I hold to be the living Power and prime Agent of all human Perception, and as a repetition in the finite mind of the eternal act of creation in the infinite I AM. The secondary Imagination I consider as an echo of the former, co-existing with the conscious will, yet still as identical with the primary in the kind of its agency, and differing only in degree, and in the mode of operation. It dissolves, diffuses, dissipates, in order to recreate; or where this process is rendered impossible, yet still at all events it struggles to idealise and unify. It is essentially vital, even as all objects (as objects) are essentially fixed and dead.
>
> FANCY, on the contrary, has no other counters to play with, but fixities and definites. The Fancy is indeed no other than a mode of Memory emancipated from the order of time and space; while it is blended with, and modified by that empirical phenomenon of the will, which we express by the word CHOICE. But equally with the ordinary memory the Fancy must receive all its materials ready made from the law of association.

The fancy is the mere reshuffling of materials previously given in perception, in accordance with the "law of association." To philosophers, this will bring to mind Hume's attempts at a Newtonian theory of the mind as a forum in which "ideas" give rise to other ideas in more or less definite ways, according to relations of resemblance, contiguity, and causation. Hume clearly regarded this, at least in his earliest work, as a process subject to regularity and law. But he does not regard it as a mechanical process, at least in one sense of that term, since he stresses the "liberty of the fancy to transpose or change" its ideas. Coleridge similarly acknowledges that the fancy is "blended with, and modified by" the empirical phenomenon of choice. In other words, neither is intent on interpreting away the empirical phenomenology, in which we can exercise some control over our fancies, however banal and unimaginative they may be.

The imagination, so much more impressive, is unfortunately much harder to pin down. As a repetition in the finite mind of the "eternal act of creation in the infinite I AM," it is first associated with creation ex nihilo, a purely spontaneous eruption within the mind of materials of some kind—exactly the kind of event that engendered talk of inspiration by the muses, lunacy, or frenzy. However, it is also a "prime agent of all human perception." So right at the outset we must register that it is completely unclear how these two different suggestions hang together: Even Kant, whose philosophy is generally held to underpin Coleridge here, insisted on the receptive nature of perception, without which empirical knowledge would be impossible. But reception, or responsiveness to something that is already extant, is on the face of it inconsistent with the hyperbolic reference to the godlike creation of the cosmos from within. Presumably, Coleridge was gesturing at what contemporary philosophy would describe as the distinction between the realm of law or causation and the realm of reason. Whatever materials the world throws at us, there is the question of finding words, thoughts, or categories in which to perceive it. Then, although the first process is purely causal, the second involves the creative power of the mind, and is at least to that extent within the "realm of reason." But it dilutes any normal notion of creativity to a vanishing point to say, for instance, that someone who sees a truck at a medium distance in broad daylight and describes it as a truck is exercising creativity. We surely need to preserve some kind of polar contrast with the ordinary, unimaginative, or banal.

It is certainly no criticism of Coleridge that he falters in front of what may be the central problem of articulating or defending transcendental idealism, which is precisely that of holding together the antagonistic horses of *reception* and *creation* in its account of what pulls the mind along.[1] But it does put his whole theory of imagination into a rather dim light, and it must motivate us to ask whether the celebration of spontaneous eruption and the corresponding downgrading of mere "fancy" have distorted subsequent ideas about creativity.

We should notice that a fatal problem with Coleridge's primary imagination is that we cannot make sense of the idea that creation ex nihilo is something that we *do* as agents, as opposed to something that happens within us: an eruption that happens to occur in one head rather than another. This is a principled problem, arising because nihil offers nothing: no reason for choice and therefore for transforming it into one thing or another. It offers only a void into which things might float, but no basis for reflection, intelligence, design, or control. There is no *foothold* for choice in the void, and as soon as alternatives are presented for choice, then the work of the imagination is already done. Something has floated into our minds. This has happened in us or to us, but it is not something we *did*, any more than catching a cold is, strictly speaking, something we do (unless we set about it, for instance by deliberately going where there is an epidemic). In the dark with senses numbed and memory unsummoned, it is only the imagination that *could generate* scenarios between which choice could be exercised, but by the time we are choosing to explore one idea or neglect another, the productive work of the imagination appears to be over, finished when it provided us with the ideas in the first place, which only then become materials about which to make choices. Coleridge is apparently insensitive to this problem, instead wanting to attribute imaginative power to the *will* of the artist, and identically in its primary and secondary form. The Greeks, cheerfully

---

[1] The problem is also the focus of recent writing. See McDowell's *Mind and World* (Cambridge, MA: Harvard University Press, 1994), or Davidson "On the Very Idea of a Conceptual Scheme," *Proceedings and Addresses of the American Philosophical Association*, 47: pp. 5–20, reprinted in Davidson, *Inquiries into Truth and Interpretation*, 2nd ed. (Oxford, UK: Clarendon Press).

admitting the passivity of the artist complemented by the active role of the muses breathing the poet's words into him, or in other words inspiring him, have the advantage here. Or perhaps Turgenev does, saying, as reported by Henry James: "As for the origin of one's wind-blown germs themselves, who shall say, as you ask, where THEY come from? We have to go too far back, too far behind, to say. Isn't it all we can say that they come from every quarter of heaven, that they are THERE at almost any turn of the road?"

2

So much for a bit of cultural context. Turning to the present, I think we should find it interesting that Coleridge's distinction, if not his wording, is echoed in the most up-to-date psychological literature.[2] Much of this acknowledges Graham Wallas's 1926 book *The Art of Thought* as its ancestor. In that book, Wallas distinguished four phases of thought involved in an exercise of insight. There is the mental preparation, the incubation of the problem, the illumination itself, and finally the verification or afterword, in which the illumination is assessed, tested, and confirmed or rejected. In these terms, one modern debate concerns the "incubation" period. This is the part that precedes the moment of insight, and the question is how much of it is "business as normal," and how much requires something potentially strange to be going on, at least in the unconscious if not in the more exalted realms of divinity and madness.

According to the former view, all we find are versions of more mundane cognitive skills: the deployments of knowledge bases, memory, search heuristics such as trial and error, analogies and associative reasonings, sensitivity to external cues, together with subsequent critical verification procedures. Perhaps the best-known work in this vein is that of Robert Weisberg, whose books include the popular 1986 work *Creativity: Genius and Other Myths*.[3] The motto of this school might be Edison's famous remark that genius is one percent inspiration and 99 percent perspiration. Apparently opposing this approach stand those descendants of Socrates who want to emphasize the difference of the "magic moment": the "aha!" or "Eureka" flash when the idea just pops into the head, the problem is reformulated, and a new perspective and solution come in a flash, exactly parallel to, and in fact modeled upon, a perceptual gestalt shift like the Necker cube or the duck-rabbit. Perhaps calling this an "uncanny" moment would be better than calling it magical, for gestalt switches

    [2] A useful anthology is *The Nature of Insight*, eds. Sternberg and Davidson (Cambridge, MA: Bradford Books, 1995).

    [3] See also Michael J. A. Howe, *Genius Explained* (Cambridge, UK: Cambridge University Press, 1999), and Colin Martindale's provocative book *The Clockwork Muse* (New York: Basic Books, 1990).

are common enough not to deserve thatdescription. And this suggests that it is difficult to make anything precise of any apparent opposition here.

First, on the "business as usual" side, nobody doubts the phenomenology of the "aha!" moment. From Archimedes to Einstein, a host of anecdotes talk of the moment of sudden illumination that hits the mind as if from nowhere, and to which the Archimedean shout of joy is the grateful response. But even the anecdotes point out that the illumination requires a thoroughly prepared mind. Gauss talks about the solution to one of his problems coming to him "so to speak by the Grace of God," and he is "unable to name the nature of the thread which connected what I previously knew with that which made my success possible." But the important point is that he is in no doubt that there exists such a thread. God's gracious injection of a way to solve one of Gauss's problems is not going to happen to you and me, who cannot even comprehend the problem in the first place.

Whether we are solving crossword puzzles or trying to find the right words for an argument or a poem, there are times when we get stuck. We meet an impasse, but then suddenly, as if from nowhere, the problem is seen differently and the solution comes. The question is only whether the "as if from nowhere" can be seen as the result of psychological processes continuous with those involved in more mundane cogitation. For after all, during cognitive "business as usual," things occur to us as if from nowhere: idle dreams obviously, but also the right words, anywhere up an index of banality from zero to 100 percent, also pop into one's head as if from nowhere. All this shows is that consciousness is not built to be privy to the causal antecedents of its own materials. That is not what it is for.

We should remember as well that "business as usual" is by no means the controlled, rational, linear process that we sometimes take it to be. In his excellent book *Personality*, Peter Goldie quotes many authors, including Nietzsche, Conrad, and Virginia Woolf, who have marveled at the bubbling, chaotic, and strange vortices in our stream of consciousness even in mundane, everyday moments of life.[4] About lying in bed, for instance, vaguely aware that we ought to turn over to be more comfortable, Robert Musil talks of the opacity of the action, which is not the upshot of any very definite act of willing, but at some point "just happens." We find ourselves turning over, just as in Conrad's novel Jim finds himself in the lifeboat, or we find odd thoughts coming to mind or odd dreams and memories besetting our waking hours.

A second softening of the contrast is that on the "uncanny moment" side, nobody really doubts the importance of the prepared mind. Presumably, anybody can work themselves into a bacchic frenzy, but then there is nothing creative about it (in the story of the Bacchae, it was purely destructive). In contrast, the narratives of creativity in the literature tend to focus on mathematicians like Gauss and Poincaré,

---

[4] Peter Goldie, *Personality* (London: Routledge, 2004), pp. 95–108.

scientists like Darwin or Watson and Crick, musicians like Mozart, polymorphous artists like Picasso, or writers like James and Turgenev. In every case, there is a long apprenticeship, a painstaking mastery of craft skills learned from, and often imitative of, those who have so far led the field, and preceding any great leap forward. The pianist's answer to a fan who gushed how lucky he was—"yes, and the more I practise the luckier I get"—pretty much sums it up. You and I are not going to repeat Poincaré's sudden insight into Fuchsian functions and non-Euclidean geometries without doing an awful lot of higher mathematics, nor could anyone have solved the structure of DNA without first mastering the very considerable technical state of play that very nearly led Linus Pauling, Maurice Wilkins, Rosalind Franklin, and others there at the same time.

Perhaps some of the more excitable and less academic literature in the area, such as that purveyed by "lateral thinking" and "brainstorming" gurus, comes close to suggesting that creativity works by casting aside preparedness as merely a hindrance, a rut out of which the adept must thankfully climb. It is certainly true that an impasse in solving a problem may demand a rethinking of the whole problem space. But it is hardly likely to require jettisoning significant quantities of education, training, and experience. To solve a cryptic crossword puzzle typically requires finding a different "take" on the clues from any they are built to suggest. But it also requires a good deal of practice and the deployment of huge resources of knowledge and especially knowledge of the language. I challenge anyone to solve, say, an Araucaria puzzle in the *Guardian* without them.[5]

One avenue toward downplaying anything strange about the incubation period is already evident. It consists in magnifying the extent of the preparation that precedes it. If that is great enough, then there is nothing so very surprising about someone who is in the right place at the right time being able to push things a little further. We might be reminded of Thomas Henry Huxley's remark on reading Darwin's mechanism of evolution by natural selection: "how extremely stupid not to have thought of that." And given all the surrounding work and the intensity of 19th-century interest in evolution, perhaps it was.

Another equally important tack is to emphasize the importance of Wallas's final stage, the verification and checking. Weisberg gives many examples in which a work hailed as the result of a lightning strike of creative genius turns out to have been worked upon, modified, altered, and refined over a much longer period of sustained critical attention. Artists' and composers' notebooks show the work involved. Even the most celebrated narratives of the creative moment are not sacrosanct. So, for instance, Coleridge's famous account of his drug-induced vision of the complete poem of "Kubla Khan," together with the intrusion on business of the man from Porlock who apocalyptically destroyed the bulk of it, is almost certainly false, since

---

[5] The late Araucaria ("monkey puzzle") was the acknowledged doyen of crossword puzzle creators.

the poem exists in earlier forms that Coleridge then worked over, quite apart from the fact that some of its tropes are already present in books that Coleridge had been reading.[6] Just as it suits the magician to emphasize the innocence of his movements and the emptiness of the hat before he pulls out the rabbit, so it suits the Socratic-Coleridgian self-image of the artist (or scientist or inventor) to downplay the preceding and subsequent labors their work required.

Other fantasies may be wished upon artists by well-meaning or malicious others, as in the well-known forged Mozart letter of 1815, in which Mozart is alleged to have said that he composed in a dreamy state in which "the whole composition, though it be long, stands almost finished and complete in my mind, so that I can survey it, like a fine picture or a beautiful statue, at a glance." Exciting, were it true, and greedily sucked up, as reports of miracles so often are. But it is completely belied by genuine letters of Mozart concerning what the recent editor of the new Köchel Catalogue calls the "practical concerns, conscious deliberations, and sustained effort that Mozart brought to composition." And taking away the miracle ought only to increase our admiration for the achievement.[7]

Another example of less than candid authorial reflection comes from Henry James's introduction to *Portrait of a Lady*, where he tells us that

> [t]rying to recover here, for recognition, the germ of my idea, I see that it must have consisted not at all in any conceit of a "plot," nefarious name, in any flash, upon the fancy, of a set of relations, or in any one of those situations that, by a logic of their own, immediately fall, for the fabulist, into movement, into a march or a rush, a patter of quick steps; but altogether in the sense of a single character, the character and aspect of a particular engaging young woman, to which all the usual elements of a "subject," certainly of a setting, were to need to be super added.

James is nothing if not artful, and he carefully adds that

> [q]uite as interesting as the young woman herself at her best, do I find, I must again repeat, this projection of memory upon the whole matter of the growth, in one's imagination, of some such apology for a motive,

suggesting a fairly skeptical attitude toward the creator's own narrative of the genesis of the creation. But although he goes on to elaborate the novelistic work that it takes to allow the original vision to grow, it is hard not to suspect an element of misdirection. For among all this candor, the elephant in the room is the extent

---

[6] R. Weisberg, *Creativity* (Hoboken, NJ: Wiley, 2006), p. 77.

[7] See http://www.mozartproject.org/essays/zaslaw.html.

to which the Isabel Archer/Osmond story is a direct reworking of George Eliot's Gwendolen Harleth/Grandcourt relationship in *Daniel Deronda*, about which, in the introduction, James is completely silent. Far from floating windblown or God-given into James's mind, Isabel Archer is irresistibly interpreted as a direct riposte to Eliot, although this says nothing important about the relative merits of the two novels.

3

I incline, then, to agree with Weisberg that the stories people tell about their own creative moments, like James's "projection of memory," do not give us as much data as we might wish. This is so even when the creator talks, as Poincaré did, of the work of his unconscious: Poincaré said that the illumination is "the manifest sign of long, unconscious, prior work." But this is not so much a theory or explanation of anything as much as it is a confession that Poincaré, like the rest of us, does not know what brought the "aha!" moment about. It is hidden from the subject as much as it is from us. Or, if Poincaré had moments of conscious thought, musings, and doodlings preceding his breakthroughs, then they were not unconscious. They were the kind of process we all go through and of which we are all aware, but happening in a supremely gifted and practiced mathematical mind.

I am not here pronouncing on the very idea of a non-conscious "workspace." I do not know what goes on during the periods when consciousness takes time off. And I do not doubt that sometimes this time off is valuable, and that often time taken in conscious deliberation is substantially wasted. Deposits of experience and emotion, for instance, seem to guide us to good snap decisions just as well as periods of orga-nized conscious cogitation.[8] Perhaps neurophysiological measurements will open up a sense of the constant activity of the brain, even when consciousness is absent, that casts light on this. But I do not believe that at present there is anything theo-retically useful to say about "the unconscious," conceived of as a realm of thought parallel to that of the conscious mind, but itself hidden from awareness.

To make mental processes empirically tractable, laboratory studies need to focus on problems and solutions that are common enough for statistical analysis to get a foothold and generally replicable. Beethoven-scale creative moments are neither common nor replicable. So, instead, "insight" studies concentrate upon neat, per-plexing but soluble puzzles, and try to isolate the conditions under which solutions occur to people. Such problems might include crossword puzzles; word association puzzles, such as finding a word that goes together with each of the three words chase,

---

[8] Ap Dijksterhuis, "On Making the Right Choice: The deliberation-without-attention effect," *Science*, 311 (2006), p. 1005.

wall, and note (answer: paper); puzzles that require rethinking such as the man in the room who needs to get hold of two dangling ropes that are too far apart for him to reach, but who has a pair of pliers (answer: use the pliers as a pendulum bob and swing one of the ropes); the well-known cannibals and missionaries river-crossing problem; and others of a similar nature. Experimental variables affecting speed or likelihood of hitting on a solution can include motivations, the introduction of rest periods, availability of cues, and preceding experience with puzzles in the same domain or different domains.

I am sure that there are rich facts to uncover in these areas. But it may be a different matter to bring them to bear on precise, well-formulated theories. To give but one example, incubation periods could be interpreted in terms of opportunities for something called the unconscious mind to get to work. But they could also be described as periods of recovery from fatigue, or periods that allow the salience of some particular set of ideas that is in fact blocking the way to a solution, to diminish.

For another instance of the difficulty of formulating rival theories, in one chapter of his 2006 book, Weisberg contrasts his "business as usual" framework with an economic model, credited to Sternberg and Lubart, according to which the key to creativity is "buying low and selling high," which seems to mean doing things that people around you do not value very much, finding or making them valuable, and then profiting from the proceeds. Nice work if you can get it, certainly, but it is difficult to see why this contrasts with business as usual—indeed, it is rather obviously just what (good) business as usual consists of. Obviously, all of us, in our clothing as *Homo economicus* would *delight* in doing this. And post hoc, one can perhaps describe the successful members of our communities as *having* done that. It is actually a bit of a stretch: What was it that people did not value before, say, Raphael? Painting was valued. Ability was valued. Raphael's paintings were not valued, but then they did not exist. And if we waive that difficulty, as a psychological theory, it is tautological, and Weisberg need not have felt threatened by it. "Buy low and sell high" is tautological advice for the investor, and it is a useless post-hoc description of the fortunate persons the market or the culture then rewards and may call creative. It is, as it were, business as usual, plus being in the right place at the right time. This much is luck, not character. Character only sets someone to buy low and sell high, or to acquire the skills and knowledge that enable them to do so.

4

These remarks about the difficulty of theory are not intended to be more than suggestive. Clearly, we all believe in causality. The only question is whether we can generate theory about the causal variables, and whether it will turn out to be valuable to remain at a neurophysiological level, or to ascend to thinking in computational processes, or finally in terms of psychological variables, thought of as characterizing genuine cognitive processes at an unconscious level. I interpret this as an issue about the value of an intentional stance when the intentionality is shut out from awareness and therefore all the more subject to doubts about indeterminacy. It is, I fear, a matter on which we can only wait and see.

If one thing is certain, it is that we should remain skeptical about divine madness, poetic frenzy, and the other tropes of the Romantic artist. We should also be wary of supposing that a manifestation of genius in one dimension is any indication of equal genius in another: the kind of naïve faith that leads people to suppose that actors will make brilliant governors, or that celebrity singers are special authorities on the problems of the third world, health, diets, or child-raising. I also believe that the Romantic tropes have done enormous damage in recent culture. We need to respect genius, sure enough, but not by separating it from its roots in talent, hard work, discipline, and determination. Nor should we abandon all critical standards in the name of encouraging children's "creativity," instead of respecting ability and guiding them toward working to display it. Fortunately enough, education concerns areas such as mathematics or music, where ability is clearly identifiable. But in other areas, including writing and the visual arts, with the loss of discrimination comes a loss of everything that honors the human spirit and makes the great achievements of literature and art pinnacles of human intelligence at its best. We can be sure that the hard apprenticeships of a Bernini, a Titian, a Shakespeare, a Darwin, an Einstein, or a Mozart were a very different kettle of fish.

8

The Role of Imagination in Creativity

DUSTIN STOKES

It is perhaps an uncontroversial truth that the imagination is important for creative thought. The terms "creative" and "imaginative" are often used interchangeably, at least in popular contexts. And volumes have been written on the imaginations of creative artists, not to mention poems, films, paintings, and other depictions of the same phenomenon. Kant recognized a connection between imagination and creativity:

> So the mental powers whose combination (in a certain relation) con-stitutes *genius* are imagination and understanding. One qualification is needed, however. When the imagination is used for cognition, then it is under the constraint of the understanding and is subject to the restriction of adequacy to the understanding's concept. But when the aim is aesthetic, then the imagination is free, so that, over and above that harmony with the concept, it may supply, in an unstudied way, a wealth of undeveloped material for the understanding which the latter disregarded in its concept (Kant [1790] 1987, p. 185)

A number of important insights can be gleaned from this passage. Consider Kant's distinction between imagination used for conceptual understanding and imagina-tion used for artistic ends. By way of this distinction, Kant intimates two features of imagination endorsed today. First, imagination provides a kind of cognitive free-dom important for creative thought and action.[1] Second, imagination can be used in

---

[1] Imagination for Kant was, by most interpretations, something different than it is for philosophers and psychologists today. The Kantian imagination was the activity of both apprehending and repro-ducing the ideas and percepts from the manifold of experience. So 'imagination' for Kant, it seems, denoted what today we would think of as understanding and perceptual belief, in addition to imagery and propositional imagination.

more or less constrained ways. Kant's thesis is about aesthetic ideas and the special service that imagination provides for that particular kind of mental engagement, but it can—contrary to what Kant suggests—be generalized. Indeed, the thesis generalizes both beyond the aesthetic to creative scientific theorizing and problem-solving and beyond radical creativity or genius to more mundane, everyday creativity.

The thesis advanced here is that imagination is important for even the most minimally creative thought. This general claim may also be a truism, but it would be nice to have in hand some reasons for thinking it so. Very few philosophical analyses have been offered to this or some similar end. And though psychologists have researched both imagination and creativity, studies that attempt identification or testing of a link between the two phenomena have been sparse.[2]

So, how might creative thought and imagination be connected in an architecture of the mind? This chapter addresses this question, centrally from the perspective of philosophy, but with empirical assistance from cognitive and developmental psychology. In addition to illuminating the connection between the two phenomena, consideration of recent work on imagination helps us to better understand creative processes.

1. Artistic Creativity and Truth-Boundedness

Kant was right: Imagination, when used to aesthetic ends, provides a free play of ideas, a "wealth of undeveloped material for the understanding." And contrary to Kant, imagination has this feature whether or not it is used for aesthetic ends. With respect to the range of contents that one can take a certain cognitive attitude toward, imagination enjoys a freedom that most (perhaps all) other attitudes or capacities lack.[3] One can imagine situations that have not and will never happen. One can imagine the truth of propositions of which one is uncertain. One can imagine consequences to an action before performing it. And so on. This cognitive play is important if not essential to creative art-making for the simple reason that creative

---

[2] Philosophical exceptions include Carruthers 2002 and Polanyi 1981. For analysis from psychology, see Cacciari 1997 and Ward 1994. Worth special mention is an essay by Berys Gaut (2003), who provides an analysis that explores and advances insights from Kant, in particular on artistic creativity and aesthetic ideas. The analysis offered below is generally compatible with Gaut's, since he too argues that imagination is important to "active creativity" (he claims the connection to be an a priori constitutive one). However, Gaut's analysis is distinct in at least the following ways: (a) He focuses on rich creativity, explicitly committing to a value condition for creativity; (b) he focuses very little on non-artistic creativity (e.g., creativity in theory or science); and (c) he focuses on metaphor-making as a paradigm of the creative use of the imagination, maintaining that study of the former is especially revealing of the structure of the latter. As the reader will discover, the present analysis is distinct from Gaut's analysis in at least these three ways.

[3] This is not to imply that imagination is always unconstrained. A more precise clarification of imagination, including this qualification, is offered in section 4.

things are, in part, new things. And new things are, sometimes, new combinations of old things, combinations of concepts, ideas, skills, knowledge, and so on. Or even stronger, creativity may involve thoughts or actions that are radically novel, not merely conceptual combinations of existing materials. It may involve a radical transformation of a conceptual space (Boden 2004). The strongest traditional account of novelty and creativity endorses a creation ex nihilo thesis: Truly creative ideas come from nowhere. Whatever the case, a capacity like imagination—even as sparsely described here—is needed for this kind of conceptual combination, transformation, and formation.

Consider Bach's famous work *The Well-Tempered Clavier*. The work consists of Book I and Book II, each one comprising a set of one prelude and one fugue devoted to each of the 12 major and minor keys. Grant a few simple assumptions: First, this is a creative work of art, whatever other properties one may or may not attribute to it. Second, Bach was responsible for this creation; it was not, as ancient and romantic theories might have it, merely a product of a muse or divine inspiration. Finally, part of Bach's goal, as evidenced by the title of the work, was to explore the possibilities of two musical technologies new to his day: tempered tuning for keyboard instruments and the tonal scale system.[4] Conjoining these assumptions: This is an instance of rich creativity, but one that was highly constrained in identifiable ways. A natural question to ask is simply, How did Bach do it? Tough question. One way to make headway on such a question is to identify the constraints on the artist and what sorts of cognitive maneuvering these constraints necessitated (in order for the work to be created). As will become clear, even in constrained circumstances, the creative process required the cognitive play mentioned above.

Bach knew a lot about tempered tuning technologies and, more broadly, music technologies. But he didn't know everything (he was a genius but he was, after all, human). So let's imagine a Super-Bach, one who knew *everything* there was to know—both in terms of all of the facts and all of the relevant skills—about the clavier, tempered tuning, and the 12-tone scale. This would not have been sufficient for the creation of *The Well-Tempered Clavier*. Indeed, Super-Bach might be an omniscient being, with complete knowledge of all of the music-theoretical space of the time, and would not yet have knowledge of the musical structure of *The Well-Tempered Clavier*. Super-Bach's knowledge (just like actual Bach's knowledge) of the space would indeed constrain his composition, but this knowledge alone would not amount to, afford, or even imply the musical work in question. This is for the simple reason that there is nothing in this conceptual domain, or cluster of domains, that includes or entails (by itself) *The Well-Tempered Clavier*. The general point is about how far states like knowledge (or justified true belief, if one prefers)

---

[4] In fact, some theorists hold that he created these works for largely didactic purposes (Tomita 1996, 1998).

can take us toward thinking creatively. And the suggestion is this: Any cognitive state that functions to faithfully represent the information of some conceptual space— be that cognitive state a true belief, propositional or procedural knowledge, or a memory—can at best play a necessary but insufficient role in the thinking required for an accomplishment like *The Well-Tempered Clavier*. *Truth-bound cognitive states*, as they will be called here and as will be clarified below, are rarely sufficient for creative thought.[5]

The same point can be made in simple terms of information. Given some set of information {I}, different agents will acquire different knowledge about {I}. The content of the *knowledge* had with respect to {I} derives solely from {I}, since to be knowledge of {I}, some belief or skill will have to accurately represent some element of {I}. Of course, not all thoughts about {I} amount to knowledge. Some will be false beliefs; some will be true but unjustified; and others will be false and unjustified. Still others will be non-doxastic: One might have entertainings, desires, intentions, curiosities, doubts, and imaginings, among other states, with respect to {I}. Among these latter states, many are *non*-truth-bound.

"Truth-boundedness" denotes the accuracy function of a class of cognitive states. And so "truth" is here used in a broader, stipulated sense since, in addition to propositional states, it must accommodate procedural kinds of knowledge or skills—one learns more or less *accurately*, not truly, how to make an omelet or fix a flat tire.[6] Beliefs of course can be false, and we can inaccurately learn skills. But when properly functioning, these kinds of states accurately represent whatever features of the world they aim to represent. They are essentially inflexible in this way.[7] The same goes, on recent philosophical accounts, for remembering and seeing. This implies a working schema for truth-boundedness:

> Truth-boundedness: A cognitive state Φ is truth-bound if a proper function of Φ is to accurately represent (some part of) the world.

This definition, although perhaps unhappily imprecise, provides a sufficient mode of distinction useful enough to demarcate two classes of cognitive states and capacities. Any type of state that satisfies this condition is truth-bound. States that do not

---

[5] This claim is apparently supported by empirical study on practice and expertise. See Meinz and Hambrick 2010, Campitelli and Gobet 2011, and Hambrick and Meinz 2011.

[6] We might instead say "accuracy-bound" or "accuracy-functioning," but these terms simply aren't as snappy. And there are a number of terms in current philosophical usage: "factive," "truth-aptness," "truth-functional," "truth tracking," "truth committal." Each of these terms may be related to the notion that "truth-bound" aims to capture. But each is certainly distinct and with connotations that would likely distract from present purposes. So "truth-bound" it shall be.

[7] For one important discussion of this feature of belief, see Velleman's "The Aim of Belief" in Velleman 2000.

satisfy the condition, that lack this representational function and are relevantly flexible, are *non- truth-bound.*[8]

Although not a complete catalogue, the following states all appear to be non-truth-bound: imaginings, suppositions (many philosophers take supposition to be just an impoverished form of imagining), curiosities, desires, hopes, wishes, fears, and many other emotions. Perhaps all of the states just mentioned lack an (exclusive) mind-to-world direction of fit. Desires, hopes, and wishes, for example, instead have a world-to-mind fit (Searle 1983). But to be clear, "non-truth-bound" does not just mean states with world-to-mind fit, as opposed to the mind-to-world fit of doxastic states. Following some cognitive accounts of emotion, we might think of emotions as having both directions of fit, since (on such accounts) the emotional state is (partly) constituted by both a belief and a desire-like state (De Sousa 1987, Oatley 1992, Oatley and Johnson-Laird 1987). Fear, for example, may be constituted by a belief that there is some danger to oneself and a desire to remove oneself from that very threat. So fear would be characterized by both mind-to-world and world-to-mind fit.

Imaginings are not inherently constrained in either direction, instead possessing a direction of fit (or not) relative to the context of imagination. So, for example, if one is reading a fictional narrative and one is attempting to follow the imaginative prescriptions of that narrative, one will imagine just the propositions that the story makes (fictionally) true. One's imaginative states in such instances have a kind of mind-to-world fit, where the world is just the fictional world of the story (Walton 1990). Alternatively, if one thinks that some imaginative states can be desire-like, then perhaps they enjoy a (fictional) world-to-mind direction of fit (Currie 2002, Currie and Ravenscroft 2002, Stokes 2006, Doggett and Egan 2007). So the notion of truth-boundedness is not captured by simply distinguishing directions of fit.

In Kant's terms, then, non-truth-bound states are not "subject to the restriction of adequacy to the understanding's concept." These states are necessary for richly

---

[8] We might hesitate to call many skills "states," let alone "cognitive states." And their being truth-bound, even in the broad way specified, implies they are representational to some degree. This is somewhat orthogonal, since we are primarily interested in creative *cognition*, which will surely involve representational cognitive states if anything does. But to be clear, one need only grant that in learning and executing some skills, certain states of the learning or executing agent represent features of the environment. In learning how to read music, I form beliefs and acquire concepts that represent the musical theory and notation before me. These representations may not exhaust the skill, but they are partly constitutive of it. And even an apparently non-cognitive skill can be similarly described. In practicing my tennis backhand, my motor actions (aim to) mirror those of my instructor (and I certainly think about it this way, as I practice). This skillful activity *may* be explained without appeal to mental representation, but nonetheless, some states of the system, namely my physical body, mirror features of my environment (even if those states are described in purely physiological, non-mentalistic terms), and so on. The point is just that some skillful activity involves states that function to represent their environments, where these states may be more or less accurate in performing this function.

creative thinking—for novel conceptual combinations, transformations, and for-mations—since truth-bound states fail to do the relevant work. Non-truth-bound states do not function to accurately represent the world; these states potentially, and without malfunction, involve (at least) minimal manipulation of the informa-tion they carry or (re)present. Put another, hopefully familiar, way, these states (in contrast with truth-bound states) do not aim for objectivity. As such, these states do not purport to tell us about the mind-independent world (or the facts about some subject matter) and so do not "go wrong" when they do not match the world (or those facts). Creativity, it should be no surprise, is not after all an intrinsically truth-seeking enterprise.[9]

All of this motivates hypothesizing a certain functional role as part of creative cognition. Creativity, at least of the sort that Kant had in mind and of which Bach provides one example, requires non-truth-bound cognitive states in the process that enables it (or just is it). Call this the *cognitive manipulation role*. It specifies not just the *allowance* for but indeed the *need* for non-truth-bound states in the creative pro-cess.[10] This is the lesson of the Super-Bach thought experiment: All of the relevant musical-theoretical knowledge (all of the relevant truth-bound states) would not suffice for the composition of *The Well-Tempered Clavier*.

Imagination serves this cognitive manipulation role. Bach presumably imagined, working from within the constraints that he imposed upon himself, how certain musical combinations and structures would achieve certain goals. He did not, as it were, simply read off or abstract from the relevant music-theoretic information. He had to manipulate, by use of the imagination, that information (and perhaps add to

---

[9] A couple of important qualifications need to be made. First, the claim is that imagination is not truth-bound, in the sense that imagination does not qua imagination properly function to accurately represent the world. This is compatible with the claim, maintained by many modern and contemporary philosophers, that imagination can be *used* to determine or reason about modal truths. Indeed, if one maintains the strong position that imagination is, by its nature, bound to provide information about modal truth, then the mention of "world" in the definition of "truth-boundedness" becomes impor-tantly operative: Present interest is in a distinction between mental states that are bound versus not bound to accurately represent truths about the *actual* world. (A reason to doubt this strong position is that, as some have argued, imagination in the context of fiction appears to allow for contradiction, incoherence, and incompleteness. See Walton 1990, pp. 57–67). The second qualification concerns the claim that creativity is not intrinsically truth-seeking. One may worry here about creative processes and products in the theoretical and scientific domains. The scientist is, after all, aiming at truth. Does the present account preclude her thoughts and behaviors from being creative? This concern raises big issues about discovery versus creation, some of which will have to be skirted here. But the first thing to say is that some of scientific discovery is presumably not creative. However, much of it is creative, and the present analysis is committed to the claim that when theorizing *is* creative, even if the broad enter-prise is a truth-seeking one, *some* of the process that leads to the theory or result will involve cognitive manipulation and, necessarily, inclusion of non-truth-bound states. This implication will hopefully become clearer in the sections that follow.

[10] This role will be further characterized in section 2.

it) in ways unbound to accurately representing it. This oversimplifies Bach's creative process, but the general point should be clear. There is, for richly creative achievement in the arts and sciences, a cognitive manipulation role, and imagination serves it well. This is part of Kant's insight. This insight is extended to more mundane creativity in section 2 and then made more precise in sections 3 and 4.

2. Minimal Creativity and Cognitive Manipulation

One reason for thinking that creative processes require cognitive manipulation is that the creativity of Bach and other geniuses involved a *cognitive breakthrough* (or several). Bach began with a conceptual space—in this case a new music-theoretic space—and had to *do* something with it, importantly, something that had never been done before. In this way, Bach's creativity is radical, since at the very least his work is novel relative to the entire history of music in a way that is exciting, valuable, and instructive. This kind of change is not possible using inflexible, truth-bound cognition. Cognitive breakthroughs, however, can be much more banal. But even the everyday breakthrough, as will now be argued, implies that some cognitive faculty plays the role of cognitive manipulation.[11]

From the standpoint of philosophy, psychology, and cognitive science, radical creativity does not exhaust theoretical interest. It may in fact be the last place to look if giving a cognitivist or naturalistic analysis of creativity. A number of theorists have acknowledged this general point. Margaret Boden, for example, makes an influential distinction between *historical* and *psychological* creativity (Boden 2004). The first is just as the name implies: An idea or act is novel if it is new relative to the history of ideas (or, broadening the notion, relative to some class of behavior or culture). Psychological creativity involves ideas that are novel relative to some individual mind. Others too have suggested weaker, mundane, or minimal senses of creativity.[12] The thread common to these analyses is this: Creativity is not exclusive to minds like Bach's or Beethoven's. All human thinkers have some capacity for thinking in ways that are relatively original, for taking on novel skills and information, for solving problems in surprising and unexpected ways. What conditions, then, are there on a more everyday sense of creativity?

Boden's distinction is really one between two different types of novelty: F is historically or psychologically creative by virtue of being, respectively, historically novel or psychologically novel. A novelty condition captures our most basic of intuitions about creativity: Creative Fs are novel Fs. Boden's important insight is that our interest in creative thought outstrips historical novelty or novelty simpliciter.

---

[11] See Stokes 2011 for more on cognitive breakthroughs.

[12] See Barsalou and Prinz 1997, Prinz and Barsalou 2002, Bird and Stokes 2006, Carruthers 2002, Nanay, chapter 1, this volume, Stokes 2007, 2008, 2011, and Weisberg 1986, 1999.

A child who works out a difficult mathematical theorem in a surprising way, even if the theorem is well known and established (but unbeknown to the child), has done something we rightly acknowledge as importantly novel, namely, novel *for the child*. If Borges's character Menard manages to rewrite parts of Cervantes's *Don Quixote* without copying the text, then he has done something psychologically novel (Borges 1964).[13] In both of these cases, the thoughts and actions of the agent are, even if not novel relative to the history of ideas, novel relative to the cognitive histories of the relevant agents. This difference in novelty needn't be one in kind, but instead a difference in the scope of the comparison class; the child's mathematical solution is novel relative to a narrow class of ideas (namely, that child's), while Godel's incompleteness proofs were novel relative to a much broader class (say, all ideas before Godel). In any case, psychological (or, we might say, *behavioral*) novelty provides one necessary condition for a minimal concept of creativity.

A second plausible condition is agency, which captures the fact that creative thoughts and behaviors are ones for which we are responsible, as evidenced by their general praiseworthiness. Sunsets and cloud figures may be aesthetically interesting, but they are not the kinds of things that we count as creative. One withholds an attribution of creativity here by the same token as one grants it for an artwork or scientific thesis: Creative Fs are the results of agency. Moreover, creative Fs have to be linked with agency in the right way: We don't judge happy accidents to be creative, even if interesting and valuable. An agency condition, suitably sharpened, is thus a necessary condition for minimal creativity. Conjoining these two conditions:

> MC*: Some thought (or action) x is minimally creative only if, for some agent A, x is the non-accidental result of the agency of A and x is psychologically (or behaviorally) novel relative to A[14]

It will be assumed here that a novelty condition and an agency condition are conditions on any sense, minimal or rich, of creativity. These conditions are necessary, but unlikely sufficient even for mundane, everyday creativity.[15] But they are sufficient to

---

[13] Psychologically novel at the very least: Were Menard to accomplish such a task, he may well have done something historically novel. And, if Borges's theorizing is accurate, Menard would thus have created an entirely distinct work and one with different aesthetic properties. For discussion of the ontological implications of a case like this, see, among others, Goodman and Elgin 1986, Currie 1991, Davies 2004.

[14] "MC*" is used here to flag a weaker characterization of my MC (Stokes 2011). See that discussion for extended analysis of an agency condition plus a third (modal) condition, argued to be conjointly sufficient for minimal creativity. And see Gaut 2009 for related discussion of agency and skill.

[15] For alternative, additional conditions (or simply alternative analyses), see Boden 2004, Gaut 2003, Gaut and Livingston 2003, Nanay, chapter 1, this volume, Novitz 1999; and for analyses from an empirical perspective, see Sternberg 1999. One condition commonly posited (indeed by most if not all of the just-mentioned theorists) as necessary for rich creativity is a value condition: An x is richly creative only if it is valuable (or useful). See my 2008, 2011 for worries about the theoretical value of a value condition.

characterize creativity for present purposes. That is, even with this incomplete definition, we can ask important questions about creative cognition. We can ask what kinds of cognitive faculties are needed to generate thoughts and action that meet these two basic conditions. So grant that MC* provides a working characterization of minimally creative thought, and grant further that minimal creativity is a common phenomenon.

Even minimally creative thought and behavior require cognitive manipulation. To see this, consider two independent sets of studies in experimental psychology, both of them on figurative thought.

First, consider three related studies on drawing capacities. Annette Karmiloff-Smith solicited drawings of nonexistent houses, people, and animals from children ranging in age from four to 11 (Karmiloff-Smith 1990, 1992, pp. 155–161). Christina Cacciari and colleagues solicited drawings of nonexistent houses and animals from children in the same age range (Cacciari et al. 1997). Thomas Ward performed similar studies on adults, asking them to imagine and draw nonexistent creatures (Ward 1994, 1995). One hypothesis, motivated by all three sets of data, is that children and adults alike are highly constrained by their existing concepts; concepts, like HOUSE, PERSON, or ANIMAL, significantly constrain how a person is able to depict novel instances of such concepts. Although frequency of cross-category combination increases with age, the properties from any one category are relatively stable. Ostensibly then, individuals "retrieve a specific instance of a given category and pattern the new creation after it, regardless of whether they were required to imagine and draw an artifact such as a house or a natural kind such as an animal" (Cacciari et al. 1997, p. 157).

So even given invitations to create nonexistent things, the drawings were quite predictable—largely generated in line with the relevant conceptual schemes; nothing radically novel here. However, a question remains: Are any of these drawings possibly enabled *merely* by the relevant conceptual knowledge? We know that the subjects consistently deployed their concepts of HOUSE, PERSON, etc., to make their drawings; was this knowledge sufficient? No. The concepts of HOUSE and PERSON, no matter how rich, will not (by themselves) enable a child to draw a house with eyes for windows, a mouth for a front door, and arms and legs. These cross-category changes require the child to cognitively manipulate, rather than faithfully mirror, the conceptual space in particular, albeit minimal, ways. These drawings require non-truth-bound cognitive states.

Consider a second set of studies on the development and acquisition of figurative linguistic competence—comprehension of metaphors, idioms, proverbs, and the like. Children as young as seven years of age are able to understand and use figurative language. The development of this competence is not based in rote learning mechanisms. One plausible reason for this is that metaphoricity co-varies with abstraction:

As with nouns, verbs that are understood at a higher level of abstraction are rated as more metaphorical than when the same verbs could be interpreted at the basic (literal) level. Furthermore, this effect is graded: the higher the level of abstraction, the higher the rated metaphoricity. These findings suggest that people use level of abstraction as a cue to metaphoricity for both nominal and predicative metaphors

(Torreano, Cacciari, and Glucksberg 200, p. 259)

And recognizing metaphors as abstractions is not accomplished simply by observing adult usage of metaphor.[16] Instead, one must suspend the literal meanings of the relevant terms and phrases.[17] Learning and recognizing metaphors thus consists in the acquisition of what some call *figurative competence*. This suite of abilities includes the apprehension of a variety of meanings for a single lexical item, suspension of purely literal or referential linguistic strategies, awareness of linguistic conventions, and the importance of the context of utterance (Cacciari et al. 1997, p. 159).[18]

The relevant moral is that learning figurative linguistic types is not enabled by straightforward rote learning: One does not just memorize a meaning and syntactic role for the lexical item(s). This learning requires more than truth-bound cognitive states, more than entertaining and assenting to the information contained in the relevant conceptual space. It requires some consideration of and simple hypothesis formation about the potential for multiple meanings, multiple syntactic roles, conventional and contextual factors, among other things. These considerations involve more than the formation of true beliefs and accurate skills. Or better put, even if the development of beliefs and skills—and thus the acquisition of propositional and procedural knowledge of figurative language—is the end result, this result involves as its means some non-truth-bound states. The lesson of this rich set of research is that this result is not enabled by "merely reading off" the information contained in the conceptual space.

The drawing and figurative language behaviors possess two marks of creativity: agency and novelty. The cognitive behaviors of the subjects are effortful and involve thoughts (at least some of them) that are novel relative to the minds of those subjects. Behaviors that, in this way, meet the conditions of MC* are not *richly* creative, but if there is a continuum of creative cognition, they lie at the end opposite

---

[16] See Levorato et al. 2004, p. 304, which cites the following studies in support of this thesis: Kempler, Van Lancker, Marchman, and Bates 1999; Levorato and Cacciari 1992, 1995; Nippold and Martin 1989; Nippold and Rudzinski 1993; Van Lancker and Kempler 1987.

[17] As Levorato et al. 2004, p. 304, puts it, what's required is "the ability to suspend, if not suppress, contextually inappropriate meanings." In the case of idioms, the reader has to suppress the constituent word meanings that are irrelevant to the figurative interpretation. According to Gernsbacher and Faust 1991 and Gernsbacher, Varner, and Faust 1990, "poorer performances in reading for comprehension in adults (and children) might be due to the deficient suppression mechanisms possessed by less skilled readers...."

[18] See also Cacciari and Levorato 1989; Gibbs 1987, 1991, 1994; Levorato and Cacciari 1992, 1995, 1999, 2002.

the cognitive behaviors of Bach and Beethoven. In simple terms, they involve *doing something* with the information in the relevant spaces, and in (agent-relative) psychologically novel ways. Note that this is consistent with resisting an attribution of any rich sense of "creative" in these instances.

Both the drawing behavior and the figurative language behavior require non-truth-bound cognitive states. The subjects must manipulate the information in that space and use it in cross-categorical ways, even if only in the minimal ways required to humanize a house or comprehend a phrase like "Lawyers are sharks." And so these cognitive behaviors, like Bach's composition, require cognitive manipulation. From here, we might derive an empirical generalization. If these cognitive behaviors are minimally creative, then minimally creative cognition requires cognitive manipulation. The inference here is an inductive one, a generalization from two classes of novel cognitive behavior to all minimally creative cognition. As an empirical generalization, the inference is strong to the degree that the novelty in these behaviors typifies (psychologically) novel behavior. The cognition involved—concept deployment and combination in the first set of studies, and non-literal linguistic learning in the second set—is general and basic, and so any psychological novelty that emerges would also be basic. Another way of putting the point is this: The degree or quantity of non-truth-bound resources needed to behave in psychologically novel ways—either in the drawing tasks or the figurative learning tasks—is quite low. And so, plausibly, any minimally creative cognition would require at least this much of the same non-truth-bound resources.

This empirical generalization may be combined with the earlier conceptual considerations. Novel cognition—be it radical historical novelty or mere psychological novelty—requires more of an agent than accurately representing a conceptual space, even when the tasks are simple and mundane. Novelty implies cognitive manipulation. It is thus the novelty in the studied behaviors that does the work of motivating the claimed need for cognitive manipulation. Creative behaviors qua novel behaviors reasonably require whatever resources enable the psychologically novel behaviors in these studies (even if one denies the creativity of the latter). These resources have been distinguished as non-truth-bound cognitive manipulation, in contrast with truth-bound beliefs and skills. So, if these behaviors require cognitive manipulation, and creative cognition requires at least this much (by way of non-truth-bound cognitive resources) of its agents, then creative cognition requires cognitive manipulation. This generates a thesis:

> Cognitive manipulation thesis (T): Creative thought and behavior (rich or minimal) requires cognitive manipulation. Cognitive manipulation involves thinking about the contents of some conceptual space in non-truth-bound ways.

This thesis is so far pretty thin; only the notions of truth-boundedness and minimal creativity have been adequately clarified. And so in order to better hone in on the best candidate cognitive faculty or faculties for the cognitive manipulation role, a more thorough analysis of the cognition typical of creative processes is needed.

3. Enriching the Cognitive Manipulation Role

Whether it is creativity in the category of genius or the everyday, a number of cognitive (or at least *mental*) features typify a creative process. Although these features may not be possessed by every instance of creativity, they do (and usually in some combination) typify a great deal of creativity. Indeed, very plausibly, any instance of creativity will involve some combination of this cluster of cognitive features. Here is the strategy: Identify a cluster of typifying cognitive features. To identify this cluster of features is to enrich the cognitive manipulation role. In terms of explanation, it is to identify desiderata for any theory of creative cognition, features that on balance should be explained by the mechanisms posited or invoked by the theory. And if one type of cognitive faculty best serves this role, then that faculty is plausibly necessary for much if not all of creativity. As should be clear by this point, the concluding thesis (section 4) is that imagination is the relevant faculty.

One brief qualification before proceeding: The central explanandum for this chapter is the active, conscious component/s of the creative cognitive process. The term "cognitive manipulation" is intended to make this perspicuous. Although much of the traditional literature on creativity focuses instead on either (or both) (a) implicit cognition (sometimes called *incubation* or, less technically, *insight*) or (b) free association, a great deal of creativity results from deliberate and active cognitive effort. Indeed, if it is minimal creativity in question, it is plausible that active creativity is (part of) the norm. That said, the analysis given below is compatible with the inclusion of these other, less active and/or less conscious, cognitive aspects in a complete explanation of the creative process. Indeed, the present analysis can work in tandem with explanations of (a) and (b), if not partly explain the importance of (a) and/or (b). More on this later.

Begin by considering an uncontroversial instance of creativity, Picasso's *Guernica*. If one visits the Museo Reina Sofía in Madrid, one will find displayed in conjunction with the massive painting itself over 300 of Picasso's preparatory sketches and (at least this was true a few years ago) a photojournalistic study of Picasso creating the piece. From these photos, one quickly learns that Picasso's process included removing or covering components that he had already painted on the final canvas. The process involved not just exhaustive prepping before painting but, essentially, erasing. A case like this reveals the silliness of traditional divine inspiration theories of creativity. Picasso's execution was long, deliberate, and arduous.[19]

---

[19] For related debate in the psychological literature, see Weisberg 1995, 2004 and Simonton 1999, 2007 (and the critical commentary accompanying the latter target article).

So unless the traditional theory explains this case by positing a divinely inspired Picasso-automaton (and moreover, where the inspiring deity was apparently regularly changing its mind), the traditional theory cannot explain a paradigm case of creativity. Kicking dead theories to one side, the lesson to glean here is that Picasso produced his work through careful and deliberate thought. This suggests the first desideratum.

Voluntariness: The creative process typically involves a cognitive faculty or faculties that *may* be engaged voluntarily by the creating agent. Very often, even if not always, a person decides to take on a certain project—produce a painting or poem or melody; introduce a new scientific thesis or a new way of testing it; improve or invent a technology; identify a new way of solving a puzzle—and in taking on this project must deliberate, hypothesize, scrutinize, test, try, tweak, and revise. The same is true, even if to lesser degree, for instances of minimal creativity (or, if one prefers, psychological novelty). For example, the subjects of the studies on figurative language had to actively play with the contents of the relevant linguistic or conceptual space. In all such cases, the cognition involved was ostensibly under the will of the agent: Whatever cognitive faculty or faculties she used, at least a significant portion needed to be the sort that she could voluntarily and relatively immediately control. To be clear, this imposes no requirement that the relevant faculty *always* be under voluntary control. And indeed, given so-called Eureka! moments and free-associative insight, a faculty that is generally but not always under voluntary control may be preferable.[20]

Affect and motivation: Creative products, especially artworks, are often emotional in character, both in what they express and what they evoke in their audience. And artists (and generally, any person acting creatively) are emotionally moved by their creative productions and, importantly, before their productions are finished. The point here is not just one about being motivated and emotionally affected by "getting the job done." Of course, the creative person feels this. But plausibly, in working through the creative process, a person gets emotionally caught up with and in turn motivated by the deliberation, hypothesis-generation, attempts and failures, and so on. This provides another desideratum for a theory of creative cognition: Creative processes often involve mental mechanisms that causally interact with affective and motivational systems.

---

[20] *Working memory* is plausibly relevant here. Information must be made available for manipulation and further processing, and this is generally how psychologists understand the theoretical role of working memory. However, the latter is not going to do the work of explaining (or serving) the cognitive manipulation role as it is understood here, in particular given the features of non-truth-boundedness, affect, and free association. At most, working memory will be a *necessary* but insufficient condition for cognitive manipulation.

Inference and decision-making: Although the creative process (typically) requires flexibility in the form of non-truth-bound cognition, it also requires cognition that can contribute to decision-making and inference. After testing and deliberation, the scientist will draw certain conclusions about how the theorizing should proceed, or about what methods of testing are possible. After considering a variety of possible media or techniques for this or that element of a work, an artist will ultimately select the medium or technique she deems best (by some criterion). Consider the child who is learning the metaphor "Lawyers are sharks." After reflecting on relevant contextual factors and non-literal possibilities for these words, while suppressing distracting literal meanings, the child will infer an interpretation. So the output of an inference or decision is, typically and respectively, a belief or an action. One forms a belief that "*This* hypothesis/testing method is possible" or that "The phrase can be used *this* way." Or one forms an intention on how to proceed at a juncture in the process. But the output does not exhaust the inferential or decision-making process: There is always some cognitive means that fills out the inferential or decisional procedure. The suggestion here is that creative processes are no exception; insofar as these processes often involve inferences drawn and decisions made, whether intermediary or final, these processes will need to involve cognitive faculties that connect in appropriate ways with inferential systems.

Free association: This may just be an extension of the non-truth-boundedness already identified. But the notion of free association has figured so largely in philosophical and psychological theorizing about creativity that it deserves separate mention. Here a romantic characterization is instructive rather than distracting. Kekulé's discovery of the benzene molecule may be the most popular of anecdotes in creativity theorizing. One of Kekulé's own descriptions of the discovery goes as follows:

> Again the atoms were gambolling before my eyes. This time the smaller groups kept modestly in the background. My mental eye, rendered more acute by repeated visions of this kind, could now distinguish larger structures, of manifold conformation; long rows, sometimes more closely fitted together; all twining and twisting in snakelike motion. But look! What was that? One of the snakes had seized hold of its own tail, and the form whirled mockingly before my eyes. As if by a flash of lightning I awoke.
>
> (quoted in Boden 2004, p. 26)

A common and reasonable way to describe Kekulé's mental activity here is as free-associative: He was allowing, without much mental effort, ideas and concepts to combine without active direction or correction. Atoms mingled with snakes, twisting, turning, biting, and so on. If one introspects one's own mundanely novel behavior—say, if one is asked to draw a humanized house—one will sometimes plausibly find similar free-associative activity. The idea to turn some hedges into a beard or some opened window shutters into ears might come simply by randomly mixing house concepts and person concepts, letting these "ideas float around in one's head" as we might say. This provides another desideratum: Creative processes often involve this kind of conceptual freedom, and so a faculty suitable for free association should plausibly be part of an explanation of creativity.

In addition to these four desiderata, non-truth-boundedness has already been identified and defined. Conjoining these five features of creative processes provides a more robust job description, a richer characterization of cognitive manipulation. The enriched thesis is this:

> Cognitive manipulation thesis (R): Creative thought and behavior (rich or minimal) requires cognitive manipulation. Cognitive manipulation typically involves voluntarily thinking about the contents of some conceptual space in non- truth-bound ways. In creative processes, this cognitive activity often causally interacts with affective, motivational, inferential, and free associative capacities.

Although perhaps not every instance of creativity will be enabled by or require this cognitive profile in full, much (perhaps all) of creativity seems typified by some combination of these features.[21] To the degree that a cognitive faculty is capable of possessing all of these features, this faculty is a good candidate to fill the role of cognitive manipulation (now more richly understood). And if there is one type of faculty that possesses more (or all) of these features, in contrast with other cognitive faculties, then that faculty very plausibly is *the* faculty to play the role.

4. Creativity, Cognitive Manipulation, and Imagination

Imagination is the best candidate for serving the cognitive manipulation role. This claim is motivated by considering two contrasting aspects of imagination: *cognitive playfulness* and *cognitive workfulness*.[22] Understanding these two aspects of the

---

[21] Two additional putative aspects of creativity, insight (understood as resulting, apparently unwilled, from unconscious or subconscious thought) and free association, are discussed at the end of section 4.

[22] There are other candidate mental faculties that may serve the role of non-truth-bound cognition. For examples of relevant naturalistic accounts, see Campbell 1960, 1965; Martindale 1989, 1995, 1999; Simonton 1999; Thornton 2002. There isn't space to carefully analyze these theories here, but the main worry is that they all posit mechanisms that plausibly enough explain creativity when it ostensibly results from unconscious or subconscious mental activity, but seem to fall short of explaining creativity that occurs during conscious, deliberate mental activity. Although many traditional accounts would indicate otherwise, the latter phenomenon, not the former, is by far the most prevalent. But even if one resists this claim, the central explanandum for this chapter *is* the latter phenomenon.

imagination reveals how an imagination-based account of creative process satisfies the theoretical desiderata identified in the previous section.

Arguing for the playfulness of imagination is fairly easy work. Imagination answers to names like "pretence," "pretend play," "role-playing," and "make-believe."[23] To engage in imaginative activity is to engage in a cognitive activity that generally, as it were, carries smaller stakes for epistemic and bodily action. In fact, on one plausible model of imagination, this is one of the very features that distinguish it from other cognitive states like belief, desire, and intention. Imaginings do not, qua imaginings, immediately cause action. Neither do imaginative states function to accurately represent the world.

Simple conceptual analysis suffices for this point. As contrasted with beliefs and intentions, imaginings lack intrinsic commitment to truth and ends. It is a conceptual fact that beliefs aim for the end of truth and intentions aim for the end of action. These types of states are, in some sense, bound to these ends or results: To believe that P is to be committed to the truth of P and to intend to do Q is to be committed, ceteris paribus, to doing Q. Similarly, perceptual experience is *assertoric*. Although perception can go awry, as it does in cases of illusion and hallucination, it properly functions to provide information about the world. Barring some special reason for doubt, perceptual experience purports to show one features and objects in the world. Imagination bears, by itself, no such commitments. Berys Gaut (2003) offers a compelling test case to this end. Moore's paradox tells us that it is problematic to assert "I believe that it is Tuesday, but it isn't Tuesday." Analogously, an assertion like the following is problematic: "I intend to go to the islands, but I won't go to the islands if given the chance." In contrast, there is nothing paradoxical about either of the following: "I imagine that it is Tuesday, but it isn't Tuesday"; "I imagine going to the islands, but I won't go to the islands if given the chance." Imagination thus enjoys a freedom that other states lack. Therefore, imagination possesses the first feature of cognitive manipulation as characterized above; imaginative states are non-truth-bound.

This feature of imagination likely explains another: One generally can control one's imagination at will. Imagine your favorite fictional character sitting beside you

---

[23] There may be important differences between the states or capacities that such terms denote. Differences aside and for present purposes, all of these capacities are similar enough in the relevant way—namely, with respect to cognitive freedom or flexibility—to be categorized under the general "imagination." It should also be noted that philosophers distinguish (and debate) various forms of the imagination and related capacities: sensory imagery versus propositional imagination, rich or engaged imagination versus mere supposition, and so on. Various features of the imagination are clarified below. But again, the working assumption here is that in spite of putative differences between these distinguished types, they all fall broadly under a general capacity (or perhaps a family of capacities) that can be reasonably be called "imagination." For discussion, see Currie and Ravenscroft 2002; Gendler 2000, 2003, 2011; Kind 2001; McGinn 2004; Nichols 2004, 2006; Walton 1990, among others.

as you read this. Imagine s/he (or it) speaking to you about the philosophy of creativity and then offering you a cup of tea. Now that you are off and running, carry on the imagining however you wish. So, one can imagine objects, properties, and events that one has never perceived and the existence of which one does not believe. One can willfully imagine propositions one believes to be false. One can imagine doing certain actions that one has no intention of doing. And so on. The voluntariness of imagination is explained by its non-truth-boundedness. Here also, the contrast with belief is useful: One does not, with any immediacy, decide to believe. And this involuntariness is explained by the fact that belief is committed to truth. In this way, belief is sensitive to evidence. And though the irresponsible epistemic agent may do her best to attend to *this* evidence, and ignore *that*, if the evidence is before her, she forms the belief (or not) unwillingly. Imagination, in contrast, is not committed to truth. It is "evidence-indifferent" (McGinn 2004, p. 132). And so we can imagine with a freedom of will that belief and perception do not enjoy. Imagination is therefore suitably voluntary to serve the cognitive manipulation role.[24]

Just as imaginings are decoupled from truth, imaginings are typically decoupled from action. Some have argued that some imaginative states, say, in a child's game of pretence, may result directly in action.[25] However, imaginative states do not, in contrast to intentions, stand in any deep conceptual relation with (bodily) action. The analogous behavioral point is that imaginings often, perhaps most typically, result in no relevant action. This feature may be connected with another important feature of imagination, its relation to affect. Consider one compelling explanation for our affective response to fictions. I seem to fear the vampire as I watch a horror film. In spite of my apparent fear, I do not flee the theatre in self-defense but squirm in cinematic enjoyment. The fact that I do not flee is taken as evidence for an imagination-based explanation. I do not believe that the vampire is a real threat, nor do I desire to remove myself from danger, since if I did, I would flee. Instead, I form some imaginative states about the fictional vampire that result in an affective response. The physiology of this affect is often adequately characterized in ways similar to a reality-directed fear: My heart rate rises, my muscles tense, I cling to my seat, etc. The same can be said for imagining past events, possible future events,

---

[24] There is a lot to be said here. One issue concerns whether it is a mere psychological fact or a stronger conceptual fact that beliefs are not under voluntary control. On this issue—doxastic involuntarism—see classic essays by Alston 1989, Bennett 1990, Williams 1973. A second related qualification is this: Assuming that beliefs are not under voluntary control (at least as a psychological fact about humans), this does not imply that beliefs cannot sometimes play something like the cognitive manipulation role. We can and do form false beliefs, and these sometimes may be the (indirect) result of fanciful or wishful thinking. But the latter kinds of beliefs deviate from norms of epistemic rationality. And so, unless creativity is regularly the result of irrational thought processes or malfunctioning reason, belief is an implausible candidate to explain cognitive manipulation in the bulk of creative processes.

[25] On this debate, see Currie and Ravenscroft 2002, Funkhouser and Spaulding 200,; Nichols and Stich 2000, 2003, and Velleman 2000.

or counter-actual events: I may feel temporarily sad upon imagining the death of a loved one, even as she simultaneously sits across the table from me. Imaginative states, then, causally interact with affective systems.[26]

There is an apparent tension here. The suggestion is that imaginative states can engage with affective systems. But part of the motivation for this explanation, in the context of fictional-directed affect, is that the relevant affective responses do not result in action, and imagination (unlike belief, desire, and intention) is conceptually and behaviorally decoupled from action. This threatens to discount imagination from possessing the affective *and* motivational features of cognitive manipulation as it typifies creative processes. However, the apparent problem dissolves if one acknowledges that the claim about affect depends upon the denial of a universal claim about imagination and action: Imagination does not always (perhaps not even typically) immediately cause action. This is the conceptual point brought out above. And this is consistent with a corresponding existential claim: Imagination may cause action. Here there are a variety of options: Perhaps imagination may cause action directly.[27] It may cause affect that is sufficient to motivate action, perhaps not in fiction-directed cases, but in future-directed or counter-actual directed cases. (Is it a belief or merely an imagining that causes the apparent fear that gets me to check behind the shower curtain for the bogeyman?) And, finally, imagination may cause other mental states that themselves typically cause action: belief, desire, intention. If one or more of these suggestions is true, then imagination can also meet the affective and motivational desideratum.

These last suggestions imply that imagination causally interacts with a rich variety of mental states and processes. Making good on these suggestions requires a careful discussion of the second aspect of imagination: cognitive workfulness. In spite of the playfulness of imagination as just established—non-truth-bound, under voluntary control, capable of generating (non-reality directed) affect—imagination can do a great deal of work for us. Philosophers have always implicitly indicated this by using the imagination (and appealing to what is imaginable) to construct arguments, thought experiments, and counterexamples. More recently, philosophers have begun to explicitly analyze these valuable features of the familiar capacity.

According to one recently defended thesis, in spite of functional differences, imagination and belief carry information in a *single code*. Thus systems that take input from

---

[26] Fiction-directed affect has received considerable philosophical attention in the past few decades. An imagination-based explanation is perhaps the most popular extant view. A related debate concerns whether these affective responses are genuine emotions. But this question is ontological (some say terminological; see Currie 1997), concerning not whether imagination can engage affective systems but instead whether the resultant affect is of the same psychological kind as reality-directed emotion or of a separate kind. See, among others, Currie 1990, Gaut 2003, Gendler and Kovakovich 2006, Walton 1990, Weinberg and Meskin 2006, and Harris 2000 for related empirical work. To be clear, the present claims are neutral with regard to this ontological question.

[27] See fn. 26.

belief can take isomorphic inputs from imagination and will process that input in broadly similar ways. A system receiving input from an *imagining* that P or a *belief* that P will produce similar (though not identical) output. The framework inspired by this thesis is supposed to solve a number of philosophical problems about the imagination and fiction and enjoys both philosophical and empirical support.[28] One can take a lesson from this approach without commitment to the single code thesis: The representational (or information-carrying) nature of imaginative states is such that these states can be processed by a variety of mental and cognitive systems. And those systems (at least some of them) are the same systems that process belief representations.

Imaginings can, in a familiar way, drive or serve as premises in inference. We often subject our imaginings to ordinary inferential practice, drawing inferences about what is imagined in the same ways we would if we had beliefs with the same contents. If I imagine that P, and I imagine that *if P then Q*, then I am disposed to imagine Q just as I would in actual circumstances of reasoning. And we often supplement our imaginings with actual beliefs in order to render the imaginative project coherent and consistent. If I am told by a narrative that Holmes has blood on his shirt and the story has been (at least implicitly) a realistic one about humans, I am disposed to infer that Holmes has *red* stains on his shirt, given my beliefs about the actual world.[29] Imaginings can also be used to supplement reasoning about the actual world. One theory of folk mindreading ability requires precisely this: In explaining or predicting another person's behavior, I imaginatively simulate the (relevant) mental states I take the person to have. From this simulation, I draw inferences about her actions, why she did what she did or what she may do next (Currie 1995, 1996; Goldman 1989, 1992; Gordon 1986).

In the theoretical domain, there is a long tradition of supposing an important relation between conceivability—understood broadly as imagination—and possibility. So although few today would maintain that P's being imaginable is constitutive of P's being possible, many do maintain an inferential relation between the two. Imagining that P is, in some importantly qualified sense, a guide to modal truth; the first gives one good reason to believe that *possibly P*. Here again, we are using imaginings alongside beliefs to draw inferences, in this case about possible worlds (Chalmers 2002, McGinn 2004, Van Inwagen 1998, Yablo 1993).

These considerations suffice to show that imagination displays another feature identified in section 3 above; it figures in theoretical and everyday inference.[30]

---

[28] See Harris 2000, Leslie 1987, Nichols 2004, Nichols and Stich 2000, Weinberg and Meskin 2006.

[29] Nichols and Stich (2000, 2003) call this "non-inferential elaboration"; Gendler (2003) calls this "mirroring."

[30] Both Nichols and Stich (2000, 2003) and Gendler (2003) use "inferential elaboration" to describe these general relations. It should also be noted that none of this is meant to imply that imaginative states are always subject to rational rules of inference. We can and do use imagination in ways immune or blocked from normal inferential practice.

But the connections between the imagination and other elements of the mind go deeper, and some of them show how imaginings may drive decision and action.

Beliefs and perceptual experience on the one hand, and propositional imaginings and mental images on the other, have the same type of content. But we typically keep these mental states appropriately distinguished. For example, we generally do not confuse imaginings with beliefs; introspectively, we identify imaginings *as* imaginings. Imaginings are in this way *weakly quarantined* from other mental states. Further, imaginings are often *strongly quarantined* insofar as they do not cause perceptions, actual beliefs, or desires or a change in intentions, values, or other cognitive states.[31] However, there are exceptions to both sorts of quarantine, more commonly to the strong sort.

Imaginings do influence or cause other mental states. I might vividly imagine that it will rain and come to believe that it will rain. I might visually imagine the sofa fitting through the doorway and judge that the sofa will fit through the doorway (and then act upon this judgment). I might imagine a bowl of ice cream and quickly find myself, driven by a newly formed desire, on the way to the ice cream shop. In spite of weak cognitive quarantine, imaginings are causally efficacious in these respects, enjoying a kind of *cognitive contagion*. And even weak quarantine can sometimes be violated. For instance, people sometimes mistake mental images for perceptions, or have trouble determining if a perceptual memory is one of something perceived or something merely imagined (Segal 1970, Kosslyn 1994, p. 55, Reisberg et al. 1986; see Currie and Ravenscroft 2002 for further discussion).[32]

Imaginative states thus integrate with other states in inference, causally influence our doxastic commitments, desires, and intentions, and in turn influence (even if indirectly) how we decide and act. Given its voluntary nature, there is significant freedom in how one uses and directs the imagination. One can use the imagination in a playful way, potentially engaging affective systems; or one can use it in a thinner and more constrained way, making suppositions only as robust as is needed for hypothesis generation. This is evident in the quotation from Kant given earlier: Imagination may be constrained by the cognitive task and conceptual domain for which it is employed, and will accordingly connect with inferential and other mental mechanisms. Thus imaginative states may play a rigorous and purposive role in human cognition. Imagination is not all play and no work.

To this point, the conclusion is that imagination has four of the identified features of cognitive manipulation typical of creative cognitive

---

[31] "Cognitive quarantine" and "cognitive contagion" are the terms of Gendler (2003, 2006). "Weak quarantine" and "strong quarantine" are my terms.

[32] Currie and Ravenscroft (2002) propose another exception to weak quarantine, arguing that schizophrenics and other patients experiencing so-called delusional beliefs suffer from a failure to recognize imaginings as imaginings, treating them in ways more like belief (Currie and Ravenscroft 2002, pp. 161–184). Gendler offers an extended analysis of the phenomenon of imaginative contagion (Gendler 2006). For recent and possibly relevant research in neuroscience, see Buda et al. 2011.

processes: non-truth-boundedness, voluntariness, affect and motivation, and inference and decision-making, as they were named above. The final feature, free association, must now be discussed. How should one think about the relation between imagination and free association?

On a liberal account of the imagination, free association is just imagination in one of its many guises. Imagination bears no intrinsic commitment to truth or action. So one might think that free association is just imagination that is unconstrained and, relative to deliberate imaginative projects, undirected. This encourages a distinction between active and passive imagination and keeps both free association and deliberate pretence under the same general category of mental process. However, on a more conservative account of imagination, imagining involves actively *doing* something (mentally): imagining a counterfactual proposition and then actively filling out details around that proposition, forming rich visual images of how one will construct a snow fort, and so on. Recalling Kekulé's story, free association is comparatively passive: One does not control the ideas and images, one let's them "gambol" before one's mind's eye. But even if, as this analysis would have it, the two faculties are distinct, they are not incompatible. And importantly, they plausibly may work together. So, even granting the difference in deliberate control, both mental activities are non-truth-bound. This similarity is crucial since imagination may then be used, in a truth- and evidence-insensitive way, to seize upon ideas that result from free association. Plausibly, this is what Kekulé did: When certain images from his reverie surprised or interested him, he continued to actively use and play with them in imagination. It is the combination of the two faculties that helped enable his final inferences about his task, namely, the nature of the benzene molecule.[33] So even if imagination does not subsume free association, it suitably engages with free associative activity and in the ways typical of creative cognition.

This last point generalizes to address some possible worries. At least part of the ordinary conception of creativity, one might urge, involves something very different from deliberate, conscious thought. Instead, creativity involves free association (as in Kekulé's reverie) or insight that results from some kind of subconscious or implicit cognition (sometimes called "incubation") or both. And many traditional theories of creativity have placed greater emphasis on these features of creativity. This could motivate various worries: The present account fails to explain important features of creativity. Or the present account fails to explain a large sample of paradigmatic creative acts and persons. Or the present account misses the core of creativity; the non-deliberate and unconscious stuff is where the action is!

First, a note of caution and then a response. There is an assumption that often underlies worries and theses like the ones just articulated, namely, that creative thought or behavior is a single act, occurring at one time (or in a small window of

---

[33] This line of thought is compatible with a recent model of creative processes—the Geneplore model. See Finke, Ward, and Smith 1992.

time). This assumption is misguided. Of course, we might accept that important insights come at a moment, or that some particular daydream or free associative episode is essential to a creative breakthrough. But by the same token, we should insist that *some* conscious, deliberate thought (and/or action) is essential to a creative breakthrough. Kekulé, for example, would not have had his famous insight *at all*, had he not already done a great deal of thinking, deliberating, hypothesizing, and indeed imagining about the chemistry of his day and the problem at hand. Some of these cognitive events, then, are necessary to Kekulé's creative process (in addition to his reverie-induced insight). The general lesson is that it is far more plausible to think of creativity in terms of a multifaceted cognitive *process*, which occurs over time and often involves the cognitive manipulation that is the focus here and the insight and free association that has been the focus in much of the creativity literature.[34]

Finally, can the present account offer any explanation of these additional, putative aspects of creativity? Although it is unclear what psychological mechanisms are supposed to constitute insight and free association, these processes are, prima facie, good candidates for non-truth-bound cognitive states or processes. And so one advantage of the present account is that it identifies the need for processes like these: Non-truth-bound cognition is needed for creativity since creativity involves novelty. And these two processes can, in addition to imagination, provide non-truth-bound content. Beyond this, the present emphasis on cognitive manipulation highlights conscious, deliberate thought and its role in the creative process. But this too, as prior discussion suggests, is compatible with acknowledging the importance of insight and free association. Rarely does an artist or scientist gain a breakthrough by insight or free association without both some important antecedent and consequent cognitive work. Preparation must precede the breakthrough (here one might think of Picasso's preparatory sketches for *Guernica* or Kekulé's arduous research prior to his famous insight). And after the insight, the agent will explore and further consider the apparent breakthrough prior to committing to it (e.g., before putting brush back to canvas or articulating a decisive scientific thesis). In these cases, cognitive manipulation performed by the imagination is (part of) the rest of the story. It is important both before and after the insight. So while the present account does not fully explain these other putative aspects of creativity, it does provide some explanation for their importance and encourages a general account of the creative process, whereby it is broadly individuated in a way that may include a variety of non- truth-bound states and processes.

To conclude, imagination serves, and plausibly *best* serves, the cognitive manipulation role. According to the richer thesis offered in section 3, this role as it is typically found in

---

[34] For a naturalized explanation of incubation (or insight) in creativity, see Stokes 2007. For a metaphysics of creativity that treats creativity as a process, see Stokes 2008. For an empirically grounded process-model of creativity, see Finke et al. 1992, who see "creativity not as a single unitary process but as a product of many types of mental processes" (p. 2).

a creative process is typified by at least five features. Imagination—at least when broadly characterized as above—displays all of these features. Imagination is non-truth-bound, and this (partly) explains why it is generally under immediate voluntary control. Directly or indirectly, it engages with affective and motivational systems. And it is cognitively rigorous enough to drive inference and decision-making. Finally, even if it is not itself free associative, both mental activities are similarly non-truth-bound, such that imagination can interact with ideas generated by free association. Taken together, this provides a powerful explanation for what we may take to be an obvious truth: Imagination is important if not necessary for creative thought. This is true, it has been argued, for both the creativity of genius and everyday minimal creativity.

5. A Concluding Worry and a General Lesson

The analysis offered above, which attempts to provide reasons for the commonly assumed connection between creativity and imagination and, in turn, explain part of the creative process in terms of imagination, may evoke the following pair of worries. Simplifying the analysis and focusing just on truth-boundedness for the moment, the basic suggestion is that, given the novelty of creative thought, creative processes require (at least typically) non-truth-bound cognition. And so the first worry is that the explanation is one of novel cognition and not of creativity more broadly understood. Novel cognition, the worry would proceed, is a relatively mundane phenomenon. And what we thought we were getting was an explanation of something far more elusive, namely, creative cognition. The second worry builds on the first. The proposal is that imagination best serves the role of cognitive manipulation. And, again focusing just on non-truth-boundedness, it serves this role (at least in part) because it allows for the cognitive freedom that seems needed in even the most mundane of novel thought. But then we are saddled with the conclusion that imagination is needed for much of (if not all of) novel thought. Forming new beliefs and concepts, learning, and acquiring new skills are partly explained in terms of imaginative activity. And these commonplace mental acts, we might have expected, are simply not particularly imaginative.

These are not challenges to but instead virtues of the present account. Assuaging the first worry does require granting the claim that creativity, or at least a central component of it, is an everyday phenomenon. Human beings all have the capacity for frequent creative thought qua novel thought for what above was termed "minimal creativity." Once this is granted, the worry disappears with the following qualification. The above explanation does not attempt to explain all features of creativity. It attempts to explain a central one, novel creative thought (that appropriately depends upon agency), by appeal to imagination. And in addition to this, a number of features typical of creative processes—voluntariness, affect and motivation, and so on—fill out the cognitive manipulation role and further support the claim that imagination is deeply important, if not necessary, for creative thought and behavior. This does not, to be clear, explain all features or degrees of creativity. But it does explain some central features in a way that is broadly naturalistic and ripe for future research in philosophy and cognitive science.

What of the second worry, that on this account, the imagination is important for a remarkable variety of mental acts? This should be no problem. First, recall that imagination can vary significantly in richness. One can imagine an entire scenario in rich perceptible detail, or one can baldly imagine a proposition and mechanically run it through a process of inference. So while it may seem initially surprising that mundane cognitive acts like forming a belief or desire, acquiring a concept, or learning a simple skill may require imaginative activity, the proposal does not require rich imagination in its explanans: Some of these mundane acts of novel cognition presumably involve more bald imagination.

This is a point echoed in contemporary epistemology. On one standard line of reasoning, skeptical doubts are generated by considering possibilities that are incompatible with a proposition P believed (or under consideration for belief). From the first-person perspective, whether these skeptical possibilities are salient, and thus whether one recognizes a threat to one's certainty that P, depends upon imagination. Belief deliberation, formation, and maintenance, if they involve any of this kind of consideration, involve the cognitive manipulation that imagination offers us. Of course, the degree of imaginative engagement shifts with both the epistemic agent and the context: Given certain contexts, some epistemic agents let their imaginations rip (Lewis 1996). Given other contexts, the imaginings are fewer in number and narrower in scope. Some agents let their imaginations rip all the time; some aren't very imaginative, ever. Moreover, as mentioned above, imagination plausibly plays a central role in the formation of modal beliefs. Upon clearly imagining that P (perhaps above some threshold for clarity, consistency, completeness, etc.), one may well form the belief that *possibly P*, and oppositely upon the failure to (suitably) imagine that P. The point here is that we should be happy to accept that rational processes of belief formation and maintenance involve imagination.

The point generalizes; there is nothing particularly special about belief in this regard. Desires, intentions, and other propositional attitudes are often the result, in part, of imaginative activity. Cross-categorical concept application and skill acquisition require imagination—this was one of the morals of the empirical studies discussed in section 2. So one should not take the mundaneness of a mental state to be an indication that it did not require the use of imagination for its formation.[35]

To conclude, recognizing that imagination and creativity (of at least some limited richness) are commonplace does not strip them of their value. Nor is the claim

---

[35] Indeed, on one recent account, imagination is fundamental to all of cognition since it is fundamental for grasping meaning (McGinn 2004).

incompatible with what seem to be obvious facts: Some people are more imaginative than others, and some people are more creative than others. Instead, the analysis proposed here identifies connections between imagination and more minimal creativity. This is something that we can study without appeal to the romantic traditions that have so often thwarted good explanations of creativity; the analysis instead encourages explanations from contemporary philosophy and cognitive science. These attempts at explanation, one would hope, may ultimately contribute to explaining the presumed target of those romantic theories, namely, our most imaginative and creative minds. But the first step taken here has been to identify architectural features common to the minds of Bachs, Picassos, and (perhaps) more ordinary minds like yours and mine.

Acknowledgments

Thank you to Dom Lopes for feedback on a much earlier draft of this paper, and the editors of this volume for very helpful suggestions.

References

Alston, W. 1989. "The Deontological Conception of Epistemic Justification," in *Epistemic Justification* (Ithaca, NY: Cornell University Press).

Barsalou, L. W., and Prinz, J. 1997. "Mundane Creativity in Perceptual Symbol Systems," in T. Ward, S. Smith, and J. Vaid (eds.) *Creative Thought: An Investigation of Conceptual Structures and Processes* (Washington, DC: American Psychological Association).

Bennett, J. 1990. "Why Is Belief Involuntary?" *Analysis*, 50: pp. 87–107.

Bird, J., and Stokes, D. 2006. "Evolving Minimally Creative Robots," in S. Colton and A. Pease (eds.) *Proceedings of The Third Joint Workshop on Computational Creativity*, European Conference on Artificial Intelligence, pp. 1–5.

Boden, M. 2004. *The Creative Mind*, 2nd ed. (London: Routledge).

Borges, J. L. 1964. "Pierre Menard, Author of *Quixote*," in D.A. Yates, and J. E. Irby (eds.), *Labyrinths: Selected Stories and Writings* (New York: New Directions).

Buda, M., Fornito, A., Bergström, Z. M., and Simons, J. S. 2011. "A Specific Brain Structural Basis for Individual Differences in Reality Monitoring," *Journal of Neuroscience*, 31(40): pp. 14308–14313.

Cacciari, C., and Levorato, M. 1989. "How children understand idioms in discourse," *Journal of Child Language*, 16: pp. 387–405.

Cacciari, C., Levorato, M., and Cicogna, P. 1997. "Imagination at Work: Conceptual and Linguistic Creativity in Children," in T. Ward, S. Smith, and J. Vaid (eds.) *Creative Thought: An Investigation of Conceptual Structures and Processes* (Washington, DC: American Psychological Association).

Campbell, D. 1960. "Blind variation and selective retention in creative thoughts as in other knowledge processes," *Psychological Review*, 67: pp. 380–400.

———.1965. "Variation and selective retention in socio-cultural evolution," in H. Barringer, G. Blanksten, R. Mack (eds.) *Social Change in Developing Areas* (Cambridge, UK: Schenkman).

Campitelli, G., and Gobet, F. 2011. "Deliberate Practice: Necessary But Not Sufficient," *Current Directions in Psychological Science*, 20: pp. 280–285.

Carruthers, P. 2002. "Human Creativity: Its Cognitive Basis, its Evolution, and its Connections with Childhood Pretence," *British Journal for the Philosophy of Science*, 53: pp. 225–249.

Chalmers, D. 2002. "Does Conceivability Entail Possibility?" in T. Gendler and J. Hawthorne (eds.) *Conceivability and Possibility* (Oxford, UK: Oxford University Press).

Currie, G. 1990. *The Nature of Fiction* (Cambridge, UK: Cambridge University Press).

——. 1991. "Work and Text," *Mind*, 100: pp. 326–340.

——. 1995. "Imagination and Simulation: Aesthetics Meets Cognitive Science," in M. Davies and T. Stone (eds.) *Folk Psychology* (Oxford, UK: Blackwell).

——. 1996. "Simulation-theory, Theory-theory, and the Evidence from Autism," in P. Carruthers and S. Smith (eds.) *Theories of Theories of Mind* (Cambridge, UK: Cambridge University Press).

——. 1997. "The Paradox of Caring: Fiction and the Philosophy of Mind," in M. Hjort and S. Laver (eds.) *Emotion and the Arts* (Oxford, UK: Oxford University Press).

——. 2002. "Desire in Imagination," in T. Gendler and J. Hawthorne (eds.) *Conceivability and Possibility* (Oxford, UK: Oxford University Press).

Currie, G., and Ravenscroft, I. 2002. *Recreative Minds* (Oxford, UK: Oxford University Press).

Davies, D. 2004. *Art as Performance* (Oxford, UK: Blackwell).

De Sousa, R. 1987. *The Rationality of Emotion* (Cambridge, MA: MIT Press).

Doggett, T., and Egan, A. 2007. "Wanting things you don't want: The case for an imaginative analogue to desire," *Philosopher's Imprint*, 9: pp. 1–17.

Finke, R., Ward, T., and Smith, S. 1992. *Creative Cognition* (Cambridge, MA: MIT Press).

Funkhouser, E., and Spaulding, S. 2009. "Imagination and Other Scripts," *Philosophical Studies*, 143: pp. 291–314.

Gaut, B. 2009. "Creativity and Skill," in M. Krausz, D. Dutton, K. Bardsley (eds.) *The Idea of Creativity* (Leiden, NL: Brill).

——. 2003. "Creativity and Imagination," in B. Gaut and P. Livingston (eds.), *The Creation of Art* (Cambridge, UK: Cambridge University Press).

Gaut, B., and Livingston, P. 2003. "The Creation of Art: Issues and Perspectives," in B. Gaut and P. Livingston (eds.) *The Creation of Art* (Cambridge, UK: Cambridge University Press).

Gendler, T. 2000. "The Puzzle of Imaginative Resistance," *Journal of Philosophy*, 97: pp. 55–81.

——. 2003. "On the Relation Between Pretense and Belief," in D. Lopes and M. Kieran (eds.) *Imagination, Philosophy and the Arts* (London: Routledge).

——. 2006. "Imaginative Contagion," *Metaphilosophy*, 37: pp. 183–203.

——. 2011. "Imagination," in E. Zalta (ed.), *The Stanford Encyclopedia of Philosophy*, http://plato.stanford.edu/archives/fall2011/entries/imagination/.

Gendler, T. S., and K. Kovakovich. 2005. "Genuine Rational Fictional Emotions," in M. Kieran (ed.), *Contemporary Debates in Aesthetics and the Philosophy of Art* (Oxford, UK: Blackwell).

Gernsbacher, M. A., and Faust, M. 1991. "The mechanism of suppression: A component of general comprehension skill," *Journal of Experimental Psychology: Learning, Memory, and Cognition*, 17(2): pp. 245–262.

Gernsbacher, M. A., Varner, K. R., and Faust, M. 1990. "Investigating differences in general comprehension skill," *Journal of Experimental Psychology: Learning, Memory, and Cognition*, 16: pp. 430–445.

Gibbs, W. 1987. "Linguistic Factors in Children's Understanding of Idioms," *Journal of Child Language*, 14: pp. 569–586.

——. 1991. "Semantic Analyzability in Children's Understanding of Idioms," *Journal of Speech and Hearing Research*, 34: pp. 613–620.

——. 1994. *The Poetics of the Mind: Figurative Thought, Language, and Understanding* (Cambridge, UK: Cambridge University Press).

Goldman, A. 1989. "Interpretation psychologized," *Mind and Language*, 4: pp. 161–185.

——. 1992. "In defense of simulation theory," *Mind and Language*, 7: pp. 104–119.

Goodman, N., and Elgin, C. 1986. "Interpretation and Identity: Can the Work Survive the World?" *Critical Inquiry*, 12: pp. 567–574.

Gordon, R. 1986. "Folk psychology as simulation," *Mind and Language*, 1: pp. 158–170.

Hambrick, D., and Meinz, E. 2011. "Limits on the Predictive Power of Domain-Specific Experience and Knowledge in Skilled Performance," *Current Directions in Psychological Science*, 20: pp. 275–279.

Harris, P. 2000. *The Work of the Imagination* (Oxford, UK: Blackwell).

Kant, I. 1987(1790). *Critique of Judgment*, trans. W. S. Pluhar (Indianapolis, IN: Hackett).

Karmiloff-Smith, A. 1990. "Constraints on representational change," *Cognition*, 34: pp. 57–83.

——. 1992. *Beyond Modularity* (Cambridge, MA: MIT Press).

Kempler, D., Van Lancker, D., Marchman, V., and Bates, E. 1999. "Idiom comprehension in children and adults with unilateral brain damage," *Developmental Neuropsychology*, 15(3): pp. 327–349.

Kind, A. 2001. "Putting the Image Back in Imagination," *Philosophy and Phenomenological Research*, 62: pp. 85–109.

Kosslyn, S. 1994. *Image and Brain: The Resolution of the Imagery Debate* (Cambridge, MA: MIT Press).

Leslie, A. 1987. "Pretense and Representation: The Origins of 'Theory of Mind,' " *Psychological Review*, 94(4): pp. 412–426.

Levorato, M., Nesi, B., and Cacciari, C. 2004. "Reading comprehension and understanding idiomatic expressions: A developmental study," *Brain and Language*, 91: pp. 303–314.

Levorato, M., and Cacciari, C. 1992. "Children's Comprehension and Production of Idioms: The Role of Context and Familiarity," *Journal of Child Language*, 19: pp. 415–433.

——. 1995. "The Effects of Different Tasks on the Comprehension and Production of Idioms in Children," *Journal of Experimental Child Psychology*, 60: pp. 261–283.

——. 1999. "Idiom comprehension in children: Are the effects of semantic analyzability and context separable?" *European Journal of Cognitive Psychology*, 11: pp. 51–66.

——. 2002. "The creation of new figurative expressions: Psycholinguistic evidence on children, adolescents and adults," *Journal of Child Language*, 29: pp. 127–150.

Lewis, D. 1996. "Elusive Knowledge," *Australasian Journal of Philosophy*, 74: pp. 549–567.

Martindale, C. 1989. "Personality, Situation, and Creativity," in J. Glover, R. Ronning, and C. Reynolds (eds.) *Handbook of Creativity* (New York: Plenum).

——. 1995. "Creativity and Connectionism," in S. Smith, T. B. Ward, and R. Finke (eds.), *The Creative Cognition Approach* (Cambridge, MA: MIT Press).

——. 1999. "Biological bases of creativity," in R. Sternberg (ed.) *Handbook of creativity* (Cambridge, UK: Cambridge University Press).

McGinn, C. 2004. *Mindsight: Image, Dream, Meaning* (Cambridge, MA: Harvard University Press).

Meinz, E., and Hambrick, D. 2010. "Deliberate practice is necessary but not sufficient to explain individual differences in piano sight-reading skill: The role of working memory capacity," *Psychological Science*, 21: pp. 914–919.

Nichols, S. 2004. "Imagining and Believing: The Promise of a Single Code," *The Journal of Aesthetics and Art Criticism*, 62: pp. 129–139.

—— (ed.) 2006. *The Architecture of the Imagination: New Essays on Pretense, Possibility, and Fiction* (Oxford, UK: Oxford University Press).

Nichols, S., and Stich, S. 2000. "A Cognitive Theory of Pretence," *Cognition*, 74: pp. 115–147.

——. 2003. *Mindreading* (Oxford, UK: Oxford University Press).

Nippold, M. A., and Martin, S. T. 1989. "Idiom interpretation in isolation versus context. A developmental study with adolescents," *Journal of Speech and Hearing Research*, 32: pp. 59–66.

Nippold, M. A., and Rudzinski, M. 1993. "Familiarity and transparency in idiom explanations: A developmental study of children and adolescents," *Journal of Speech, Language and Hearing Research*, 36: pp. 728–737.

Novitz, D. 1999. "Creativity and Constraint," *Australasian Journal of Philosophy*, 77: pp. 67–82.

Oatley, K. 1992. *Best Laid Schemes: The Psychology of Emotions* (Cambridge, UK: Cambridge University Press).

Oatley, K., and Johnson-Laird, P. 1987. "Towards a cognitive theory of the emotions," *Cognition and Emotion*, 1: 29–50.

Polanyi, M. 1981. "The Creative Imagination," in D. Dutton and M. Krausz (eds.), *The Concept of Creativity in Science and Art* (Boston: Martinus Nijhoff).

Prinz, J., and Barsalou, L. 2002. "Acquisition and Productivity in Perceptual Symbol Systems: An Account of Mundane Creativity," in T. Dartnall (ed.), *Creativity, Cognition, and Knowledge* (Westport, CT: Praeger).

Reisberg, D., Culver, L., Heuer, F., and Fischman, D. 1986. "Visual Memory: When Imagery Vividness Makes a Difference," *Journal of Mental Imagery*, 10: pp. 51–74.

Searle, J. 1983. *Intentionality: An Essay in the Philosophy of Mind* (New York: Cambridge University Press).

Segal, S. 1970. "Imagery and Reality: Can they be Distinguished?" in W. Keup (ed.), *Origins and Mechanisms of Hallucinations* (New York: Plenum Press).

Simonton, D. 1999. *Origins of Genius* (Oxford, UK: Oxford University Press).

———. 2007. "The Creative Process in Picasso's Guernica Sketches: Monotonic Improvements versus Nonmonotonic Variants," *Creativity Research Journal*, 19: pp. 329–344.

Sternberg, R. (ed.) 1999. *Handbook of Creativity* (Cambridge, UK: Cambridge University Press).

Stokes, D. 2006. "The evaluative character of imaginative resistance," *The British Journal of Aesthetics*, 46: pp. 247–405.

———. 2007. "Incubated Cognition and Creativity," *Journal of Consciousness Studies*, 14: pp. 83–100.

———. 2008. "A Metaphysics of Creativity," in K. Stock and K. Thomson Jones (eds.), *New Waves in Aesthetics* (London: Palgrave Macmillan).

———. 2011. "Minimally creative thought," *Metaphilosophy*, 42: pp. 658–681.

Thornton, C. 2002. "Creativity and Runaway Learning," in T. Dartnall (ed.), *Creativity, Cognition and Knowledge* (Westport, CT: Praeger).

Tomita, Y. 1998. "The Sources of J. S. Bach's Well-Tempered Clavier II in Vienna, 1777–1801," *Bach*, 29/2: pp. 8–79.

———. 1996. "The Well-Tempered Clavier, Book 1," http://www.music.qub.ac.uk/~tomita/essay/wtc1.html.

Torreano, L., Cacciari, C., and Glucksberg, S. 2005. "When Dogs Can Fly: Level of Abstraction as a Cue to Metaphorical Use of Verbs," *Metaphor and Symbol*, 20: pp. 259–274.

Van Inwagen, P. 1998. "Modal Epistemology," *Philosophical Studies*, 92: pp. 67–84.

Van Lancker, D., and Kempler, D. 1987. "Comprehension of familiar phrases by left but not by right hemisphere damaged patients," *Brain and Language*, 32: pp. 265–277.

Velleman, D. 2000. *The Possibility of Practical Reason* (Oxford, UK: Oxford University Press).

Walton, K. 1990. *Mimesis as Make-Believe* (Cambridge, MA: Harvard University Press).

Ward, T. B. 1994. "Structured Imagination: The role of category structure in exemplar generation," *Cognitive Psychology*, 27: pp. 1–40.

———. 1995. "What's old about new ideas?" in S. M. Smith, T. B. Ward, and R. A. Finke (eds.), *The Creative Cognition Approach* (Cambridge, MA: MIT Press).

Weinberg, J., and Meskin, A. 2006. "Puzzling Over the Imagination: Philosophical Problems, Architectural Solutions," in S. Nichols (ed.), *The Architecture of the Imagination: New Essays on Pretense, Possibility, and Fiction* (Oxford, UK: Oxford University Press).

Weisberg, R. 1986. *Creativity: Genius and Other Myths* (New York: W. H. Freeman).

———. 1995. "Case studies of creative thinking: Reproduction versus restructuring in the real world," in S. M. Smith, T. B. Ward, and R. A. Finke (eds.), *The creative cognition approach* (Cambridge, MA: MIT Press), pp. 53–72.

———. 1999. "Creativity and Knowledge: A Challenge to Theories," in R. Sternberg (ed.), *Handbook of Creativity* (Cambridge, UK: Cambridge University Press).

———. 2004. "On structure in the creative process: A quantitative case-study of the creation of Picasso's Guernica," *Empirical Studies of the Arts*, 22: pp. 23–54.

Williams, B. 1973. "Deciding to Believe," in *The Problems of the Self* (Cambridge, UK: Cambridge University Press).

Yablo, S. 1993. "Is Conceivability a Guide to Possibility?" *Philosophy and Phenomenological Research*, 53: pp. 1–42.

9

Creativity and Consciousness

Evidence from Psychology Experiments

ROY F. BAUMEISTER, BRANDON J. SCHMEICHEL, AND C. NATHAN DEWALL

How should one understand the role of the conscious human mind of the artist in the creative process? Multiple possible views have been suggested. Probably the most influential and popular theoretical tradition has regarded creativity as something that occurs outside of consciousness so that, if anything, conscious thought and conscious selfhood have been regarded as impediments to creativity. Against that view, we shall argue that conscious thought plays an essential and constructive role in many creative processes.

We assume that the human mind contains multiple parts and processes, and these differ widely as to how conscious they are. Some functions and processes seem utterly and irrevocably outside of consciousness. Others are outside of consciousness but are potentially accessible to conscious attention. And others occur in the full spotlight of consciousness.

Creative work has been one of the highest and most inspiring accomplishments of the human race. Creativity in science and technology has contributed mightily to the progress of human culture and the general betterment of the human condition. Despite the benefits of creativity, the creative process remains somewhat mysterious. Our goal is to spell out and conduct experimental tests of different ideas about whether consciousness plays any sort of role to help or hinder the creative process.

1. Four Standard Theories

The idea that conscious thought is irrelevant if not inimical to the creative process has a long tradition behind it. In Western intellectual and artistic history, the idea that creative inspirations originated with external, supernatural beings (such as a muse) was reiterated in many places for centuries. Most likely it was meant metaphorically in many cases rather than literally. Even so, the usage of a muse as a metaphor still signified that the conscious self of the artist was not the source of the creative work but rather received it as a gift.

More recent versions invoking the irrelevance of conscious thought have tended to emphasize the unconscious mind as the wellspring of creativity. Freudian thought was one of the most influential movements of 20th-century intellectual history, and it regarded creativity as stemming from unconscious processes (e.g., Russ 1993, Freud 1916). Indeed, Freud proposed that creative success may depend on deep unconscious processes and even defense mechanisms such as sublimation that redirect the energy of the basic instincts (geared toward aggression and sexuality, in his theory) into the relatively harmless, socially approved forms of creative work. Philosophers such as Dennett (2003) have depicted the conscious mind as irrelevant to the creative process, emphasizing unconscious processes instead, albeit not the same ones proposed by Freud. Creative artists themselves (see discussion by Wegner 2002) have often embraced the view that the conscious mind gets in the way of the creative process and that creativity flourishes when unconscious processes are permitted to flow and blossom undisturbed by conscious interference. The perennial popularity of alcohol and drugs among creative artists can be considered a means of clearing away the structures of conscious selfhood (see Baumeister 1991) to allow freer play to the creative unconscious. Some artistic movements, such as Surrealism, involved explicit efforts to diminish conscious guidance and let the unconscious run free in the hope of maximizing creativity. Indeed, some Surrealists tried to enter trance states prior to writing or painting, on the assumption that trances would improve their creativity by getting rid of consciousness and letting the unconscious operate unfettered (e.g., Breton 1969).

Although the view that conscious thought is irrelevant or detrimental to creativity has been dominant, other views have been asserted. Pressing (1988) articulated a severely contrary view that emphasized conscious processes and free will as the essential core of creativity. In this view, conscious, deliberate choices are what create something new. Relatively few theorists embrace the view that creativity is purely or exclusively conscious, but it is a useful counterpoint to the reigning view that creativity is purely unconscious. One supportive observation is that, of all the species on the planet, creative art is mainly found among humans, who are also presumably more conscious or conscious in a more advanced way than other species. If consciousness were an impediment to creativity, humankind should seemingly be the least creative species.

Two alternative, intermediate theories could also be proposed, and these have influenced our work. One is that conscious and unconscious processes play separate but complementary roles. Creative inspirations may emerge from unconscious processes, but it is only by virtue of conscious thought that they are fashioned into a creative product. Morsella (2005) proposed that consciousness evolved to resolve conflicts between competing impulses or responses as to how muscles should move bones. Applied to creativity, one could suggest that automatic, unconscious processes might generate an assortment of possible options, but consciousness is necessary to choose among them. For example, a composer in the middle of a piece might think of several possible alternatives for how to fashion the next few measures, and only by virtue of conscious thought would he select one to be written and played instead of the other possibilities. We concur with Morsella.

The last theory is that external cues activate internal, unconscious processes that automatically produce creative results. This view is based on the auto-motive theory by Bargh (1990). It differs from the Freudian sorts of theories in that it does not assert that unconscious contents are essential to creativity. Rather, the unconscious has motivations and processes, but these are set in motion chiefly by external cues that activate them. Thus some event or stimulus in the situation can activate the motivation to be creative. Conscious processing could be one means by which these cues enter the mind, though in some cases, cues could enter unnoticed by conscious attention. Indeed, a growing body of evidence has suggested that conscious and unconscious processes are equally viable as means to activate the unconscious processes that do the bulk of the mind's work (e.g., Bargh, Gollwitzer, Lee-Chai, Barndollar, and Troetschl 2001; Chartrand and Bargh 1996; Shah 2005). This view offers one potential role for consciousness, as a conduit by which the initial cue enters into the mind to set in motion the unconscious processes that do the rest of the work to produce the creative product. We suspect that this view is also correct. However, this role would be nonessential, insofar as the cue could enter the mind by unconscious processes, in which case, some theorists might conclude that the entire creative process could occur without conscious help or input. We are less sympathetic to that implication, and our experimental results (see next section) will indicate why. Still, we do agree that consciousness is an important and potent means by which important ideas enter the mind (Baumeister and Masicampo 2010).

2. Experimenting on Creativity

Our approach has been to use controlled laboratory experiments to test these competing theories (see Baumeister, Schmeichel, DeWall, and Vohs 2007). We have used standard procedures to investigate conscious and unconscious processes. The logic of experimental design in psychology emphasizes the importance of randomly assigning research subjects to different treatment conditions. Random assignment is needed in order to average out all the differences that occur among people. This permits one to assume that the different treatment groups start out roughly equal on all relevant factors. The only difference among them is therefore the treatment itself. The experimental design permits causal conclusions.

In two of the studies we conducted, the treatment groups were further equalized by having each research participant do every treatment condition. In this case, we randomized the sequence, so some people did condition A first while others did condition B first. That would prevent effects of accumulated practice from biasing the results.

In general, the so-called cognitive load procedure has been the most popular way of manipulating conscious thought. It is based on the assumption that the conscious mind can only do one thing at a time (see, e.g., Lieberman, Gaunt, Gilbert, and Trope 2002). Therefore, researchers try to keep it preoccupied so it cannot intrude on what is being measured. One common method is to require the person to remember a phone number, which for most people entails having to keep mentally repeating the sequence of digits. We have used variations on this, such as having people count backward by six or seven or listen to music and keep a tally of how often a particular word appears in the lyrics. People can perform many other tasks while under such a cognitive load, but their performance sometimes changes, and these changes are assumed to reflect the unavailability of conscious attention.

3. The Guitar Experiment

The first experiment we conducted on the role of consciousness in creativity used musical improvisation. One of the authors is an amateur jazz musician. One evening he was playing his guitar in his usual fashion, which is to say that he had recorded chord accompaniments that could be replayed electronically while he would improvise a melody across them (live). On a lark, he thought to try improvising under cognitive load, and so he counted backwards by seven from 1,000 while playing. He found he was able to continue playing effectively in some ways, such as by producing a steady stream of notes, keeping up with the beat, and playing notes that were correct. However, he sensed that his creativity had suffered. His wife, who appreciates his music despite being somewhat tone-deaf, came out from the other room to comment on the difference. He tried harder to be creative while continuing the counting exercise, but noticed that his strategy amounted to something like cheating: He would count a couple numbers, then turn attention to his playing, then back to the counting. It seemed that he could not produce a creative solo while performing the load task correctly.

After discussing this with colleagues, we set out to do a systematic experiment along these lines. We recruited relatively accomplished musicians: They were all graduate students in the music program at Florida State University. We recruited only those who specialized in guitar. We prepared recorded accompaniments and asked them to jam along by improvising a solo across these chords. They got to practice on one accompaniment and then did a new one with each treatment condition. In essence, they were improvising a melody while hearing the song for the first time. For experienced musicians, this is somewhat challenging but entirely possible, as long as the chord sequence is predictable enough, so that after they have heard one verse, they know what is coming.

For those unfamiliar with jazz and music theory, let us provide a quick introduction to the task. Essentially all the music one hears in the modern Western world uses the basic set of 12 different notes. These same notes are repeated over and over up and down the piano keyboard: These are simply higher and lower versions of the same notes. A musical key is a subset of those notes, usually just seven of them. While in a key, only those seven notes are appropriate for use, and the others will sound wrong to various degrees, though a couple of them may be sneaked in occasionally for dramatic effect. To illustrate, beginning musicians learn to play scales, which are sets of eight notes, and the first and last are the same note, just at different levels. Chords are combinations of notes, typically three or more.

A typical musical piece has three components. First, it has a rhythm or beat, which sets the speed and is usually, though not always, organized in groups of four. If you tap your feet to any song on the radio, you will usually get the groups of four beats. Second, it has a melody, which is what the lead instrument or singer will render. If you hum along to the radio, you are usually humming the melody. Last, there are sets of chords, which form the backdrop of the music. If you subtract the melody and the drums, the rest of the band is typically playing chords. Each verse plays the same sequence of chords.

In blues, jazz, and other music involving improvisation, the usual practice is as follows. The beat starts right away and stays about the same. The song starts (possibly after a warm-up measure or two of introduction) with the band playing the melody and the chords together. After this, the band plays the same sequence of chords over and over but abandons the melody, and instead, the musicians take turns improvising new melodies called solos. Their improvising is constrained by the chords. As we said, the chords determine what the key is and which notes will sound good, better, and best—and which ones will sound horribly wrong.

Improvising is thus a bit like quickly crossing a fast-moving stream by jumping from stone to stone. There may be multiple pathways, so one has to keep choosing which stone to jump toward. Different stones may work equally well, but you want to end in one of the same places, and there are certainly many wrong possible steps that will get your feet soaked.

We did not tell our musicians what the chords were. Also, to trip them up, we slipped in a change of key in the middle of each piece. Accomplished musicians can typically handle this, because even without knowing exactly what happened, they can somehow sense that something is different, and the set of seven notes they have been using has to be revised somewhat when a particular chord entails a change of key. We wanted to see how much of this, if any, depended on conscious processing. They were hearing the song for the first time while they jammed to it, so there was no chance to practice, rehearse, or memorize.

There were three conditions in our experiment. Each musician did one solo in each condition. We scrambled the order randomly, in case people got better at our tasks with practice. In the pure control condition, we had the musician simply play a solo. In the low-load condition, we had them count forward aloud by one starting with 15 while they were improvising a solo. And in the high-load condition, we had them play the solo while counting backward aloud by six from 913. (Counting backward by seven proved to be too difficult for our sample of musicians.)

All solos were recorded, and we had two reasonably accomplished musicians listen to them and rate them on various measures. The judges did not know which solo was done in which condition (i.e., counting forward or backward or not counting) to ensure that everything was fair and impartial.

When we added everything up, we found evidence that creativity depends on consciousness. The solos that had been improvised under high cognitive load (counting backward by six) were rated significantly worse than the solos produced in either of the other conditions. Creative quality was about the same in the other two (i.e., counting forward or not counting). Thus it is not the act of counting that is the problem; it is the consciousness-consuming task of counting backward by six. Most adults can count forward by one rather automatically, which is to say without paying much attention to what they are doing, and so it did not interfere with creative musical improvisation.

Counting backward did not ruin everything. Au contraire, the musicians were remarkably adept at performing despite the counting. The musicians kept the beat flawlessly. They also stayed on key quite well, playing from among the seven correct notes and avoiding the other wrong-sounding ones (impressive, considering that they were hearing the piece for the first time while playing it). They even navigated the surprise key change quite effectively, deftly exchanging their set of seven notes for a slightly different set when the chords dictated doing so. (Essentially, this involves rearranging the mental pattern one projects onto the neck of the guitar that indicates which places are good and which, like a misstep in crossing the stream, are to be avoided.) In order to do that, it was necessary to perform a fairly complex set of mental operations: The musician had to hear the incoming chords, notice that one of the chords did not fit in the same key as the previous chords, deduce that he[1] had to change the set of notes from which to draw during his solo, and select a new set of notes to use while continuing his solo. And yet they all did this while counting backward by six. This suggests that all these cognitive operations can be performed with little or no help from the conscious mind.

Our findings thus testify to the impressive capacities of the automatic, unconscious mind. Yet they also showed that consciousness was vital for creativity. When

---

[1] All participants in this study were male. Indeed, the large gender asymmetry in jazz and musical composition has been a puzzling challenge to theories about gender and creativity; see Baumeister, 2010.

their conscious minds were hampered and preoccupied by a mental arithmetic task, the musicians continued to do most things well—but the quality of their creative improvisation was a conspicuous exception, in that it alone seemed to suffer.

Several additional observations are instructive. First, the results did not seem to be due to any sort of self-fulfilling prophecy. If anything, the musicians themselves tended to subscribe to the theory that consciousness gets in the way. Several of them expressed surprise and dismay afterward, saying they had expected to do even better when counting backward because the conscious ego would be out of the way and the creative unconscious would be able to operate unfettered. They noticed that they had done worse, but it was not what they had expected.

Second, our results, though statistically significant, probably understated the size of the true effect. The experimenter noticed that several participants attempted to cope with the dual task in the same way that the first author had done in his living room when the idea for this procedure first occurred to him. That is, a couple musicians were observed to say several numbers rapidly, then play a string of notes, then revert back to counting. This allowed them to be somewhat more creative, but with respect to the hypothesis, it was cheating because they effectively stole some conscious attention away from the number task to invest it in the music. All of this provides further evidence that one cannot really do mental arithmetic and improvise creatively at the same time. Creative work apparently needs the conscious mind.

In terms of music, then, our results suggest that rhythm is unconscious whereas melody is conscious. Participants were able to keep the beat effectively, regardless of cognitive load.[2] This meshes with everyday intuition: Someone might well tap her foot to a beat without even realizing she is doing so and still keep perfect time. To create a new melody, however—for that is what improvisation does—full conscious awareness is needed, and a cognitive load is ruinous.

What were the melodies like when improvised while counting backward? They were certainly far from random notes. Our impression is that they tended toward repetition and simple, stilted phrases. The unconscious tends to operate in established patterns. It thrives on habit and doing familiar things again and again. It may generate multiple ideas, including creative ones, but it does not seem to have any basis for preferring the creative ones over staying with tried-and-true ones. This argument can thus be made consistent with the view that creative ideas originate in the unconscious. When the conscious mind is preoccupied with mental arithmetic, the unconscious can still generate some possible melody lines, and the body can play them effectively. What is lacking is the tendency to stop oneself from falling into a rut and playing a similar kind of phrase or sequence over and over ad nauseam.

---

[2] Humming, whistling, singing, or perhaps playing a well-rehearsed and memorized melody may also be unconscious, of course. When we say that melody is conscious, we refer specifically to the genesis of melody. Consciousness may also be required to learn a melody, but that is another issue.

One might extend these findings further and suggest that part of the contribution of the conscious mind to the creative process is its keen ability to get bored. Boredom may be a conscious feeling, something largely alien to the unconscious. The unconscious would therefore be more or less immune to boredom, and so it is content to find a good phrase or pattern and keep working at it. The unconscious genesis of creative ideas is perhaps less a passionate quest for novelty than simply finding a viable solution to a problem. Once it has a solution, in the sense of a way to play some eligible notes, it has no urge to swap it out for another, different solution and then another and another. Only with full conscious awareness does the mind reject repetition and continue to exchange different patterns until a fully, pleasingly creative result is obtained.

4. The Picture Drawing Experiment

One is rarely confident about drawing strong conclusions from a single experiment. We did not want to put much faith in what we had learned from the guitar study, at least not until we could check whether similar conclusions would emerge from another experiment with different procedures.

Our next experiment therefore sought to get the same result as the guitar study but with as many changes as we could manage. Instead of using a selected population of near experts, we used a general sample of college students. Instead of an all-male sample, we used a mostly female sample. Instead of improvising music, the creative task was to draw a picture. Instead of counting backward, the cognitive load was created by a listening vigilance task.

In this experiment, each participant donned headphones and listened to music while drawing two pictures. For one of the songs, the participant had to count how many times the word "time" occurred in the lyrics. For the other song, there was no instruction, and the participant just heard it play while drawing. The songs ("Time Zone" and "48 Hours," both by the rock band Negativland) were complex and cacophonous, with multiple levels of vocals, so it was necessary to pay rather close attention in order to keep track of how often the word "time" was sung. We randomly assigned the sequence, so some people did the counting task first and others did it second. To make sure people were focusing on the lyrics as instructed, we had them report their tallies. We had decided in advance to omit the data from anyone whose count was way off, as that would indicate failing to attend to the cognitive load task and hence possibly devoting conscious attention to the drawing task. Fortunately, nobody furnished a tally that fell outside the target area. Apparently, everyone paid attention as instructed.

The two drawing tasks involved using colored pencils on paper. For each drawing, four required elements were presented (i.e., house, car, person, and tree for one;

building, flower, airplane, and face for the other). The participant could draw these in any manner he or she wished, and with any other images he or she wanted, as long as these four were all included. They were told to stop when the song ended and that the song would last about five minutes. In between the two drawing tasks, participants took a brief break and filled out a mood report scale.

As usual, we collected the drawings and had them rated by judges who did not know what treatment condition had produced them, or even what the experiment was about. Then we matched the ratings up with the pictures and ran statistical analyses to find out how pictures produced under the different experimental conditions stacked up.

Once again, the results suggested the value of conscious attention for creativity. The pictures drawn while attending to and counting the song lyrics were rated as less creative than the ones drawn while merely listening to background music. In additional ratings, they were also rated as less unique and were liked less by the judges than the pictures drawn by people who could focus their entire conscious minds on the task, without having to count song lyrics.

In this study, we also had participants rate their own pictures at the end of the study. They largely agreed with the judges. They rated their drawings made under cognitive load as less creative than their other drawings.

Moreover, and also parallel to the guitar study, we found that preoccupying the conscious mind did not simply degrade everything. Pictures were rated for coherence, but there was no difference. The mood ratings showed no difference, so it was not that drawing with cognitive load produced some boost in positive or negative emotion.

We also recruited two more judges who went through all the different pictures and laboriously counted how many different colors had been used in each one. We did this because it seemed possible to us that the cognitive load had made people not bother to use as many different colors, and we thought perhaps using fewer colors would explain the creativity difference. But it did not. Subjects in both conditions used an average of about seven out of 18 different colors. Also, there was no correlation between number of colors and creativity rating. In this sample, at least, more creative did not mean more colorful.

When studies with very different procedures converge on the same conclusion, confidence in that conclusion is increased—indeed, increased considerably more than if two studies with identical procedures yielded the same result. In social science research, one can never be sure whether a particular result might derive in some peculiar way from the particular method or sample. The odds of such peculiar effects leading to the same conclusion from different methods are quite long, however.

Hence these findings greatly encouraged us to conclude that consciousness plays an important role in creativity. In both picture drawing and musical improvisation, creativity suffered when the conscious mind was preoccupied.

5. The Popcorn Story Title Experiment

The first two studies showed that creativity suffered when consciousness was pre-empted. We turned next to exploring whether we could increase creativity rather than decrease it. For this, we used two different pathways. One relied on conscious processing, and the other relied on unconscious processing. The latter allowed us to test the auto-motive theory (see above), which suggests that external cues are sufficient to activate creative motivations and increase creativity. Also, for this one, we did not do anything to encumber either conscious or unconscious processes during the task.

The task for this experiment involved formulating possible titles for a brief short story. The story (adapted by Eisenberger and Rhoades 2001, from Seyba 1984) was one paragraph long and told in the second person. It invites the reader to imagine being a kernel of popcorn in a frying pan amid a cluster of other kernels. The heat increases, the reader hears the popping, and then undergoes the exhilarating trans-formation of popping. Soon the heat and noise subside.

Each participant was instructed to write a title for the story. To engage the moti-vation to be creative, we used two different methods. Each participant underwent one of those or was in the control condition that had no manipulation other than reading the story and writing the titles.

The instructions for the control condition read: "On the lines below, try to come up with five titles for the short story." In the conscious motive condition, the word "creative" was inserted before the word "titles." That one word change was the entirety of the manipulation. It cannot be much more subtle than that. Still, we assumed that inserting that word would be sufficient to convey the conscious understanding that the person was expected to try extra hard to be creative in doing the task.

The unconscious goal condition was necessarily more elaborate. For this, we added a separate procedure prior to reading the story. Every subject did this, includ-ing in the control condition, but a subtle change accomplished the manipulation. The procedure was based on prior research that has sought to activate motivations unconsciously (e.g., Srull and Wyer 1979, Chartrand and Bargh 1996). Each person is given a series of 15 groups of four words, and the assignment is to cross out one word from each group and make a phrase with the remaining three words. Some of the clusters of words are designed to contain words that activate the idea and motivation desired by the researcher. Although the task is done consciously, people generally do not realize that the words are actually activating some motivation, and so this is considered an effective way to manipulate unconscious strivings.

In the present study, some subjects received sets of word puzzles that contained words relating to creativity (e.g., "boating your imagination use" or "originality near is cool"). Eight of the 15 word groups contained a word or phrase designed to invoke the idea of creativity. Meanwhile, participants in the other two conditions received sets of words that did not have any particular theme and none that invoked creativity (e.g., "he dishes the wash" and "mice pencil like cats"). Subjects did not rate the task as easier or more difficult in either condition. More important, nobody detected any theme running through the word-unscrambling task.

Titles were rated for creativity. As usual, this was done by judges who did not know which person or what condition was associated with each title. We got plenty of titles. Some were rather clever and creative, such as "PANdemonium," "Popcorn Puberty," and "A-pop-calypse." Others were quite mundane, such as "Popcorn Kernels."

When we matched up the titles with the conditions, we found that the conscious instruction to be creative had indeed significantly increased creativity. Thus, engaging the conscious mind, even by merely changing one word in the task instruction, was effective at raising the level of creative output.

In contrast, the manipulation designed to activate the unconscious motivation to be creative had no effect. Subjects who had unscrambled phrases that referred to creativity were no more creative than other subjects. Even though they had received eight separate cues for creativity, the manipulation failed to raise creativity, in contrast to the single word delivered with conscious instruction.

To be fair, one might wonder whether the unconscious priming manipulation had simply failed to have any effect. We had used procedures quite similar to what had successfully produced changes in behavior in previous studies, so there was reason to think we were doing what was appropriate for activating unconscious motivations. Still, it is hard to draw conclusions from null results. Maybe our experimenters had somehow failed to get the unconscious cues to function. Maybe our subject population was somehow lower than others in their unconscious receptivity to creativity cues.

To address this problem, we ran an additional experiment. It started off with the same unconscious priming task we had used—exactly the same, including the same eight groups of words containing a creativity cue in one condition and not in the other. After this, however, we tested everyone to see whether the idea of creativity was active in his or her mind. This was done (again using standard procedures) by having people fill in the blanks to make new words. We gave people a list of word fragments to be completed with either creative or noncreative words. For example, _ _ _ ENT could be completed to read "invent" (creative) or "repent" (not creative). If the idea of creativity is prominent in someone's mind, then that person is likely to complete more fragments with the words referring to creativity. We were careful to ensure that none of the words used in this task were the same words used in the phrase-making task.

Sure enough, the phrase-making task had in fact activated the idea of creativity. People who had done the phrase-making task with groups of words that invoked creativity later made more word completions that referred to creativity, as compared to people who had done the phrase-making task with neutral words.

Thus the phrase-making task was effective at activating the idea of creativity. But this was not enough to increase the creativity of their performance. Only the conscious instruction to try to be creative accomplished that.

6. Summary and Conclusions

We began by noting four different possible theories about the possible role of consciousness in the creative process. The results of several experiments have contradicted two of the theories and seem most compatible with one of the others.

Our findings showed repeatedly that consciousness plays a vital role in creativity. This contradicts the view—which we have depicted as the dominant, preferred one among a wide swath of psychologists, artists, and other thinkers—that consciousness is irrelevant or even an impediment to creativity. We noted that many guitarists in our first study remarked that they had expected creativity to improve when their conscious minds were preoccupied, and they were surprised to find the opposite. Both the guitar and the picture drawing study yielded clear evidence that preoccupying the conscious mind with an irrelevant task led to reductions in creativity, noticeable to both the creative artists themselves and to third-person judges who knew nothing of the procedures or hypotheses and simply made ratings of the various drawings and musical recordings on a case-by-case basis.

Taking consciousness elsewhere detracted from creativity. Conversely, engaging the conscious mind with a deliberate, explicit, conscious goal to be creative led to improvements in creativity. In the popcorn story title study, changing just one word in the instructions was sufficient to increase creativity. Apparently, having the conscious goal of being creative is helpful to creativity.

Meanwhile, activating an unconscious goal of creativity was not sufficient to increase creativity. In the popcorn story title study, some participants received eight separate cues to activate the idea of creativity unconsciously. Our follow-up study showed that this procedure was indeed effective at activating the idea of creativity. But it did *not* make people more creative. Indeed, eight separate words aimed at the unconscious were less effective than a single word directed toward the conscious mind.

Hence the present results also speak against explaining creativity with an extension of Bargh's (1990) auto-motive model. We hasten to add that these results do not reflect negatively on his model in general. In fact, ample research has supported it in many contexts. Subtle cues do activate unconscious motivations and thereby influence many behaviors. Our studies revealed that creativity is apparently not one of them, though some recent evidence using different methods found that subliminal cues may increase creativity among individuals who are chronically motivated to be creative (see Fitzsimons, Chartrand, and Fitzsimons 2008).

How about the other two theories? We noted one view holding that creativity is essentially or exclusively a conscious process. Our results fall far short of being able to support any such extreme claim. Indeed, a recent literature review examining all manner of effects of conscious processes on behavior concluded that consciousness does have plenty of behavioral consequences—but these are mostly indirect, and seemingly all operate in complementary cooperation with unconscious processes (Baumeister, Masicampo, and Vohs 2011). It went so far as to conclude that it seems likely that almost all human behaviors emerge from a combination of conscious and unconscious processes.

The present results seem most compatible with that integrative view. We do not dispute the insight that may have motivated the reigning view, which is that creative inspirations and ideas may all originate outside of consciousness. Our point is only that conscious processes are powerfully helpful, and very possibly indispensable, for the fulfillment of the creative process.

Our best guess is therefore that creative ideas do indeed originate in the unconscious mind. Indeed, multiple ones may be generated at each choice point. The unconscious is not a single, unified process but rather a welter of separate, independent processes. A creative artist may be aware of an assortment of options for what to do next at each point in composing a work. Consciousness is needed to select among them, integrate the best ones, and thereby fashion a coherent, pleasing, novel product.

This view fits recently emerging theories of consciousness. The idea that consciousness is required to resolve disputes is central to the analysis by Morsella (2005). He also noted that almost all recent theorists have asserted that one function of consciousness is to integrate assorted information (what he calls the "integration consensus"). Baars (2002) and others have pointed out that the unconscious can effectively process single words but consciousness is apparently needed to process incoming groups of words, including sentences and paragraphs. These observations and others led Baumeister and Masicampo (2010) to speak of "consciousness as the place where the unconscious mind constructs meaningful sequences of thought."

In that view, the contents of the conscious mind are all the products of unconscious processes—yet they accomplish something that the unconscious alone could not accomplish. Complex ideas and integrative thoughts can best (and perhaps only) be assembled in the conscious mind.

The view of conscious and unconscious as separate, competing processes that do similar things has dominated psychology in recent decades. Our sense is that that is slowly being replaced with an understanding that conscious and unconscious do different things and complement each other. The old view would look at each task and wonder whether it was done consciously or unconsciously. The new view instead assumes that every complex task emerges as a mixture of both kinds of processes. Our work suggests that creativity should be regarded as an instructive example of that kind of cooperation. The unconscious generates the pieces, but consciousness puts them together into a creative product.

References

Baars, B. J. 2002. The conscious access hypothesis: Origins and recent evidence. *Trends in Cognitive Science*, 6, pp. 47–52.

Bargh, J. A. 1990. "Auto-motives: Preconscious determinants of social interaction," in E. T. Higgins and R. M. Sorrentino, eds., *Handbook of motivation and cognition* (vol. 2, pp. 93–130). New York: Guilford.

Bargh, J. A., P. M. Gollwitzer, A. Y. Lee-Chai, K. Barndollar, and R. Troetschel. 2001. "The automated will: Nonconscious activation and pursuit of behavioral goals." *Journal of Personality and Social Psychology*, 81, pp. 1014–1027.

Baumeister, R. F. 2010. *Is there anything good about men? How cultures flourish by exploiting men*. New York: Oxford University Press.

Baumeister, R. F., and E. J. Masicampo. 2010. "Conscious thought is for facilitating social and cultural interactions: How mental simulations serve the animal-culture interface." *Psychological Review*, 117, pp. 945–971.

Baumeister, R. F., E. J. Masicampo, and K. D. Vohs. 2011. "Do conscious thoughts cause behavior?" *Annual Review of Psychology*, 62, pp. 331–361.

Baumeister, R. F., B. J. Schmeichel, C. N. DeWall, and K. D. Vohs. 2007. "Is the conscious self a help, a hindrance, or an irrelevance to the creative process?" *Advances in psychology research*, 53, pp. 137–152.

Breton, A. 1969. *Manifestoes of Surrealism* (R. Seaverand and H. Lane, trans.). Ann Arbor, MI: University of Michigan Press.

Chartrand, T. L., and J. A. Bargh. 1996. "Automatic activation of impression formation and memorization goals: Nonconscious goal priming reproduces effects of explicit task instructions." *Journal of Personality and Social Psychology*, 71, pp. 464–478.

Dennett, D. 2003. *Freedom evolves*. New York: Viking.

Eisenberger, R., and L. Rhoades. 2001. "Incremental effects of reward on creativity." *Journal of Personality and Social Psychology*, 81, pp. 728–741.

Fitzsimons, G. M., T. L. Chartrand, and G. J. Fitzsimons. 2008. "Automatic effects of brand exposure on motivated behavior: How Apple makes you 'think different.'" *Journal of Consumer Research*, 35, pp. 21–35.

Freud, S. 1916. *Leonardo da Vince: A psychosexual study of an infantile reminiscence* (A. Brill, trans.). New York: Moffat, Yard.

Lieberman, M. D., R. Gaunt, D. T. Gilbert, and Y. Trope. 2002. "Reflection and reflexion: A social cognitive neuroscience approach to attributional inference." *Advances in Experimental Social Psychology*, 34, pp. 199–249.

Morsella, E. 2005. "The function of phenomenal states: Supramodular interaction theory." *Psychological Review*, 112, pp. 1000–1021.

Pressing, J. 1988. "Improvisation: Methods and models," in J. Sloboda, ed., *Generative processes in music: The psychology of performance, improvisation, and composition* (pp. 129–178). New York: Oxford University Press.

Russ, S. 1993. *Affect and creativity*. New York: Erlbaum.

Seyba, M. E. 1984. *Imaging: A different way of thinking*. Hawthorne, NJ: Educational Impressions.

Shah, J. 2005. "The automatic pursuit and management of goals." *Current Directions in Psychological Science*, 14, pp. 10–13.

Srull, T. K., and R. S. Wyer Jr. 1979. "The role of category accessibility in the interpretation of information about persons: Some determinants and implications. *Journal of Personality and Social Psychology*, 37, pp. 1660–1672.

Wegner, D. 2002. *Illusion of conscious will*. Cambridge, MA: MIT Press.

10

The Origins of Creativity

ELIZABETH PICCIUTO AND PETER CARRUTHERS

1. Introduction

The goal of this chapter is to provide an integrated evolutionary and developmental account of the emergence of distinctively-human creative capacities. Our main thesis is that childhood pretend play is a uniquely human adaptation that functions in part to enhance adult forms of creativity. We review evidence that is consistent with such an account, and contrast our proposal favorably with a number of alternatives.

Most theorists assume that creativity requires ideas, behavior, or products that are both novel and valuable. Thus construed, creativity appears to be uniquely human. Indeed, it seems to be fairly rare even among humans. Given that no animals and not all humans exhibit this kind of creativity, it can seem mysterious how the capacity for creativity might have evolved, and how it might emerge in the course of childhood development. However, Boden (2004) draws an important distinction between *historical* creativity (when the novelty is relative to an entire society or historical tradition) and *psychological* creativity (when the novelty is relative to a single individual). While historical creativity is rare, psychological creativity is quite widespread and is perhaps a trait that almost all human adults possess to a significant degree.

We suggest that psychological creativity can be subdivided still further, by relativizing the value component also to a single individual. The result is a distinction between what might be called "agent-relative" and "agent-neutral" forms of psychological creativity. Agent-neutral creativity is novelty of ideas, behavior, or products that are valuable in an objective or communally agreed-upon sense while not rising to the level of historical creativity. Agent-relative creativity, in contrast, would be an idea, behavior, or product that is both novel and valuable from the perspective of the agent alone. The concept of agent-relative creativity is theoretically fruitful, we suggest, in enabling us to see at least a form of creativity displayed in the behavior of some non-human animals. This can help us to see how agent-neutral and historical kinds of creativity might evolve.

It is fair to say that most of the interest in creativity on the part of philosophers has been directed toward its historical form, for, of course, we care especially about the sorts of creativity that result in great art, literature, and science. Even cognitive scientists have for the most part been interested in the factors that can transform mundane (and presumably pan-human) forms of psychological creativity into historical creativity. Hence they have focused on the extensive knowledge of historically creative people, together with the motivations, personalities, and institutional frameworks that encourage such people to flourish. However, even psychological creativity (in its agent-neutral form) is arguably uniquely human (with perhaps a few isolated exceptions that we will note in due course). Focusing on agent-relative forms of psychological creativity may enable us to see what makes it possible for historical creativity to emerge, in both phylogeny and development. Not only is this a topic worthy of interest in its own right, but it may help us to understand the components and characteristics of uniquely human forms of psychological creativity (which in turn, of course, make historical creativity possible).

Our discussion is organized around one widely accepted account of the structure of psychological creativity. This is the so-called Geneplore (for "generate and explore") model of creative cognition (Finke et al. 1992, Finke 1995, Ward et al. 1999). On this account, most instances of creativity can be divided into two main phases: a generative phase, in which novel ideas or hypotheses are created and entertained, and an exploratory phase, in which those ideas or hypotheses are explored, evaluated, and/or implemented. (Arguably, these two phases collapse into one another in connection with some in-the-moment forms of creativity such as jazz or dance improvisation, or in swift, witty conversation when it seems that novel actions are undertaken immediately, coincident with the activation of the corresponding motor plans, without prior rehearsal or evaluation. See Carruthers 2011.) This enables us to separate questions about the emergence of generative capacities in infants and nonhuman animals, on the one hand, from questions about the development of exploratory-evaluative reasoning, on the other.

In section 2, we address the evolutionary precursors of psychological creativity. We suggest that a capacity to generate novelty can be found quite commonly in the animal kingdom, but only in ways that are either limited in scope or domain-specific. We also suggest that the exploratory component can be found in at least nascent form in some nonhuman animals, as well as much more robustly in earlier species of hominin. Yet nonhuman animals are not (or only very rarely) creative in an agent-neutral sense. Moreover, there is very little evidence of agent-neutral creativity in the hominin line prior to the emergence of *Homo sapiens*. This leads us to ask what it is that makes human creative capacities unique. Various possible answers are considered in section 3. The hypothesis that we settle on (and begin to explore and evaluate in comparison with alternatives in section 4) is that the function of pretend play in human infancy is to develop capacities for agent-neutral creativity. Finally, section 5 examines the mechanisms through which pretense enhances creativity. We suggest that it not only encourages us to generate novelty in an unrestricted and domain-general way, but that it also exercises the abilities to suppress habitual or obvious responses and to select and hold in mind more unusual possibilities, thus enabling those ideas to be developed and evaluated.

2. Precursors of Agent-Neutral Creativity

Most phenotypic characters evolve gradually in small increments. Moreover, evolution often works by co-opting and reusing existing mechanisms for new functions. This is known in the literature as "exaptation." We suggest that creativity does not burst suddenly onto the evolutionary scene with humans but is exapted from mechanisms present in many animals. In the present section, we consider some precursors of psychological creativity, separating our discussion into parts in accordance with the Geneplore model sketched in section 1.

2.1. Precursors of generativity

The generative components of creativity are actually quite common in the animal kingdom. Consider protean forms of escape behavior, for example, which are widespread among prey animals (Driver and Humphries 1988, Miller 1997). A moth that detects the presence of bat ultrasound, for example, will go into a looping, tumbling flight path that appears random (and that is certainly unpredictable to the bat; Roeder and Treat 1961, Roeder 1962, May 1991). Likewise, a gazelle or other prey animal fleeing from a lioness will be apt to use an unpredictable sequence of leaps and bounds and sudden changes of direction. It is likely that the cognitive mechanism underlying such protean behavior involves some sort of noisy, quasi-random process for selecting from among a constrained set of motor instructions. (The set is constrained, of course, by the need for speed; and only motor instructions for generating motion are relevant—the gazelle won't also twitch its tail in a quasi-random manner while fleeing.) Thus animals do generate novel behavior. Further, their behavior is valuable to them if not to anyone else.

Such behavior may not be what we have in mind when we think of creativity (not even psychological creativity). In part, this may be because the behavior doesn't have the sort of agent-neutral value that people associate with creativity; but it may also be because the trigger for such behaviors is innate, and the behavior itself is limited to a single domain. It is unclear, however, that there is any significant difference between such protean behavior and immediate improvisation in jazz or dance, at least in terms of the cognitive underpinnings. Both involve stochastically selected sequences of movement subject to a variety of contextual constraints (Carruthers

2011). And improvised movements of these latter sorts, of course, would unques-tionably be described as creative. The difference between them is that the creativity of a jazz musician or dancer is valuable to others. Thus a jazz musician or a dancer is capable of agent-neutral creativity, while a gazelle's creativity is agent-relative.

Some animal behavior can be much more readily seen as creative because it is agent-neutral. Consider the elaborate, decorative bower-building behavior of some species of bower bird. While the behavior as a whole is innately triggered, each individual bird constructs and decorates its own form of bower. It selects and arranges eye-catching materials in a way that humans can quite readily recognize as valuable, with the details of the arrangement depending partly on the happen-stance of the materials that the bird finds in its immediate environment and partly on preferences inherent in the bird's own personality. Consider also the songs of some species of bird and whale. The Australian butcher bird, in particular, seems to have remarkable musical talents, improvising songs from a wide repertoire of song fragments in a way that would truly be worthy of a jazz musician (Taylor 2008a, 2008b). But while these do seem to be instances of agent-neutral creativity, they are specific to only a single domain. It is also likely that they are heavily innately channeled.

Given that domain-specific forms of the generative component of psychological creativity are widespread in the animal kingdom, it is reasonable to suppose that they might also be present in some earlier species of hominin (and also in our-selves). It seems likely that the generative capacities of earlier hominins too were highly constrained, because there is no evidence in the archaeological record of psy-chological creativity of any general sort prior to the emergence of *Homo sapiens* in Africa some 150,000 years ago. Certainly there is no evidence of creative technolog-ical innovation. On the contrary, we find complete stasis in stone tool-making, with designs remaining unchanged for hundreds of thousands of years (Coolidge and Wynn 2009). Admittedly, earlier hominins might have put their generative capaci-ties to use in specific domains that have left no mark on the archaeological record, engaging in creative forms of song or dance, for example. But it is plain that they did not possess the sort of domain-general creativity that is distinctive of our species. It follows, then, that some significant change must have taken place within our lineage at some point during the transition from the common ancestor of ourselves and the Neanderthals. In section 3, we consider some possible suggestions for what that change might have been.

2.2. Precursors of cognitive exploration

The exploratory component of psychological creativity involves a number of related capacities. One is an ability to inhibit immediate responses and to rehearse or sustain potential solutions in mind so that they can be elaborated and evaluated before a choice is made. This requires both "executive function" (to inhibit prepotent responses) and some form of controlled working memory in which the ideas in question can be explored. Evidence of both can be found in the literature on "insight learning" in comparative psychology.

Consider the New Caledonian crow that was able to solve the problem of retrieving some meat from within a cage on the first trial, after examining the experimental setup for over a minute before acting (Taylor et al. 2010). In order to solve the problem, the bird had to pull up a string to retrieve a short stick attached to the end, which could then be used to retrieve a long stick that was otherwise inaccessible behind some bars to retrieve the meat. The crow might have reasoned thusly: "To get the meat, I need to use a stick to reach it. There are two sticks available. The one on the string is too short. The one in the cage is long enough. But I need a stick to reach it. The one on the string is long enough for that. So I'll get it." Although remarkably smart, and displaying good understanding of the physical properties of sticks, as well as sound judgments of distance, there is nothing here to suggest the presence of the generative component of creativity. It seems to result from a "chaining" of conditional beliefs, rather than from the sort of constrained stochasticity that is arguably the hallmark of the cognitive processes underlying psychologically creative behavior (Simonton 2003). But undoubtedly, the birds have to inhibit their initial tendency to approach the meat straight away, and they have to manipulate representations of the task setup in such a way as to work out a solution in advance of acting.

While insight learning in other animals is observed only infrequently, we know that by 400,000 years ago, *Homo heidelbergensis* made regular use of the executive and working memory components of creative cognition when knapping finely wrought stone tools (Coolidge and Wynn 2009). In fact, we know quite a lot about the cognitive processes that are required for stone knapping. One source of evidence is provided by contemporary knappers who have acquired the skills in question and can give us introspective reports. But another source of evidence derives from those instances where all or most of the products of a particular tool-making episode have been discovered together in the archaeological record and can be retrofitted to provide an exact account of the sequence of blows involved in manufacture (Schlanger 1996). We know that in order to produce three-dimensional symmetries, hominins from this time must have been capable of visually rotating their image of what would happen to a stone if it were struck in a particular way, to imagine how it would then look from the other side. And we know that tool production from this era involved complex hierarchically ordered sequences of action that required the knapper to plan several steps ahead and inhibit prepotent or habitual strikes every so often in order to shift to a different phase of the activity (Coolidge and Wynn 2009). These seem to be essentially the same capacities for executive control and working memory that are required for the "explore" component of psychological creativity.

2.3. Putting the components together

In addition to evidence that the two separate components described by Geneplore models of creativity are present in other animals, there are some examples of insight behavior among apes that suggest that both components might sometimes be at work together. These are cases where it is hard to see how the animals could arrive at their solutions by a process of chaining conditionals. It therefore seems that apes might sometimes be capable of generating novel ideas and evaluating them before putting them into practice. The animals might sometimes try out in imagination actions from their repertoire in a process of unguided or quasi-random search until they happen to hit on one that can be predicted to yield a solution.

For example, something of this sort seems like a plausible explanation for one of the findings of an experiment described by Menzel (1974). One ape, Belle, was taken alone into an enclosure and shown where some food was buried before all the apes were then released into the enclosure together. Whenever the alpha male saw Belle digging up the food, he pushed her out of the way and bit her, taking her food. Belle tried a variety of strategies to elude him, but without success. But then she used a different tactic. On one occasion, she walked purposefully to a location where there was no food and began to dig. After the male pushed her away and began digging there himself, she took advantage of his absorption and traveled swiftly to the location where the food was really buried. She dug it up and was able to consume it before the male arrived. It seems possible that Belle might have hit on this idea using both of the components of agent-relative creative cognition (i.e., generation and exploration), mentally rehearsing various actions from her repertoire and considering what might happen if she were to perform them. When she hit on one that might succeed, she was able to see that this was so and put the plan into operation.

Although examples like this are suggestive, we really have no solid evidence that both the generative and exploratory components of creativity are ever employed together by members of other species. Even in connection with the fine stone tools made by members of closely related species—*Homo heidelbergensis* and the Neanderthals—it is by no means clear that ideas needed to be generated *creatively* prior to their development, transformation, and evaluation in working memory, because experienced knappers had extensive knowledge of the properties of their materials and the sequences that were necessary to achieve their goals. They may therefore have been capable of discerning the affordances provided by a particular stage in tool-making without having to generate and rehearse alternative actions in a creative way. Although members of these species were remarkably smart on many different levels, it is by no means clear that they were capable of even agent-relative forms of Geneplore creativity.

Moreover, even if forms of psychological creativity are sometimes present in other species, what we know for sure is that they are only manifested in highly restricted circumstances. We don't see bower birds or butcher birds turning their creative capacities to other forms of problem-solving, for example (nor do gazelles). And as we noted earlier, up until the advent of *Homo sapiens* some 150,000 years ago, we see no signs of creativity of products in the archaeological record either (Coolidge and Wynn 2009). Although there may be psychological creativity of a very limited sort in nonhuman animals and earlier species of *Homo*, there is certainly no historical creativity. What, then, explains the remarkable creative abilities of humans? What cognitive processes enable us to take the capacities for executive function, working memory, and creative idea and behavior generation that we share with some other animals and then "boost" and deploy them across many different types of context, in such a way that the result is so qualitatively (and not just quantitatively) different? This is the question that we address in section 3.

3. What Makes Humans Unique?

We are not here asking what makes humans unique in general, but rather what makes them uniquely creative. Since other species share (or have shared, in the case of earlier hominins) capacities for constrained generativity of the sort that are characteristic of creative cognition, while also having the necessary powers of working memory, it is natural to wonder whether human creativity results from some combination of these with some other distinctively human capacity or capacities. At any rate, this is the hypothesis that we propose to consider.

3.1. Language

Bickerton (1995) suggests that our distinctive capacities for creative thought are a byproduct of language. This is a natural enough idea, for we know that the large vocabulary and recursive grammar of natural language together provide us with an almost unlimited representational resource (even allowing for limitations in working memory). And we know that we can, at will, combine together words in novel ways—thereby entertaining novel thoughts—and that we often do so (e.g., in humor and in metaphor).

However, it is one thing to possess a recursive representational system that makes it *possible* for people to formulate thoughts that neither they nor anyone else has entertained before, but it is quite another thing to have a disposition to use it thus and to use it relevantly. And we can see no way that the former could in any sense be sufficient for the latter. Moreover, it is highly implausible that language should underlie all forms of distinctively human creativity, as there are many kinds of creativity that seem wholly unrelated to language, such as musical, kinetic, or visual creativity. And indeed, painters and other artists who suffer from aphasia may show no diminishing of artistic creativity (Mell et al. 2003, Seeley et al. 2008).

3.2. Highly developed working memory

Coolidge and Wynn (2009) argue that the distinctive adaptation separating highly creative *Homo sapiens* from the otherwise extremely successful (but uncreative) Neanderthals is an increase in working memory. They point out that the evidence from cranial anatomy suggests that the only difference between the two species that has relevance for brain function is a distinctive enlargement in the posterior parietal cortex (Bruner 2008, 2010). This is an area known to be deeply implicated in human working memory function (Jonides et al. 2008). Moreover, the parietal cortex in general is heavily involved in the control of action, and the posterior parietal has recently been shown to be distinctively implicated in the *manipulative* (as opposed to short-term retentive) aspects of working memory (Koenigs et al. 2009).

These enhancements in working memory capacities probably extended a trend that had been taking place throughout hominin evolution toward increased capacities for executive function and attentional control, because it is well known that the main seat of these capacities lies in the frontal lobes, which have been significantly expanded relative to other brain areas during hominin evolution (Coolidge and Wynn 2009). And recent theories of working memory place special emphasis on attentional capacities and related executive functions in their accounts (Engle 2002, Postle 2006, D'Esposito 2007). Moreover, as we will see in section 5, these capacities are vital for sustaining creativity. But sustaining is one thing; generating is another.

These changes in executive function and working memory would no doubt have greatly enhanced the "explore" component described by Geneplore models of creativity. They would have led to an increased capacity to rehearse and evaluate potential ideas and actions in advance of accepting or implementing them. But it is very doubtful whether they are sufficient by themselves to explain the emergence of domain-general forms of psychological creativity of the sort that humans distinctively exhibit. This remains true even if we suppose that sophisticated language capacities were already in place among the common ancestors of ourselves and the Neanderthals, thereby conferring on them an enhanced capacity for generating and entertaining novel thoughts across all domains. For again, it is one thing to be *capable* of generating novelty in a domain-general manner, and quite another thing to be *disposed* to do so regularly and in relevant ways. Put differently, it is one thing to possess capacities that *enable* creative cognition (such as language and a powerful form of working memory). It is another thing to put those capacities to use. The disposition to do so has not yet been explained.

3.3. Cultural construction

It might be suggested that the disposition to be creative could be a culturally constructed one. Perhaps it depends on cultural frameworks that reward creativity and that consequently instill in people the explicit goal of being creative. In support of this suggestion, it might be said that it can explain the gap of more than 100,000 years between the first emergence of *Homo sapiens* in Africa and the so-called cultural explosion of creative products that didn't begin until after 50,000 years ago. It may be that the latter didn't depend upon any new biological adaptation, but rather on some suitable set of cultural practices and expectations.

However, it seems unlikely that the disposition to create is entirely culturally constructed. For one thing, there is reason to think that the cultural explosion is illusory, an impression created by an overemphasis on Europe in archaeological research, combined with the fact that high population densities are necessary for cultural innovations to be transmitted reliably enough to show up in the archaeological record (McBreaty and Brooks 2000, Shennan 2000, 2001, Henrich 2004). Also, while the kinds and degree of exhibited creativity vary from culture to culture (Lubart 1990), people in every culture display significant amounts of creativity. Metaphor, poetry, dance, music, myths, body adornment, and narratives are among the creative endeavors that appear cross-culturally and are universal among humans (Pinker 2003).

3.4. Convergent and divergent thinking

Gabora and Kaufman (2010) argue that what is distinctively human is the capacity for both divergent and convergent thinking. Divergent thinking is associated with defocused attention, which involves more intuitive thought. Out-of-left-field generation of ideas comes about via divergent thinking. Convergent thinking is more rigorous and analytical and is associated with focused attention. Consideration and fine-tuning of ideas are part of convergent thinking. Gabora and Kaufman suggest that divergent and convergent thinking can function independently depending on context. They can also work together in the case of creativity, where divergent thinking maps onto the generation of ideas described in Geneplore, and convergent thinking maps on to exploration.

We think this view is largely right. We aim to offer an explanation of how divergent and convergent thinking become a habitually paired process as they do in the case of creativity (first divergent, followed by the refinements of convergent). And again, we also wish to explain the *propensity* of humans to deploy these abilities for creative thought.

3.5. Is creativity adaptive?

With the exception of Gabora and Kaufman (2010), each of the proposals considered briefly above seems to assume that distinctively human creative capacities aren't a biological adaptation, for it isn't plausible to claim that either language or enhanced working memory evolved specifically to make us more creative. (In contrast, social constructivists who believe in cultural evolution might be able to claim that creativity is a *cultural* adaptation.)

Our own proposal is to link creativity to another distinctively human tendency, the disposition to engage in pretend play. While the young of many other species engage in rough-and-tumble play and also in the playful execution of species-characteristic adult behaviors (especially running and hunting), none engages in *pretend* or *symbolic* play in natural circumstances. In contrast, pretend play is a human universal, occurring in all typical infants. Moreover, it emerges spontaneously without encouragement or teaching. Since the pretend play of children is sometimes itself creative in nature, it is natural to wonder whether the adaptive function of pretense might be to encourage and enhance adult forms of creativity. This is the hypothesis that we propose to explore, beginning in section 4. But since our proposal is that pretense is an adaptation for creativity, it presupposes that creativity itself is adaptive. This question is addressed briefly here.

It is surely very plausible that incremental increases in creativity would result in increases in fitness; it seems quite likely that creative individuals would be better able to solve problems and overcome obstacles and would thus be more effective in seeking sustenance, securing mates, providing for offspring, and avoiding danger. And indeed, there is evidence that creative hypothesis generation plays a vital role among hunter-gatherers who are tracking prey (Liebenberg 1990, Carruthers 2002). Of course, it might be objected that other animals get along just fine without evolving domain-general creative capacities. But this is easily explained if, as we have suggested, enhancements in creativity depend upon increases in executive function and working memory. It may be that the latter had to evolve first, before increases in creativity would even be possible, let alone adaptive.

Miller (1999) suggests, in contrast, that creativity of an agent-neutral sort is not adaptive for survival but has rather been sexually selected. He states: "The most dramatic examples of human culture, such as ritual, music, art, ideology, and language-play, seem like energetically expensive wastes of time, to someone thinking in terms of the survival of the fittest. From the viewpoint of indicator theory, that sort of wasteful display is exactly what we would expect from traits shaped for reproductive competition." Miller proposes that since creativity is an indicator of intelligence and youthful vigor, and is expensive to produce, creative displays (such as music, dance, witty conversation, and body adornment) that seem prima facie less than apt to help us survive are actually fitness advertisements. One cannot easily fake creative ability, so one's advertisement of creativity is an honest indicator that one is reproductively fit.

In fact, it may be that both accounts are true. If one sees creative cultural endeavors as one manifestation of a cognitive process of constrained generativity and exploration that underlies much everyday problem-solving, as well as scientific creativity (as we do), then music, say, is less clearly an expensive waste of time. Rather, it is an exercise of an ability that is quite useful in many situations. And it may be that such endeavors are sexually attractive, in part, because of this. But we don't need to settle this issue here, because all of these accounts agree that creativity is an adaptation. They disagree only about the adaptive pressures that produced it.

4. Why Do Children Pretend?

Why do nearly all children, cross-culturally, engage in pretend play? The question is ambiguous since it can be interpreted in either a proximal (motivational) or distal (evolutionary or functional) sense. The answer to the proximal question is, we believe, quite obvious. Children pretend because they enjoy it. More specifically, we think that young children begin with a disposition to find pretend play intrinsically rewarding (Picciuto 2009). The mere act of entertaining a suppositional representation is pleasurable for its own sake, leading children to begin exploring pretend scenarios. When they do so, they are likely to discover additional rewards, since by representing themselves as engaged in some desirable or admired activity, their emotional systems will respond with positive affect (in the manner outlined by Damasio 1994), despite the fact that they know full well that the actions in question aren't real (Carruthers 2006). As a result, the disposition to engage in pretend play will be further reinforced.

It is the distal question that interests us here. What is the evolutionary and/or developmental *function* of pretend play, if any? We consider a number of possible answers.

4.1. Functionless pretense

Two prominent theorists in the first half of the 20th century denied that pretense has any function. They suggested that, essentially, children pretend for lack of anything better to do. Maria Montessori considered pretense a waste of a child's developmental time (Lillard 2005, p. 187). She concluded from the fact that children prefer to use a real object rather than a substitute (e.g., that they prefer cutting with a real knife rather than a pretend knife) that instances of pretense occur because children are not able (or permitted) to perform real actions. Likewise, Piaget (1962) regarded pretense as a stage that would be cast aside as children develop logic and rationality.

Few theorists today would be likely to consider a child who fails to pretend as unusually competent and fulfilled. Most think that pretense at least co-occurs with, and more likely helps develop, some cognitive faculty—that children pretend for an important developmental reason. It is well known that the pretense of autistic children is extremely limited, and it is natural to think that there is some connection between the absence of pretense behavior and the other impairments seen in autism. Moreover, given that play interventions can actually improve executive function, emotion regulation, and divergent thinking in typically developing children (Fisher 1992, Galyer and Evans 2001, Moore and Russ 2009), as well as improving behavior, social cognition, and language in developmentally disabled and autistic children (Greenspan 1992), it seems likely that pretense has a causal role in optimal development.

4.2. Social schemata

A more recent suggestion is that the function of pretense is to help children practice social schemata and acclimate themselves to the wider culture in which they live (Bogdan 2005). The idea is that pretense functions to enhance social functioning and familiarity with social roles and scripts. And it is true that in many cultures, parents use pretend play to teach children how to behave in social situations (Haight et al. 1999). But much pretense does not involve social schemata. While the account has some plausibility for instances of pretend cooking or pretend childcare, it is much harder to map onto such paradigm cases of pretense as talking with an imaginary friend or pretending that a block of wood is a fire truck. Taking one object for another does not necessarily involve social or cultural rehearsal. Moreover, it is far from clear how this proposal could work, even in those cases where it initially seems most plausible, because one needs to have a mental representation of a social schema in order to pretend to enact it. So how could the latter help to inculcate the former? Further, there are many instances of social pretense where it is hard to see them as an aid to cultural acclimation. A pretense that is especially outlandish and fantastical is not the easiest route for learning about cultural conformity. Pretending one is a superhero (as many children do, particularly in Western cultures) and pretending to leap tall buildings in a single bound do nothing to rehearse useful schemata for everyday social interactions—which tend not to involve leaping over tall buildings.

In addition, the proportion of pretense devoted to rehearsing social schemata seems to vary from culture to culture. Irish-American children spend much less time rehearsing everyday social situations than do Chinese children in Taiwan (Haight et al. 2003); Anglo-American preschoolers do it less than Korean-Americans (Farver and Shin 1997). If pretense were a cognitive activity whose function is to inculcate cultural conformity and practice social roles, then it would be likely to function similarly across cultures (i.e., children in all cultures would pretend their culture's particular schemata).

4.3. Developing mindreading

Yet another suggestion is that the function of pretend play is to facilitate the development of our so-called mindreading capacity. (This is the ability to attribute mental states to other people and to explain and predict their behavior in the light of such states.) On some accounts, mindreading is fundamentally a *simulative* capacity in which one adopts in imagination the perspective of another person and then thinks and reasons within the scope of that pretense, attributing the outcomes to the target individual (Currie and Ravenscroft 2002, Goldman 2006). So early pretense (beginning at 18 months) may be a necessary precursor for later mindreading (emerging in the third and fourth year of life). Additional support for this suggestion can be derived from the finding that pretend play is largely absent in autistic children; indeed, everyone accepts that autism involves a deficit in mindreading (Baron-Cohen 1995, Goldman 2006). Hence it may be that it is the early failure to engage in pretend play that is responsible for later failures in mindreading tasks such as the false-belief task.

A rapidly expanding body of recent research makes this suggestion untenable, however, for it shows that children have intact mindreading capacities far earlier than the age at which they successfully pass verbal false-belief tests, and also earlier than or coincident with the onset of pretend play. We now know that infants in the first year of life attribute goals to other agents and form appropriate expectations in light of those goals, while at the same time drawing appropriate inferences when agents have or lack perceptual access to an event (Woodward 1998, Johnson 2000, Csibra et al. 2003, Luo and Baillargeon 2005). Moreover, we also know that infants in their second year of life (almost certainly by the age of 18 months and perhaps as early as 13 months) can identify and form appropriate expectations about the false belief of another agent, while also understanding that other people can be misled by appearances (Onishi and Baillargeon 2005, Southgate et al. 2007, Surian et al. 2007, Song et al. 2008, Scott and Baillargeon 2009, Buttelmann et al. 2009). Since infants do not begin to engage in pretense until around the age of 18 months, it is plain that the function of pretense cannot be to enable the development of mindreading. On the contrary, some aspects of mindreading, at least, are in place prior to the onset of pretend play, while others seemingly co-occur with the latter. Even infants' understanding of the pretend behavior of other agents seems to co-occur with the onset of first-person pretending (Onishi et al. 2007).

In addition, mindreading is a capacity that is restricted to a single domain. Both pretense and creativity, however, are (at least in humans) domain-general. It seems more plausible that a domain-general behavior serves to develop a domain-general capacity, rather than a domain-specific capacity.

What, then, is the connection between the mindreading problems that are characteristic of autism and the absence of pretend play in autism if pretense doesn't serve to facilitate mindreading? There are a number of possibilities. One is that it is pretense that depends upon mindreading, rather than vice versa. This could happen either directly (pretending requires knowing that you are pretending) or indirectly (the pleasures of pretense depend upon seeing one's own actions in a certain light). But another possibility is that both utilize similar cognitive resources, which Leslie

(1987) calls "decoupling." This is the capacity to entertain and reason with a suppositional or counterfactual representation (either one's own pretense or the false belief of another). Hence it may be this common capacity that is damaged in autism.

Yet another possibility is that both pretense and mindreading happen to depend on networks of long-range neural connections in the brain, which are known to be less prevalent in autism (Belmonte et al. 2004, Courchesne et al. 2007). As we will see in section 5, pretense uses executive control and attention (known to be located in the frontal lobes) to suppress interpretations arising naturally from perceptual input (located in the occipital and temporal lobes in the case of vision). Likewise, the mindreading system involves a long-range network including regions of frontal, temporal, and parietal lobes (Frith and Frith 2003, Saxe and Powell 2006, Saxe 2010). Hence, on this account, the co-occurrence of mindreading deficits with an absence of pretend play in autism wouldn't be causal. Rather, both would be products of the same underlying neuro-developmental cause.

4.4. Pretense is for creativity

So far in this section, we have considered a number of suggestions concerning the function of pretend play (or lack thereof) and have found each of them to be problematic to various degrees. Our own suggestion, in contrast, is that the function of pretense is to enhance creativity. Practicing pretense as a child, we suggest, makes one a more creative adult. This is an intuitive connection suggested by, among others, Vygotsky ([1934] 1965). There are also recent empirical data that are consistent with it.

Pretend play has been found to predict creativity four years later, and early imaginative play predicts later divergent thinking (Russ et al. 1999). Moreover, when children are given play opportunities, as opposed to repetitive copying, their subsequent creativity in unrelated domains is boosted when tested a few minutes later (Howard-Jones et al. 2002). In addition, just as our account predicts, it turns out that people with autism, who show a marked absence of pretend play in infancy, are also less creative than typical people in adulthood (as well as having well-known mindreading deficits). People with autism are less generative overall, while also producing less novelty and showing less imagination (Craig and Baron-Cohen 1999). They also do far worse at generating novel uses of an object and generating novel interpretations of a meaningless line drawing, and there is evidence of both impaired generation of new ideas and failure to inhibit impermissible or repeated responses (Turner 1999).

None of this evidence is probative, of course. Indeed, each set of data also admits of an alternative explanation. Thus the reason why pretense abilities predict creativity some years later may be that both are manifestations of a common innate mechanism (such as Leslie's "decoupler") that varies in efficiency between people; and essentially the same explanation can be given for the deficits in creativity found in autism. If so, then it needn't be the *function* of pretense to enhance creativity; and earlier pretense might fail to have any causal impact on later creativity. Moreover, although the short-term effects of play on creativity are surely causal, they might be mediated by the well-known effects of positive mood on creative performance (Baas et al. 2008). It may be that play puts children into a good mood (or repetitive copying puts them into a bad one), and it is the latter that then impacts their creative performance a few minutes later. However, our account does have the advantage of providing a single unifying explanation of the data, in contrast with the disparate explanations sketched here.

Gaut (2010) suggests a possible critique of the view that the function of pretense is to enhance creativity. Some animals seem to pretend. For example, kittens engage in hunting and stalking behavior that is similar to, but importantly different from, the hunting and stalking behavior that occurs in the presence of actual prey. If some animals pretend, then pretense is not the uniquely human behavior that can explain uniquely human forms of creativity. However, the pretense behavior of animals is restricted to a single domain. Kittens pretend to hunt, but they don't pretend to eat, or to groom themselves, or that they can fly, or that they are dogs. If indeed animals do pretend, it is in a very different way than the variegated, domain-general pretending that human children engage in. It is this type of domain-general pretense that would be likely to give rise to the domain-general capacity of creativity.

In addition to being consistent with and providing a unifying explanation of the evidence, our account has one crucial feature that the common-cause explanations canvassed earlier lack: It can explain why children engage in pretense in the first place. This should not be taken for granted. On the contrary, were it not so familiar, the fact that human infants begin to engage in pretend play at around 18 months would be a striking species-typical behavior, and would cry out for some sort of adaptionist explanation. For even if infants' emotional reactions to their pretend episodes can explain why they continue pretending once they have begun (Carruthers 2006), we need to explain why they ever begin in the first place. Since cultural explanations (in terms of imitation of others, for example) are highly implausible, the most reasonable suggestion is that human infants are innately disposed to begin engaging in pretense, and that they find these episodes somehow intrinsically rewarding (Picciuto 2009). If this is so, then it requires an explanation. This is what our account can provide, and it is the only one of those canvassed that can do so while being consistent with the full range of evidence.

Our account would be greatly strengthened, however, if we could specify the mechanisms through which pretend play in infancy enhances creativity in later life. (As generally happens in science, the capacity of a theory to provide a satisfying and detailed explanation of phenomena can provide us with good reason for embracing it, even if alternative accounts are not yet ruled out.) This will require us to characterize some of the cognitive mechanisms involved in pretense, as well as the processes involved in psychological creativity, demonstrating how an innate disposition to engage in the former might lead to enhancements in the latter. This is the topic of section 5.

5. How Pretense Enhances Creativity

There are a number of ways in which pretense might enhance creativity, and there are a number of cognitive factors that are common to each. We propose to discuss these in turn, drawing attention when appropriate to empirical evidence that bears on our proposal. These are not competing hypotheses, however. Rather, we believe that pretense helps develop several capacities that are required for creativity.

5.1. Pretense and generativity

A natural initial thought is that the function of pretense may be to encourage and enhance the generative component of creativity. Perhaps the initial disposition to pretend, combined with the further encouragement and rewards provided by frequent pretense, are what explain why humans generate so much more novelty than do other animals, and why they do so across a wide range of domains. One initial problem with this suggestion, however, is that many forms of pretense are, in themselves, only minimally creative. Most instances of pretense fail to be historically novel, and many won't even be psychologically new. Children frequently return to the same or similar pretend scenarios, for example, which would not seem useful for exercising the mere ability to come up with unorthodox suppositions. Moreover, children in some cultures most often pretend quotidian scenarios (Farver and Shin 1997, Haight et al. 2003).

We suggested in section 2 that capacities for constrained stochastic selection of actions and ideas may be a preserved feature deriving from our nonhuman animal ancestors. But we noted that other animals don't use this capacity very much, or only do so within highly restricted domains. Hence, even if pretense is only sometimes creative, it can still have the function of helping to develop adults who are more creative than are nonhuman animals and who are creative in a general way, not restricted to a specific sort of context or activity. Moreover, recall that it is *imaginative* play in childhood that predicts adult creativity (Russ et al. 1999). Since individual differences in creativity of play co-occur with individual differences in adult creativity, this is quite consistent with the idea that the function of childhood pretense is to produce at least pan-human levels of creativity among adults. The proposed role for pretense in encouraging widespread generativity is also consistent with the finding that people suffering from autism not only fail to engage in pretense during childhood, but also grow up to be much less creative than other adults.

5.2. Supposition

A further natural suggestion arises from the fact that pretense and creative thinking both involve forms of *supposition*. During play, children may *suppose* that the banana is a telephone or that the teddy bear is alive and likes to drink tea, and they reason and act accordingly (up to a point). Likewise in science, researchers creatively generate explanatory hypotheses or possible experiments, in each case *supposing* that the hypothesis is true or that the experiment is conducted as described, in order to evaluate those suggestions. Similarly in the arts, composers and painters might entertain imagistic representations of the consequences of certain actions or of those actions themselves, in such a way that one might naturally express their thoughts in the form: "Suppose the melody continued like *this*…" or "Suppose I painted a red oval *there*.…" Perhaps what pretense does, then, is provide practice in making suppositions and reasoning within their scope, thus supporting both the "generate" and "explore" components of Geneplore creativity. Indeed, some of the standard tests of an individual's creativity invite the test-taker to "just suppose" (e.g., to just suppose that people never had to sleep anymore). Subjects are then graded on their responses to measure their abilities for divergent thinking (Plucker and Makel 2010, p. 53).

It might be objected that there are forms of creativity that this model doesn't fit so easily. These include some kinds of performance art, where creativity is displayed in the moment, as well as spontaneous athletic, musical, and dance improvisation, and witty conversation. The supposition model only fits those forms of creativity where ideas are first *rehearsed* before being evaluated or put into practice. This is central to Geneplore forms of creativity, but as we noted earlier, there seem to be many instances in which no real distinction can be drawn between the two phases postulated by such models. As we will see in sections 5.3 and 5.4, however, there are other ways in which pretense can enhance even in-the-moment forms of creativity. And in any case, it can be true that pretense is, in part, an adaptation to enhance Geneplore creativity while also having the function of encouraging more widespread use of our generative capacities (as outlined in section 5.1).

One piece of evidence consistent with the proposed connection between the suppositional nature of pretense and adult forms of creativity is the finding that people with autistic-spectrum disorders (who fail to engage in pretend play in infancy and show deficits in creativity as adults) also have problems in entertaining and reasoning with counterfactual or suppositional thoughts more generally (Peterson and Bowler 2000, Grant et al. 2004). It may thus be that difficulties in suppositional reasoning (which are manifested initially in an absence of pretend play) are what result in the reduced creativity of people with autistic-spectrum disorders.

5.3. Bypassing the obvious

In addition, a further common factor in both pretend play and creative thought and behavior is that in each, the agent has to bypass prepotent, habitual, and/or more obvious responses. In playing with a banana as if it were a telephone, for instance, a child has to bypass, and keep bypassing, the thought that it is really a banana—despite the fact that her senses will be screaming out at her that it is. She must ignore the fact that the object is really a banana and explore what opportunities are afforded by the premise that it is a telephone—all the while conscious of the fact that it is a banana. Likewise, in generating creative titles for a story or unusual things that one might do with a brick, one has to suppress the obvious responses. And the same is true even in cases of creativity that don't fit the Geneplore model. In dance or jazz improvisation, for example, one has to bypass "too obvious" or habitual continuations. Perhaps this ability is part of what play enhances. Note that it is an ability that requires executive function, akin to that involved when one attempts *not* to think of a polar bear (Mitchell et al. 2007).

Moreover, Baumeister et al. (2012) discuss a study that required guitar players to count backward by six while playing improvised guitar solos. Such counting absorbs the resources of working memory. The guitar soloists were able to keep the beat and remain in key, even when the key changed. This suggests that such abilities do not require much in the way of conscious attention. However, the creativity of soloists who were asked to count was ranked lower than those who were not asked to perform such a task. Creativity seems to require conscious attention. An exercise of executive function, such as that provided by pretense, could thus serve to enhance creative ability.

Since in both pretense and creativity one has to bypass the obvious, most salient, reality-oriented construal or response, it may be part of the function of the disposition to pretend that it should enhance such a capacity. This suggestion is consistent with the finding that creative adults are indeed better at bypassing irrelevant information, responding faster and more accurately in Stroop-like tasks (Groborz and Necka 2003). (These are tasks in which, for example, one has to name the color of a presented word, where the word itself can indicate a color that is either congruous or incongruous with the color of the letters shown, such as "RED" printed in blue letters. In the incongruous case, one has to ignore the irrelevant semantic content of the word in making one's response.) Although we know of no evidence that the same is true of children who play more often, it at least serves to confirm that creativity does indeed involve some sort of generalized ability to bypass unwanted or irrelevant information. Ideally what one would like, however, is evidence that children who play more often and with greater elaboration in childhood would turn out to be less sensitive to the Stroop effect as adults. This is what our account predicts.

5.4. Selecting the non-obvious

Another factor that is common to both pretense and creativity is closely related to the above while being almost its inverse. In order to embark on a pretense and in order to come up with a creative idea or behavior, one has to *not* bypass the *non*-obvious, seemingly irrelevant possibilities. On the contrary, pretense and creativity are each possible only if there is a range of non-literal, non-obvious, and non-routine possibilities that are available for the agent to select from. (Indeed, Bristol and Viskontas [2006] cite a number of memory studies that show that creativity requires not only working memory, but also decreased cognitive and cortical inhibition.) So representations of these possibilities need to be active. Note that it does no good for them to be stored in long-term or semantic memory, because then, of course, one could not search for and activate any one of them in particular without already having determined its potential usefulness. But that would mean that the idea had *already* occurred to one. Nor would a more generalized query like "Give me something new" be likely to activate these representations in particular. Hence novelty, in both pretend play and adult creativity, is only possible if the agent can maintain a range of activated non-obvious representations to select from.

It may then be part of the function of pretense to foster the availability of such representations in adulthood, thereby supporting creativity. Consistent with this suggestion, it has been found that high levels of creative achievement in adults are linked with low levels of what psychologists call "latent inhibition" (Peterson et al. 2002, Carson et al. 2003). The latter is measured by giving subjects a learning task in which there are recurring but irrelevant distractor stimuli. When the task is completed, subjects are given a follow-up assignment that depends on detection of those very same types of stimuli. Subjects high in latent inhibition find the second task difficult to solve; having learned of the irrelevance of the stimuli, they have ceased to attend to them. Subjects who have low latent inhibition, in contrast, perform significantly better on the follow-up task. Although they, too, were able to succeed on the first task, they have continued to pay attention to details that they have learned are irrelevant. What this seems to show is that creative individuals tend to pay attention to seemingly irrelevant details and maintain a range of activated representations that aren't obviously relevant to the task at hand.

One might think that having one's mind filled with irrelevant ideas would be maladaptive. And indeed, in some circumstances and when taken to extremes, it is. For example, there is extensive literature documenting low levels of latent inhibition in people suffering from schizophrenia (Baruch et al. 1988a, 1988b, Lubow and Gevirtz, 1995). Carson et al. (2003) posit that one difference between the two groups, however, is that people in psychotic states or prone to psychotic states tend to be of lower general intelligence than creative controls. They find that creativity requires low inhibition specifically in combination with high general intelligence. They also point out that schizophrenia is associated with deficits of working memory. One needs both the ability to summon ideas that are seemingly irrelevant and the working memory to select and explore a valuable one. Moreover, one might think that there is a big difference between someone who has a range of activated representations *available* to be selected and entertained, and someone who *actually* entertains such representations on a regular basis. It seems that normal creative individuals might be in the first situation while people suffering from psychotic states are in the second.

Consistent with these ideas is the finding that creativity can be enhanced by the conscious intention to be creative (Baumeister et al. 2007). It can also be primed by a symbol of insight, such as the proverbial lightbulb (Slepian et al. 2010). It seems that ordinary individuals, while normally ignoring active representations that aren't immediately relevant, can adopt the strategy of paying attention to and entertaining such representations when they have the goal of being creative. Arguably, what adults do in such circumstances is to "think playfully," even though they are way beyond the age of engaging in pretend play. People suffering from schizophrenia, in contrast, may be unable to prevent themselves from entertaining bizarre or irrelevant representations.

5.5. Exploring and evaluating

In addition to requiring both bypassing more obvious responses and openness to non-obvious ones, in both play and creativity, there is also an element of evaluation and development. These are, of course, crucial to the "explore" component of Geneplore models of creativity. For example, a scientist who thinks of a novel hypothesis must initially evaluate its consistency with the evidence and its coherence with things that she already believes. She then needs to consider ways to test the hypothesis, how those experiments should be designed, and so on. The path from initial idea to final evaluation may take many years of hard work. Likewise, a painter who has a novel idea for a painting has to undertake an initial evaluation of the idea before considering the many different ways in which the idea could be implemented, what paints to use, what size canvas would work best, and so forth.

Similarly, it is not the case that simply any non-obvious or non-habitual response will do in a pretense—some are better than others. For example, objects used in pretend play generally at least suggest a perceptual resemblance to an imagined object. And while scenarios can get increasingly elaborate with age, there still seem to be both inappropriate and appropriate additions to pretend episodes. When pretense becomes social, it requires an openness to surprise additions made by others; yet it seems that even in social pretense, it isn't the case that simply anything goes. So there seems to be an initial evaluation taking place at the outset of a pretend episode, just as there is at the outset of a creative episode in adulthood.

Moreover, pretense, like creativity, often involves a capacity for sustained focus while working within the scope of an initial supposition. Pretending generally takes time and involves a number of intermediate stages. Hence, during that time, the child needs to keep in mind the relevant pretend suppositions and maintain her focus while the pretense is acted out. It may thus be part of the function of pretense to enhance people's capacity to focus on an idea or activity while it is being explored, evaluated, or implemented. Although there are few hard data involving controlled experiments to support this claim, it is in fact one of the central tenets of the "Tools of the Mind" educational program (Bodrova and Leong 2006) based on the ideas of Vygotsky, who believed that pretend play enhances both creativity and executive function. He claimed that participation in structured forms of pretend play in preschool enhances children's executive function abilities during their later school years, and especially that it enhances their ability to keep focused on a task. This is just what our analysis would predict.

The capacity for persistent focus on a task is of much more general value, however, playing an important part in many aspects of characteristically human life, both creative and uncreative. So even if the capacities for sustained focus are required in both pretense and creativity, and even if the former contributes materially to the latter, it may be the case that pretense helps develop other abilities in addition to creativity. It may be an adaptation for enhancing goal-directed and executively controlled behavior as well.

5.6. Pulling together the strands

A number of the ideas canvassed above are supported by the main conclusions of Christoff et al. (2007), as well as Bristol and Viskontas (2006). They find that a kind of defocused attention combined with cognitive control is especially distinctive of creative thought, combining together aspects of focused problem-solving (cognitive control) with unguided thinking (or "mind-wandering"). This is surely consistent with the main components of our earlier task analysis of creative cognition. To be creative, one has to allow oneself to attend more widely and be open to alternative ideas or behaviors, but at the same time, one has to bypass more obvious ideas and behavior and maintain focus while alternative possibilities are explored and evaluated. Since the same would appear to be true of pretend play, this is quite consistent with the claim that the latter is an adaptation designed to enhance the former.

We have to concede that the evidential base for our claim is presently somewhat slim, and much of it only supports, at best, a *correlation* between pretense and creativity. But the evidence is at least consistent with the proposal that enhancing creativity is what pretend play is *for*. Moreover, recall that the species specificity of pretend play behavior cries out for explanation. Our hypothesis gains considerable plausibility, in our view, from its capacity to provide such an explanation, as it is the only proposal among those canvassed that does so.

6. Conclusion

We have argued that pretend play in children is an adaptation whose function is, at least partly, to enhance creativity in adults. There is evidence that some animals exhibit a limited and domain-specific creative ability that may have been exapted by humans—in whom creativity seems to be an adaptation. We suggest that a primary reason that typical human infants universally engage in pretend play is to develop the capacities that encourage and allow for creative thought. This is a more plausible account of the function of pretense than theories that suggest that pretend play develops mindreading capacities or more sophisticated social schemata. By encouraging the development of several different common capacities (such as generativity, supposing, bypassing the obvious, and selection of the valuable but less obvious), childhood pretense paves the way for creativity in adulthood.

References

Baas, M., De Dreu, C., and Nijstad, B. 2008. "A meta-analysis of 25 years of mood-creativity research: Hedonic tone, activation, or regulatory focus?" *Psychological Bulletin*, 134, pp. 778–806.

Baron-Cohen, S. 1995. *Mind-Blindness*. Cambridge, MA: MIT Press.

Baruch, I., Hemsley, D., and Gray, J. 1988a. "Differential performance of acute and chronic schizophrenics in a latent inhibition task," *Journal of Nervous and Mental Disease*, 176, pp. 598–606.

Baruch, I., Hemsley, D., and Gray, J. 1988b. "Latent inhibition and 'psychotic proneness' in normal subjects," *Personality and Individual Differences*, 9, pp. 777–783.

Baumeister, R., Schmeichel, B., DeWall, N., and Vohs, K. 2007. "Is the conscious self a help, a hindrance, or an irrelevance to the creative process?" *Advances in Psychology Research*, 53, pp. 137–152.

Baumeister, R., Schmeichel, B., and DeWall, N. 2012. "Creativity and consciousness: evidence from psychology experiments," E. S. Paul and S. B. Kaufman (eds.), *The philosophy of creativity*. New York: Oxford University Press.

Belmonte, M., Allen, G., Beckel-Mitchener, A., Boulanger, L., Carper, R., and Webb, S. 2004. "Autism and abnormal development of brain connectivity," *Journal of Neuroscience*, 24 (42), pp. 9228–9231.

Bickerton, D. 1995 *Language and Human Behavior*. Seattle: University of Washington Press.

Boden, M. 2004. *The Creative Mind: Myths and mechanisms*, 2nd ed. London: Routledge.

Bodrova, E., and Leong, D. 2006. *Tools of the Mind: A Vygotskian approach to early childhood education*. Upper Saddle River, NJ: Prentice Hall.

Bogdan, R. J. 2005. "Pretending as imaginative rehearsal for cultural conformity," *Journal of Cognition and Culture*, 5, pp. 191–213.

Bristol, A., and Viskontas I. 2006. "Dynamic processes within associative memory stores: piecing together the neural basis of creative cognition," in J. Kaufman and J. Baer (eds.), *Creativity and Reason in Cognitive Development*. New York: Cambridge University Press.

Bruner, E. 2008. "Comparing endocranial form and shape differences in modern humans and Neanderthals: a geometric approach," *PaleoAnthropology*, 2008, pp. 93–106.

Bruner, E. 2010. "Morphological differences in the parietal lobes within the human genus: a neurofunctional perspective," *Current Anthropology*, 51, pp. S77–S88.

Buttelmann, D., Carpenter, M., and Tomasello, M. 2009. "Eighteen-month-old infants show false belief understanding in an active helping paradigm," *Cognition*, 112, pp. 337–342.

Carruthers, P. 2002 "The roots of scientific reasoning: infancy, modularity, and the art of tracking," in P. Carruthers, S. Laurence, and S. Stich (eds.), *The Cognitive Basis of Science*. New York: Cambridge University Press.

Carruthers, P. 2006. "Why pretend?" in S. Nichols (ed.), *The Architecture of the Imagination*. New York: Oxford University Press.

Carruthers, P. 2011 "Creative action in mind." *Philosophical Psychology*, 24, pp. 347–361.

Carson, S., Peterson, J., and Higgins, D. 2003. "Decreased latent inhibition is associated with increased creative achievement in high-functioning individuals," *Journal of Personality and Social Psychology*, 85, pp. 499–506.

Christoff, K., Gordon, A., and Smith, R. 2007. "The role of spontaneous thought in human cognition," in O. Vartanian and D. Mandel (eds.), *Neuroscience of Decision Making*. London: Psychology Press.

Coolidge, F., and Wynn, T. 2009. *The rise of Homo sapiens: The evolution of modern thinking*. Hoboken, NJ: Wiley-Blackwell.

Courchesne, E., Pierce, K., Schumann, C., Redcay, E., Buckwalter, J., Kennedy, D., and Morgan, J. 2007. "Mapping early brain development in autism," *Neuron*, 56, pp. 399–413.

Craig, J., and Baron-Cohen, S. 1999. "Creativity and imagination in autism," *Journal of Autism and Developmental Disorders*, 29, pp. 319–326.

Csibra, G., Bíró, S., Koós, O., and Gergely, G. 2003. "One-year-old infants use teleological representations of actions productively," *Cognitive Science*, 27, pp. 111–133.

Currie, G., and Ravenscroft, I. 2002. *Recreative Minds: Imagination in philosophy and in psychology*. New York: Oxford University Press.

Damasio, A. 1994 *Descartes' Error*. London: Papermac.

D'Esposito, M. 2007. "From cognitive to neural models of working memory," *Philosophical Transactions of the Royal Society B*, 362, pp. 276–772.

Driver, P., and Humphries, N. 1988. *Protean Behavior: The biology of unpredictability*. New York: Oxford University Press.

Engle, R. 2002. "Working memory capacity as executive attention," *Current Directions in Psychological Science*, 11, pp. 19–23.

Farver, J. A. M., and Shin, Y. L. 1997. "Social pretend play in Korean- and Anglo-American preschoolers," *Child development*, 68: pp. 544–556.

Finke, R. 1995. "Creative realism," in S. Smith, T. Ward, and R. Finke (eds.), *The Creative Cognition Approach*. New York: Cambridge University Press.

Finke, R., Ward, T., and Smith, S. 1992. *Creative Cognition*. Cambridge, MA: MIT Press.

Fisher, E. 1992. "The impact of play on development: A meta-analysis," *Play and Culture*, 5, pp. 159–181.

Frith, U., and Frith, C. 2003. "Development and neurophysiology of mentalizing," *Philosophical Transactions of the Royal Society of London B: Biological Sciences*, 358, pp. 459–473.

Gabora, L., and Kaufman S. B. 2010. "Evolutionary approaches to creativity," in J. C. Kaufman and R. J. Sternberg (eds.), *The Cambridge Handbook of Creativity*. New York: Cambridge University Press.

Galyer, K., and Evans, I. 2001. "Pretend play and the development of emotion regulation in preschool children," *Early Child Development and Care*, 166, pp. 93–108.

Gaut, B. 2010. "The philosophy of creativity," *Philosophy Compass*, 5, pp. 1–13.

Goldman, A. 2006. *Simulating Minds*. New York: Oxford University Press.

Grant, C., Riggs, K., and Boucher, J. 2004. "Counterfactual and mental state reasoning in children with autism," *Journal of autism and developmental disorders*, 34, pp. 177–188.

Greenspan, S. I. 1992. *Infancy and early childhood: The practice of clinical assessment and intervention with emotional and developmental challenges*. Madison, CT: International Universities Press.

Groborz, M., and Necka, E. 2003. "Creativity and cognitive control: Explorations of generation and evaluation skills," *Creativity Research Journal*, 15, pp. 183–197.

Haight, W. L., Wang, X. L., Fung, H. H., Williams, K., and Mintz, J. 1999. "Universal, developmental, and variable aspects of young children's play: A cross-cultural comparison of pretending at home," *Child development*, 70, pp. 1477–1488.

Henrich, J. 2004. "Demography and cultural evolution: Why adaptive cultural processes produced maladaptive losses in Tasmania," *American Antiquity*, 69, pp. 197–214.

Howard-Jones, P., Taylor, J., and Sutton, L. 2002. "The effect of play on the creativity of young children during subsequent activity," *Early Child Development*, 172, pp. 323–328.

Johnson, S. 2000. "The recognition of mentalistic agency in infancy," *Trends in Cognitive Sciences*, 4, pp. 22–28.

Jonides, J., Lewis, R., Nee, D., Lustig, C., and Berman, M. 2008. "The mind and brain of short-term memory," *Annual Review of Psychology*, 59, pp. 193–224.

Koenigs, M., Barbey, A., Postle, B., and Grafman, J. 2009. "Superior parietal cortex is critical for the manipulation of information in working memory," *Journal of Neuroscience*, 29 (47), pp. 14980–14986.

Leslie, A. 1987. "Pretence and representation," *Psychological Review*, 94, pp. 412–426.

Liebenberg, L. 1990. *The Art of Tracking: The origin of science*. Cape Town: David Philip.

Lillard, A. S. 2005. *Montessori: the science behind the genius*, Oxford, UK: Oxford University Press.

Lubart, T. I. 1990. "Creativity and cross-cultural variation," *International Journal of Psychology*, 25, pp. 39–59.

Lubow, R., and Gewirtz, J. 1995. "Latent inhibition in humans: Data, theory, and implications for schizophrenia," *Psychological Bulletin*, 117, pp. 87–103.

Luo, Y., and Baillargeon, R. 2005. "Can a self-propelled box have a goal? Psychological reasoning in 5-month-old infants," *Psychological Science*, 16, pp. 601–608.

May, M. 1991. "Aerial defense tactics of flying insects," *American Scientist*, 79, pp. 316–328.

McBrearty, S., and Brooks, A. 2000. "The revolution that wasn't," *Journal of Human Evolution*, 39, pp. 453–563.

Mell, J., Howard, S., and Miller, B. 2003. "The influence of frontotemporal dementia on an accomplished artist," *Neurology*, 60, pp. 1707–1710.

Menzel, E. 1974. "A group of young chimpanzees in a one-acre field: leadership and communication," in A. Schrier and F. Stollnitz (eds.), *Behavior of Non-Human Primates*. Waltham, MA: Academic Press.

Miller, G. 1997. "Protean primates: the evolution of adaptive unpredictability in competition and courtship," in R. Byrne and A. Whiten (eds.), *Machiavellian Intelligence II: extensions and evaluations*. New York: Cambridge University Press.

Miller, G. F. 1999. "Sexual selection for cultural displays," in R. Dunbar, C. Knight, and C. Power (eds.), *The evolution of culture*. Edinburgh, UK: Edinburgh University Press, pp. 71–91.

Mitchell, J., Heatherton, T., Kelley, W., Wyland, C., Wegner, D., and Macrae, C. 2007. "Separating sustained from transient aspects of cognitive control during thought suppression," *Psychological Science*, 18, pp. 292–297.

Moore, M., and Russ, S. 2009. "Follow-up of a pretend play intervention: Effects on play, creativity, and emotional processes in children," *Creativity Research Journal*, 20, pp. 427–436.

Onishi, K., and Baillargeon, R. 2005. "Do 15-month-olds understand false beliefs?" *Science*, 308, pp. 255–258.

Onishi, K., Baillargeon, R., and Leslie, A. 2007. "15-month-old infants detect violations in pretend scenarios," *Acta Psychologica*, 124, pp. 106–128.

Peterson, D., and Bowler, D. 2000. "Counterfactual reasoning and false belief understanding in children with autism," *Autism*, 4, pp. 391–405.

Peterson, J., Smith, K., and Carson, S. 2002. "Openness and extraversion are associated with reduced latent inhibition: replication and commentary," *Personality and Individual Differences*, 33, pp. 1137–1147.

Piaget, J. 1962. *Play, dreams and imitation in childhood*, trans. Gettegno, C., and Hodgson, F. M. New York: Norton.

Picciuto, E. 2009. "The pleasures of suppositions," *Philosophical psychology*, 22:4, pp. 487–503.

Pinker, S. 2003. *The blank slate*. New York: Penguin.

Plucker, J. A., and Makel, M. C. 2010. "Assessment of creativity," in J. C. Kaufman and R. J. Sternberg (eds.), *The Cambridge Handbook of Creativity*. New York: Cambridge University Press.

Postle, B. 2006. "Working memory as an emergent property of the mind and brain," *Neuroscience*, 139, pp. 23–38.

Roeder, K. 1962. "The behavior of free-flying moths in the presence of artificial ultrasonic pulses," *Animal Behavior*, 10, pp. 300–304.

Roeder, K., and Treat, A. 1961. "The detection and evasion of bats by moths," *American Scientist*, 49, pp. 135–148.

Russ, S., Robins, A., and Christiano, B. 1999. "Pretend play: Longitudinal prediction of creativity and affect in fantasy in children," *Creativity Research Journal*, 12, pp. 129–139.

Saxe, R. 2010. "Theory of mind (neural basis)," *Encyclopedia of Consciousness*. Cambridge, MA: MIT Press.

Saxe, R., and Powell, L. 2006. "It's the thought that counts: Specific brain regions for one component of theory of mind," *Psychological Science*, 17, pp. 692–699.

Schlanger, N. 1996 "Understanding levallois: Lithic technology and cognitive archaeology." *Cambridge Archaeological Journal*, 6, pp. 75–92.

Scott, R., and Baillargeon, R. 2009. "Which penguin is this? Attributing false beliefs about object identity at 18 months," *Child Development*, 80, pp. 1172–1196.

Seeley, W., Matthews, B., Crawford, R., Gorno-Tempini, M., Foti, D., Mackenzie, I., and Miller, B. 2008. "Unravelling Boléro: progressive aphasia, transmodal creativity and the right posterior neocortex," *Brain*, 131, pp. 39–49.

Shennan, S. 2000. "Population, culture history, and the dynamics of culture change," *Current Anthropology*, 41, pp. 811–835.

Shennan, S. 2001. "Demography and cultural innovation: a model and its implications for the emergence of modern human culture," *Cambridge Archaeological Journal*, 11, pp. 5–16.

Simonton, D. 2003. "Scientific creativity as constrained stochastic behavior: the integration of product, person, and process perspectives," *Psychological bulletin*, 129, pp. 475.

Slepian, M., et al. 2010. "Shedding light on insight: Priming bright ideas," *Journal of Experimental Social Psychology*, 46, pp. 696–700.

Song, H., Onishi, K., Baillargeon, R., and Fisher, C. 2008. "Can an actor's false belief be corrected by an appropriate communication? Psychological reasoning in 18.5-month-old infants," *Cognition*, 109, pp. 295–315.

Southgate, V., Senju, A., and Csibra, G. 2007. "Action anticipation through attribution of false belief by 2-year-olds," *Psychological Science*, 18, pp. 587–592.

Surian, L., Caldi, S., and Sperber, D. 2007. "Attribution of beliefs by 13-month-old infants," *Psychological Sceince*, 18, pp. 580–586.

Taylor, A., Elliffe, D., Hunt, G., and Gray, R. 2010. "Complex cognition and behavioral innovation in New Caledonian crows," *Proceedings of the Royal Society B*, 277, pp. 2637–2643.

Taylor, H. 2008a. "Towards a Species Songbook," Ph.D. dissertation, University of Western Sydney, Australia.

Taylor, H. 2008b. "Decoding the song of the pied butcherbird," *Transcultural Musical Review*, 12 <http://www.sibetrans.com/trans/>.

Turner, M. 1999. "Generating novel ideas: Fluency performance in high-functioning and learning disabled individuals with autism," *Journal of Child Psychology and Psychiatry*, 40, pp. 189–201.

Vygotsky, L. S. [1934] 1965. *Thought and language*, ed. and trans. Hanfmann, E., and Vakar, G. Cambridge, MA: MIT Press.

Ward, T., Smith, S., and Finke, R. 1999. "Creative cognition," in R. Sternberg (ed.), *Handbook of Creativity*. New York: Cambridge University Press.

Woodward, A. 1998. "Infants selectively encode the goal object of an actor's reach," *Cognition*, 69, pp. 1–34.

11

Creativity and Artificial Intelligence:

A Contradiction in Terms?

MARGARET A. BODEN

1. Introduction

Many philosophers, and many otherwise hardheaded scientists too, deny the possibility of a computer's ever being creative. But that denial can mean two very different things.

Sometimes, such people are saying that a computer could not generate *apparently* creative performance. That's an empirical claim—and it's mistaken. There are many examples of seemingly creative artificial intelligence (AI) programs. Some of their novel results have been exhibited in major museums like the Tate, the Victoria and Albert Museum, and the Museum of Modern Art; others have been awarded patents (in U.S. law, they are only given for ideas not "obvious to a person skilled in the art").

It doesn't follow that AI scientists will ever be able to engineer a neo-Chopin or a neo-Mozart (although that goal has been approached more closely than most people imagine; Cope 2001, 2006). It's even less likely that there will ever be an AI Shakespeare; the richness of the poet's world knowledge and, even more important, the subtlety of his (and his readers') judgments of *relevance* will not, in practice, be matched (Sperber and Wilson 1986, Boden 2006, 7.iii.d). However, such individuals are the crème de la crème. Respectable, albeit lesser, examples of (apparent) AI creativity already abound (Boden 2004).

But sometimes, the skeptics are saying that *irrespective of its performance*, which might even match superlative human examples, no computer could "really" be creative. The creativity, we are told, lies entirely in the programmer. This is a philosophical claim, not an empirical one. On this view, it follows from the very nature of creativity that a creative computer is not a mere practical impossibility, but a contradiction in terms.

The case for that position can be made from opposite directions. On the one hand, it may be said that computers *possess* some specific property that prevents them from being creative. On the other hand, it may be said that they *lack* some specific properties that humans have that are necessarily involved in genuine creativity. The commonest candidate in the first category is that they are programmed (see section 3). Common candidates in the second category include autonomy, intentionality, consciousness, values, and emotion (see section 4).

I have put the question in this way (i.e., speaking of "computers") because that is the way in which most philosophers (and others) express it. However, the question would perhaps be better put in terms of *computer-based systems, computing mechanisms*, or *information-processing systems* in general. That's because, for most people, the term "computer" brings to mind a familiar and relatively simple type of machine—perhaps the one on your lap or the living room table.

Granted, the simplicity of these familiar machines is only relative. The variety of information-processing functions carried out by today's computers is very much wider than most people believe. Not every current computing system is neatly GOFAI or connectionist (the only types of computation usually considered by philosophers). Even a desk-top PC harbors unsuspected complexities.

For example, some computational architectures cannot be simulated by a Turing machine (TM), because they have a number of interacting subsystems running concurrently and asynchronously. A humble PC has a number of concurrently active subsystems, controlling (and responding to) devices such as the hard drive, DVD reader, internet connection, mouse, and keyboard. Each one delivers an "interrupt" signal when the relevant device is ready to process; whenever two or more interrupts happen to occur simultaneously, they may be handled according to pre-assigned priority rules, or they may be dealt with in random order. Less humble computer systems, such as those controlling an airliner, are even more complex. In general, computers that interact in some deep way with the many asynchronous changes happening in their physical environment will not behave like TMs, unless that environment is equivalent to a TM—which is unlikely to be true of chemical processes, weather systems, human brains, or the Internet. (These computers are very predictable most of the time, however, because computer scientists have developed ways of making them interact harmoniously and in accordance with specific rules.)

Nevertheless, and despite these often-ignored complexities, it may well be impossible—given current technology—to build *a single computer* with sufficient power to meet all the requirements for creativity that are outlined below. Perhaps we'd need thousands of them linked in a tightly integrated network.

More to the point, our current computers, with their diverse hardware attachments (sensors, effectors, and communication channels), merely skim the surface of the huge variety of information-processing mechanisms—including chemical information-processing mechanisms—that are probably required for human-level, and much animal, intelligence. Future computer-based systems will doubtless be different in various ways. For instance, a pioneering computer model of the modulatory effects of diffusing chemicals in the brain reflects the fact that the *computational functions* of certain neurones may be temporarily altered, even though their *connectivities* remain unchanged (Smith et al. 2002). In other words, in a neuroscientifically realistic network, the anatomical pattern of neuronal connections *is not* all there is to it. Similarly (and pace critics of AI such as John Haugeland 1978), the diffuse effects of chemically induced moods, for instance, *are not* beyond simulation in computer models.

In short, the widespread skeptical intuitions about the creative limitations of computers *as we now know them* may well be largely correct. But they need not apply to all possible computer-based systems.

In sections 3 to 5, I address some of those skeptical intuitions. But first, we need some clarification about the notion of creativity.

2. What Is Creativity?

I said above that the denial of computer creativity can mean two different things. I should rather have said that it can mean *many* different things, for there is no universally accepted definition of creativity.

That's not surprising. Most concepts cannot be given hard-and-fast definitions that capture all the sub-varieties and that make non-arbitrary decisions about near-misses and borderline cases. To understand the concept, then, we need to focus on the similarities and differences among those varieties, near-misses, and borderline cases. In other words, dichotomous questions like "Is this an X, yes or no?" and essentialist disputes about "What is X, really?" are usually misguided (see sections 4 and 5).

However, if quibbling about spurious dichotomous distinctions is a waste of time, comparing alternative definitions is not. For it helps us to map the logical geography of the concept—or, better, the phenomenon—in question. The possible candidates for the attribution of "creativity" differ from each other in at least as many ways as do instances of "game" or "chair" (Wittgenstein 1953). As a result, what people understand by the term—when they do try to give a hard-and-fast definition—can differ on a number of dimensions.

Some people, for instance, use it to mean the production of novel ideas and/ or artifacts—*whether or not* these are valuable in any way, and (if so) *whether or not* their originator recognizes their value. On this view, a schizophrenic's word salad is creative purely on account of its novelty. Its potential (for third-party use) as a source of poetic imagery is irrelevant—as is the person's own inability to recognize and value that potential. Likewise, Johannes Kepler is here seen as being no less creative when he declared his new idea about noncircular planetary orbits to be "a cartload of dung" than when, several years later, he realized its value ("Oh, what a foolish bird I have been!").

Others do include a value criterion (with or without a requirement that the originator recognize that value), so that mere novelty isn't enough to qualify for creativity. This implies that the identification—and explanation—of creativity is not a purely scientific matter, because science makes no value judgments. To be sure, it might be able to explain why we accept certain values: Evolutionary psychology suggests why there is such a widespread tendency to prize shininess, for instance (Coss and Moore 1990, Coss 2003, pp. 86–90). But showing that a feature is very useful for certain purposes (e.g., for life and/or evolutionary survival) is not, in itself, to show that those purposes are indeed valuable.

The values concerned in our judgments of creativity range very widely. Most are differentially accepted by distinct social groups, so that disagreements on attributions of creativity arise accordingly. Some are relatively long-lasting, whereas others are subject to quick-changing fashions. Moreover, many are domain-specific: The values considered appropriate to judgments of creativity in physics, say, differ from those applied in painting or poetry. Whether any values (perhaps symmetry?) are universally accepted and/or applicable to domains as different as physics and art are further contentious questions (see Boden 2006: 8.iv.b).

Yet other people interpret "novelty" very strongly, so that if it turns out that Bloggs had the idea in question before Robinson did, then Robinson's idea wasn't truly creative after all. And as for Bloggs and Robinson themselves, some philosophers insist that no individual should be marked out by this honorific, because creative ideas arise within human groups (some of whose members are systematically overlooked in attributions of creativity or even "discovery"; Schaffer 1994).

Finally, if one takes the terms *ideas* and *artifacts* literally, then biological evolution cannot properly be called creative. Yet it's often regarded as a hugely creative process.

In short, the concept of creativity is highly slippery. Since it is used in so many very different ways, discussions often founder because the discussants are talking at cross-purposes. As remarked above, none of these can be pronounced "right" or "wrong": All reflect some aspects of the phenomena being discussed. Nevertheless, it will be helpful here to pick one reasonably clear definition of the concept, with which to structure the argument.

My own definition sees creativity as the ability to generate creative ideas (a shorthand term that includes artifacts)—where a creative idea is one that is *novel, surprising, and valuable*. We've just seen that "valuable" can be given multiple interpretations. But the other terms also have more than one meaning: "novel" has two, and "surprising" has three.

First, an idea may be new *to the originator*; in that case, it is psychologically creative (P-creative for short). Or it may be, as far as is known, new *to the whole of human thought*; in that case, it is historically creative (or H-creative). Clearly, P-creativity includes H-creativity, because a historically new idea must also be new to the individual concerned. H-creativity is the more glamorous phenomenon and (as noted above) is sometimes assumed to be essential to creativity properly so-called. For our purposes here, however, P-creativity is the more interesting. That's because it leads us to consider the psychological mechanisms that underlie originality and that may, or may not, be simulated or even instantiated in computers.

Those mechanisms underlie the second aspect of my definition, namely, *surprise*. Phenomenologically, there are three types of surprise that we may feel on first encountering a creative idea (whether our own or someone else's).

One is the surprise we feel on seeing something happen that, because it is statistically unusual, we didn't expect, but that we always knew (or would have allowed, if we'd been asked) to have been possible. An example is the 100:1 outsider winning the horserace. The second is the surprise of seeing something that we didn't expect and had never even considered, but that, once it arises, we can see to fit into some previously familiar pattern; for instance, a new painting or musical composition by an artist who has already mastered an established style. And third is the shock we experience when presented with a new idea that is seemingly not just improbable and/or unexpected, but downright *impossible* (closed-ring molecules, for instance, at the time when molecules were still thought of as being open strands).

These three forms of surprise correspond to three types of creativity generated by different psychological mechanisms (Boden 2004). The first is *combinational* creativity, which involves the unfamiliar juxtaposition of familiar ideas. (Think of poetic imagery, musical "quotations," or visual collage.) The generative processes here are those of associative memory.

The other two types of originality are closely related, since each springs out of a previously accepted style of thinking or conceptual space. In *exploratory* creativity—which, on a first encounter, elicits the second type of surprise distinguished above—some familiar style/space is explored by generative processes that construct novel structures informed, and limited, by the constraints defining them. (Think of a novel fugue or the synthesis of a new molecule within a known chemical family.) Sometimes, the exploration is deliberately aimed at discovering and/or exhibiting individual constraints, and even at testing their limits. Those sorts of exploration can be done not only by the creator, but by the "audience" too. This is why the (structurally based) *surprisingness* of a Bach fugue, for instance, may continue to engage us, even though the initial *feeling* of surprise is no longer aroused.

The third type is *transformational* creativity, wherein the novel structure does not fit into any known style—and even seems *impossible on first acquaintance*. Typically, transformation follows on conscientious exploration. Pure exploration gives way to transformation when the originator alters (or drops) some previously recognized constraint or adds one or more new ones. This enables *fundamentally* new structures to be generated that were impossible relative to the previous (untransformed) style. The psychological mechanisms concerned are both exploratory (generative) and constraint-altering—where certain classes of alteration (e.g., constraint negation) can happen to many different constraints in many different domains.

Transformation is not creation ex nihilo. Some of the previous generative constraints will remain; and the novel constraints may show traces of their pre-alteration ancestors. Even the most shocking novelties will be somehow related to an old style. This relationship may not be immediately apparent, and still less well understood. Acceptance of the new structures as being "valuable" may take some time, for the stylistic similarities and differences must be both recognized and tolerated. (Pablo Picasso's cubist canvas *Les Demoiselles d'Avignon* was initially rejected even by his artist friends; when it was finally exhibited a few years later, it caused a public scandal.)

In other words, if one includes value within the concept of creativity, then structural change in thinking style is not sufficient for attributions of transformational creativity. Fresh judgments about value are required since (by definition) some previously accepted/valued constraints will have been ignored. And some of the new value judgments may depend on the extent to which the newly transformed style can support further *exploratory* creativity of an interesting kind (see the comparison of two graphics programs in section 3).

3. What Creativity-Denying Features Do Computers Possess?

It's commonly said that computer creativity is a contradiction in terms because the computer is programmed. It does what it has been told to do—or, better, *what it has been empowered to do*—by its programmer. (The qualification is needed partly because the human being often cannot predict the machine's performance. Even more to the point, the program may enable the machine—perhaps in contact with the external world, including the Internet—to learn/develop/evolve preferences very different from, perhaps even antithetical to, those of the programmer.)

In other words, being programmed is the antithesis of being autonomous— which (so this objection runs) is a necessary feature of creativity. Whatever *genuine* creativity is involved in so-called computer creativity, then, must pertain only to the human programmer.

People making this objection may allow that combinational and exploratory creativity can at least be *simulated* by computers. But they typically draw the line at transformational creativity because this involves not just a new thought but a new way of thinking—and that, it is claimed, cannot even be simulated by AI. After all, the skeptic will say, the rules/instructions specified in the program determine the computer's possible performance, and there's no going beyond them.

That remark is correct. But what it ignores is that the program may include rules *for changing itself.* For example, it may be able to learn—perhaps on the basis of unpredictable input from the environment, or perhaps due to its self-monitoring of internal "experimentation" of various kinds. Or, more to the point for our purposes here, it may contain genetic algorithms (GAs; see Boden 2006, 15.vi).

GAs can make random changes in the program's own task-oriented rules. These changes are similar to the point mutations and crossovers that underlie biological evolution. Many evolutionary programs also include a *fitness* function, which selects the best members of each new generation of task programs for use as "parents" in the next round of random rule-changing. In the absence of an automated fitness function, the selection must be made by a human being.

Evolutionary programming can result in prima facie examples of transformational AI. For example, Karl Sims's (1991) graphics program produces images that often differ radically from their predecessors, with *no* visible family resemblance. That's possible because its GAs allow not only point mutations (e.g., changing a numeral) within single programmed instructions, but also concatenations and/or hierarchical nestings of entire image-generating programs. So the program often arouses *impossibilist* surprise in the human beings observing it.

Whether Sims's computer system could deliver transformed *styles*, as well as transformed *items*, is another matter, for family resemblance is the essence of style. A style is a general pattern of ideas/artifacts that is sustained over time by the people adopting it. Sims's program cannot sustain a style, because a relatively fundamental mutation may occur at anytime. Indeed, human selectors who try to steer the system toward certain colors or shapes are always frustrated; sooner or later, unwanted features appear. In brief, Sims's program is almost *too* transformational. Other evolutionary programs exist that allow only minor mutations and correspondingly minor transformations. For instance, a GA program inspired by the sculptor William Latham can generate a sustained visual style (Todd and Latham 1992). However, this is new-ish rather than new, being highly reminiscent of the style of its human programmer/selector.

I said that various prima facie examples of transformational AI involve evolutionary programming. Why that cautious "prima facie"? Sims's program, after all, does generate radically transformed images. And Latham's program generates new-ish visual styles. Moreover, many highly efficient algorithms have been automatically evolved from *random* beginnings (for an early example, see Hillis 1992). If that's not transformation, what is?

Well, the objection here is a variant of the familiar argument that a computer can do only what its program tells it to do. It is posed by people who take the biological inspiration for evolutionary programming seriously (Pattee 1985, Cariani 1992; see also Boden 2006, p. 15.vi.c). They point out that programs are abstract systems and as such are logically self-contained. Even evolutionary programs, like those discussed above, are essentially limited to the possibilities inherent in the GAs and other rules supplied by the programmer. Genuine, truly radical transformations can arise in an evolving system, these objectors argue, only if it interacts *physically* with actual processes in the outside world.

Their favorite example concerns the origin of new organs of perception. They allow that once a light sensor has arisen in a biological organism, it can become more powerful as a result of genetic mutations that can be approximated in AI programs. So an inefficient computer vision system might, thanks to GAs, evolve into a better one. But the *first* light sensor, they insist, can arise only if some mutation occurs that causes a bodily change that happens to make the organism sensitive to light for the very first time. The light—considered as a physical process—was always out there in the world, of course. But only now is it "present" for the organism. One might say that only now has it passed from the world into the environment. That acceptance of light as part of the organism's environment depends crucially on physical processes—both in the world and in the living body. And these processes (so the argument goes) have no place in AI.

These skeptics (and many others) assume that AI is either simulation in a purely virtual world or abstract programming that defines all the interactions that can happen between program and world—as in computer vision, for example. It follows, they say, that the generative potential of a computer program is accordingly constrained. So although much-improved artifacts can result from evolutionary computing, no fundamentally new capacities can possibly arise. For instance, if the physical parameters foreseen by the programmer as potentially relevant don't happen to include light, then no artificial eye can ever emerge. In general, there can be no *genuine* transformations in AI.

That may be true of AI systems that are purely virtual simulations with no representation of physical parameters—as both Sims's and Latham's programs are. But (for reasons explained below) it need not be true of all virtual simulations. And it's demonstrably not true of all AI systems—in particular, of some work in so-called embodied AI. Indeed, recent research in this area has resulted in the evolution of *a novel sensor*: the very thing that these critics claim can happen only in biology.

In brief, a team of researchers was using a GA to evolve oscillator circuits—in hardware, not in simulation (Bird and Layzell 2002). To their amazement, they ended up with a primitive radio receiver. That is, the final (automatically selected) circuit acted as a radio antenna—a "radio-wave sensor"—that picked up and modified the background signal emanating from a nearby PC monitor.

On investigation post hoc, it turned out that the evolution of the radio-wave sensor had been driven by unforeseen physical parameters. One of these was the aerial-like properties of all printed circuit boards, which the team hadn't previously considered. But other key parameters were not merely unforeseen but unforeseeable, because the oscillatory behavior of the evolved circuit depended largely on accidental—and seemingly irrelevant—factors. These included spatial proximity to a PC monitor; the order in which the analogue switches had been set; and the fact that a soldering iron left on a nearby workbench happened to be plugged into the mains.

If the researchers had been aiming to evolve a radio receiver, they would never have considered switch order or soldering irons. Nor would either of these matters necessarily be relevant outside the specific (physical) situation in which this research was done. On another occasion, perhaps, arcane physical properties of the surrounding wallpaper might have played a role. So we can't be sure that even research in *embodied* AI could confidently *aim* to evolve a new sensor. The contingencies involved may be too great and too various. If so, doubt about (non-accidental) genuine transformations in AI still stands. But that they can sometimes happen unexpectedly is clear.

As suggested above, unexpected transformations might even happen in a *purely virtual* simulation, provided that it modeled the relevant interactions with the physical environment. For example, when Sims (1994) used GAs to evolve the anatomy and behavior of creatures made up of "blocks" of varying shapes and sizes, he found that some moved in lifelike ways whereas others, although equally efficient, did not. Their style of movement was hugely different from anything seen in biology—indeed, it was biologically *impossible.* On inspection, it turned out that Sims had mistakenly omitted a specific physical parameter from the simulated physics, and some creatures had evolved to take advantage of this. When he added it and restarted the experiment, no non-lifelike behavior appeared. So environmentally based transformations might be, in principle, impossible in a purely virtual model *only if* they depend on specific features of the physical world that could never be included, because they resist algorithmic simulation. In sum, it's true that *insofar as* a computer's performance is caused by its program, everything it does is somehow implicit in the instructions (perhaps including GAs) provided by its programmer. Only insofar as it can be affected by unforeseen events can genuinely new types of results emerge. Many of those events will be external to the system itself. However, they might be cultural/semantic, as well as physical: Accidental interactions with text or imagery on the Internet, for instance, might occasion creative transformations very different from what the programmer envisaged (see Boden forthcoming.) Moreover, they could also include internal events, if the system could perform information-processing internally, playing around in various ways (e.g., making novel combinations and exploring existing styles) with the structures already present in it.

4. What Essential Features of Creativity Might Computers Lack?

We've already seen that the concept of creativity is complex and highly slippery. But the kinds of slipperiness identified in section 2 are only part of the philosophical story here. Creativity is normally taken to be a property of new ideas and artifacts and/or of the people who originate them. Now, we must ask whether it involves features that computers—or, better, computer-based systems (see section 1)—lack.

Specifically, does it imply autonomy, intentionality, consciousness, value, and emotion—all of which are commonly assumed to be denied to computers?

Two different questions arise here. One (the topic of this section) asks whether each of those concepts is indeed crucial to creativity. The other (addressed in section 5) asks whether each is indeed necessarily lacking in computers.

A caveat: These questions are posed in essentialist terms ("*crucial to* creativity" and "*necessarily* lacking"). Yet in section 1, I repudiated essentialist approaches. Hard- and-fast definitions generating dichotomous distinctions aren't available for any concept of interest, and certainly not for creativity—nor, in turn, for autonomy, intentionality, consciousness, value, and emotion. It follows that each of the questions expressed above can be misleading. Nevertheless, they will be helpful in structuring our discussion—much as focusing on a particular definition of creativity can be helpful too.

The notion of *autonomy* or self-direction is implicit in talk of someone's "originating" an idea. Indeed, creativity is often thought of as a species of freedom. This need not be understood (although it often is) as freedom in a strongly individual sense. We saw in section 2 that some philosophers stress the social sources of originality and are wary of ascribing the creative responsibility to individuals. (For a psychologist's defense of this position, see Csikszentmihalyi 1999.) Even so, each member of the group of interacting, and perhaps deliberately cooperating, people is assumed to share the general human property of freedom or autonomy.

My own definition of creativity (in section 2) tacitly assumed that the novel idea was freely generated by the person concerned. Or rather, it assumed this with respect to H-creative ideas. The case of P-creative ideas is sometimes rather different. Sometimes, the origin of a P-creative idea can be predicted by a third party, or even largely brought about by their influence. Think of Socratic dialogue, for instance. Here an idea that has never occurred to the pupil is deliberately eased into existence by the tutor. There's a real sense in which the student *was not* wholly autonomous in coming up with the P-creative idea.

In the normal case, however, the person realizes the (perhaps very old and/ or very widespread) idea for the first time without such direct intervention. The P-creative idea may, of course, be suggested or triggered by some environmental cue. But that's just to say that the thought isn't random—not that it isn't autonomous.

In short, all H-creativity, and almost all P-creativity, is autonomous. It's made possible partly by idiosyncratic personal experience and partly by powerful (including meta-cognitive) information-processing mechanisms provided by evolution. The same is true of "free choice" in practical and moral reasoning (see below). In short, and despite all the many socio-cultural (and physical) influences on thinking, creative ideas are freely generated.

What of intentionality (a.k.a. "aboutness" or meaning)? This is, by definition, an essential property of *ideas*. And it's essential to *artifacts* too, for an artifact is not merely a physical thing many of whose features have been caused by a human being; that description would fit a collapsed tomato, accidentally trodden under-foot. Rather, it is a physical thing whose existence and/or some of whose features have been brought about by human action—typically, by deliberate human action. (Drop the "human" here and one could allow that artifacts might be made by the actions of chimps or by tool-using crows; Weir et al. 2002, Kacelnik et al. 2006.)

Some artifacts, to be sure, are not brought about by deliberate action: many poems and paintings of the Surrealists in the 1920s, for example. These artists engaged in automatic writing and painted while in trance states in order to priori-tize the unconscious mind—which Andre Breton declared to be "by far the most important part [of our mental world]." Indeed, Surrealism was defined by Breton as "Pure psychic automatism by which one proposes to express...the actual function-ing of thought, in the absence of any control exerted by reason, exempt from all aesthetic or moral preoccupations" (Breton 1969). Even if one accepts this descrip-tion at face value, however, one must grant that these artifacts arise from intentional, albeit involuntary, processes—namely, unconscious ideas and/or "automatic" (but meaningful) psychological processes.

So if creativity is defined—as it usually is—by reference to ideas and artifacts, it must be intentional. (Biological evolution could not then be classed as truly cre-ative, despite the many near-impossibilist surprises in phylogenesis; see section 2 above. For it produces new organs and new species, not new artifacts; and it does this by means of non-intentional processes.)

The third item in our list of key concepts here is consciousness. What of that? Does creativity necessarily involve consciousness?

Well, one might doubt this, because it's not only the Surrealists, with their explicit stress on the artist's unconscious ideas and automatisms, who have suggested that consciousness is *not* essential to creativity. It has long been noted that creative ideas are often generated without consciousness—much to the surprise of the person concerned.

For instance, they may "pop up" during artistic work or problem-solving with-out the originator's being able to say how this happened. Or they may arise in the so-called incubation phase of creativity, while the person is consciously thinking about something entirely different or even asleep (Boden 2004, pp. 29–35, 256–261). Moreover, they are *always* generated without full consciousness of the pro-cesses involved. But so too are the sentences we use in everyday conversation, and the perceptual, motor, and intellectual judgments that we make. (That's hardly sur-prising: If all such data, on every processing-level, were consciously available, they would present a paralyzing information overload.) The partial unconsciousness of creativity isn't a special case—although people often speak of it with awe as though it were.

Why, then, is it so widely believed that creativity requires consciousness (see Baumeister, Schmeichel, and DeWall, this volume)? The reason, I suggest, is that many of the creative activities of adults (in art, craft, and science) are consciously monitored throughout, sometimes in a highly self-conscious way (Harrison 1978). Even more to the point, they typically involve a conscious judgment that the final idea is valuable. Indeed, that's why some people are willing to ascribe "creativity" only if the creator recognizes the value of their own idea—as Kepler, at first, did not (see section 2) and as young children, despite their high P-creativity, in general do not. When Pablo Picasso declared proudly "*Je ne cherche pas, je trouve!*" he was denying only sustained deliberation (and error) on his part, not conscious appreciation of the *trouvaille*.

This consideration suggests that the fourth item on our list is included within the third. In other words, valuation is one of the many species of consciousness. According to the Surrealists (and their inspiration, Sigmund Freud), valuation is sometimes unconscious. But even they allowed that their unconsciously generated artworks attracted their conscious approval once they had been formed. Breton (1937, pp. 31ff.), for instance, spoke of the artist as a vigilant watchman (*guetteur*) in preconscious waters (*les eaux pre-conscientes*). Whether or not someone explicitly includes positive value in their definition (as I do; see section 2), people discussing creativity are in practice interested only in those novel ideas that someone approves. In brief, positive value is normally treated as an essential aspect of the concept.

Similar remarks apply to *emotion*, the last item on the list. I don't know of anyone who explicitly defines creativity with reference to emotion. My own intuition here is that a P-creative idea might perhaps be produced, and might even be recognized as valuable by its originator, without any specific emotion being involved. If that's so, then identifiable emotions (as distinct from the positive affect involved in judging something to be "valuable") aren't strictly necessary for creativity.

However, creativity in the arts is often associated with deep, and deeply personal, emotions. A poet's or architect's grief at losing a lover may inspire a masterpiece that's admired for hundreds of years. And emotions of many different kinds appear to be involved in other cases of artistic creativity. Nor is scientific creativity immune to emotion. Perhaps it's rarely driven by grief, but it's sometimes driven by jealousy, even if of a relatively superficial kind. And it's often inspired by a passionate desire for recognition or monetary gain. The selfless quest for knowledge is less common than scientists like to make out. Perhaps intellectual curiosity drove Archimedes and led him to leap from his bath in excitement on originating his novel and highly valuable idea—but even he expected to be rewarded by the king.

Indeed, positive valuation normally involves some emotional tone, howsoever mild that may be. And many creative thinkers have reported strong emotions as an aspect, even a driving aspect, of their work. So creativity typically, if not necessarily always, involves emotion.

As that word "driving" suggests, an emotion is *not* purely a matter of conscious feeling. To the contrary (as we see in section 5), emotions involve complex mechanisms deeply embedded in our mental architecture and are needed for scheduling activities in complex multi-motivated creatures (Boden 2006, 7.i.d-f). Grief, for example, and its gradual assuagement through mourning, involves obsessional memories, sudden interrupts, and frequent distractions of goal-driven activities. However, it also involves intense feelings of sadness, desolation, and loss. It is these conscious aspects of emotion, or emotional qualia, which people normally have in mind when they speak of emotions in creative thinking. In the context of our discussion, then, emotion—like value—is a species of consciousness.

In sum: Autonomy, intentionality, and consciousness (including valuation and emotion) are indeed—with minor qualifications—typical of creativity. It's not surprising that philosophers of an essentialist disposition regard them as *essential* to creativity.

5. So Could a Computer Really Be Creative?

To ask whether a computer could "really" be creative is to ask whether any of the concepts considered in section 4 is forever barred to computers (or to computer-based information-processing systems). The answer is clear in only one case, that of autonomy.

The presumption of autonomy as a sine qua non of creativity is what drives the objection that a computer can do only what its programmer tells/enables it to do. That objection was broadly accepted above (in section 3)—although it was also pointed out that a computer's performance may be unpredictable and may even involve the development of values/preferences very different from those of the programmer. So we must allow that, *in that strictly limited sense*, no programmed system can be truly autonomous. In that sense also, then, computers cannot be truly creative either.

This claim might be challenged on the grounds that some AI scientists—and some computer artists too—actually make a point of describing their systems as "autonomous." In saying this, they are highlighting certain interesting features of the ways in which their machines function. That is, they are all (reasonably) distancing their computer's performance from an unalterable program written by a human programmer, and thus (reasonably) asserting some degree of independence on the machine's part. But they are not all focusing on the same features, so they are using the term "autonomous" in three very different senses to denote distinct types of processing—only one of which is at all analogous to human freedom (Boden 2010).

Fortunately, we need not enquire here just how close that analogy is—I say "fortunately" because the concept of freedom is itself highly contentious. Like most cognitive scientists, I interpret it in computational terms, as marking a particular type of cognitive/motivational complexity (Boden 2006, 7.i.g, Dennett 1984). Some philosophers would regard this view as not merely mistaken, but profoundly absurd (see below). Yet if we allow, as argued in section 3, that programmed systems do not possess autonomy—because the program, *even if* it's one that bears some resemblance to human freedom, was originated by a human being—that philosophical disagreement can be ignored.

Comparable philosophical disagreements arise with respect to the other key concepts here, however. And they cannot be sidelined so quickly. Intentionality and consciousness (and values and emotion too) are hugely controversial. Indeed, they are so problematic that we don't understand them well enough to be able to ask the question about "real" creativity sensibly, never mind answer it.

Some philosophers will disagree. They deem it obvious, even near-axiomatic, that computers lack these key properties. This is true of writers in the broadly neo-Kantian tradition, from phenomenologists to postmodernists, and recently, some analytical philosophers too (e.g., McDowell 1994, Morris 1991, 1992). Martin Heidegger, for example, glossed intentionality and consciousness as *Dasein*, which he ascribed only to human beings. For orthodox Heideggerians, even nonhuman animals lack *Dasein* (a point disputed by some of his more scientifically minded followers; Wheeler 2005, pp. 157–160). The notion that it could be possessed by computers is rejected by neo-Kantians as a fortiori absurd. So is the notion that intentionality could ever be explained by science—even by evolutionary theory and/or neuroscience. They argue that intentionality is the ground of all our conceptual thought, science included, so a naturalistic psychology is impossible (Boden 2006, 16.vi-viii).

Notoriously, the split between neo-Kantian and naturalistic/empiricist views is the deepest split within Western philosophy. That's true even though analytically trained philosophers now take neo-Kantianism more seriously than they did 20 years ago (cf. Williamson 2007). Not only does it affect discussion on all philosophical questions (cf. Blackburn 2005), but it cannot be definitively settled: There is no knockdown argument on either side.

Jerry Fodor, responding to John McDowell's version of the anti-naturalist position, declared that McDowell was "as good a contemporary representative of this philosophical sensibility as you could hope to find," but insisted that "it's all wrong-headed. Science isn't an enemy, it's just us" (Fodor 1995, p. 8). Praising McDowell's book for raising "a number of our deepest perplexities," he defiantly added, "Which, however, is not to say that I believe a word of it" (Fodor 1995b, p. 3). Notice that telltale expression: *I [don't] believe a word of it.* Fodor was admitting that he couldn't actually disprove McDowell's account. Certainly, he had identified several aspects of McDowell's core concept of "second nature" that he felt were mistaken, unjustified, or merely metaphorical. (What is it, for instance, to "resonate" to meaning?) And he'd offered his own, alternative claims. But even the supremely self-confident Fodor didn't suggest that these were strictly provable.

One brave—or perhaps foolhardy?—philosophically minded computer scientist, Brian Cantwell Smith (1996), has tried to bridge the gap by rolling intentionality and computation together within his basic metaphysical definition. The philosopher Haugeland is quoted on Smith's book cover as saying: "Smith recreates our understanding of objects essentially from scratch—and changes, I think, everything." If Smith is right, then that is true. But it's by no means clear that he is right. (My own view is that Smith helped himself to the "dynamic flux," his version of Kant's noumenal world, without proper license—see Boden 2006, 16.ix.e. He claims, in his final 60 pages, that he's pulled this concept up by its own bootstraps to form a "constructivist" metaphysics of objects and intentionality—cf. also pp. 188f. But it seems to me that he begs this fundamental philosophical question instead of answering it.)

Nor is this naturalist/neo-Kantian split the only problem here. On each side of the split, people disagree among themselves. The naturalists, for instance—whom I, like Fodor, believe must be basically correct—offer several radically different accounts of intentionality.

A few, like Smith, offer highly eccentric theories wherein intentionality and/ or information is made metaphysically basic (i.e., not confined to minds, whether human or animal; e.g., Chalmers 1996). But even the less eccentric approaches vary significantly. For example, some naturalists define intentionality as a causal phenomenon (Dretske 1984, 1995); others gloss it as computational (Sloman 1986, 1987b); while yet others see it as somehow rooted in biological evolution (Dennett 1969, Millikan 1984, Papineau 1987).

None of these positions is free of difficulties. The evolutionist Ruth Millikan, for instance, argues that a miraculously assembled molecule-for-molecule replica of a person (the so-called swamp-man), with causal powers identical to those of a real human being, would lack intentionality. Although the swamp-man's verbal responses would be just like ours, his/its words would lack all meaning—simply because he/it had been nanoassembled, not biologically evolved. My own view (as someone sympathetic to Millikan's approach) is that this highly counterintuitive claim cannot be contradicted but may be ignored, much as in practice we ignore the theoretical possibility—according to statistical thermodynamics—of there being, if only for a split second, a snowball in Hell. Nevertheless, it must be admitted that swamp-man is something of an embarrassment. And swamp-man isn't the only problem. Causal theories of intentionality, for instance, have difficulty accounting for non-veridical content. In short, there is no theory of intentionality that satisfies all naturalists.

But at least those disputatious philosophers can understand each other. The situation is even worse with respect to consciousness. Not only do the naturalists and neo-Kantians locate it on opposite sides of the split, asking very different questions accordingly, but those within the naturalist camp are far from mutual intelligibility, never mind agreement (Boden 2006, 14.xxi, 16.iv.b). This is especially true with regard to what David Chalmers (1996) has called the "hard" problem, namely, the analysis/explanation of conscious sensations, or qualia.

The competing naturalist accounts of consciousness include a number that are expressed in relatively traditional terms (e.g., Block 1995, 2001, Searle 1992) and even more that appeal to science. Some recent analyses lean heavily on neuroscience (e.g., Baars 1988, 2001, Dehaene and Naccache 2001, Edelman and Tononi 2000, Edelman and Seth 2009), while others are based in speculations about quantum physics—thus inviting the charge of attempting to solve one mystery by citing another (e.g., Chalmers 1996, Penrose 1989, 1994, Walker 2000). One philosopher of strong scientific sympathies argues—a position that is possibly correct, but in my view unnecessarily defeatist—that the mystery here is permanent, because the human mind simply lacks the cognitive capacity to achieve a scientific understanding of consciousness, much as dogs lack whatever's needed to understand language or physics (McGinn 1991).

Besides all those candidates is a clutch of scientifically influenced theories that strike many people, including other naturalists, as even more counterintuitive than swamp-man. They're regarded as especially bizarre, even as unintelligible, when they're applied to qualia. These are the various computational theories of consciousness. Not all of them focus on the key question of this section, namely, whether there can be such a thing as "machine consciousness" (Holland 2003). However, anyone who offers a computational account of (any aspect of) human consciousness must admit that suitably similar computer-based information-processing systems could, in principle, be conscious too.

Two of these theories are especially interesting: the analyses of human and animal consciousness developed over many years by Marvin Minsky (1985, 2006) and by Aaron Sloman (1999, 2000, 2010a,b; Sloman and Chrisley 2003). Both focus on the computational architecture of the mind as a whole, and they are similar in a number of ways. But Sloman's account is more systematic than Minsky's (and is closely related to his discussions of philosophical problems like cause, freedom, possibility, reference, and intentionality).

Sloman points out—what is often stated, but also often forgotten—that the noun "consciousness" is highly misleading. We'd do far better to consider cases where a subject is "conscious of" X or Y. There are many such cases in both humans and animals that differ considerably from each other. They don't differ merely in intensity; nor do they fall on a continuous spectrum. Rather, they differ in their essential computational structure. In other words, the multitudinous varieties of consciousness are aspects of the multidimensional virtual machines that we call "minds."

Like virtual machines in computers (Sloman argues), these aspects of mind are real and have real causal effects. Qualia, for example, are internal computational states that have various effects on behavior and/or on other aspects of the mind's information processing. They can exist only in virtual machines of significant structural complexity (he outlines the types of computational resources that are required). They can be accessed only by some other parts of the particular virtual machine concerned and do not necessarily have any behavioral expression. In particular, they cannot always be described (by higher, self-monitoring levels of the mind) in verbal terms. So whereas some computationalists—such as Daniel Dennett (1991, 1995)—deny the reality of qualia, *even in human minds*, Sloman does not. (This doesn't mean that he identifies them with brain processes. Some computational states cannot be defined in the language of physical descriptions— even though they can exist, and have causal effects, only when implemented in some underlying physical mechanism.)

We saw in section 4 that the aspects of consciousness that are closely related with and perhaps even essential for creativity are emotions, value judgments, and deliberate self-monitoring. According to Sloman, in order to generate such phenomena, the virtual machine that is the mind needs to be of a certain kind.

Emotions, for instance, involve scheduling mechanisms that are necessary in multi-motive creatures acting in a complex and largely unpredictable world (Sloman 1978, 1987a, 1993). (So the emotionless Mr. Spock of *Star Trek* is an evolutionary impossibility.) That's true even of grief, which has driven every Renaissance *Pieta* and many other works of art besides. This emotion, with its characteristic and diverse effects, can—and inevitably will—arise only in minds architecturally capable of deep personal love (Fisher 1990). Sloman has explained the psychology of this phenomenon and its alleviation through mourning in computational terms (Wright et al. 1996).

More accurately, grief and other emotions have been broadly outlined by him (and by Minsky 2006) in computational terms, using theoretical concepts and insights drawn from AI. Functioning computer models based on his and Minsky's ideas are very few on the ground. Indeed, most so-called computer models of emotion are based on very superficial psychological theories. These normally assume, for instance, that emotion must have behavioral effects (which precludes allowing that grief can endure for years even though it is often temporarily dormant or seemingly eclipsed by mirth). However, a few varieties of the emotion of anxiety have been simulated by Sloman's group (Wright 1997,; Wright and Sloman 1997; see also Boden 2006, 7.i.f).

The types of anxiety concerned are among those that a nursemaid might experience while left in sole charge of a dozen hungry, attention-demanding, and active babies—in a nursery where two open doors lead onto a busy road and a garden stream. Crucially, "might experience" here doesn't primarily mean "might feel." (In other words, this is not intended as a model of qualia.) For these distinct species of anxiety enable the nursemaid to prioritize her motives and schedule her actions appropriately.

They reflect the facts that some goals cannot be pursued simultaneously (she has only two hands, after all, and can't be in two places at once); some goals conflict in a stronger sense, so that at most one of them can be achieved; some are hugely important, but never urgent; others are both important and urgent; some are relatively unimportant, but must be attempted urgently if they are to be attempted at all; some goals may be postponed (perhaps only for a limited period) while another is given priority; and others, which cannot be postponed indefinitely, must be abandoned if they can't be achieved quite soon.

Clearly, these facts apply to all tasks that require multi-motive scheduling, where conflicts between motives can arise for many different reasons. So this isn't merely a model of (some types of) anxiety. It illustrates the nature of emotion in general.

That's not to say that it fully reflects the architectural complexity of the human case. The emotional demands on the simulated nursemaid, who has only seven motives to follow, are much more complex than those represented in other current simulations of emotion. To that extent, they are a significant advance. But real nursemaids, besides satisfying the seven motives represented in this model, have to also worry about cuddling the babies, bathing them, changing them, singing to them, protecting them from live electric plugs…and so on.

The psychology of grief and of many other emotions is more challenging still. The necessary structural complexity is orders of magnitude greater than that of any current computer system. Even more to the point, it involves architectural distinctions that we are only just beginning to understand. So to attempt even to model (never mind instantiate) grief in a computer-based system today would be hugely premature.

It follows that a computational understanding of how some examples of human creativity are driven by grief is available to us only in the sketchiest terms. Nevertheless, these ideas help us to understand how grief is possible—and how among its many manifestations, there may be a drive to commemorate the lost love in painting, poetry, or song.

6. Conclusion

The previous few paragraphs will strike some readers as ridiculous, because the notion that there could be a *computational* theory of consciousness (including emotions and valuation) seems, to many people, to be intuitively absurd or even unintelligible (see Nanay, this volume). (It's worth mentioning, however, that Sloman's account of grief appeared in a journal whose editor, as a consultant psychiatrist, is all too familiar with the ravages of grief and mourning.) As already remarked, that reaction can occur even on the naturalist side of the philosophical fence—and is de rigueur on the neo-Kantian side.

To reject computationalism, however, is not to agree on an alternative. As we saw in section 5, even the non-computationalist naturalists differ hugely about the nature of intentionality and consciousness. Should one appeal to neuroscience or to quantum physics? Or to neither? Should one favor a maverick philosophical position in which intentionality/information is metaphysically basic? Or should one throw up one's hands in despair, proclaiming that these matters lie forever beyond human ken?

In sum, the question of whether a computer could ever "really" be creative is currently unanswerable, because it involves several highly contentious philosophical questions. If we take the argument about autonomy seriously, then we can agree that "AI-creativity" is a contradiction in terms, even though a computer's performance may be very much more independent of its program than is usually assumed. But if we appeal rather to intentionality or consciousness, the question must remain open.

References

Baars, B. J. 1988. *A Cognitive Theory of Consciousness.* Cambridge, UK: Cambridge University Press.

Baars, B. J. 2001. *In the Theatre of Consciousness: The Workspace of the Mind.* Oxford, UK: Oxford University Press.

Bird, J., and Layzell, P. 2002. "The Evolved Radio and its Implications for Modeling the Evolution of Novel Sensors," *Proceedings of Congress on Evolutionary Computation,* CEC-2002, pp. 1836–1841.

Blackburn, S. W. 2005. *Truth: A Guide for the Perplexed.* The Gifford Lectures 2004. London: Allen Lane.

Block, N. 1995. "On a Confusion About a Function of Consciousness," *Behavioral and Brain Sciences,* 18(2): pp. 227–287.

Block, N. 2001. "Paradox and Cross Purposes in Recent Work on Consciousness," *Cognition,* 79: pp. 197–219.

Boden, M. A. 1990(2004). *The Creative Mind: Myths and Mechanisms.* 2nd ed., expanded/revised. London: Routledge.

Boden, M. A. 2006. *Mind as Machine: A History of Cognitive Science.* Oxford, UK: Clarendon Press.

Boden, M. A. 2010. "Autonomy, Integrity, and Computer Art," in M. A. Boden, *Creativity and Art: Three Roads to Surprise* (Oxford, UK: Oxford University Press), chap. 9.

Boden, M. A. (forthcoming). "Can Evolutionary Art Provide Radical Novelty?" in M. A. Boden and E. A. Edmonds, *Perspectives on Computer Art* (provisional title), ch. 11.

Breton, A. 1937. *L'Amour Fou.* Paris: Gallimard.

Breton, A. 1969. *Manifestoes of Surrealism,* trans. R. Seaver and H. R. Lane. Ann Arbor: University of Michigan Press.

Cariani, P. 1992. "Emergence and Artificial Life," in C. G. Langton, C. Taylor, J. D. Farmer, and S. Rasmussen (eds.), *Artificial Life II.* Redwood City, CA: Addison-Wesley, pp. 775–797.

Chalmers, D. J. 1996. *The Conscious Mind: In Search of A Fundamental Theory.* Oxford, UK: Oxford University Press.

Cope, D. 2001. *Virtual Music: Computer Synthesis of Musical Style.* Cambridge, MA: MIT Press.

Cope, D. 2006. *Computer Models of Musical Creativity.* Cambridge, MA: MIT Press.

Coss, R. G. 2003. "The Role of Evolved Perceptual Biases in Art and Design," in E. Voland and K. Grammer (eds.), *Evolutionary Aesthetics.* London: Springer, pp. 69–130.

Coss, R. G., and Moore, M. 1990. "All that Glistens: Water Connotations in Surface Finishes," *Ecological Psychology,* 2: 367–380.

Csikszentmihalyi, M. 1999. "Implications of a Systems Perspective for the Study of Creativity," in R. J. Sternberg (ed.), *Handbook of Creativity.* Cambridge, UK: Cambridge University Press, pp. 313–335.

Dehaene, S., and Naccache, L. 2001. "Towards a Cognitive Neuroscience of Consciousness: Basic Evidence and a Workspace Framework," *Cognition,* 79: pp. 1–37.

Dennett, D. C. 1969. *Content and Consciousness: An Analysis of Mental Phenomena.* London: Routledge & Kegan Paul.

Dennett, D. C. 1984. *Elbow Room: The Varieties of Free Will Worth Wanting*. Cambridge, MA: MIT Press.

Dennett, D. C. 1991. *Consciousness Explained*. London: Allen Lane.

Dennett, D. C. 1995. "The Unimagined Preposterousness of Zombies: Commentary on Moody, Flanagan, and Polger," *Journal of Consciousness Studies*, 2: pp. 322–326.

Dretske, F. I. 1984. *Knowledge and the Flow of Information*. Oxford, UK: Blackwell.

Dretske, F. I. 1995. *Naturalizing the Mind*. Cambridge, MA: MIT Press.

Edelman, G. M., and Seth, A. 2009. "Animal Consciousness: A Synthetic Approach," *Trends in Neurosciences*, 9: pp. 476–484.

Edelman, G. M., and Tononi, G. 2009. *Consciousness: How Matter Becomes Imagination*. London: Allen Lane.

Fisher, E. M. 1990. *Personal Love*. London: Duckworth.

Fodor, J. A. 1995. "Review of John McDowell's *Mind and World*," *The London Review of Books*, 17:8, April 20th, pp. 10–11. Reprinted in J. A. Fodor, *In Critical Condition: Polemical Essays on Cognitive Science and the Philosophy of Mind* (Cambridge, MA: MIT Press, 1998), pp. 3–8.

Harrison, A. 1978. *Making and Thinking: A Study of Intelligent Activities*. Sussex, UK: Harvester Press.

Haugeland, J. 1978. "The Nature and Plausibility of Cognitivism," *Behavioral and Brain Sciences*, 1: pp. 215–226.

Hillis, W. D. 1992. "Co-Evolving Parasites Improve Simulated Evolution as an Optimization Procedure," in C. G. Langton, C. Taylor, J. D. Farmer, and S. Rasmussen (eds.), *Artificial Life II* (Redwood City, CA: Addison-Wesley), pp. 313–324.

Holland, O. (ed.) 2003. *Machine Consciousness* (Exeter, UK: Imprint Academic). Special issue of the *Journal of Consciousness Studies*, 10 (4–5).

Kacelnik, A., Chappell, J., Weir, A. A. S., and Kenward, B. 2006. "Cognitive Adaptations for Tool-Related Behaviour in Caledonian Crows," in E. A. Wasserman and T. R. Zentall (eds.), *Comparative Cognition: Experimental Explorations of Animal Behaviour*. Oxford, UK: Oxford University Press, pp. 515–528.

McDowell, J. 1994. *Mind and World*. Cambridge, MA: Harvard University Press.

McGinn, C. 1991. *The Problem of Consciousness*. Oxford, UK: Basil Blackwell.

Millikan, R. G. 1984. *Language, Thought, and Other Biological Categories: New Foundations for Realism*. Cambridge, MA: MIT Press.

Minsky, M. L. 1985. *The Society of Mind*. New York: Simon & Schuster.

Minsky, M. L. 2006. *The Emotion Machine: Commonsense Thinking, Artificial Intelligence, and the Future of the Human Mind*. New York: Simon & Schuster.

Morris, M. R. 1991. "Why There Are No Mental Representations," *Minds and Machines*, 1: pp. 1–30.

Morris, M. R. 1992. *The Good and the True*. Oxford, UK: Clarendon Press.

Papineau, D. 1987. *Reality and Representation*. Oxford, UK: Basil Blackwell.

Pattee, H. H. 1985. "Universal Principles of Measurement and Language Functions in Evolving Systems," in J. Casti and A. Karlqvist (eds.), *Complexity, Language, and Life: Mathematical Approaches*. Berlin: Springer-Verlag, pp. 168–281.

Penrose, R. 1989. *The Emperor's New Mind: Concerning Computers, Minds, and the Laws of Physics*. Oxford, UK: Oxford University Press.

Penrose, R. 1994. *Shadows of the Mind: A Search for the Missing Science of Consciousness*. Oxford, UK: Oxford University Press.

Schaffer, S. 1994. "Making Up Discovery," in M. A. Boden (ed.), *Dimensions of Creativity*. Cambridge, MA: MIT Press, pp. 14–51.

Searle, J. R. 1992. *The Rediscovery of the Mind*. Cambridge, MA: MIT Press.

Sims, K. 1991. "Artificial Evolution for Computer Graphics," *Computer Graphics*, 25 (no. 4): pp. 319–328.

Sims, K. 1994. "Evolving 3D-Morphology and Behavior by Competition," *Artificial Life*, 1: pp. 353–372.

Sloman, A. 1986. "What Sorts of Machines Can Understand the Symbols They Use?" *Proceedings of the Aristotelian Society*, Supp., 60: pp. 61–80.

Sloman, A. 1987a. "Motives, Mechanisms, and Emotions," *Cognition and Emotion*, 1: pp. 217–233. Reprinted in M. A. Boden (ed.), *The Philosophy of Artificial Intelligence*. Oxford, UK: Oxford University Press, 1990, pp. 231–247.

Sloman, A. 1987b. "Reference Without Causal Links," in J. B. H. du Boulay, D. Hogg, and L. Steels (eds.), *Advances in Artificial Intelligence—II*. Dordrecht NL: North Holland, pp. 369–381.

Sloman, A. 1993. "The Mind as a Control System," in C. Hookway and D. Peterson (eds.), *Philosophy and the Cognitive Sciences*. Cambridge, UK: Cambridge University Press, pp. 69–110.

Sloman, A. 1999. "Review of [R. Picard's] *Affective Computing*," *AI Magazine*, 20:1 (March), pp. 127–133.

Sloman, A. 2000. "Architectural Requirements for Human-like Agents Both Natural and Artificial (What Sorts of Machines Can Love?)," in K. Dautenhahn (ed.), *Human Cognition and Social Agent Technology: Advances in Consciousness Research*. Amsterdam: John Benjamins, pp. 163–195.

Sloman, A. 2010a. "An Alternative to Working on Machine Consciousness," *International Journal of Machine Consciousness*, 2(1), available at www.cs.bham.ac.uk/research/projects/cogaff.

Sloman, A. 2010b. "Phenomenal and Access Consciousness and the "Hard" Problem: A View from the Designer Stance," *International Journal of Machine Consciousness*, 2(1), available at www.cs.bham.ac.uk/research/projects/cogaff.

Sloman, A., and Chrisley, R. L. 2003. "Virtual Machines and Consciousness," in O. Holland (ed.), *Machine Consciousness*. Exeter, UK: Imprint Academic, pp. 133–172.

Smith, B. C. 1996. *On the Origin of Objects*. Cambridge, MA: MIT Press.

Smith, T., Husbands, P., and O'Shea, M. 2002. "Neuronal Plasticity and Temporal Adaptivity: Gas Net Robot Control Networks," *Adaptive Behavior*, 10: pp. 161–183.

Sperber, D., and Wilson, D. 1986. *Relevance: Communication and Cognition*. Oxford, UK: Blackwell.

Todd, S. C., and Latham, W. 1992. *Evolutionary Art and Computers*. London: Academic Press.

Walker, E. H. 2000. *The Physics of Consciousness: The Quantum Mind and the Meaning of Life*. Cambridge, MA: Perseus.

Weir, A. A. S., Chappell, J., and Kacelnik, A. 2002. "Shaping of Hooks in New Caledonian Crows," *Science*, 297: p. 981.

Wheeler, M. W. 2005. *Reconstructing the Cognitive World: The Next Step*. Cambridge, MA: MIT Press.

Williamson, T. 2007. *The Philosophy of Philosophy* (Oxford, UK: Blackwell).

Wittgenstein, L. 1953. *Philosophical Investigations*, trans. G. E. M. Anscombe (Oxford, UK: Blackwell).

Wright, I. P. 1997. "Emotional Agents," Ph.D. diss., School of Computer Science, University of Birmingham, available at http://www.cs.bham.ac.uk/research/cogaff/.

Wright, I. P., and Sloman, A. 1997. *MINDER1: An Implementation of a Protoemotional Agent Architecture*. Technical Report CSRP-97-1, University of Birmingham, School of Computer Science (available at ftp://ftp.cs.bham.ac.uk/pub/tech-reports/1997/CSRP-97-01.ps.gz)

Wright, I. P., Sloman, A., and Beaudoin, L. P. 1996. "Towards a Design-Based Analysis of Emotional Episodes," *Philosophy, Psychiatry, and Psychology*, 3: pp. 101–137.

PART SIX

PHILOSOPHY OF SCIENCE

12

Hierarchies of Creative Domains

Disciplinary Constraints on Blind Variation and Selective Retention

DEAN KEITH SIMONTON

Creativity comes in many flavors. As a first cut, we can clearly distinguish creativity in the arts from creativity in the sciences. Yet surely not all forms of artistic creativity are the same. The creativity of an academic or classical artist must depart from that of an expressive or romantic artist, for example (Ludwig 1998). Even within the sciences, we can separate the creativity of the natural sciences (e.g., physics) from the creativity of the social sciences (e.g., sociology). Moreover, within each discipline or sub-discipline, we can easily make finer distinctions. According to Kuhn's (1970) analysis of scientific history, there are two types of scientists: (1) practitioners of normal science who engage in "puzzle-solving" research confined within a given paradigm, and (2) scientific revolutionaries who propose a new paradigm to replace the old. Presumably, the creativity of the normal scientist operates in a different manner from the creativity of the revolutionary scientist (Ko and Kim 2008, Sternberg 1999b).

Now, granting the existence of these varieties of creativity, we can then ask the following questions: Do creative domains differ systematically or do they differ willy-nilly? If the former holds, what is the basis for the differences? Can the inter-domain contrasts have logical and even psychological foundations? If so, what are the repercussions of those foundations for understanding creativity? I address these questions by integrating two rather distinct philosophical traditions.

The first concerns whether we can array the creative domains into a hierarchy, an issue that has roots in Plato's (ca. 360 B.C.E.) *Republic*, Immanuel Kant's (1790) *Critique of the Power of Judgment*, Auguste Comte's (1830–1842) *Positive Philosophy*, and Thomas Kuhn's (1970) *Structure of Scientific Revolutions*. This tradition can be best styled as Comtean.

The second tradition regards whether creativity and discovery can be conceived as involving a blind variation and selective retention (BVSR) process (Martindale 2009). The BVSR position has antecedents in Alexander Bain (1855), William

James (1880), Ernst Mach (1896), and Henri Poincaré (1921), and then continued with Karl Popper (1959) and Donald T. Campbell (1960). This tradition can be somewhat more generously referred to as Bainian.

I will then show that domains can be ordered according to the extent to which creativity in that domain operates in a BVSR manner. That conclusion then has implications for the kinds of dispositional traits and developmental experiences that are most typical of creators in various domains. These traits and experiences are relevant insofar as they influence the degree to which a person engages in BVSR creativity.

1. Comtean Disciplinary Hierarchies

The ancient Greeks assigned muses to major domains of creativity. According to legend, Zeus, the reigning god in the Greek pantheon, fathered nine daughters who were responsible for heroic or epic poetry, lyric and love poetry, sacred poetry, tragedy, comedy, music, dance, astronomy, and history. That each domain required a distinct goddess hints that the source of inspiration depends on the type of creativity. Some philosophers went a step further by arguing that some domains were superior to other domains. For instance, Plato made it clear in his *Republic* that mathematics was superior to the visual arts. While mathematicians discovered genuine truth in the ideal world of "forms," artists did no more than make facsimiles of mere appearances—copies of shadows—and thus the artistic creators were sadly two steps removed from those forms. Of course, the relative status of domains would be contingent on the criteria used. These criteria would differ across thinkers and across history. Thus, in the Middle Ages it was theology that became proclaimed as the "queen of the sciences," providing the capstone to a complete university education.

Kant put forward a more enduring distinction in his *Critique of the Power of Judgment*. Having defined genius as the capacity to produce ideas that are both original and exemplary, he then made the bold claim that such genius could only be manifested in the fine arts. Creativity in the sciences had no need of genius because scientists confine themselves to fact and logic—the "scientific method"—rather than give free reign to their imaginations. Even Isaac Newton was denied genius status. Although Kant overstated his case, this contrast between artistic and scientific creativity will prove to be central later in this chapter.

Yet even within the sciences, distinctions might be made. Kuhn (1970) distinguished between pre-paradigmatic and paradigmatic sciences. In the former, scientists have not yet attained a consensus on the theoretical concepts and methodological techniques that define the discipline. Such scientific disciplines are plagued by contending schools that represent distinct theories and methods. Paradigmatic sciences, in contrast, exhibit a strong theoretical and methodological consensus. This consensus is often centered on certain exemplars, such as Newton's *Principia*

Mathematica in physics or Darwin's *Origin of Species* in biology, which provide models of scientific excellence. The contrast I mentioned earlier between revolutionary and normal scientists can only apply in any meaningful way to paradigmatic sciences. In a sense, there are three kinds of science: pre-paradigmatic, paradigmatic but normal, and paradigmatic but revolutionary. The revolutionaries are not anti-paradigm, but rather are motivated to provide the discipline with a more successful paradigm that can once again guide practitioners of normal science.

Naturally, instead of viewing sciences in dichotomous terms, we can array them according to the degree to which they are paradigmatic. Physical sciences are noticeably more paradigmatic than the biological sciences, and the biological sciences, in turn, are more paradigmatic than the social sciences, most of which are largely if not entirely pre-paradigmatic (classical macroeconomics marking a possible exception). This conception would then allow the main scientific disciplines to be ordered into a hierarchy. The resulting hierarchy, in fact, would probably be reminiscent of Comte's (1839–1842) speculation that the main sciences could be placed in the following order: astronomy, physics, chemistry, biology, and sociology. To be sure, Comte's own ordering was not predicated on the degree to which creators adhere to a paradigm, but rather according to whether one discipline is contingent upon another (e.g., chemistry depends on physics just as biology depends on chemistry). Even so, the correspondence remains striking. In Comte's day, astronomy and physics were already highly paradigmatic, courtesy of Newton and Pierre-Simon Laplace, while chemistry was slowly catching up after the anti-phlogiston paradigm shift introduced by Antoine Lavoisier. With the advent of Charles Darwin still decades away, biology was largely pre-paradigmatic, while sociology did not yet exist as an organized discipline—indeed, it was Comte who coined the discipline's name!

These observations now take us to the key question that drives this chapter: Can we extend this ordering even further to encompass the principal domains of creative achievement? By principal domains, I mean those that have the most persistent and most omnipresent manifestations in the history of civilization, namely, the major sciences, humanities, and arts (see, e.g., the main categories in Cox 1926, Galton 1869, Kroeber 1944, Murray 2003). Given the Comtean hierarchy of the sciences and the Kantian distinction between scientific and artistic creativity, it would seem that the arts might be appended to the hierarchy somewhere after the social sciences. Furthermore, it might also be possible to insert the humanities into the disciplinary sequence, presumably somewhere between the sciences and the arts. The possibility of an extended hierarchy is certainly suggested by Henry Bliss's (1935) influential bibliographic classification system. Nonetheless, as said before, the order of the disciplines in any such configuration must depend on the criteria by which those disciplines are assessed. If the goal is to understand how creativity varies across domains, then I argue that the optimal criterion is the extent to which the creative process in a given domain depends on blind variation and selective retention. It is to that second intellectual tradition that we now turn.

2. Bainian BVSR Creativity

Charles Darwin's *Origin of Species* provided the first completely naturalistic explanation for the appearance of what can be referred to as *adaptive originality* (Simonton 2009a). New species emerge from old species not through divine creation or Lamarckian "inner strivings," but rather variations are spontaneously generated that are then subjected to natural selection. Darwin was insistent that the variations produced could be maladaptive, as well as adaptive—there was no prescience in the process. The less fit variations would be simply weeded out in the "struggle for existence" driven by Malthusian population pressures. In a sense, Darwin was providing a theory of the creative process in nature. Creativity is frequently defined as an idea or behavior that has the joint properties of novelty and utility, but these two qualities might be replaced with originality and adaptiveness without a major shift in meaning. One is thereby led to wonder whether human creativity operates by a similar process of variation and selection.

As a naturalist, of course, Darwin had no interest in this question. The closest he came to discussing human creativity appeared in his (1871) *Descent of Man*, and then it was just to speculate on how the capacity for certain kinds of creativity might have been the result of sexual selection. However, William James (1880), the American psychologist and (later) pragmatist philosopher, made a more direct connection. He began by claiming that

> social evolution is a resultant of the interaction of two wholly distinct factors: the individual, deriving his peculiar gifts from the play of psychological and infra-social forces, but bearing all the power of initiative and origination in his hands; and, second, the social environment, with its power of adopting or rejecting both him and his gifts. (p. 448)

James then went on to describe the processes by which the person creates this originality:

> Instead of thoughts of concrete things patiently following one another in a beaten track of habitual suggestion, we have the most abrupt cross-cuts and transitions from one idea to another, the most rarefied abstractions and discriminations, the most unheard of combination of elements, the subtlest associations of analogy; in a word, we seem suddenly introduced into a seething cauldron of ideas, where everything is fizzling and bobbling about in a state of bewildering activity, where partnerships can be joined or loosened in an instant, treadmill routine is unknown, and the unexpected seems only law. (p. 456)

This first attempt at a Darwinian theory of creativity has many flaws, but two stand out (cf. Campbell 1974). First, James makes the individual creator the unit of selection, in close parallel with the individual organism in Darwin's theory. Second, James assumes that the creator acquires originality via an almost random process— most akin to chaotic mutations.

In 1960, Donald Campbell provided a far superior conception: the blind variation and selective retention (BVSR model) of creative thought. Campbell's conception departed from James's in two ways. First, the unit of selection was the "thought trial" or ideational variation. Second, these variations are not necessarily generated randomly, although they can be. Instead, Campbell only requires that the variations be *blind*. Blindness occurs when (a) "the variations emitted [must] be independent of the environmental conditions of the occasion of their occurrence" (p. 381), and (b) "the occurrence of trials individually [must] be uncorrelated with the solution, in that specific correct trials are no more likely to occur at any one point in a series of trials than another, nor than specific incorrect trials" (p. 381). As Campbell pointed out, this definition permits perfectly deterministic or systematic processes to produce blind variations. He gave the specific example of radar scans, which are necessarily blind but unquestionably systematic. The same principle applies to other systematic searches (Simonton 2011b).

Campbell never developed BVSR as a comprehensive psychological theory of creativity, instead preferring to move into two related (but not equivalent) areas, namely, socio-cultural evolution and evolutionary epistemology (Campbell 1965, 1974). Campbell's switch may account for why he initially seemed to influence the philosophy of science far more than the psychology of creativity. This impact was certainly facilitated by the strong correspondence between Campbell's views and those of Karl Popper (1963, 1979). Still, the philosophical response has been both antagonistic (e.g., Kronfeldner 2010, Thagard 1988) and supportive (e.g., Bradie 1995, Briskman 1981, Kantorovich 1993, Nickles 2003, Stein and Lipton 1989, Wuketits 2001). Later, when psychologists began to develop the BVSR position, a parallel division took place between opponents (e.g., Gabora 2005, 2010; Sternberg 1998, 1999a; see also Dasgupta 2004) and proponents (e.g., Simonton 1999a, 1999b; Staw 1990). However, much of the debate pro and con has been based on fundamental misconceptions of the BVSR theory of creativity (Simonton 2011b, 2013). Most of these misconceptions stem from the incorrect assumption that Campbell's theory is predicated on an *analogy* with Darwin's theory of biological evolution. Campbell actually makes only two rather tangential references to Darwin and does not even list any of Darwin's publications in the reference section of his essay.

In contrast, Campbell made it clear that the antecedents of the BVSR theory of creativity lie elsewhere. For instance, he showed that the physicist and philosopher Ernst Mach (1896), as well as the mathematician Henri Poincaré (1921), count among the anticipators of the theory. Yet the earliest antecedent, according to Campbell, can be found in *Senses and the Intellect* published by philosopher Alexander Bain four years before Darwin came out with *Origin of Species*.

For instance, Bain claimed that "the greatest practical inventions [are] so much dependent upon chance [that] the only hope of success is to multiply the chances by multiplying the experiments" (p. 597). Bain is quoted extensively throughout Campbell's work. There is a certain irony in this priority, because while Darwin was working on his *Origin*, he had been advised by a family member ("Fanny H.") to read Bain's work, but never managed to do so, even though he had bought a copy for his personal library (Simonton 2010b). If Darwin had gotten around to reading Bain, we might now be wondering whether a theory of evolution could have been based on an analogy with a theory of creativity! Is organic evolution really Bainian?

In any case, it is evident that the biggest source of controversy concerns the concept of blindness. Most BVSR opponents, whether philosophers or psychologists, argue that ideational variations are guided, directed, or sighted rather than blind (e.g., Sternberg 1998, Thagard 1988). Most recently, Kronfeldner (2010) argued that the appropriate criterion of blindness is what the philosopher Elliot Sober (1992) proposed to identify whether a mutation is directed or undirected. This criterion is essentially equivalent with what philosopher Stephen Toulmin (1972) referred to as variant generation being *decoupled* from selection. Decoupling occurs when "the factors responsible for the selective perpetuation of variants are entirely unrelated to those responsible for the original generation of those same variants" (p. 337).

However, I have already shown that Sober's formal definition can be readily applied to ideational variations (Simonton 2010a). Yet unlike biological evolution, where variants are either blind or not blind in a dichotomous manner, the ideational variants in creativity fall along a continuum from the totally blind to the completely sighted (Simonton 2011a, 2013). Indeed, it is possible to define a measure that equals one under perfect sightedness (or coupling) and equals zero under absolute blindness (or decoupling). Although values of zero would be extremely rare relative to values of one, variations that are 100 percent sighted are far less likely to be creative.

Nor is this the only departure. Unlike biological evolution, ideational variants may be subject to either simultaneous or sequential selection (biological is always simultaneous) and to either external or internal selection (biological is always external). For example, in creativity it is possible for ideas to be generated one after another and tested against an inner cognitive representation of reality (e.g., the Popperian and Gregorian "creatures" described in Dennett 1985). Because creativity enjoys the capacity to maximize the exploitation of previously acquired knowledge and skill, including expertise acquisition based on other BVSR processes, such as operant conditioning (Campbell 1960, Dennett 1995), the phenomenon is not only more complex than biological evolution, but also vastly superior as a generator of adaptive originality (Simonton 1999b). The argument has been advanced that the ability of *Homo sapiens* to generate creative ideas greatly excels evolution's capacity to generate novel life forms (Basalla 1988). After all, human creativity has generated all of the diverse cultures and civilizations (both extinct and extant) scattered across Earth, each crammed with mythologies, religions, philosophies, ideologies, inventions, techniques, artistic products, musical compositions, customs, laws, fashions, games, and sports, and a host of other artifacts having no parallels in the organic world. In contemporary times, organic evolution has probably created fewer new multi-cellular species than the human mind has devised new video games.

3. Empirical Integration

Below, I engage in three tasks. First, I show that major domains of creativity can indeed be placed in a hierarchy, one that encompasses the arts and humanities, as well as the sciences. This hierarchical arrangement will be interpreted in terms of the extent to which creators operating in the domain depend on BVSR creativity. Second, I show that creators differ in the extent to which they use BVSR and that these individual differences correspond to contrasting dispositional traits and developmental experiences. Third and last, I indicate how the previous two demonstrations interconnect: Creators whose traits and experiences favor BVSR will be more likely to be found in domains where reliance on BVSR is more extensive.

3.1. Domains

There can be no doubt that the principal empirical sciences can be arrayed into a hierarchy extending from the "hard" natural sciences to the "soft" social sciences (Simonton 2002, 2004; see also Ashar and Shapiro 1990, Börner 2010, Fanelli 2010). For example, numerous objective criteria put five core disciplines in the following order: physics, chemistry, biology, psychology, and sociology. Once allowance is made for the omission of astronomy and the insertion of psychology, this ordering echoes the Comtean hierarchy. The objective criteria underlying a discipline's placement can be roughly grouped into three levels:

1. *Ideas*—The sciences at the top of the hierarchy display an impressive agreement on the concepts and methods that define the discipline. In Kuhnian terms, these sciences are highly paradigmatic (Kuhn 1970). Both the concepts and methods tend to be logical, formal, precise, and objective. In sciences further down in the hierarchy, the core concepts and methods tend to become more intuitive, imprecise, ambiguous, and subjective, with considerably more freedom for idiosyncratic construal. Another way of expressing the contrast is to say that domains vary greatly in the extent to which creators rely on "strong" methods versus "weak" methods (Klahr and Simon 1999). An example of a strong method is an algorithm that guarantees a solution through the application of a

straightforward method (e.g., solving a second-order polynomial using the quadratic formula), whereas an instance of a weak method would be some rule of thumb or heuristic that helps reduce the possibilities but without any assurance of a solution (e.g., hill climbing or trial and error).

2. *Products*—Given the greater conceptual and methodological rigor of the hard sciences, it comes as no surprise that sciences at the top of the hierarchy show a stronger disciplinary consensus on the merits of specific contributions. The field not only agrees on what constitutes the "research frontier" or the "leading edge," but also concurs on what constitutes a major solution to the central questions that define the research front. As a result, citations tend to concentrate on a proportionately small number of publications, and the front advances so fast that knowledge becomes quickly obsolete, requiring that citations focus on more recent publications. The softer sciences lack this degree of disciplinary agreement. Not only are citations more evenly distributed across publications, but the citations also include a larger percentage of older contributions—the rate of knowledge obsolescence becomes much slower.

3. *Persons*—What holds for single publications also holds for the scientists responsible for those publications. That is, fields at the top of the hierarchy display a stronger consensus concerning who among their colleagues are credited with high-impact contributions to the domain. Not only is agreement indicated by peer evaluations, which tend to concentrate on a relatively small number of colleagues, but also the consensus shows up in the citation patterns. Particularly striking is the fact that the "up-and- coming" scientists can be identified much earlier in the hard sciences. It is no accident that a scientist's age when receiving the Nobel Prize corresponds to his or her discipline's placement in the hierarchy (i.e., physics < chemistry < physiology or medicine < economics).

Two points must be added to the above criteria (Simonton 2009b). First, the hierarchical configuration can be *interpolated* within specific sciences to account for intradisciplinary differences. For instance, psychologists can be separated into the natural science-oriented and the human science-oriented (cf. Wilhelm Dilthey's classic distinction between *Naturwissenschaften* and *Geisteswissenschaften*). The former is clearly situated higher in the hierarchy than the latter (Simonton 2000). In fact, radical "Skinnerian" behaviorism, which was staunchly natural science in orientation, was by some criteria comparable to the hard sciences (Cole 1983).

Second, the hierarchy can indeed be *extrapolated* to encompass the humanities and arts, where the humanities are placed after the social sciences and the arts after the humanities. In this extrapolation, the disciplines highest in the hierarchy feature creativity that is highly constrained by logic, data, objectivity, conceptual and methodological precision, formal presentation, and a strong collective consensus, whereas disciplines lowest in the hierarchy feature creativity that gives considerable rein to subjectivity, emotion, and individualistic expression. Moreover, just as differentiations can be made among the several sciences, so are differentiations observed among the various humanities and arts. Creativity in history operates under more logical, factual, and formal constraints than does creativity in poetry. These contrasts bear an obvious connection with Friedrich Nietzsche's (1872) notable distinction between the Apollonian and Dionysian arts, where the former stresses reason, logic, thinking, self-control, and order and the latter stresses irrationality, instinct, emotion, passion, and chaos.

It is my contention that almost all of the attributes that determine placement in this extended hierarchy entail the degree to which creativity depends on BVSR. As already noted, ideational variations (thought trials) can vary along a scale from the 100 percent sighted to the 100 percent blind. For disciplines at the top of the hierarchy, the ideational variations are predominantly at the sighted end of the continuum, whereas for disciplines at the bottom of the hierarchy, the ideational variations are chiefly at the blind end of the continuum—with aleatoric art and music marking an extreme in blindness. The more logical, factual, objective, precise, formal, and consensual the creativity, the more sighted it must necessarily be. The more irrational, imaginary, subjective, ambiguous, expressive, and individualistic, the more the thought trials must be blind.

Yet it is manifest that the discipline is not what engages in BVSR but rather the individual who does so in the process of contributing creative ideas to that discipline. It is these creators that we must examine next.

3.2. Creators

Colin Martindale (1990) has linked BVSR with two cognitive processes that he identifies as primordial thought versus conceptual. These two processes were derived from the Freudian or psychoanalytic distinction between primary and secondary process, respectively (Martindale 1975). Whereas primordial thought is associated with increased variational blindness, conceptual thought is associated with increased variational sightedness. This twofold involvement is important because too often researchers have followed Freud (1908) and other psychoanalysts (e.g., Kris 1952) in assuming that primary process was what generated creativity (Ochse 1989, Suler 1980). According to Martindale (1975, 1990), both primordial (primary process) and conceptual (secondary process) thought are involved, albeit the precise mix will depend on the nature of the creativity, a point that I come back to shortly.

The issue that must be addressed is the existence of individual differences in the capacity and/or propensity to engage in BVSR. Empirical research suggests that a creator's leaning toward sighted or blind variations may be contingent on both dispositional traits and developmental experiences (reviews in Simonton 1999b, 2009a, 2010a). These findings can be summarized as follows:

1. *Dispositional traits*—The ability or inclination for BVSR should be associated with (a) stronger faculty for remote and rare associations, divergent thinking, and allusive or over-inclusive thought; (b) higher openness to experience, a variable that encompasses having diverse interests and defocused attention (e.g., reduced latent inhibition); (c) lower conformity, conventionality, and conservatism; and (d) higher incidence of subclinical psychopathological traits (e.g., as manifested in psychoticism or schizotypy scores). Negative BVSR inclinations should be lined with the opposites of these personal attributes, such as convergent and directed thinking, narrower interests, highly focused attention, higher conformity and conventionality, and lower tendencies toward psychopathology (i.e., superior mental health).

2. *Developmental experiences*—The capacity or propensity for BVSR should be associated with (a) exposure to homes that are more unconventional, unstable, and heterogeneous (e.g., orphanhood, divorce, parents with conflicting religious, ethnic, or geographical backgrounds); (b) later-born status in the family sibling configuration; (c) bilingualism and/or multiculturalism (e.g., first- or second-generation immigrants); (d) inferior scholastic performance, less formal education, and more marginal professional training; (e) more numerous and more heterogeneous role models and mentors; and (f) more politically unstable and culturally heterogeneous societal conditions. In comparison, creators with minimal proclivity for BVSR will come from the opposite environments, such as highly conventional and stable homes, firstborn status, exceptional scholastic performance and formal training, fewer and more homogeneous role models and mentors, and societal conditions characterized by political stability and cultural homogeneity.

We now have all the pieces of the puzzle ready to put in place.

3.3. Domain-creator congruence

If placement on the expanded disciplinary hierarchy negatively correlates with the prominence of BVSR thinking, and if the individual creator's penchant for BVSR thought is congruent with specific dispositional traits and developmental experiences, then the creators active in a given domain should exhibit traits and experiences that correspond with that domain's position in the disciplinary hierarchy. That is, domains requiring more BVSR cognition will be populated by creators having traits and experiences more conducive to BVSR thinking. There is abundant evidence that this is the case for all relevant dispositional traits and developmental experiences (Simonton 2009b).

With respect to dispositional traits, the empirical support is perhaps strongest regarding the incidence and intensity of psychopathology. For example, one historiometric study found that "persons in professions that require more logical, objective, and formal forms of expression tend be more emotionally stable than those in professions that require more intuitive, subjective, and emotive forms" (Ludwig 1998, p. 93). In particular, (a) artists display more emotional instability than do scientists; (b) within the sciences, social scientists display more instability than do natural scientists; (c) within the arts, artists in the expressive arts (e.g., visual arts and literature) have higher rates of instability than those in the performing arts (e.g., dance and music), who in their turn have higher rates of instability than those in the formal arts (e.g., architecture); (d) within a particular expressive art like literature, poets exhibit higher rates of instability than do fiction writers, who in their turn have higher rates of instability than do nonfiction writers; and (e) within any given artistic domain (e.g., sculpture or painting), those who create in an emotive style will exhibit higher rates of instability than those creating in a symbolic style, and the latter exhibit yet higher rates of instability than those creating in a formal style. It may be apparent that these results display a fractal pattern of "self-similarity" where the same contrasts appear at successive levels of magnification, starting at the art-versus-science contrast and focusing down to the emotive-symbolic-formal contrast (Ludwig 1998).

Another illustration concerns the distinction between practitioners of normal science and those who engage in revolutionary science. In line with what was said earlier, the latter should require more BVSR thinking than the former, a differential that should show up in the presence of psychopathology. A recent empirical investigation endorses this inference (Ko and Kim 2008). After dividing a large sample of eminent scientists into paradigm-preserving and paradigm-rejecting creators, the investigators then assessed the scientists according to four levels of mental illness: none, personality disorders, mood disorders, and schizophrenic disorders. In the case of the paradigm-preserving scientists, eminence was negatively correlated with the magnitude of psychopathology. But for the paradigm-rejecting scientists, the correlation between eminence and psychopathology was positive rather than negative.

With respect to developmental experiences, creators active in disciplines lower in the hierarchy are indeed more likely to come from homes that are more unstable, unconventional, and heterogeneous, to be later-borns, to do less well in school, receive less formal education and more marginal professional training, to have more numerous and diverse mentors and role models, and to emerge from more culturally heterogeneous and politically unstable societal conditions. To illustrate the very first effect, the home environment, consider the results from a study of Nobel laureates (Berry 1981). If we confine attention to those awarded Nobels in physics, chemistry, and literature (the "physiology or medicine" Nobel covers too many disciplines, both pure and applied), then we find that position in the hierarchy corresponds with two critical familial experiences. First, whereas only 6 percent of the literature laureates had fathers who were academic professionals, the percentage increases to 17 percent for chemistry laureates and to 28 percent for physics laureates. Second, whereas 17 percent of the creative writers lost their father during their minority years, the percentage of parental loss decreased to 11 percent for the chemists and to 2 percent for the physicists. The differential between the writers and the physicists is especially salient. In contrast to the literature laureates, 30 percent of whom "lost at least one parent through death or desertion or experienced the father's bankruptcy or impoverishment," "the physicists...seem to have remarkably uneventful lives" (p. 387; see also Raskin 1936).

Again, many more examples could be given of the parallels between the domain's placement in the hierarchy and the traits and experiences of the domain's creators, parallels that relate to the domain's dependence on BVSR thinking (Simonton 2009b). Still, the above instances should suffice to make the point.

4. Conclusion

In this chapter, I have tried to merge two separate intellectual traditions concerning the nature of creativity. The first (Comtean) tradition concerns the hierarchy of the sciences, and the second (Bainian) tradition concerns the blind variation and selective retention of thought trials. In the former case, the hierarchy was shown to have empirical validity, one based on objective criteria regarding creative ideas, products, and persons. Furthermore, this hierarchy could be both interpolated within disciplines and extrapolated to disciplines in the arts and humanities. It was then argued that the empirical criteria that determine a discipline's placement in this extended and differentiated hierarchy could be understood in terms of its dependence on BVSR processes. Those domains at the top of the hierarchy rely more on sighted variations, whereas domains at the bottom of the hierarchy depend more on blind variations. The next step was to indicate how a creator's capacity and propensity for BVSR thought was related to certain dispositional traits and developmental experiences. Given these relations, the following deduction was obvious: A discipline's ordinal position in the hierarchy will correspond with the traits and experiences of the creators contributing to that discipline. Empirical evidence was cited that endorses that inference.

Returning to Kant's distinction between creativity in the fine arts and creativity in the sciences, we must now recognize that the distinction has some justification both logically and empirically. Because artistic creativity is less constrained than scientific creativity, the former is more dependent on BVSR than the latter. The only valid objection to his dichotomous split is that he did not make enough distinctions. Besides drawing a line between art and science, Kant needed to draw additional lines separating the various arts and the several sciences, as well as the humanities—including his own domain of philosophy—that reside between the arts and sciences. The multiple cuts would then divide the many disciplines into a unidimensional series, where a discipline's specific placement is decided by the degree to which creators in that discipline depend on BVSR. To be fair of course, in 1790, the creative disciplines were not yet in the state they are today or even near their current state when Comte compounded his hierarchical system about 50 years later. It took almost two centuries to establish, using objective criteria, that the sundry disciplines vary so consistently, to the degree that they can be considered paradigmatic in a Kuhnian sense. Poetry may have started before physics, but it still comes in last.

That said, this chapter must be considered no more than the roughest sketch of a necessarily detailed and complicated integration of the Comtean and Bainian traditions. Even so, as a psychologist, I cannot help but believe that this preliminary synthesis gains in plausibility because it is cemented by what we know about the psychology of creativity. A creator's dispositional traits and developmental experiences provide the empirical link between the disciplinary hierarchy and BVSR creativity.

References

Ashar, H., and Shapiro, J. Z. 1990. "Are retrenchment decisions rational? The role of information in times of budgetary stress," *Journal of Higher Education*, 61, pp. 123–141.

Bain, A. 1855 (1977). *The senses and the intellect* (D. N. Robinson, ed.). Washington, DC: University Publications of America.

Basalla, G. 1988. *The evolution of technology*. Cambridge, UK: Cambridge University Press.

Berry, C. 1981. "The Nobel scientists and the origins of scientific achievement." *British Journal of Sociology*, 32, pp. 381–391.

Bliss, H. E. 1935. "The system of the sciences and the organization of knowledge," *Philosophy of Science*, 2, pp. 86–103.

Börner, K. 2010. *Atlas of science: Visualizing what we know*. Cambridge, MA: MIT Press.

Bradie, M. 1995. "Epistemology from an evolutionary point of view," in E. Sober (ed.), *Conceptual issues in evolutionary biology* (2nd ed., pp. 454–475). Cambridge, MA: MIT Press.

Briskman, L. 1980 (2009). "Creative product and creative process in science and art," in M. Krausz, D. Dutton, and K. Bardsley (eds.), *The idea of creativity* (2nd ed., pp. 17–41). Leiden, NL: Brill.

Campbell, D. T. 1960. "Blind variation and selective retention in creative thought as in other knowledge processes," *Psychological Review*, 67, pp. 380–400.

Campbell, D. T. 1965. "Variation and selective retention in socio-cultural evolution," in H. R. Barringer, G. I. Blanksten, and R. W. Mack (eds.), *Social change in developing areas* (pp. 19–49). Cambridge, MA: Schenkman.

Campbell, D. T. 1974. "Evolutionary epistemology.," in P. A. Schlipp (ed.), *The philosophy of Karl Popper* (pp. 413–463). La Salle, IL: Open Court.

Cole, S. 1983. "The hierarchy of the sciences?" *American Journal of Sociology*, 89, pp. 111–139.

Comte, A. (1839–1842) 1855. *The positive philosophy of Auguste Comte* (H. Martineau, trans.). New York: Blanchard.

Cox, C. 1926. *The early mental traits of three hundred geniuses*. Stanford, CA: Stanford University Press.

Dasgupta, S. 2004. "Is creativity a Darwinian process?" *Creativity Research Journal*, 16, pp. 403–413.

Dennett, D. C. 1995. *Darwin's dangerous idea: Evolution and the meanings of life*. New York: Simon & Schuster.

Fanelli, D. 2010. "'Positive' results increase down the hierarchy of the sciences." *PLoS ONE* 5(4): e10068. doi:10.1371/journal.pone.0010068.

Freud, S. 1908 (1959). "Creative writers and day-dreaming," in J. Strachey (ed. and trans.), *Standard edition of the complete psychological works of Sigmund Freud* (vol. 9, pp. 141–153). London: Hogarth Press.

Gabora, L. 2005. "Creative thought as a non-Darwinian evolutionary process." *Journal of Creative Behavior*, 39, pp. 262–283.

Gabora L. 2010. "Why blind-variation and selective-retention is an inappropriate explanatory framework for creativity." *Physics of Life Reviews*, 7, pp. 182–183.

Galton, F. 1869. *Hereditary genius: An inquiry into its laws and consequences.* London: Macmillan.

James, W. 1880. "Great men, great thoughts, and the environment." *Atlantic Monthly*, 46, pp. 441–459.

Kant, I. 1790 (2000). *Critique of the power of judgment.* Paul Guyer and Eric Matthews (trans. and eds.). Cambridge, UK: Cambridge University Press.

Kantorovich, A. 1993. *Scientific discovery: Logic and tinkering.* Albany, NY: State University of New York Press.

Klahr, D., and Simon, H. A. 1999. "Studies of scientific creativity: Complementary approaches and convergent findings." *Psychological Bulletin*, 125, pp. 524–543.

Ko, Y., and Kim, J. 2008. "Scientific geniuses' psychopathology as a moderator in the relation between creative contribution types and eminence." *Creativity Research Journal*, 20, pp. 251–261.

Kroeber, A. L. 1944. *Configurations of culture growth.* Berkeley, CA: University of California Press.

Kronfeldner, M. E. 2010. "Darwinian 'blind' hypothesis formation revisited." *Synthese*, 175, pp. 193–218, doi: 10.1007/s11229-009-9498-8.

Kuhn, T. S. 1970. *The structure of scientific revolutions*, 2nd ed. Chicago: University of Chicago Press.

Ludwig, A. M. 1998. "Method and madness in the arts and sciences." *Creativity Research Journal*, 11, pp. 93–101.

Mach, E. 1896. "On the part played by accident in invention and discovery." *Monist*, 6, pp. 161–175.

Martindale, C. 1975. *Romantic progression: The psychology of literary history.* Washington, DC: Hemisphere.

Martindale, C. 1990. *The clockwork muse: The predictability of artistic styles.* New York: Basic Books.

Martindale, C. 2009. "Evolutionary models of innovation and creativity," in T. Rickards, M. Runco, and S. Moger (eds.), *Routledge companion to creativity* (pp. 109–118). London: Taylor & Francis.

Murray, C. 2003. *Human accomplishment: The pursuit of excellence in the arts and sciences, 800 B.C. to 1950.* New York: HarperCollins.

Nickles, T. 2003. "Evolutionary models of innovation and the Meno problem," in L. V. Shavinina (ed.), *The international handbook on innovation* (pp. 54–78). New York: Elsevier Science.

Nietzsche, F. 1872 (1956). *The birth of tragedy* (F. Golffing, trans.). Garden City, NY: Doubleday.

Ochse, R. 1989. "A new look at primary process thinking and its relation to inspiration." *New Ideas in Psychology*, 7, pp. 315–330.

Plato. 360 B.C.E. (1952). *The Republic*, in R. M. Hutchins (ed.), *Great books of the Western world* (vol. 7, pp. 295–441). Chicago: Encyclopaedia Britannica. Poincaré, H. (1921). *The foundations of science: Science and hypothesis, the value of science, science and method* (G. B. Halstead, trans.). New York: Science Press.

Popper, K. 1959. *The logic of discovery.* New York: Basic Books.

Popper, K. 1963. *Conjectures and Refutations.* London: Routledge.

Popper, K. 1979. *Objective knowledge: An evolutionary approach* (rev. ed.). Oxford, UK: Clarendon Press.

Raskin, E. A. 1936. "Comparison of scientific and literary ability: A biographical study of eminent scientists and men of letters of the nineteenth century." *Journal of Abnormal and Social Psychology*, 31, pp. 20–35.

Simonton, D. K. 1999a. "Creativity as blind variation and selective retention: Is the creative process Darwinian?" *Psychological Inquiry, 10*, pp. 309–328.

Simonton, D. K. 1999b. *Origins of genius: Darwinian perspectives on creativity*. New York: Oxford University Press.

Simonton, D. K. 2000. "Methodological and theoretical orientation and the long-term disciplinary impact of 54 eminent psychologists." *Review of General Psychology, 4*, pp. 13–24.

Simonton, D. K. 2002. *Great psychologists and their times: Scientific insights into psychology's history*. Washington, DC: American Psychological Association.

Simonton, D. K. 2004. "Psychology's status as a scientific discipline: Its empirical placement within an implicit hierarchy of the sciences." *Review of General Psychology, 8*, pp. 59–67.

Simonton, D. K. 2009a. "Creativity as a Darwinian phenomenon: The blind-variation and selective-retention model," in M. Krausz, D. Dutton, and K. Bardsley (eds.), *The idea of creativity* (2nd ed., pp. 63–81). Leiden, NL: Brill.

Simonton, D. K. 2009b. "Varieties of (scientific) creativity: A hierarchical model of disposition, development, and achievement." *Perspectives on Psychological Science, 4*, pp. 441–452.

Simonton, D. K. 2010a. "Creativity as blind-variation and selective-retention: Constrained combinatorial models of exceptional creativity." *Physics of Life Reviews, 7*, pp. 156–179.

Simonton, D. K. 2010b. "Reply to comments." *Physics of Life Reviews, 7*, pp. 190–194.

Simonton, D. K. 2011a. "Creativity and discovery as blind variation and selective retention: Multiple-variant definitions and blind-sighted integration." *Psychology of Aesthetics, Creativity, and the Arts, 5*, pp. 222–228.

Simonton, D. K. 2011b. "Creativity and discovery as blind variation: Campbell's (1960) BVSR model after the half-century mark." *Review of General Psychology, 15*, pp. 158–174.

Simonton, D. K. 2013. Creative thought as blind variation and selective retention: Why sightedness is inversely related to creativity. *Journal of Theoretical and Philosophical Psychology*. Advance online publication, doi: 10.1037/a0030705

Sober, E. 1992. "Models of cultural evolution," in P. Griffiths (ed.), *Trees of life: Essays in philosophy of biology* (pp. 17–39). Dordrecht, NL: Kluwer.

Staw, B. M. 1990. "An evolutionary approach to creativity and innovations," in M. A. West and J. L. Farr (eds.), *Innovation and creativity at work: Psychological and organizational strategies* (pp. 287–308). New York: Wiley.

Stein, E., and Lipton, P. 1989. "Where guesses come from: Evolutionary epistemology and the anomaly of guided vision." *Biology & Philosophy, 4*, pp. 33–56.

Sternberg, R. J. 1998. "Cognitive mechanisms in human creativity: Is variation blind or sighted?" *Journal of Creative Behavior, 32*, pp. 159–176.

Sternberg, R. J. 1999a. "Darwinian creativity as a conventional religious faith." *Psychological Inquiry, 10*, pp. 357–359.

Sternberg, R. J. 1999b. "A propulsion model of types of creative contributions." *Review of General Psychology, 3*, pp. 83–100.

Suler, J. R. 1980. "Primary process thinking and creativity." *Psychological Bulletin, 88*, pp. 144–165.

Thagard, P. 1988. *Computational philosophy of science*. Cambridge, MA: MIT Press.

Toulmin, S. 1972. *Human understanding: The collective use and evolution of concepts*. Princeton, NJ: Princeton University Press.

Wuketits, F. M. 2001. "The philosophy of Donald T. Campbell: A short review and critical appraisal." *Journal Biology and Philosophy, 16*, pp. 171–188.

PART SEVEN

PHILOSOPHY OF EDUCATION
(AND EDUCATION OF PHILOSOPHY)

13

Educating for Creativity

BERYS GAUT

1. Introduction

The claim that one can teach a person to be creative has understandably been met with a great deal of skepticism. It conjures up images of business seminars where one is invited to figure out the solution to an arcane and trivial problem, perhaps how to cross a river using some minimal amount of equipment, and somehow this exercise is supposed to make one more creative. More weightily, the teachability claim encounters a long tradition that holds that creativity is an innate capacity that cannot be learned.

I argue that the innateness view is mistaken: One can teach people to be creative. More specifically, one can *educate* them, in a sense to be explained, to be creative.[1] I will show that the arguments against the possibility of teaching creativity are flawed; having clarified the teachability claim, I develop a positive argument that shows that one can educate people to be creative. Next, I show how creativity can be enhanced in two disparate domains, mathematics and fiction writing, demonstrating how a heuristic approach is effective. Finally, I reflect briefly on how creativity can be taught in philosophy.

2. The Imitation and Rules Arguments

Two straightforward arguments can be extracted from historical sources against the possibility of teaching someone to be creative. The historical discussion was

---

[1] Even at the level of popular suspicion, there are reasons to temper one's doubts. The foremost populariser of the teachability of creativity is Edward de Bono, whose methods have been empirically tested, and there is some evidence that they are effective (Nickerson 1999, pp. 402–403). Nickerson also discusses the generally positive results of investigations of other programs designed to enhance creativity.

generally conducted in terms of the notion of genius, creativity at a very high level; I broaden the arguments to creativity in general. The first is the imitation argument:

1. All learning is a form of imitation.
2. Imitating someone or something is incompatible with being creative.
3. So one cannot learn to be creative.

The second is the rules argument:

1. All learning consists in the following of rules.
2. Following rules is incompatible with being creative.
3. So one cannot learn to be creative.

Since teaching something successfully requires the person taught to have learned what is taught, both arguments entail that creativity cannot be taught. The first argument derives its force from the thought that "imitative" is an antonym of "creative" and the claim that when we learn something, we imitate someone (for instance, in learning how to speak, we imitate those around us) or something (for instance, we may copy a sample of handwriting in learning how to write). The second argument derives its force from the thought that learning is a matter of internalizing the rules of the activity that is learned (for instance, the rules constituting the vocabulary and grammar of a language) and the claim that one is not creative if one follows rules, for creativity is a matter of breaking or making rules, rather than following them.

Before assessing the soundness of these arguments, it is helpful to flesh them out with a brief discussion of their role in the work of two seminal thinkers on creativity: Edward Young and Immanuel Kant.

Young's *Conjectures on Original Composition*, first published in 1759, is arguably the earliest sustained discussion of originality and genius. Young describes originality in organic terms: "An *Original* may be said to be of a *vegetable* nature; it rises spontaneously from the vital root of genius; it *grows*, it is not *made*..." (1918, p. 7). Originality is something natural and given, not susceptible to teaching, any more than one can instruct a vegetable. We possess it naturally; each is born with a unique mind and features, and learning cannot advance originality, though it may destroy it: "Born *Originals*, how comes it to pass that we die *Copies*? That meddling ape *Imitation*...destroys all mental individuality..." (p. 20). And learning, he holds, is "a great lover of rules...and sets rigid bounds to that liberty, to which genius often owes its supreme glory" (p. 13).

Though Young's claims suggest both the imitation and rules arguments, he also qualifies his claims, or perhaps advances some not wholly assimilated counterclaims. Having attacked imitation and advised us to shut out the ancients from our thoughts when we write, he then qualifies this by suggesting that we should imitate not the composition but the man, particularly the man's spirit and taste (p. 11). And he distinguishes two species of genius: the adult genius, such as Shakespeare, who "comes out of nature's hand...at full growth, and mature" (p. 15) and the infantine genius, such as Swift, who must be nursed and tutored by learning, though Young warns that this learning may smother the infantine genius. So it seems that imitation may play a role in some respects and for some lesser geniuses, albeit a restricted and perilous one. Likewise, having criticized adherence to rules, Young advocates two rules, though highly general ones, for original composition: Know yourself and reverence yourself. Such rules encourage one to know the full originality of one's mind (p. 24). I return to consideration of Young's qualifications later.

Kant, with fewer qualifications, also advances something very like the imitation and rules arguments. Genius occurs only in the fine arts; it is innate, being "the talent (natural gift) that gives the rule to art...the inborn predisposition of the mind (*ingenium*) *through which* nature gives the rule to art" (Kant 2000, p. 307).[2] Kant justifies this claim by stating that "genius is entirely opposed to the *spirit of imitation*. Now since learning is nothing but imitation, even the greatest aptitude for learning, facility for learning (capacity) as such, still does not count as genius" (p. 308).[3] So, he holds, genius cannot be learned: "such a skill cannot be communicated, but is apportioned to each immediately from the hand of nature and dies with him" (p. 309). Not only can one not learn from another person, one cannot learn from his product: "the product of a genius (in respect of that in it which is to be ascribed to genius, not to possible learning or schooling) is an example, not for imitation (for then that which is genius in it and constitutes the spirit of the work would be lost), but for emulation by another genius, who is thereby awakened to the feeling of his own originality" (p. 318).

Kant also appears to endorse something like the rules argument. When one learns something, there is always a rule that one follows in learning it. For instance, a scientist such as Newton cannot be a genius, since although he thinks independently and even invents things, "just this sort of thing *could* also have been learned, and thus still lies on the natural path of inquiry and reflection in accordance with rules" (p. 308). But the genius is someone who gives the rule to art; so he does not follow rules, but rather creates them. Thus one cannot learn to be a genius. Kant allows for some role for learning and rule-following, but only in respect of academic correctness (i.e., the mastery of the technical aspects of fine art, such as knowledge of correct diction and meter for poetry [p. 303]). These are indispensable for genius but are a long way from sufficing for it. The genius also requires taste (i.e., sensitivity to the beautiful) and spirit (i.e., the ability to present aesthetic ideas), and there are no rules for either of these that can be captured in a formula (p. 309). In contrast

---

[2] The page numbers referred to are in the fifth volume of the *Akademie* edition of Kant's works.

[3] Kant's claim here is that genius is not the same as the great ability to learn; this is compatible with the claim that one can learn to be a genius. However, Kant takes the observation as an "elucidation and confirmation" of his innateness account of genius, so he believes the account to be justified by it.

to formal rules, there exist rules that can be abstracted from individual works of art (models), but they are, in modern terms, only rules of thumb. They are followed by the apprentice seeking to imitate his master (p. 309), but not by the genius; the genius may be the founder of a school, "a methodical instruction in accordance with rules" (p. 318), but he does not follow rules either as formulas or as abstracted from models.

3. Assessing the Arguments

Though the two arguments have significant intuitive force and impressive historical provenance, they should be rejected.

Both arguments are invalid, since they fail to respect the distinction between learning creatively and learning for creativity. The former concerns *how* one learns and the latter *what* one learns. They are logically independent of each other. I can learn creatively without learning to be creative: For instance, I may learn biology creatively by studying plants on my own, rather than by reading and memorizing a biology textbook. I learn creatively, but I am learning about plants, not learning to be creative. Conversely, I can learn to be creative but do so in an uncreative fashion: If there is an effective textbook that teaches one how to be creative, then I can learn to be creative by reading it, but I am not learning creatively, since I am simply absorbing what is written. Correspondingly, teaching creatively is not the same as teaching for creativity. If a classroom teacher simply expounds the creativity textbook just mentioned, he is not teaching creatively but is teaching his students to be creative. Conversely, he can teach creatively things other than how to be creative: For instance, he could find a creative way (perhaps by motivating them in original ways) to get his students to learn simple addition by rote.

The premises of both arguments entail that one cannot learn creatively, but they do not entail that one cannot learn to be creative. If learning is a form of imitation and imitation is incompatible with creativity, it follows that learning cannot be creative; but even if that were true, it would not follow that one cannot learn to be creative, as the creativity textbook example shows. Likewise, if learning consists in following rules and following rules is incompatible with creativity, it follows that learning cannot be creative, but it would not follow that one cannot learn how to be creative. Make the distinction between learning creatively and learning for creativity (and, correspondingly, teaching creatively and teaching for creativity), and the apparently plausible arguments are shown to be fallacious.

There are also problems with the premises of both arguments. The first premise of the imitation argument holds that all learning is a form of imitation. This, however, is false when it comes to learning from experience: A child who discovers that touching a hot stove is painful has (hopefully) not learned this by imitating his mother. Scientists also learn from experience, albeit not generally in the simple, observational manner of the unfortunate child, but by developing and testing hypotheses against experience. When we learn from others, imitation generally plays an important role: A child learns a language by imitating others speaking, learns to swim by imitating adults swimming, and so on. But imitation is not mere copying. To copy something is to reproduce another of that thing, ideally so that it is indiscriminable from the original, as in a well-functioning photocopier. But when a child learns by imitating her parents' speech, we would not count it as learning if she merely reproduced exactly the same sentences as her parents; that would be unintelligent imitation or parroting (Kant calls it *aping* [2000, p. 318]). Rather, learning by imitation requires intelligent and flexible copying of the relevant aspects of a behavior. In the case of language acquisition, learning is demonstrated not by the reproduction of type-identical sentences, but by a grasp of the underlying grammatical rules and vocabulary, and the production of new sentence types employing these rules and words. So imitation is not the production of exactly the same thing that is imitated, but the production of relevantly similar things, and this requires judgment, skill, and bringing something of one's own to bear.

Turning to the second premise, we can agree that mere copying is incompatible with creativity, but mere copying is not identical to imitation, as just noted. Imitation, as the selective and intelligent production of similar entities to those imitated, can be creative: The comedian who impersonates a politician for satiric purposes is imitating him, but may also be creative in his selective presentation and exaggeration of his victim's persona.[4] So if imitation is construed as mere copying, the first premise is false and the second premise true; if imitation is the selective use of similarities, the first premise has some support when restricted to learning from others, but the second premise is false.[5] Construed either way, the argument is unsound.

There is a further problem with the second premise. Recall that Young suggests an original person might imitate the man rather than the composition, and in particular, the man's taste and spirit. This naturally raises the question of *what* is being imitated. Imitating some aspect of a person or his work places limits on the degree to which one can be creative in that respect; imitating someone's style, for instance, places limits on how far one can be creative in one's own style. But suppose that one imitates not a person's style, subject matter, etc., but her creativity. Then, if one is successful in one's imitation, one has been creative; so imitating someone does not entail that one cannot be creative. The supporter of the imitation argument may protest that he denies that one can imitate creativity, for creativity cannot be learned. And so he does; but now the question is begged in favor of the innateness view, rather than an argument having been provided for it. Moreover, there is no

---

[4] I owe the example to Dan Cavedon-Taylor.

[5] Kant distinguishes between copying and imitation, and holds that the apprentice imitates but does not copy his master (2000, p. 309), but he does not note that imitation can be creative.

incoherence in the idea of imitating someone's creativity. A coherent view about creativity is that being creative consists in having certain skills and a motivation to employ them; since skills and motivations can be imitated, one can imitate someone's creativity on this view.[6] Likewise, one might imitate the creativity of a product, rather than merely its style or subject matter, etc.

The rules argument is also unsound. Consider its first premise, which states that all learning consists in the following of rules. Learning cannot consist simply in following rules, for even when there are rules in some domain, following them is insufficient to capture all aspects of how we learn. For any rule, there are potentially hard cases—cases where it is unclear whether they fall under the rule or not—and in such cases, one has to exercise judgment in applying the rule. One cannot appeal to a further rule for adjudicating such hard cases, for there could be hard cases for that further rule, and so one must exercise judgment in the case of the rule for applying rules, and so on. There must be an ineliminable role for judgment in learning.[7]

The second premise should also be rejected. Following some kinds of rules is incompatible with being creative. An algorithm is a completely determinate rule, the following of which leads to a predetermined outcome. Following an algorithm is incompatible with being creative, since it allows no room for individual judgment and choice. Painting-by-numbers kits employ an approximation of algorithms (e.g., brush this color onto this marked area of the canvas), and they are incompatible with creativity in painting. But most rules are not algorithms, and allow room for individual judgment and choice, and so a degree of creativity. Even recipes in cookbooks are to some degree like this: The instructions to add a pinch of salt or to fry until lightly browned allow for individual discretion and so for a small degree of creativity in following them.

The second premise also rules out a coherent possibility: that there are rules to enhance creativity. Young, in an apparent qualification of his anti-rules view, offers two candidates for rules: Know yourself and reverence yourself. They are grounded on his belief that we are all naturally original, and getting in touch with our natures will enhance our originality. Whether or not they are effective, they are rules for enhancing creativity. At a far more specific and mundane level, there are also rules, in the sense of rules of thumb, for inventing new recipes (which give the rule to cookery, so to speak): One should extrapolate from successful combinations of flavors, tasting and varying ingredients according to the results, for instance. And there is an entire tradition of thought—heuristics—that offers a set of rules to enhance creativity, which I discuss later. So in simply rejecting the possibility of there being rules to enhance creativity, the second premise begs the question against the view that one can educate for creativity.

---

[6] See Gaut 2009; I briefly defend the teachability of creativity on pp. 96–97.
[7] This is one way of construing Wittgenstein's (1978, sections 138f.) rule-following argument.

4. The Teachability Claim

To show that some or even all arguments against a view are unsound is not to show that the view is correct. How might one argue that one can educate people to be creative?

We need first to clarify the claim. To show that one can teach people to be creative, we do not need to show that one can teach *everyone* to be creative. One can teach people to swim; that claim is not falsified by noting that some physically disabled people and people with hydrophobia cannot be taught to swim. So background abilities and motivations may be required to learn some capabilities. These cannot always be specified, as the swimming example might suggest, in terms of having normal physical capacities and not being subject to phobias or neuroses. One can teach advanced calculus, but the required abilities include superior intelligence, and the motivation is a good degree of interest in mathematics; physical abilities play no role. So the prerequisite abilities and motivations vary depending on what is taught. We can sidestep the problem of having to offer a general characterization of these by noting that one can show that creativity can be taught if one can show that one can teach *some* people to be creative. This is the claim that we should target.

Creativity is a scalar concept, a matter of degree: People or achievements can be more or less creative. When one says that someone or something is creative simpliciter, one sets some threshold of degree of creativity that is satisfied, at which creativity is *salient*, and this varies with the context: Children have to display less originality to be artistically creative than do adults, and untrained adults less than do professional artists. So the fundamental usage of "creative" is a scalar one, and its binary or threshold use is derivative from this. In the same way, the notion of intelligence is scalar: People are more or less intelligent, and when one says that someone is intelligent, one sets some threshold that is context-dependent: To be intelligent, a child need not be as intelligent as an intelligent adult, and to be intelligent, an adult need not be as intelligent as an intelligent physicist. Since the scalar use of the concept is more fundamental than the threshold use, we should construe the teachability of creativity claim as: One can teach *some* people to be *more* creative. Doing so also avoids the problem that the satisfaction of the binary usage varies with context.[8]

How might one argue that one can teach some people to be more creative? One way is by exemplification: Produce some examples of successfully teaching people to be creative. Examples of teaching creativity in mathematics and writing are discussed later. A different way is to produce a general argument to show that creativity can be taught, and it is to this task that I now turn.

---

[8] One might object that the scalar usage weakens the teachability claim too much to be interesting. However, the binary claim that one can teach *some* people to be creative follows from the scalar claim that one can teach some people to be *more* creative, given a plausible assumption. For, whatever threshold of creativity one sets, there will be some people who are just below that threshold; if some of these are ones who can be taught to be more creative, then one can teach some people to be creative in the binary sense.

5. The Constitutive Argument

Consider the concept of creativity. Creativity is a kind of disposition: A creative person will, in suitable circumstances, produce creative things. Simply having the ability to create is not sufficient: When Rimbaud, disillusioned, abandoned writing poetry by the age of 21, he ceased to be creative, even though he presumably still possessed the ability to write creative poetry. An ability is a constituent of a disposition, but does not suffice for it: a person must also be motivated to act on that ability. So we can think of a disposition in an agent as a motivated ability. Teaching someone to be creative thus involves teaching both the motivation and the ability.

It is not hard to teach people to be motivated to be creative. It is in general easy to teach people to be motivated to exercise their abilities if the resulting actions are highly valued, and creativity is one of the most admired qualities in contemporary society. A good deal of research has suggested that intrinsic motivation (i.e., being motivated to perform an action for its own sake rather than merely as a means to another end) is conducive to creative activity (Amabile 1996, Hennessey 2010, Kieran, this volume). Since achieving creative outcomes is often enjoyable, and high value is placed on creativity, teaching people to be intrinsically motivated in their creative endeavors is not hard. According to the same research, extrinsic motivations also play a role under certain conditions in motivating people to be creative. Creative achievement has many rewards in most fields of endeavor, so cultivating extrinsic motivations for being creative is not hard either.[9]

Turning to the ability component of the creative disposition, it is generally acknowledged that it involves an ability to generate or produce new things. "Things" here refers widely to concepts, thoughts, hypotheses, theories, and artifacts of various kinds, including paintings, sculptures, buildings, and so on. Things can be more or less new, so creative ability is a scalar notion, and when we talk of something being creative simpliciter, we appeal to some notion of salient newness. But it is easy to produce saliently new but worthless things (e.g., dancing a jig while singing extracts from Kant's works), and to avoid such "silly" activities being counted as creative, we have to add a value condition. Value too comes in degrees, since things can be more or less valuable, so creativity is scalar in respect of value too. Putting together these conditions, creative ability, understood in the scalar sense, is the ability to produce new and valuable things. But not just any way of producing things counts as creative. One may produce new and valuable things purely by luck (e.g., stumbling accidentally, I spill paint onto a canvas and produce a new and valuable form), but this would not be an instance of creativity, for deeming an act to be creative involves

---

[9] The psychological research is problematic in certain respects (Gaut forthcoming), but all that is required here is that both intrinsic and extrinsic motivations are involved in creativity and that both are teachable.

according it a kind of credit, and we do not give credit for pure luck (though we do give credit for the *use* of luck). So one must act purposively in being creative; more specifically, one must act purposively in respect of the value of what one produces. If my purpose is to leave the room and in doing so I accidentally spill the paint and that is all I do, I am still not creative. I must have aimed at producing (including selecting) at least some of the valuable features of the painting to count as creative. Hence one must also have an evaluative ability in the relevant domain, accept these values as reasons for producing certain features, and have some understanding of the values (Gaut 2012). Second, as noted earlier, one is not creative if one produces a new and valuable item by following precisely specified rules or instructions, such as algorithms, that permit no role for individual judgment or choice. So the sort of production involved in creativity must be purposive production that involves the exercise of choice, evaluation, understanding, and judgment (Berys Gaut 2010).

So creative ability involves producing new and valuable things in the way just indicated. The component ability to produce new things can be taught. For instance, one may look for similarities between disparate areas by seeking analogies; the history of scientific invention is replete with examples of the productivity of analogies in achieving new insights, from Harvey's analogy of the heart to a pump, to Rutherford's analogy of the atom to the solar system. Analogies have a role not only in science but also in art. One may generate new works, for instance, by constructing fictional worlds that display analogies with other successful works: A well-known example is how features of the plot of *Romeo and Juliet* were deployed in the very different context of 1950s New York in *West Side Story* to create a saliently different and successful work, which nevertheless owed a strong debt to Shakespeare. One can also generate new ideas in art by a close attention to experience; as Goethe points out, writing from one's own experience guarantees a degree of originality: "while you content yourself with generalities, every one can imitate you; but, in the particular, no one can—and why? because no others have experienced exactly the same thing" (Eckermann 1906, p. 30). The focus on particular events and their specifics is important in generating new approaches not only in art but also in some scientific domains: For instance, introspective attention to how one's mind works can be a valuable source of insight in psychology. Introspective reports by notable thinkers, most influentially Poincaré, have played an important role in the psychology of creativity (Weisberg 2006, ch. 8). We later consider many examples of heuristics for generating new approaches.

One can also teach the second component ability of creativity, for one can teach people to produce valuable things. This in general is the role of skills, which include physical ones like swimming, cooking, plumbing, and piano playing, and cognitive ones like the ability to use critical reasoning, to express oneself clearly, and so on. One can also teach propositional knowledge, and such knowledge enhances the ability to produce worthwhile things: If I am entirely ignorant of how heating systems work, my efforts to repair the boiler are highly unlikely to be successful; and if I understand nothing of mathematics, even an original mathematical result that I produce would not count as creative, since it could only have been the product of mere luck. Nothing that is creative in any domain can be accomplished unless one has some knowledge and experience in that domain, and there is a good deal of evidence that to be creative at a high level in a domain, one must have spent years mastering it.[10]

So if one analyses creativity—a disposition to produce, in a certain way, new and valuable things—into its component motivation and abilities, one can show that creativity can be taught, because the motivation to be creative, the ability to produce new things, and the ability to be produce valuable things can all be taught. Let's call this the *constitutive argument* for the teachability of creativity.[11]

One may object that this argument commits a fallacy of composition. The parts of a thing may possess properties that the whole does not, so the fact that one can teach the components of creativity does not show that one can teach creativity itself. However, to allege a fallacy is not to prove that it has been committed: One needs an argument to show this. In the case of teaching, one can standardly teach a combination of skills if one can teach its components: If I can teach you mathematics and economics, I can teach you mathematical economics; and if I can teach you French and how to interpret novels, I can teach you to give your interpretations in French. The exception to this claim is when exercising the abilities conjointly would be impossible. This may be logically impossible—I can teach you to form a visual image of a circle and a visual image of a square, but I cannot teach you to form a visual image of a round square. Or it may be physically impossible—I can teach you to sing and I can teach you to hold your breath, but I cannot teach you to sing while holding your breath. But this cannot be the ground for maintaining a fallacy of composition in the case of creativity, since being creative is not impossible in any sense, as there are numerous actual instances of it. So one needs another argument for why the combination cannot be taught; but that is just to say that, in order to show that there is a fallacy of composition, one needs an argument to show that creativity cannot be taught. Without this, the assertion of a fallacy is simply question begging. I earlier criticized two influential arguments for the claim that creativity cannot be taught. Absent any successful argument against the teachability of creativity, the constitutive argument stands. So the constitutive argument is defeasible, but not defeated.

Second, one may object that the argument proves too much. Does it not show that one can teach everyone to be creative, for each of its components is teachable

[10] The "10-year rule" holds that significant creativity in a domain requires considerable exposure to and knowledge of that domain, in many cases amounting to 10 years, though the exact length of time varies with the domain (Weisberg 1999).

[11] For a different constitutive argument for the teachability of creativity that analyses creativity in terms of patterns of thinking and values, see Perkins 1990.

to everyone? But the argument does not show this. Even if everyone could be taught to be more creative in a domain, it would not follow that everyone could be taught to be creative simpliciter in that domain, since that is a threshold notion, and some people might not be capable of crossing that threshold. Moreover, the argument does not in fact show that one can teach everyone to be more creative in any domain; as already noted, one can exhibit a degree of creativity in a domain only if one has some understanding of that domain, and not everyone is capable of understanding some domains. One cannot be a creative mathematician if one is not intelligent or well trained enough to understand mathematics, for instance. So creativity in some domains may require abilities that some people cannot acquire, and this is consistent with the constitutive argument, since all that is required is that the component abilities are teachable (i.e., they can be taught to *some* people). Likewise, to say that one can teach people to be more motivated is not to say that one can teach anyone, in any area, to be more motivated: If a person is irrefragably hostile to or indifferent about some aspect of human endeavor, one may be unable to do anything to endow her with appropriate motivations.

Third, the argument may look unsound because it ignores the role of luck in creative production. One cannot teach people to be lucky if this is genuine luck (i.e., fortunate randomness). One cannot, for instance, teach people how to roll a six with an unbiased dice. Different theories assign different degrees of importance to luck in creativity: It plays a significant role in at least some domains according to Darwinian theories (Simonton, this volume), but it plays a lesser role according to expertise theories of creativity (Weisberg 2006). But whatever its judgment of the importance of luck, no theory should deny it some role, for there are many examples (such as Fleming's chance discovery of penicillin) of luck playing a part in creative activities. However, this fact does not constitute an objection to the constitutive argument. It is true that insofar as luck plays a role in creativity, one cannot teach people how to be creative in that respect. But creative outcomes cannot be the outcome of pure luck, as already noted. And one can teach the other factors that promote creativity in various domains, such as the use of analogies, attention to the specifics of experience, employing heuristics, domain knowledge, etc. Also, even insofar as luck is involved, one can teach people how to increase the chance of something lucky happening to them by, for instance, persisting in making attempts at some creative endeavor—the equivalent of rolling the dice several times—and trying to produce the outcome in many different ways. One can also teach them how to use luck when it occurs: Had Fleming not had significant biological knowledge and been looking for a way of killing bacteria, he would not have recognized the significance of the lucky chance that befell him; as Louis Pasteur famously remarked, "chance favours only the mind that is prepared" (Perkins 2000, pp. 202–203). So to acknowledge that not every factor that may contribute to a creative outcome can be taught is not to deny that one can teach people to be more creative.

The constitutive argument allows us to refine the claim that one can teach people to be creative. In a broad sense of the term, "educating" is synonymous with "teaching." But there is also a narrower usage, in which educating is one sort of teaching. Stimulation is one kind of teaching: Stimulating someone is motivating her to be interested in some area. To be stimulated does not require one to understand the appropriate area. Mere stimulation has its value, but will not get one far: If one is merely enthused, without understanding what one is doing, it is unlikely that one will produce anything valuable or therefore creative. A second kind of teaching is training: Training is a matter of drilling someone to respond in predictable ways to inputs. One can train people how to march in the army, or how to respond correctly to factual questions, and so on. Training, like stimulation, does not require the trainee to understand what she is learning. It has some indirect role in teaching for creativity, for competence in some domains may require skills that are best acquired by drilling; but its role is a limited one, since responding in predictable ways tends to make one less creative. A third kind of teaching is education. Education encompasses motivating the student, but it is also essential that one get her to understand what she is doing. In this, it differs from stimulation and training: One can motivate a horse and train it, but one cannot educate it. As we have seen, creativity in some domain requires a degree of understanding of that domain. So teaching for creativity is specifically *educating* for creativity. And education, as its etymology suggests, is a matter of drawing-out someone's abilities and enhancing them, and this fits the constitutive argument well, since we have argued that one can teach people to be more creative and so develop their capabilities. Teaching for creativity is educating for creativity.

6. Heuristics and Mathematics

I have argued that one can educate people to be more creative. However, the argument is likely to encounter skepticism unless some plausible illustrations of this possibility are provided. Moreover, as we saw, one can also argue that creativity can be taught by producing examples of its successful teaching. So I now consider examples of educating for creativity in two disparate domains: mathematics and creative writing. Discussing these examples will also enrich our account of how educating for creativity works and show how its techniques may vary across domains.

George Pólya's *How to Solve It*, first published in 1945, is an exercise in heuristics, the aim of which is "to study the methods and rules of discovery and invention" (Pólya 1990, p. 112). The study of problem-solving encompasses "not merely routine problems but problems requiring some degree of independence, judgment, originality, creativity" (Pólya 1962, p. viii). Pólya gives a structured list of 15 questions or suggestions, subdivided into many others, to help the student solve mathematical problems. They are classified into four stages: understanding the problem, devising a plan to solve it, carrying it out, and looking back to see what one can learn from the solution. His questions are all commonsense ones, but are formulated in a general fashion so that they can be generally applied and could have occurred to the student himself (Pólya 1990, pp. 1–3). They also break down a complex task into simpler ones, so that progress is made easier. The questions or suggestions are linked to or specify heuristic strategies (termed "heuristics" for short). These include drawing a figure, considering special cases, considering extreme cases, generalizing a problem, looking for a related problem, and many more.

For instance, consider the strategy of looking at a related problem if one cannot solve a given one. Since very many problems are similar to the target problem, one should seek relevantly similar problems: problems that have the same unknown or that exhibit a structural analogy with the given problem. Suppose that one has the problem of determining the length of the diagonal running from the one top corner to the opposite bottom corner of a rectangular parallelepiped (for instance, a classroom). The solution is to construct a triangle within the parallelepiped that has as its hypotenuse the diagonal whose length one is seeking to determine, and the base of which runs between the opposite corners of the rectangle constituted by the "floor" of the parallelepiped; one then uses the Pythagorean theorem to determine the length of this diagonal. To help get to this solution, one may either look for a related problem with a similar unknown (the hypotenuse of a right-angle triangle [Pólya 1990, pp. 9–12]) or consider an analogy (between solid and plane geometry [pp. 19–20]).

The role of the questions and suggestions is to connect the problem with the student's formerly acquired knowledge and experience, so that solutions found to be effective in similar situations can be considered in new ones (pp. 33–36). But this spotting of similarities requires detailed knowledge, experience, and judgment: There are no mechanical rules. This is why, as Ian Stewart notes in the foreword to Pólya's book, these heuristic techniques have resisted algorithmic formulation in computer programs (p. xvi). The questions asked are ones that are "typically useful" (pp. 172), but there are no guarantees. Pólya also stresses that the first questions the teacher poses to the student should be the most general; only if students are unable to guess the solution should a more specific question be employed. For instance, in the parallelepiped problem, "Do you know a related problem?" is the best starting question, and "Could you apply the theorem of Pythagoras?" is the worst. The latter gives the game away, and the goal of the questioning procedure is to give the student as great a share of the work as possible (pp. 21–22). Besides employing these cognitive techniques, the teacher needs to motivate the student; problem-solving is also "education of the will" (p. 94). The means of doing this are to stimulate students' curiosity by giving them interesting problems that are within their reach and helping them to solve them by stimulating questions; by so doing, the teacher "may give them a taste for, and some means of, independent thinking" (p. xxxi). The picture of creative problem-solving offered is ultimately of a skill whose effective exercise requires motivation: "Solving problems is a practical skill like, let us say, swimming. We acquire any practical skill by imitation and practice" (p. 4).

These pedagogical techniques illustrate and support some of the general claims that we have made about educating for creativity. Creative problem-solving is a motivated skill that requires imitating the right models, and it employs rules, in the sense of rules of thumb. So, rather than imitation and rule-following being antithetical to creativity, as the imitation and rules arguments claim, their employment is an important part of learning to be creative. The goal of the teacher is to help the students become increasingly creative thinkers, and she does this by building on their preexisting capacities for this kind of thought, which is why questions should stay as general as possible initially and why they should be such that they could have occurred to the students. Indeed, for Pólya, there is no qualitative difference between the mathematics student being educated in this fashion and a research mathematician: The students should solve the problem as independently as they can, albeit with the teacher's guidance; and they learn by doing, for they are given extensive opportunities for practice. Both students and researchers employ much the same set of questions, though the latter have internalized them: Thinking, says Pólya, is a kind of conversation with oneself (p. 133). New solutions to problems are found mainly by seeing their similarity to old solutions and problems, exploiting devices such as analogies (structural similarities) and noticing similar unknowns. Awareness of these similarities requires deep knowledge and experience of the relevant domain, and is not something that can be captured by algorithmic or mechanical rules. Finally, students seek to produce solutions to worthwhile problems, ones that not only are interesting, but also further advance their problem-solving abilities. The student, in short, is being equipped to become a thinker who can make new and valuable discoveries, building on her preexisting capacities, by imitation of good models and practice under the guidance of a teacher.

Pólya's heuristic method has been enormously influential on mathematics education, though it has also been criticized and modified. Alan Schoenfeld, probably the most important mathematical educator to develop Pólya's work, notes that to be taught effectively, Pólya's 24 or so strategies have to be more precisely specified so that students can learn to apply them effectively, with their resulting multiplication into about two or three hundred strategies. For instance, knowing that an effective way to solve a problem is to consider special cases leaves undetermined what counts as a special case in any instance. In the case of mathematical series constructed recursively, the special cases best considered initially are the values of zero and one; but in solving polynomial equations, the special cases are easily factorable polynomials; and so on (Schoenfeld 1987a, esp. pp. 288–290). Schoenfeld also stresses the importance of metacognition for problem-solving—that is, thinking about thinking, a notion adopted from cognitive science. Metacognition includes both cognitive self-monitoring (monitoring one's thinking to discover what works and what does not) and self-regulation (modifying one's thinking in light of what has proved successful). Metacognitive strategies include not pursuing an attempted solution to a problem unless one has thought about it at length (novices typically plunge in with the first attempt at a solution that occurs to them); generating a large number of ideas for solutions before one examines one in detail; asking oneself at frequent intervals whether the attempted solution is going anywhere and being prepared to abandon it if it is not; and so on (Schoenfeld 1987b). Schoenfeld's adjustments to Pólya's methods are more refinements than fundamental changes. As we saw, Pólya stresses the importance of detailed knowledge and experience in applying heuristics, and so would acknowledge that they should vary with context; and metacognitive strategies are a kind of heuristic strategy, though they are ones that take one's thinking processes rather than the problem-situation as their objects.

So there is a rich tradition in mathematics of teaching students how to be more creative in their problem-solving, and there are good reasons to think that heuristic methods are effective. *How to Solve It* has sold more than a million copies and has been widely used in mathematics classes, in both high schools and universities. And Pólya knew what he was talking about: Not only a distinguished researcher, he was also an outstanding teacher, and research mathematicians have testified that his methods capture how they think (Stewart 1990, p. xii). Many studies have confirmed the effectiveness of mathematical heuristics.[12] Schoenfeld (1982) has produced evidence of the success of his particular methods, demonstrating the increased problem-solving abilities of students taking an intensive one-month course in problem-solving, compared to a control group who took a course in structured programming. The best proof of the effectiveness of heuristic methods in the end is to read *How to Solve It*, try its exercises, and see whether it does indeed show one how to be more creative in mathematics. I for one can testify to its success: I first came across the book when studying mathematics at school and found it to be immensely valuable.

However, even if creativity in mathematics is enhanced by heuristic techniques, one may object that nothing general is learned about how to teach people to be creative, so Pólya's work is of limited utility. But, even if this were true, the concession would suffice for our main purpose: A single well-grounded example is enough to establish that one can teach people to be more creative. However, Pólya's techniques do generalize to some other domains, with various adaptations. For instance, many of them apply to practical problems, such as an engineer building a dam, though the unknowns, data, and conditions are likely to be more complex and less sharply defined than in the mathematical case (Pólya 1990, pp. 149–154). But in considering the broadness of the application of heuristic methods, it is more useful, rather

---

[12] Silver and Marshall (1987, p. 277) summarize the results of several studies supporting the success of heuristics, including one meta-analysis of 33 research studies.

than discussing disciplines close to mathematics, to consider one that is very far removed from it. Let us turn to the teaching of creative writing.

7. Creative Writing

Skepticism that one can teach people to be more creative is likely to increase when one turns from the sciences to the arts: In the latter, the idea of innate genius is strongly rooted in popular thought and, as we saw, it was specifically to the arts that Young and Kant applied their innateness claims.[13] This claim, however, stands in tension with the fact that creative writing is now taught extensively in both schools and universities. Many successful writers have emerged from these courses and have testified to their effectiveness. There is also a plethora of creative writing textbooks, which exhibit a good deal of convergence in the advice they offer.[14] Such courses and books are evidently committed to the teachability of creative writing. Malcolm Bradbury, the cofounder of the first U.K. graduate creative writing course at the University of East Anglia, said that its premise was that "students can be taught to write like they might be taught to mend a car" (Bell and Magrs 2001, p. 377).

Creative writing courses are mainly directed at teaching students how to write fiction, but they are not limited to this. They also include teaching poetry, and many poems are not fictional works since they describe real experiences. Such courses also often cover "life writing"—writing non-fictional works such as memoirs, biographies, and even travel writing. So the sort of writing covered encompasses both fictional and some narrative writing. I use the term "writing" to cover both types.

The advice offered ranges from the most general (to avoid perfectionism) to the most specific (real-world locations are especially effective in crime fiction) (Anderson 2006, pp. 22, 93). Regular practice is urged as essential, and the keeping of a writer's notebook in which one can experiment and record is strongly recommended (Anderson 2006, pp. 33–43, Bell and Magrs 2001, pp. 3–19). Wide reading and analytic attention to what is read are encouraged. In addition to imitation and practice, various rules for creative writing are recommended and exercises are provided to develop proficiency with them. Consider a small sample of these rules. First, to help generate new ideas, one should use free association: Write whatever comes to mind without inhibition, perhaps using a visual diagram of linked ideas; or write for

[13] Kant thinks that in science one can educate people to make discoveries, though for this reason he calls those who do so "great minds" rather than "geniuses"; and he holds that this fact explains why science progresses and art does not (2000, pp. 308–309).

[14] As a representative sample, I discuss Anderson (2006), Bell and Magrs (2001), and Maybury (1967). The first is the textbook for an Open University creative writing course; the second is based on the University of East Anglia's undergraduate creative writing course; the third is a school textbook intended for the teaching of 7-to-11-year-olds.

a short period each morning immediately after one has awoken (Anderson 2006, ch. 1, pp. 38–39). Second, one should write about what one knows, and when doing so, record the full range of one's sense experience, being as specific as possible and making as many distinctions as one can in one's descriptions of it (Anderson 2006, pp. 44–55, Bell and Magrs 2001, pp. 20–24, Maybury 1967, pp. 13–14). Third, one should try to defamiliarize one's experience, overcoming one's habitual inattention to much of what lies before one. An exercise to overcome this is to close one's eyes and write what one can recall about the scene in front of one, then open one's eyes and write down at least three items that one did not remember (Anderson 2006, pp. 45–46). Fourth, a way to create interesting characters is by combining elements of several people whom one knows, and to make these characters more interesting, combine some conflicting characteristics (Anderson 2006, ch. 5). Fifth, one should practice seeing similarities between dissimilar things: For instance, develop sustained similes and metaphors in order to view things in new ways (Anderson 2006, p. 35, Maybury 1967, pp. 139–143). Sixth, show, don't tell: i.e., avoid general exposition unless it is necessary to advance the story rapidly, and allow the general to emerge from descriptions of specific people and actions (Anderson 2006, ch. 9, Bell and Magrs 2001, p. 47).

It is striking that Pólya's basic claims about the importance of practice, imitation, motivation, and rules of thumb in creative activity all reappear. Some of these rules are the same: Pólya stresses the importance of seeking similarities and analogies, and this advice reappears in the stress on the utility of comparisons and metaphors. However, many of the heuristic rules are notably different between mathematics and writing. The use of free association in writing contrasts with the more disciplined and focused search for related problems in mathematics. The stress on the importance of attention to the particular and the specific in writing contrasts with the search for the general in mathematics. Problem-finding has a far greater role in writing than in mathematics, since a range of specific problems is established by the state of the discipline in mathematics. While Pólya's list of mathematical questions and suggestions is relatively compact and well ordered, there is a far wider range of questions and rules in creative writing.

The explanation for these differences is to be traced to differences in the subject matter and the values of the two kinds of activities. In mathematics, we value disciplined, logical thought; but in writing, wide associations of thought are valued. Mathematics studies highly general structural relationships, whereas what we seek and value in writing is in good part experience of the particular, including the writer's individual voice. Mathematics aims to discover truths, so its heuristic path is constrained by these; in fiction writing, characters and plots are invented so there is no preexisting fictional world that it tracks. The domain of mathematics is strictly limited to a class of relationships, whereas writing can take as its subject matter anything at all, so its heuristic rules are far more numerous and heterogeneous than those of mathematics. Hence differences in subject matter and values explain differences in the content of the heuristic rules.

The evidence that one can teach someone to write creatively may be disputed. First, "creative writing" courses are misnamed: What is really being taught is a particular genre of writing— mainly fiction. One can doubtless teach elements of the craft of fiction writing, but that does not show that one can teach people to be *creative* in that craft.

However, such courses clearly aim at teaching students how to be creative in fiction (and narrative) writing. Many fictional works are not significantly creative: There are popular, hackneyed romantic fictions that could be, and sometimes are, written according to a rigid template. Learning how to write uncreative fiction is not the goal of creative writing courses. Consider the six heuristic rules listed above. If one writes about what one knows, with attention to the specific and particular, one will (hopefully) not discover that one's life is like a romantic potboiler fiction, so many clichés will be avoided; and we earlier quoted Goethe on the value of close attention to one's experiences for original writing. Likewise, the defamiliarization rule aims to break down habitual modes of perceiving (or of failing to perceive), so that one sees things in a new light. Making extended comparisons is a powerful device for finding hitherto-unobserved similarities, as is the development of similes and metaphors.[15] Free association is a useful device for coming up with new ideas; indeed, some measures of creativity take as their metric the ability to generate remote associations by this method (Mednick 1962). Combining characteristics from several actual people generates new characters. Showing (not telling) forces one to attend to the particular, with all the possibilities of making interesting new observations that this fosters. So creative writing heuristics aim at creativity, and there is reason to think that they are effective.

Second, it may be objected that comparatively few participants in creative writing courses go on to be genuinely creative; most never publish anything. And many people would get nowhere if they enrolled in such courses: One needs talent to benefit from them.

However, recall that our claim is that it is possible to educate people to be more creative, and that is entirely consistent with most participants in these courses not achieving a degree of creativity that would merit publication of their works. Nor is it any part of our claim that everyone in a particular domain can have their creativity enhanced: There are basic requirements if one is to do anything of value in a domain (such as being literate in the case of creative writing), and people vary in their talent, so some will benefit more than others. All this is consistent with the fact that people are educible for creativity.

We noted differences between the heuristics employed in teaching creativity in writing and those used in mathematics; these differences do not threaten the claim that creativity is teachable, but they have some interesting implications about how

---

[15]   On the relation of metaphor to creativity, see Gaut 2003.

one does so. Learners need to practice, to imitate well, to be highly motivated, and to have an ability to see likenesses between dissimilar things in both domains. In writing, one requires sensitivity to particulars and an ability to roam widely in free association, whereas in mathematics, one must attend to general features and engage in a more disciplined search for relationships; so creative ability is realized in somewhat different lower-level abilities in the two domains. In this, it is like some other abilities, such as walking: spiders, dogs, and humans can all walk, but the more specific abilities that realize this higher-order ability are somewhat distinct. Since the numbers of legs differ between individuals of the different species, the more specific coordination and balancing abilities that instantiate the capacity to walk differ too. Analogously, the creative capacity is realized in somewhat different lower-order abilities in the different domains of mathematics and writing. Psychologists debate whether creative abilities are general or domain-specific, examining whether creative ability in one domain correlates with that in another, and whether enhancing someone's creativity in one area increases her creativity in another (for an overview, see Baer 2010). But one can also look at the accumulated practical wisdom of how to teach people to be more creative in different domains, and this shows, as we have seen, that though certain abilities that realize creative capacities are shared across domains, many are also distinct. Likewise, the motivational component of the creative disposition exhibits a degree of generality across different domains: Being hardworking and very motivated is highly advantageous, though not essential, if one is to be creative in some activity. But there are also evidently motivational differences: The creative mathematician is interested in mathematical accomplishments, not creative writing ones. These points support a complex model, which holds that creativity is in certain respects general and in other respects domain-specific.[16] Such a model also demonstrates that the ways in which one educates for creativity should vary among different domains.

8. Conclusion: Philosophy and Creativity

We have argued, then, that one can educate people to be more creative. We considered some objections, the imitation and rules arguments, against the possibility of educating for creativity and argued that they fail. We also saw that, in the practice of enhancing creativity, imitation and mastery of the relevant rules, far

[16] Baer (2010) opts for a complex model, though for different reasons. So does Amabile (1996, esp. ch. 4) in her componential model. Amabile holds that the domain-specific skills all concern competence, rather than creativity, in that domain; in contrast, I am suggesting on the basis of pedagogical evidence that some of the creativity-relevant skills may be domain-specific too.

from being inimical to the development of creativity, form an important part of it. We also developed a positive argument for the possibility of teaching creativity, which depended on showing that creativity can be analyzed into its motivational and ability components, each of which is teachable. Finally, support for the educability claim was provided by showing how creativity can be taught in two very disparate domains, mathematics and writing. We noted the importance of imitation, practice, and heuristic rules in both areas, but also saw that the content of those rules varies a good deal. This shows that the method of educating for creativity should vary somewhat among different domains, depending on the nature and value of the activity concerned; it also supports the theoretical point that creativity is to some extent a domain-specific disposition, as well as possessing some domain-general features.

How do these points apply to philosophical education? Philosophers have written surprisingly little on the philosophy of creativity until recently.[17] They have written even less on the question of how to educate students to be creative in philosophy. Yet most philosophers are not just researchers but also educators, and as a discipline committed to the importance and power of reflection, we ought to consider our own pedagogical practices and how we can teach to nurture creativity in our students.

It should be evident that similar points about enhancing creativity apply to philosophy as they do to other domains discussed earlier. Imitation of good models, practice, and motivation are vital, and heuristic rules have considerable utility. Think of the role of analogy in philosophical creativity, something that can be crucial at even very high levels. Gottlob Frege, for instance, drew deeply on an analogy between formal and natural languages in constructing his philosophy of language.[18] In aesthetics, Kendall Walton's highly influential work on mimesis is grounded in an analogy between children's games of make-believe and representational artworks.[19] There is also a variety of more specific heuristic rules that philosophers frequently employ and that are to a degree distinctive of the domain: for example, searching for counterexamples, particularly by considering extreme, imagined cases (e.g., Twin Earth scenarios); when a claim is threatened by counterexamples or other objections, searching for a distinction such that the difficulties are shown to be consistent with the threatened claim (e.g., distinguishing between conceptions of free action as actions caused by some kinds of mental

---

[17] For a discussion of this neglect and suggestions for remedies, as well as an overview of the literature, see Berys Gaut (2010).

[18] I owe this observation to Michael Beaney.

[19] Walton (2008, pp. v–viii, 63–78) discusses the central role of this analogy in the development of his theory.

states and as requiring a kind of indeterminism); considering the contrary terms when analyzing a concept (e.g., when analyzing creativity, considering the contrary or purported contrary terms: being derivative, destructive, or imitative); and developing theories dialectically by considering a simple, general claim, then subjecting it to criticism, showing either how these criticisms can be refuted or how the theory can be altered or elaborated to meet them (see also Hájek, this volume).

Showing students how to use such techniques is important in teaching them how to do philosophy and be creative in doing so. Motivating them is also vital. This is achieved in part by getting them interested in the questions that are being posed, but merely posing questions ("stimulation" as I termed it) is insufficient to enhance their philosophical abilities if they are not provided with the tools for developing their own understanding of how to answer those questions. Education, in the sense earlier described, is a matter not just of stimulation but also of providing the cognitive means to explore these questions. Nor is this sort of philosophical education something that can happen merely at undergraduate and graduate levels: Children as young as three can learn how to do philosophy, albeit at a simple level, and greatly benefit from an approach that both stimulates their curiosity and exposes them to the use of philosophical techniques like counterexamples and making distinctions.[20]

Philosophers ought not only to reflect theoretically on the question of creativity and its teachability, but should also endeavor to put their theoretical reflections into practice in their everyday educational activities. As the examples of mathematics and creative writing have shown, reflection on the practice of teaching for creativity is a rich source of data for theory construction. Educational practice and theoretical reflection form a virtuous circle when we consider how to educate for creativity.[21]

---

[20] For an application of the heuristic-based approach to teaching philosophical thinking that is grounded on the conception of the teachability of creativity defended in this chapter, see Gaut and Gaut 2011. For empirical evidence that this heuristic-based approach is effective for children as young as three and four, see Morag Gaut 2010. The heuristic approach contrasts with the more frequently employed method of merely asking children questions without providing the fine-grained cognitive feedback that helps deepen their understanding of the philosophical issues addressed.

[21] I would like to thank Sarah Broadie, Elliot Samuel Paul, and Scott Barry Kaufman for their helpful comments on this essay.

References

Amabile, Teresa M. 1996. *Creativity in Context*. Boulder, CO: Westview.

Anderson, Linda (ed.) 2006. *Creative Writing: A Workbook with Readings*. London: Routledge.

Baer, John. 2010. "Is Creativity Domain Specific?" in James C. Kaufman and Robert J. Sternberg (eds.), *The Cambridge Handbook of Creativity*. Cambridge, UK: Cambridge University Press, pp. 321–341.

Bell, Julia, and Magrs, Paul (eds.). 2001. *The Creative Writing Coursebook: Forty Authors Share Advice and Exercises for Fiction and Poetry*. London: Macmillan.

Eckermann, Johann Peter. 1906. *Conversations of Goethe with Eckermann and Soret*, revised ed., trans. John Oxenford. London: George Bell & Sons.

Gaut, Berys. 2003. "Creativity and Imagination," in Berys Gaut and Paisley Livingston (eds.), *The Creation of Art: New Essays in Philosophical Aesthetics*. Cambridge, UK: Cambridge University Press, pp. 148–173.

——. 2009. "Creativity and Skill," in Michael Krausz, Denis Dutton, and Karen Bardsley (eds.), *The Idea of Creativity*. Leiden, NL: Brill, pp. 83–103.

——. 2010. "The Philosophy of Creativity," *Philosophy Compass* 5 (12): pp. 1034–1046.

——. 2012. "Creativity and Rationality," *Journal of Aesthetics and Art Criticism*, 70: pp. 259–270.

——. forthcoming. "Mixed Motivations: Creativity as a Virtue," *Philosophy*.

Gaut, Berys, and Gaut, Morag. 2011. *Philosophy for Young Children: A Practical Guide*. London: Routledge.

Gaut, Morag. 2010. "Can Children Engage in Philosophical Enquiry?" in Barbra McKenzie and Phil Fitzsimmons (eds.), *Exploring Interdisciplinary Trends in Creativity and Engagement*. Oxford, UK: Inter-Disciplinary Press (e-Book), pp. 195–203.

Hennessey, Beth. 2010. "The Creativity-Motivation Connection," in James C. Kaufman and Robert J. Sternberg (eds.), *The Cambridge Handbook of Creativity*. Cambridge, UK: Cambridge University Press, pp. 342–365.

Kant, Immanuel. 2000. *Critique of the Power of Judgment*, trans. Paul Guyer and Eric Matthews. Cambridge, UK: Cambridge University Press.

Maybury, Barry. 1967. *Creative Writing for Juniors*. London: Batsford.

Mednick, Sarnoff A. 1962. "The Associative Basis of the Creative Process," *Psychological Review*, 69: pp. 220–232.

Nickerson, Raymond S. 1999. "Enhancing Creativity," in Robert J. Sternberg (ed.), *Handbook of Creativity*. Cambridge, UK: Cambridge University Press, pp. 392–430.

Perkins, David N. 1990. "The Nature and Nurture of Creativity," in Beau Fly Jones and Lorna Idol (eds.), *Dimensions of Thinking and Cognitive Instruction*. Hillsdale, NJ: Erlbaum, pp. 415–443.

——. 2000. *The Eureka Effect: The Art and Logic of Breakthrough Thinking*. New York: Norton.

Pólya, George. 1990. *How to Solve It: A New Aspect of Mathematical Method*, 2nd ed. London: Penguin.

——. 1962. *Mathematical Discovery: On Understanding, Learning, and Teaching Problem Solving*, vol. I. New York: Wiley.

Schoenfeld, Alan H. 1982. "Measures of Problem-Solving Performance and of Problem-Solving Instruction," *Journal for Research in Mathematics Education*, 13(1): pp. 31–49.

——. 1987a. "Polya, Problem Solving, and Education," *Mathematics Magazine*, 60(5): pp. 283–291.

——. 1987b. "What's All the Fuss about Metacognition?" in Alan H. Schoenfeld (ed.), *Cognitive Science and Mathematics Education* (Hillsdale, NJ: Erlbaum), pp. 189–215.

Silver, Edward A., and Marshall, Sandra P. 1987. "Mathematical and Scientific Problem Solving: Findings, Issues, and Instructional Implications," in Beau Fly Jones and Lorna Idol (eds.), *Dimensions of Thinking and Cognitive Instruction*. Hillsdale, NJ: Erlbaum, pp. 265–290.

Stewart, Ian. 1990. "Foreword," in George Pólya, *How to Solve It: A New Aspect of Mathematical Method*, 2nd ed. London: Penguin, pp. xi–xxx.

Walton, Kendall L. 2008. *Marvelous Images: On Values and the Arts*. Oxford, UK: Oxford University Press.

Weisberg, Robert W. 1999. "Creativity and Knowledge: A Challenge to Theories," in Robert J. Sternberg (ed.), *Handbook of Creativity*. Cambridge, UK: Cambridge University Pres), pp. 226–250.

———. 2006. *Creativity: Understanding Innovation in Problem Solving, Science, Invention, and the Arts.* Hoboken, NJ: Wiley.

Wittgenstein, Ludwig. 1978. *Philosophical Investigations*, 3rd ed., trans. G. E. M. Anscombe. Oxford, UK: Blackwell.

Young, Edward. 1918. *Conjectures on Original Composition*, ed. Edith J. Morley. Manchester, UK: Manchester University Press.

14

Philosophical Heuristics and Philosophical Creativity

ALAN HÁJEK

1. Introduction

They say that anyone of average intelligence and moderate talent can become a strong, competition-level chess player by mastering and internalizing certain heuristics. (Who are "they"? Actually, it was a friend of mine, who said it once. But I believed her.) These are captured by slogans like "castle early and often," "avoid isolated pawns," and so on. They are *chess heuristics*. Analogously, philosophy has a wealth of heuristics—I will call them *philosophical heuristics*—although they have not been nearly so well documented and studied. This chapter is partly an introduction to a larger project of mine of identifying and evaluating philosophical heuristics. I also intend it to be a contribution to the philosophy of creativity: I argue that such heuristics can enhance one's ability to make creative contributions to philosophy.

2. A Working Definition of "Creativity"

I do not have anything especially creative to say about what *creativity* consists in,[1] and defining it precisely is not essential to achieving my goals here. I am happy to take as a working definition one that is almost universally adopted by psychologists, which is focused on creative *products*. A product—an idea or artifact—is *creative* to the extent that it is (a) novel and (b) valuable.[2]

---

[1] The ensuing discussion largely follows Gaut (2010).

[2] To be sure, products are not the only things that may be creative—*people* and *acts* may be as well, but they are mostly not my concern here.

Each condition is apparently necessary. The first condition is obviously so, although we may want to follow Boden's (2004) distinction between *H*-creativity, short for *historical* creativity (nobody else has made the product before), and *P*-creativity, short for *psychological* creativity (the product is new to a particular individual, although it may have been made previously by someone else, unbeknown to the individual). The second condition is also apparently necessary: We hardly deem products that are worthless as creative, however original they might be. To be sure, we may regard some surprising but ultimately unsuccessful leaps of thought as "creative" in some sense; but the scare quotes seem appropriate, this sense being more of a pejorative one, and not my topic here. The condition may still be questioned, however, since we may want to allow for "dark" creativity, the ingenious creation of all-too-successful malevolent products. If so, our discussion is becoming somewhat terminological. Let me simply stipulate that my topic is philosophical creativity *in the good sense*; then the necessity of condition (b) comes for free.

Some philosophers contest the sufficiency of conditions (a) and (b) for creativity (see Gaut 2010). The main source of concern is that a product that is produced by the wrong sort of *process* might meet conditions (a) and (b), but still not count as creative (for example, if someone produces it by pure luck). In section 11, I downplay the importance of the psychological processes that lead to a philosophical product in our judgments of philosophical creativity, since those processes are almost always obscure to us in others and often even in ourselves. And my primary interest is in those products to which we *ascribe* creativity. In any case, the prospect of a wrong sort of process leading to a valuable product in philosophy does not seem to be as live as it is in art, say—a philosophical gem is unlikely to be produced by pure luck, for example. So my focus is on philosophical *products*—philosophical positions, arguments, analyses, counterexamples, puzzles, paradoxes, and so on— however they were produced. That's what we ultimately value. I regard them as valuable to the extent that they advance philosophical understanding, although this too is not essential in what follows.

Identifying philosophical heuristics has been an ongoing project of mine at least in the background, and sometimes in the foreground, for many years. It might help you to understand the project if I tell you some of the things that led me to it. If you are impatient to get to the heuristics themselves, you could skip the following apologia. Once we have met a few of the heuristics and seen them in action, we will be in a position to discuss their relationship to philosophical creativity.

3. Apologia

It all began when I was a graduate student. I had the chance to observe a lot of good philosophers in action, and I wanted to be one of them. Sometimes I was reading their work; sometimes I was seeing them in action in person. Often I had a feeling of wonder at what appeared to be moments of inspiration from these philoso-phers: "Wow! That was impressive." I began trying to figure out if some of their skills were learnable, and to the extent that they were, I wanted to learn them. Over the years, I have found good philosophers repeatedly using certain techniques, perhaps unconsciously much of the time, that *can* be easily learned.

After graduate school, I taught at Caltech for a number of years. I had highly talented students who typically knew little about philosophy for 10 weeks at a time. How was I to convey to my students in such a short time how philosophy is done? Of course, the main thing was to *show* them lots of good instances of philosophiz-ing—to have them read some of the classics and some of the best of the relevant recent literature—and then to get them to philosophize themselves. But that did not seem enough to me.

For consider some other skill—say, skiing. A skiing instructor does not just say: "You've seen people ski well; now do it yourself! Go on: SKI!" Rather, the instructor gives you *skiing heuristics*, breaking down skiing into manageable bits: "Shift your weight to the downhill ski," "keep your hands forward," and so on. Yet in philosophy, we typically just show our students finished pieces of philoso-phy—the classics, the recent literature—and then effectively say: "You've seen peo-ple philosophize well; now do it yourselves! Go on: PHILOSOPHIZE!" I thought we could do better.

So I began to think about identifying manageable techniques in these philo-sophical showpieces. To be sure, the teaching of such heuristics was a tiny part of my courses—they came more as quick asides as we read through the classics or the recent literature. ("Here Hume is using the 'proves too much' strategy," or what have you.) But pointing out the heuristics as they showed up along the way was certainly valuable. And it was fun.

My introductory course on metaphysics and epistemology began with Descartes, and I drew more of my inspiration from him. In my opinion, he got much of good philosophical methodology right, nearly four hundred years ago, in his *Discourse on Method* (1637). He would start with a hard problem, break it down into smaller parts, perhaps breaking them down still further, until eventually he reduced his original problem to a bunch of smaller problems of manageable size, for which he had "clear and distinct ideas." (Of course, he had much more to say about his meth-odology than that!) In my case, the hard problem starts as *doing philosophy*—which is really a set of hard problems: trying to come up with an original philosophical position, or analysis, or argument, or puzzle, or paradox; or trying to come up with a counterexample to someone else's philosophical position or analysis, or trouble for an argument of theirs, or solving a puzzle, or resolving a paradox. (There are other conceptions of philosophy, of course, but I am characterizing the kind of phi-losophy that is of most interest to me here.) The heuristics provide some tools for breaking these problems down into easier sub-problems, and the better they are at doing this, the more useful they are.

For *philosophy is hard.* I feel that I can use all the help that I can get, and I suspect that you can too. The heuristics help in various ways. The first way has an obvious connection to creativity: the heuristics are useful while you are waiting for inspiration to strike. Suppose that you have been beating your head on a problem, waiting for a lightning bolt of brilliance to strike you. I hope it does. In the meantime, some of the heuristics may help you. Or you may have a hunch that there is something wrong with a philosophical position, but you are struggling to nail what it is. Again, some of the heuristics may help. They are also useful when you want to be self-critical. Suppose you have just written a philosophical paper, thesis, or book. It is curiously difficult to be a good critic of your own work, to see problems that might be obvious to someone else; meanwhile, would-be critics are *lining up* eagerly to point them out to you. By somewhat mechanically running through the heuristics, you are more likely to find trouble spots, or ways of improving your position: a counterexample to your view here, an illicit inference that you made there, a way of strengthening an argument here, a way of generalizing your point there, or applying it to a new domain.

More generally, the heuristics provide ways of *making one's implicit commitments explicit.* (Here, "one" may be *you,* or it may be someone else with whom you are engaging.) Sometimes these commitments are unwelcome, and they should force one to rethink the views that led to them; sometimes they are welcome, and one should celebrate them! To be sure, formal and informal logic already provide some safeguards against making illicit inferences, and they may help us make one's implicit commitments explicit. But focusing solely on logic is an overly narrow conception of the ways in which philosophers reason. We have a much richer toolbox at our disposal. My project is to identify far more of our tools.

Caveats:

- There are many distinct abilities that go into making a good philosopher, and I do not pretend to provide heuristics for all of them, or even a tenth of them. As I say, and will keep saying, these are merely *heuristics.* They are not guaranteed to work, any more than avoiding isolated pawns is guaranteed to strengthen your position in a chess game. My project is not one of finding foolproof philosophical algorithms or surefire recipes for philosophical progress—there are none. But the heuristics do tend to work, often enough that I think they earn their keep, and then some.
- The heuristics are no substitute for depth. I am not promising wisdom or profound insight. But I hasten to add that what I offer is not antithetical to them either, and indeed I think it helps rather than hinders progress to such wisdom or insight. Again, compare chess. No chess instruction book is crazy enough to say that you will become a grandmaster once you have learned to castle early and to avoid isolated pawns. On the other hand, no chess instruction book apologizes for recommending that you do these things; indeed, if it didn't, it would be remiss.

Closer to home, mathematics professors explicitly teach their students various techniques for solving problems, and they often unapologetically teach heuristics for proving things (for instance, "When you want to prove something that seems obvious, try *reductio ad absurdum*"), without compromising their students' potential for deep mathematical insights. Still closer to home, teaching our students formal and informal logic provides no guarantee of leading them to wisdom or profound insight, but doing so helps rather than hinders progress to such wisdom or insight. We don't apologize for doing so, and indeed if we didn't, we would be remiss. Again, I regard the heuristics as more tools from the same toolbox.

- Choosing the right heuristic, or the best heuristic, for a given situation usually requires good judgment—and yes, creativity. And having seized upon a given heuristic, there may be many ways in which it can be applied, and again there is a role for creativity here.

Enough talking for now about this exercise in metaphilosophy—enough meta-metaphilosophy (until section 11). It is time to bring on a few of the heuristics. The list I present here is just the tip of the tip of the iceberg; I will settle for seven of them, when as I say, I have hundreds. The ones I have chosen are some of my favorites. Moreover, as we will see, some of them are conducive to "constructive" philosophizing, which might be regarded as especially creative.

Let me begin with an easy heuristic that I think is quite fruitful.

4. Check Extreme and Near-Extreme Cases

4.1. Check extreme cases

Start with a hard problem: Someone proposes a philosophical position or analysis and you are looking for trouble for it, because you suspect that there is something wrong with it. (The "someone" might be you, in which case your job is to find trouble for your own position before someone else generously does it for you.) Try this simpler problem: Look for trouble among *extreme cases*—the first, or the last, or the biggest, or the smallest, or the best, or the worst, or the smelliest, or.... It is a snappy way to reduce the search space.

Even if there are no counterexamples lurking at the extreme cases, still they may be informative or suggestive. They may give you insights that you would have missed by focusing on more run-of-the-mill typical cases.

"Check extreme cases" is a good heuristic, three times over:

- It is often easy to use. Extreme cases of the relevant kind are often easily identified.
- It is fertile. Extreme cases are often troublesome in virtue of being extreme—that is, sometimes problems that could not arise in normal cases can arise at the

extremes. (For example, sometimes it is important that normal cases are "surrounded" by other, similar cases, whereas extreme cases are isolated "loners.")

- We are liable to forget or miss extreme cases, since we tend to live our lives in the midst of normal cases.

To be sure, there will not always be extreme cases of the relevant kind. They often correspond to maxima or minima of appropriate functions. But some functions have neither—for example, those that are unbounded in both directions, or those that approach but never reach upper and lower asymptotes. It is not clear, for example, that we can make sense of Leibniz's notion of "the best of all possible worlds"—it seems that we can imagine better and better worlds without end. (Imagine a sequence of worlds in which there are successively more happy people, or more happy rabbits....) Nor can we obviously make sense of "the worst of all possible worlds." So if our topic is the goodness of worlds, we may not be able to find any extreme cases. No matter; while this heuristic is not universally applicable, it is widely so.

Pólya (1957) notes the value of this heuristic in mathematics. This reminds us that good philosophical heuristics need not be purely *philosophical* heuristics; indeed, it would be surprising if they always were. Some of them are heuristics for good thinking more generally. But I will confine myself to philosophical examples.

4.1.1

Some philosophers regard "every event has a cause" to be a necessary truth. At first, one may wonder how to argue against this claim—where should one start? The heuristic guides the search for a counterexample: Start with extreme events. For instance, start with *the start*. The *first* event is an extreme event: the big bang. There was no prior event to cause it; it surely did not cause *itself*; and it surely was not retro-caused by some later event—so we have our counterexample. To be sure, this presupposes that there was exactly one big bang. As far as I know, this is a respectable presupposition by the lights of current cosmology. But it does not matter if it is not. Whether or not there was the big bang is presumably a *contingent* matter. No necessary truth can settle the matter either way.

4.1.2

Lewis (1986b, p. 213) writes: "Some philosophers wish to believe only in entities that have some causal efficacy." For instance, Armstrong (1989) does not believe in Platonic universals for that reason; some philosophers of mathematics do not believe in numbers and in abstract objects more generally for that reason. Lewis continues: "either they must reject such totalities as the big event which is the whole of history, or else they should correct their principle." Similarly, if we regard the whole of history as an event (the ultimate one), it provides another counterexample to the dictum that every event has a cause.

4.1.3

What is it for *Fs* to be *ontologically dependent* on *Gs*? Here is a very natural analysis: It is not possible for *Fs* to exist without *Gs* existing (see Thomasson 1999). But consider an extreme case of existence: something that exists *necessarily* (not merely contingently). According to this analysis, for any *F* and for any *necessary G, F* is ontologically dependent on *G*. If the number 3 is necessary, then we are all ontologically dependent on it. Now *there's* an unexpected argument for the Holy Trinity!

Relatedly, what is it for a theory *T* to be *ontologically committed* to Gs? Here is a very natural analysis: It is impossible for T to be true without there being Gs. But then, for any theory T and any *necessary* G, T is ontologically committed to G. If God exists necessarily, then atheism is ontologically committed to Him. If numbers exist necessarily, then Field's (1980) nominalism about numbers is ontologically committed to them. Obviously, this does not capture what is distinctive about atheism or Field's nominalism.

4.1.4

According to the von Mises/Church definition (von Mises 1957, Church 1940) of *randomness*, an infinite sequence is *random, with respect to an attribute*, if every recursively selected subsequence has the same limiting relative frequency of the attribute. It is *random* if it is random with respect to every attribute. By this definition, the extreme sequences of outcomes of tossing a coin forever,

> heads, heads, heads,... .
> and
> tails, tails, tails,...

are random. After all, *every* subsequence of the first sequence has the same limiting relative frequency of heads: 1 (the limit of the sequence 1/1, 2/2, 3/3,...). And *every* subsequence has the same limiting relative frequency of tails: 0 (the limit of the sequence 0/1, 0/2, 0/3,...). Similarly for the second sequence. But they strike me as maximally *non*-random sequences.

4.1.5

According to decision theory, you should act to maximize your expected utility: the sum of products of utility and corresponding probability, for each possible state of the world, associated with your action. A gamble with *infinite* expected utility provides an extreme case. Since expected utility is a sum, we are guided to consider ways in which sums can be infinite, and so to consider gambles whose expectations are series that diverge to infinity. The St. Petersburg game is a celebrated example. A fair coin is tossed until it lands heads for the first time. The longer it takes, the better for you. Your rewards escalate exponentially according to the schedule in table 14.1 below.

Let us identify utilities with dollar amounts (or if you prefer, recast the game in terms of utilities directly). The expected utility of the game is

$$(1/2 \times 2) + (1/4 \times 4) + (1/8 \times 8) + \ldots = 1 + 1 + 1 + \ldots = \infty$$

So according to decision theory, you should be prepared to pay any finite amount to play the game once. This seems crazy. In fact, $100 seems too much to most people.

4.2. Check near-extreme cases

Extreme cases can sometimes be dismissed: We might say that we lack trustworthy intuitions about them, or that they are pathological, or even that they are not really cases of the notion in question at all. (All three things have been said about the St. Petersburg game, for example.) So it can be useful to move to *near*-extreme cases instead.

Kenny Easwaran has told me that during preparation for a mathematics competition, he was coached to look at near-extreme cases. For example, if you have to prove a statement concerning all triangles, it may be helpful to see how it would look

TABLE 14.1

First heads on toss number	Probability	Pay-off
1	$\dfrac{1}{2}$	$2
2	$\dfrac{1}{4}$	$4
3	$\dfrac{1}{8}$	$8
$\vdots$	$\vdots$	$\vdots$
n	$\dfrac{1}{2^n}$	$ 2^n$

for a triangle with, say, a 179-degree angle and two angles of half a degree. A truly extreme case might be unhelpful or even impossible—for example, a "triangle" with a 180-degree angle and two 0-degree angles is a straight line, and not really a triangle at all. So try a near-extreme case instead.

4.2.1

von Mises might reply to the all-heads and all-tails counterexamples that they are degenerate cases of random sequences—for example, they are what you get from two-headed or two-tailed coins, and they are sequences as random as such coins could possibly produce. Then consider a near-extreme case:

Tails, Heads, Heads, Heads,... .

It still passes the von-Mises/Church test for randomness, but it still looks highly *non*-random to me, and it is not degenerate. I would say the same of sequences with finitely many tails at places specified by some function, or even sequences with infinitely many tails, spaced progressively farther apart according to various non-recursive functions. Yet they all pass the test.

4.2.2

A popular defensive move in response to the St. Petersburg game is to insist that utility functions must be *bounded*. In that case, there can be no games of infinite expectation. But then consider a truncated, finite St. Petersburg game, with a very high truncation point—say, the game is called off if the first heads has not been reached by 100 tosses. There is a good sense in which this game is like the "extreme" St. Petersburg game, just not as extreme. It still seems that decision theory overvalues the game (at $100). But this problem no longer relies on unbounded utility.

So the heuristic here is two-stage: *First look to extreme cases to spot trouble for a philosophical position; then, retreat to a less extreme case, where the same trouble may still lurk.* To be sure, it may lurk to a lesser degree; but it may also be a more plausible case, and one that may resist some of the defensive moves that may work in the extreme case. This heuristic may also be useful in cases where there are no extreme cases of the relevant kind. Still, there may be cases that we regard as near-extreme, and in which trouble arises.

Having identified trouble for a philosophical position, one should try to go on to diagnose its *source*. The trouble will typically be just a symptom of a deeper underlying problem. The St. Petersburg and truncated St. Petersburg games make vivid the fact that decision theory looks only to the "location" of the distribution of the random variable associated with a given option. It pays no heed, for example, to the "spread" of the distribution, as represented by its variance. If variance (and perhaps higher moments of the distribution) are relevant to choice-worthiness, then these gambles not only provide counterexamples to decision theory; they also enhance our philosophical understanding. And so it goes with counterexamples more generally: Ideally, they do not merely serve the negative function of refuting a particular philosophical thesis; they also teach us positive lessons about some philosophical concept or issue.

5. Death by Diagonalization: Reflexivity/Self-Reference

You can't bite your own teeth, unless something has gone badly wrong for you, dentally speaking. You can't see your own eyes—not directly, anyway—unless something has gone *very* badly wrong for you, optically speaking.

The next heuristic bids us to take a philosophical thesis and to make it refer to *itself*, to plug into a function *itself* as its own argument, and more generally, to appeal to *self-referential* cases. This technique is another handy way of cutting down the search space when you are looking for counterexamples.

Let us take our cue from Cantor's "diagonalization" proof of the uncountability of the reals, or Gödel's proof of the incompleteness of arithmetic, or the halting problem, or Russell's paradox, or the liar paradox. They remind us of the august history of the technique of self-reference; its application can yield profound results.

5.1.1

I begin with a non-philosophical example that is not remotely profound as a lighthearted warm-up. My friend Alan Baker has two (aptly–named) cooking conjectures:

> *Baker's first conjecture: Everything tastes better with either chocolate or garlic added.*

(There's a putative cooking heuristic for you.) This has much prima facie plausibility. But we don't need to look far for two clear counterexamples: *chocolate* and *garlic*.

> *Baker's second conjecture: Everything tastes worse with both chocolate and garlic added.*

And here we can find another clear counterexample: *a mixture of chocolate and garlic*!

5.1.2

Sorensen (1996) opens with this sprightly instance of the reflexivity heuristic:

> Here is a debate I cannot lose. I argue that it is possible to (at least unwittingly) believe the impossible, say, that there is a largest prime number.

The *impossibilist* objects that I am mistaken. Wrong move! By trying to correct me, the impossibilist concedes that I believe a false proposition. The proposition in question (i.e., that impossibilities can be believed), if false, is necessarily false. Thus, the impossibilist would be conceding that an impossibility can be believed (p. 247).

Sorensen is a master of this heuristic more generally. His "Faking Munchausen's Syndrome" (2000) gets my vote for the funniest title in philosophy. (Munchausen's syndrome is a mental disorder wherein those afflicted fake having a disease that they do not in fact have.)

5.1.3

Realism is often stated as a thesis of mind-independence: To be a realist about X is to be committed to the mind-independence of X. But what about realists about *minds*, as most of us are? They are surely not committed to minds being mind independent.

5.1.4

Kim (1982) suggests that an *intrinsic* property is one that can belong to something unaccompanied. Lewis (1999) replies: *Unaccompaniment* is not an intrinsic property, yet it can belong to something that is unaccompanied.

5.1.5

According to the betting interpretation of subjective probability, your degree of belief in a proposition is the price (in cents) at which you are indifferent between buying and selling a bet that pays $1 if the proposition is true, and nothing otherwise. But I have degrees of belief about my own betting behavior—for instance, I am confident that I will not enter into any bets today. This degree of belief cannot be understood in terms of a betting price of mine.

5.1.6

Homework: This puzzle is due to Raymond Smullyan (2000). You can choose one of the following two offers. Which should you choose?

Offer 1. You get $10.

Offer 2. You get $10 if you say something true and something other than $10 if you say something false.

Hint: Offer 2 is *much* better!

The next heuristic is closely related.

6. Self-Undermining Views

It is an embarrassment for a philosophical position if it is *self-undermining*. This can happen when the position itself falls in the domain that it purports to cover. The proponent of the position potentially faces a charge of a kind of philosophical hypocrisy (presumably unintended).

6.1.1

Quine (1951) famously said: "Any statement can be held true...no statement is immune to revision." Stove (1991) asks: is *this* statement immune to revision? Quine's dictum is itself a statement, and as such falls in the domain of statements over which it quantifies.

6.1.2

"Truth is relative, not objective" is an oft-heard slogan in these postmodern times. But someone who says it seems to regard *it* as an objective truth.

6.1.3

There is the story of Putnam, in one of his incarnations, arguing along these lines in a lecture: Either logic is empirical, or it is a priori; but logic is not a priori, since quantum mechanics teaches us that disjunctive syllogism is an invalid argument form; thus, logic is empirical. But as an audience member pointed out, this argument assumes that disjunctive syllogism is valid (see Jammer 1974).

6.1.4

According to the verificationist theory of meaning, the meaning of a sentence is determined by the method by which it is empirically verified, and in particular, a sentence that is unverifiable is meaningless. But it seems that the very statement of this theory is itself unverifiable, and so by verificationist lights is meaningless.

6.1.5

More generally, consider a skeptic about meaning who claims that there is no fact of the matter of what our words mean. What are we to make of the sentences that he or she uses to state the position?

All of the heuristics I have considered so far might be regarded as "negative"—they are strategies for coming up with counterexamples for other philosophers' analyses, or problems for other philosophers' views or arguments, rather than for constructing such analyses, views, or arguments in the first place. Even philosophizing that is "negative" in this sense can be creative—witness Lewis's counterexample to the thesis that we should believe only in entities that have some causal efficacy, if you need any convincing of that. It is original, imaginative, ingenious, illuminating, and compelling; what more could you want? And I have noted that counterexamples may also function positively to illuminate a philosophical concept or issue.

Recall, moreover, that in order for a philosophical product to be creative, it is necessary for it to be valuable. These "negative" heuristics may provide a valuable service in evaluating an existing product—if it survives the threats that they potentially pose to it, this counts in favour of it. For example, if an analysis takes extreme cases in its stride, more power to it. If on the other hand, it succumbs to such cases, then this may prompt philosophical progress—the analysis might be modified to handle the cases, yielding a superior final product. A similar point can be made in favor of the reflexivity heuristic. Think of how fertile Russell's paradox has been as a touchstone to set theory—a creative contribution if ever there was one, albeit "negative."

And if the analysis falls by the wayside as a result, that may still lead to philosophical progress in a way that resonates with a widely endorsed model of creative thinking in psychology. According to the Geneplore model, creative thinking consists of an interaction between two kinds of processes—those involved in *generating* ideas and those involved in *exploring* ideas to assess their potential value, significance, or utility (see Ward and Kolomyts 2010, pp. 94–95.)[3] I will soon present some "positive" heuristics that are tailor-made for the generative phase of the philosopher's creative process. Meanwhile, the "negative" heuristics may be used in the exploratory or evaluative phase, as a way of assessing the positive ideas that one has already generated. To be sure, my focus in this chapter is primarily on creative products rather than on the processes leading to them. But if the heuristics may play a role that psychologists recognize in the processes as well, all the better. And the heuristics need not be used purely negatively; sometimes they may fertilize the imagination, the seed of creativity, leading to more "positive" philosophizing, whatever that might mean.

In any case, let me turn now to some more "positive" heuristics, to the extent that it makes sense to speak this way. I hope that it will be clear how they may foster creative philosophy.

7. Begetting New Arguments out of Old

Arguments are often easily transformed from one domain to another.

---

[3] Thanks here to Elliot Samuel Paul for drawing my attention to the Geneplore model and its relevance to the discussion of creativity here.

7.1. Space ←→ time ←→ modality

Arguments involving space can often be rewritten to create parallel arguments involving time; arguments involving time can often be rewritten to create parallel arguments involving modality; and we can reverse these directions.

7.1.1

Parfit (1984) has an argument for the irrationality of discounting the future that turns on the absurdity of a similar spatial discounting.

7.1.2

Lewis (1993) provides a nice example of space → time → modality transformations of arguments. He discusses Unger's (1980) "problem of the many": an object such as a cloud has various questionable spatial parts—do we count a water droplet at the outskirts of the cloud as part of it or not? But then many aggregates of droplets of various sizes are equally good candidates to be the cloud. So how many clouds are there? It looks like the answer is "many." Or maybe the answer is "none" (each candidate is ruled out by competition from the others). But we don't get the correct answer: "one."

In his discussion of this argument, Lewis shows how to convert it into one involving questionable temporal parts (those parts near the beginning or the end of an object's life), and one involving questionable other-worldly parts.

7.2. Modal notions

Various modal notions are closely related: laws of nature, causation, counterfactuals, chance, necessity, and dispositions. For this reason, we often see parallel treatments of some of them. For example, Hume's theory of causation as constant conjunction parallels the regularity theory of laws, according to which the law that all *F*s are *G*s is simply the regularity that all *F*s are *G*s; this in turn parallels the frequentist theory of chance, according to which the chance of an event type in a trial is simply the relative frequency with which that type occurs in trials of that kind. And arguments against one sort of theory of one modal notion can often be transposed to become arguments against a parallel theory of another one.

Example: According to Hume's theory of causation, whether my hand going in *this* flame caused the pain in *my* hand depends on whether there is a constant conjunction between *other* hands going in *other* flames and subsequent pains in *those* hands. But offhand (sorry!), it seems that causation is a far more localized matter: The sole protagonists are *this* flame and the pain in *my* hand, and whether or not this was a case of causation should be intrinsic to them. Similarly, according to frequentism about chance, whether *this* radium atom has a chance of roughly 1/2 of decaying in 1,500 years depends on whether roughly 1/2 of all the *other* radium atoms in the universe decay in 1,500 years. But offhand, it seems that chance is a far more localized matter: The sole protagonist is *this* radium atom, and its chance of decay should be intrinsic to it.

7.3. Rationality $\longleftrightarrow$ morality

Many problems and theses in theories of rationality can be rewritten as problems and theses for various metaethical theories.

7.3.1

The St. Petersburg paradox for decision theory can be rewritten as a problem for a natural version of consequentialism. Imagine a world in which there are denumerably many people (or other loci of value). Order them and label them by the natural numbers: 1, 2, 3,.... Consider this action: To person 1, give \$2 with probability 1/2; to person 2, give \$4 with probability 1/4; to person 3, give \$8 with probability 1/8;... If we calculate the total utility in the world by summing the expected utilities given to each person, we get $1 + 1 + 1 + ... = \infty$. Then according to a version of consequentialism that regards the moral status of an action as the total expected utility that it accrues, then this action should be judged morally superior to every action that gives with certainty a finite quantity to a finite number of people, no matter how large the quantity and the number are. This seems crazy.

7.3.2

Pollock's (1983) example of the Ever-better wine causes trouble for the principle of rationality that one should maximize expected utility. The longer you wait to open the bottle of wine, the better it gets. When should you open it? We can specify the case so that any time seems to be too soon; yet never opening it is the worst option of all. Now transform this into a moral problem: The longer you wait to administer the Ever-better drug to a patient, the greater it will benefit her. When should you administer it? We can specify the case so that any time seems to be too soon; yet never administering it is the worst option of all.

8. Some Ways to Argue that *X* Is Possible

Why care about what is possible? Because what is possible is relevant to various things that philosophers care about—claims of necessity, supervenience, entailment, validity, equivalence, and conceptual analyses, according to all of which certain things or combinations of things are *impossible*. Moreover, philosophers often deploy thought experiments in support of their positions; when they do so, they typically assume that the scenarios that they have us imagine are in some sense possible.

There are various senses of "possible" (logical, metaphysical, nomological, epistemic, doxastic, deontic, etc.), and the methods for showing that something is possible in the relevant sense vary somewhat accordingly. The first method below for showing that something is possible works for most of them; the later ones are usually targeted at metaphysical possibility, but some of them generalize. Even when they may not be decisive, they may nonetheless provide good guides to what is possible.

Suppose you want to show that something, let's call it X, is possible. (X may be a proposition, or a state of affairs, or a being, or what have you.) There are two components to the claim "X is possible": "X" and "is possible." Accordingly, there are two main ways of arguing for the claim:

1. Begin with some *other suitable property* of X, and infer that X is possible.
2. Begin with *something else*, Y, that is possible and suitably related to X, and infer that X is possible too. (Or begin with two or more things, Y, Z...)

8.1. Begin with some other suitable property of X, and infer that X is possible

8.1.1. Actuality

Actuality implies possibility for most of the modalities,[4] so if you have a good grip on what actuality is like, you have a head start on supporting various possibility claims. And actuality gets surprisingly weird—think of quantum mechanics and special and general relativity.

8.1.2. Positive probability

The next argument form is:

1. X has positive probability.
2. If X has positive probability, then X is possible.
Hence,
3. X is possible.

Different senses of probability will lead to different senses of possibility. If the probability is *objective chance*, then we may infer *physical possibility* (and hence

---

[4] Not doxastic or deontic.

metaphysical possibility). If the probability is *subjective* (of some rational agent), then we may infer *epistemic* and *doxastic* possibility (for that agent).

Example: Quantum tunneling of medium-sized dry goods is physically possible—for example, it is physically possible for you to quantum tunnel to the North Star. After all, according to quantum mechanics, this has positive probability (admittedly tiny), and it is thus possible. And knowing this fact, you should assign positive subjective probability to it (equally tiny, to be sure), and it thus should be epistemically and doxastically possible for you.

8.1.3. Conceivability

The next argument form is:

1. X is conceivable.
2. If X is conceivable, then X is possible.[5]
Hence,
3. X is possible.

Example: Chalmers (1996) argues this way for the possibility of zombies (physical duplicates of someone with a mental life, who lack mental lives).

8.1.4. Arbitrariness

Lewis (1986a, p. 103) observes that "when something seems arbitrary, we are apt to think that it might well have been different." If not-X is apparently arbitrary, that is a reason to think that X is possible.

Example: It is apparently arbitrary that the gravitational constant has exactly the value that it does—so that is a reason to think that it could have been otherwise, against necessitarians about laws such as Shoemaker (1980).

Now that we have some ways of arguing that various things are possible under our belts, we can use them as starting points to argue that various *other* suitably related things are possible. This brings us to our second main way of arguing that X is possible.

---

[5] A clause may need to be added that excludes defeaters. There is considerable controversy over this form of argument, but this is not the place to enter the fray!

8.2. Begin with something else, *Y*, that is possible and suitably related to *X*, and infer that *X* is possible too. (Or begin with two or more things, *Y, Z…*)

8.2.1. Begin with almost-X

1. Argue that almost-*X* is possible.
2. Argue that the small difference between almost-*X* and *X* does not make a difference to what's possible: Either both are possible or neither is.

Examples:

8.2.1.1
Bigelow and Pargetter (1987) argue, contra Lewis (1986a), that it is possible to have "island universes" within a given world that are not spatiotemporally related. They contend that it is possible to have a world with near-islands as parts, joined only by a wormhole. Then they argue that removing this wormhole would make these parts entirely spatiotemporally isolated from another; but the small difference that this makes does not make a difference to what's possible.

8.2.1.2
Adams (1979) argues, contra the identity of indiscernibles, that it is possible for there to be two indiscernible objects that are not identical. Clearly, there can be two *almost* indiscernible spheres that are not identical. Then, just change one of them a little bit (e.g., remove a tiny impurity on one of them) so that they are indiscernible. That change does not make a difference to what's possible.

8.2.1.3
Contra behaviorism, it seems to be possible for someone to have a mental life without any behavioral manifestation of it. Clearly, someone who is nearly completely paralyzed can have a mental life—think of Stephen Hawking. Now imagine this person becoming completely paralyzed. Notice that method 8.1.1 supports the first step: Near-total paralysis with mental life is possible, because it's actual.
    Related:

8.2.2. Extrapolation

Begin with a clear case of possibility, and work by small steps to the case at issue. Someone who doesn't like this kind of reasoning might pejoratively call it "slippery slope" reasoning; but sometimes it is effective. The method is a little different from the previous method, where there was just a single step.

8.2.2.1

Frank Jackson (in conversation) suggested the following argument that it is possible for something functionally like Blockhead—Ned Block's (1981) imaginary computer that can carry on a conversation by having all its responses preprogrammed—to be intelligent. There is no impugning your intelligence if you look up square roots in a table. Now, slowly add more things that you look up; your intelligence is still not impugned. Eventually you get to something functionally like Blockhead.

8.2.2.2

Baldwin (1996) argues that an entirely empty world is possible. Consider a possible world with just finitely many objects. Now suppose each object disappears in turn. Eventually we reach the empty world.

The last two methods of showing that something is possible are fruitful (as I hope the examples have made clear), but they must be handled with care. Beware of "showing too much" to be possible, by sequences of small steps beginning with something that is possible: Y, almost-Y, almost-almost-Y, almost-almost-almost-Y.... If the relevant space is path-connected (in a suitable sense), then we can get from anywhere in the space to anywhere else by a sequence of small steps—but we may cross the line from possibility to impossibility along the way. It is obvious that this method has its limits. In fact, *limits* in mathematics provide good examples of its limits. Think of a function approaching but never reaching an asymptote, the way that $f(x) = 1/x$ approaches but never reaches 0. It is possible for the function to *almost reach* its limit (by any standard for "almost"), but not possible for it to *reach* its limit.

Related:

8.2.3. Interpolation

Show that W and Y are each possible, and that X falls between W and Y on some relevant axis or with respect to some gradable property.

Example: Hume's missing shade of blue is possible. Take two actual—and thus possible—shades of blue, one on either side of the missing shade, and interpolate.

8.2.4. Combinatorialism

Take any things that are separately possible, and put them together in any arrangement permitted by shape and size. According to combinatorialism, the result is possible. So by these lights, it is possible for a pub to sit on the top of Mt. Everest.[6]

---

[6] Or at least a counterpart of Mt. Everest, as Lewis (1986a) would have it.

8.2.5. *Physical symmetry principles*

Physics has various symmetry principles according to which the laws of nature are preserved under various transformations. Start with a physically possible scenario, apply one of these transformations, and voilà, you have another one. For example, take a scenario that is physically possible, time-reverse it, and you get another scenario that is physically possible.

Example: John Norton (2003) imagines a mass sitting on top of a dome. The obvious solution to Newton's equations sees the mass continuing to sit there. But Norton argues that there are also infinitely many other "unexpected" solutions, according to which the mass spontaneously begins moving and slides in some direction or other down to the base of the dome. To see that this is possible, consider the time reversal of one of these trajectories: The mass starts at the base of the dome, and it is projected toward the apex with just the right initial velocity so that it makes it to the apex, but no further. This trajectory is physically possible; hence, so is its "unexpected" time-reversal. Norton concludes that classical mechanics is indeterministic.

More generally, the so-called *CPT symmetry* of physics implies that a "mirror image" of a physically possible world is physically possible—one with all objects having their positions reflected by an imaginary plane (parity inversion), all momenta reversed (time inversion), and all matter replaced by antimatter (charge inversion). This is rich material for thought experiments!

9. Trial and Error

When ingenuity fails you, sometimes you can just run systematically through the relevant cases until you find one that meets your needs.

9.1

Consider the problem of coming up with a single truth function that is expressively complete in the sense that we can express all truth-functional compounds in terms of it. Sheffer (1913) solved the problem: "Not and," otherwise known as the "Sheffer stroke", and its dual "nor", both have this property. Coming up with the problem was ingenious, but solving it need not have been. After all, there are only 16 truth functions to check. So by running systematically through them, it should not take one long to come up with the answer.

9.2

There are various ingenious counterexamples to various theories of causation. According to Lewis's original (1973) theory, c is a cause of e just in case c and e both occur, and there is a chain of counterfactual dependences (of the form "if c_i had not occurred then e_i would not have occurred") linking c to e. In cases of so-called *late preemption*, there are two potential causes of an effect, one preempting the other, and the causal process leading from the preempted cause to the effect is cut off after the successful cause has brought about the effect.

Late preemption cases are ingenious counterexamples to Lewis's theory. But one could find them by a process of trial and error. "Neuron diagrams" or "causal graphs" are two ways of representing causal structures, with nodes representing events or variables, and arrows between them representing relations of causal promotion or inhibition. One could systematically work through various such causal diagrams, starting with simple ones and gradually building up their complexity, hunting for counterexamples. Eventually, one would stumble upon late preemption cases—they require some complexity, but not that much. Similarly, the structure of many of the well-known counterexamples to other theories of causation could be found by trial and error. To be sure, having found the structure, one would then want to find a plausible real-world case that fits it. But that is not so difficult; the hard work is finding the structure that does the job in the first place. A trial-and-error approach removes the need for ingenuity there. More generally, you may find a model or structure that serves your purposes by trial and error; having found it, you may then look for a case that fits it.

And if you have some programming skills, you can write a program to do the hard work of finding the structure for you. More generally, when the search for a counterexample can be reduced to an algorithm, a computer can find it for you. (Not that you need to tell anyone that *that's* how you arrived at it!) In this way, the process of coming up with a creative philosophical product can be partly automated. Examples of using computer tools to discover philosophically interesting technical results can be found in some recent work by Branden Fitelson. His (2008) article shows how one can put to good philosophical use a user-friendly decision procedure for the probability calculus, and an as-yet unpublished manuscript shows how first-order theorem provers and model finders can yield an interesting generalization of Gibbard's theorem that, given certain seemingly plausible assumptions, the indicative conditional collapses to the material conditional.

Sometimes a *hybrid* strategy is the way to go: partly ingenuity, partly trial and error. Sometimes by ingenuity you suspect that a counterexample lurks in a certain relatively small sub-class of cases; then you can just work through them by trial and error (perhaps with the help of a computer).

Sometimes the trial-and-error heuristic can effectively work in tandem with one or more of the other heuristics. For example, you might use the "check extreme cases" heuristic to narrow the search to a few "corners" of the search space, and then go through each of them by trial and error.

The trial-and-error heuristic also serves as a meta-heuristic when you are otherwise at a loss: *Systematically run through the heuristics until you find one that helps you!* It also works internally within some of the multifaceted heuristics. For example, in the previous section, I provided a long list of heuristics for arguing that *X* is possible, through which one could work systematically. You might be pleasantly surprised at what you come up with.

10. Future Projects: Dissertations and Books Waiting To Be Written

When you are looking for a big project to work on, take some big philosophical idea or program and apply it to a new case. The scheme is to apply philosophical system *X* to specific problem *Y*, for suitable *X* and *Y*.

This is the closest I can come to offering a heuristic for producing ground-breaking philosophy. Here the thought is that, rather than merely responding to someone else's agenda, you can do some agenda-setting of your own. And if groundbreaking philosophy when it succeeds doesn't count as creative, I don't know what does. However, even if the results are not quite so dramatic, the heuristic still encourages one to look beyond entrenched ways of thinking about an issue. System *X* is illuminated if a hitherto unrecognized application of it is revealed; progress may be made on recalcitrant problem *Y* if it is approached from a fresh perspective.

10.1

Kantian ethics has been fruitfully applied to a number of moral domains; find one to which it hasn't. Ethical issues concerning new technologies may be promising places to look—for example, privacy issues raised by the new social networks, like Facebook and Twitter. If this turns out to be passé—I'm always behind the curve when it comes to all things technological—I'm sure you can do better yourself.

10.2

Apply the Rawlsian theory of justice to intellectual property—again, some recent innovations may be good places to start.

10.3

The semantic view of theories—as opposed to the "received" syntactic view—has been fruitfully applied to biology (Lloyd 1988) and to physics (Frigg 2006). As far as I know, it has not been applied to various other scientific and social-scientific theories—geology, astronomy, economics, and what have you.

10.4

The so-called *Canberra plan* is an approach to conceptual analysis according to which we identify a folk-theoretical role for a concept to play, and then look to the world for the best player of that role. Various concepts have been Canberra-planned—e.g., mental states (Lewis 1972, Jackson 1998), moral concepts (Smith 1992), and causation (Menzies 1996). I haven't heard of anyone Canberra-planning aesthetic concepts. I must tell my Canberra-based colleagues to get to work on that!

10.5

Various fictionalist accounts of problematic notions have been given—of numbers (Field 1980), unobservables in scientific theories (van Fraassen 1980), possible worlds (Rosen 1990), and morality (Joyce 2005). As far as I know, nobody has yet given fictionalist accounts of various notions in the philosophy of language, such as reference.

10.6

Closest to my heart, Bayesian confirmation theory has illuminated the confirmation of scientific theories (see Howson and Urbach 2006). I believe it has yet to be applied to the confirmation of historical theories.

And so it goes. Some of these avenues might be dead ends—I'm not sure I'd want to take on Canberra-planning aesthetics!—but some might be fertile. And you may well be able to come up with better examples. To be sure, it takes good judgment to work out which of these projects are promising. Not just any pairing of a philosophical system with a specific problem will be fruitful. This heuristic, like any heuristic, can be misused, but then so can calculus and general relativity—that's hardly *their* fault. Once again, using heuristics only takes you so far; it leaves plenty of work for more sophisticated skills. Philosophical *noûs* will not be left jobless just yet.

We are about to change gears. Before we do so, here's a trivia question for you. Which two countries in the world have the letter "x" in their names? I invite you to spend a couple of minutes thinking about this question if need be (take longer if you like). If you can't come up with the answer, so much the better. Soon I'll explain the point of this exercise.

11. Philosophical Creativity and the Heuristics

A number of philosophical heuristics are now before you. Let's step back for a moment and consider their relationship to philosophical creativity.

Most of the philosophers to whom I've spoken about this project of mine applaud it. But a handful of my interlocutors think that it should be discouraged, because they think that I will stifle the creativity of philosophy students. It's as if they have visions of my churning out legions of cookie-cutter students, tongues hanging out, parroting my heuristics at each other: "I refute your position with heuristic #17(ii)"; "No, no, no, I defend it with heuristic #328(c)…."[7] While I am flattered that my project should prompt such Orwellian fantasies, I have far less grandiose ambitions for it.

It would be strange if we had a similar concern about chess heuristics: "Yes, castling early helps—*but don't tell anyone, because it will stifle their creativity!*" Or should we be concerned that Pólya gave generations of mathematics students heuristics for solving mathematics problems, because it *stifled their creativity*? Much as I find it hard to take these imaginary concerns too seriously, I don't take the corresponding actual concerns about my project too seriously.

For starters, even after you have mastered a heuristic, or a hundred of them, there is still so much left over to challenge your philosophical acumen. There is plenty of room for creativity to come in there. Also, as I have noted, there are creative ways of using the heuristics that I offer. ("Castle early" is not like this—there are few ways in which you can execute that advice.) And the talented chess player would discover many of the heuristics for herself eventually in any case—she would notice soon enough the benefits of castling early, and so on. So it is with the philosophical heuristics. But above all, it is not as if the heuristics must *compete* for your limited cognitive resources. Surely you can *both* attend to some of the heuristics on a given occasion, *and* freely exercise your native cunning. Or if you cannot, then by all means attend to the heuristics for just a few minutes and then set them aside so that your native cunning can work unfettered. Let me assure you: *It's not that hard.* Indeed, I will soon argue that the heuristics may promote rather than inhibit creativity.

Another objection that I have heard is that students should have good philosophical intuitions and instincts on their own. To which I reply: *What is this—survival of the philosophically fittest?* If you have such students, or are such a student, more power to you. But what about students who could use some more guidance? More to the point, as I have contended, even the best of us can benefit from internalizing these heuristics. And internalizing them only helps to instill good intuitions and instincts. Once internalized, they can become second nature. This objection makes a mockery of the idea of teaching philosophy. ("Go on: PHILOSOPHIZE!") Also, it isn't at all clear that a student who comes to philosophy with good intuitions and instincts hasn't learned them.[8]

---

[7] I'm reminded of the old joke about the annual comedians' convention, at which the same comedians gather year after year. They all know the same jokes so well that they give the jokes numbers; when they get up on stage, they merely call out numbers, to gales of laughter from their audience.

[8] Thanks here to Katrina Hutchison.

The objection to my project that I take most seriously runs as follows: Sometimes one can be too self-conscious about what one is doing; it can be better just to *do* it, rather than to *think* about doing it. Once when I was playing pool with Andy Egan, he asked me whether I hold my breath while taking a shot. I had never thought about it before, and for the rest of the game I was self-conscious about my breathing, which threw me off my game—which of course was exactly his plan! And John Searle tells a story about when he was a ski racer and had an Austrian coach to whom he turned for advice after a run. The coach's advice was simple: "*Schneller!*" ("*Faster!*"). The coach's point was that Searle should not overthink what he was doing. Instead of being preoccupied with his weight distribution or hand position, he should just *think fast* and let his body do the rest. Similarly, perhaps one should not overthink the doing of philosophy either, but rather get down to *doing* it.

I take this objection seriously, but I think it can be easily answered. For starters, in both the pool and skiing cases, presumably there was at least *some* instruction: There certainly was in the case of my pool-playing, and I assume there was in Searle's case too. So the objection should not be to all teaching of heuristics, but rather to too much of it. (Eating broccoli is good for you, but you should not each too much of it.) Similarly, I advocate using the heuristics, not *overusing* them. Then one should ask to what extent the learning of heuristics interferes with rather than enhances the expression of some skill. It surely does so more in sports than in intellectual enterprises. I can see how concentrating on a heuristic could temporarily slow down more automatic mental processes, but the philosopher hardly needs the split-second reaction times of the ski racer! And as one acquires expertise in an area, explicit rules and reasoning get replaced by automatic processes. When this happens, it becomes easier to perform other tasks concurrently. If using the heuristics works this way, there is still value in recognizing and teaching them, just as there is value in explicit ski instruction. But the expert philosopher may rarely use them explicitly (and her performance might be impeded by using them), just as the expert skier rarely thinks explicitly about how to ski (and her performance might be impeded by such thinking).[9]

But I am being too defensive. Far from being an impediment to philosophical creativity, the heuristics can actually enhance it. For starters, there is some experimental evidence that conscious processes play an essential role in creativity more generally, and even that self-consciously striving *for* creativity is conducive to increasing it—see Baumeister et al., this volume. Moreover, creativity can be enhanced by constraints[10] —poetry writing, for example, is sometimes improved when it is constrained by a given rhyming pattern or meter. The heuristics are not

[9] Thanks here to Angela Mendelovici and Katrina Hutchison.
[10] Thanks here to Uriah Kriegel. See Patricia Stokes 2005.

constraints, of course (it's not as if you *must* apply any of them), but they may *focus* and *guide* the mind much as constraints do.

More importantly, many of the heuristics show how hard problems can be broken down into easier sub-problems, so that *less* cognitive horsepower is required to solve them than the original problems required. The heuristics can work like hints, leading you closer to the solutions you seek. An analogy: Reducing the distance between two pieces of metal makes it easier for a spark to jump across them. A closer analogy: Go back to the trivia question about countries with the letter "x" in their names. How did you do? If you were unable to come up with the answer, try the following. You can be confident that no country's name *starts* with the letter "x," but in any case, let me assure you that this is the case. So any "x" must be preceded by another letter, presumably a vowel. (That's not a guarantee—just a good heuristic.) Now, slowly vocalize the sounds that could be so generated, while scanning your mental country database to check whether any names have these sounds in them:

...ax...,...ex...,...ix...,...ox...,...ux...

Did a spark suddenly jump for you? If not, relax, clear your mind as much as you can, and try again. If still not, don't worry—I'll reveal the answer shortly. You should still appreciate the point of the analogy. Loading up these sounds in your mind brings you slightly closer to your targets, thus making it easier for you to find them.[11] If you have time, you could bring your mind still closer by running successively through all the consonants that might precede these sounds:

...bax...,...cax...,...dax...,...fax...

...bex...,...cex...,...dex...,...fex...

Similarly, if you reduce the "distance" of a philosophical target, it is easier for an idea to spark across to it, easier for you to make the mental leap that will complete it. *The heuristics help get you partway to your targets.* By making your tasks easier, far from interfering with your creativity, the heuristics free you up to exercise it all the more. Far from competing with your creativity, they can *cooperate* with it.

Some of the heuristics have more of a "brute force" nature, which may seem more antithetical to creativity. And yet even that may not in fact be the case. One good chess heuristic is "check every check"—by trial and error running through a relatively small number of potential moves that directly attack your opponent's king, you may hit upon a powerful move. It is a good heuristic twice over: It is easy

---

[11] David Chalmers used this strategy to answer the question successfully at a trivia night we attended.

to use, and checks greatly restrict your opponent's immediate options. Indeed, my trial-and-error heuristic is rather like this chess heuristic. Now suppose a chess player finds what looks like a brilliant queen sacrifice by systematically checking every check. Does that fact diminish the brilliance of the move? Similarly, suppose that you find what looks like a brilliant counterexample to a philosophical view by the exercise of some heuristic. Does that fact diminish the brilliance of the counterexample?

You may reply that brilliance is one thing, creativity another, and that while we may attribute brilliance to a product, creativity is essentially a matter of the process that led to it. A sterner critic of my project might go so far as to say that the very application of a heuristic diminishes to that extent the creativity of the product produced by it.

Let me begin my response with a thought experiment. Consider two philosophers who independently hit upon the same idea, one that we judge to be creative. Then we learn that one of them came to the idea directly by pure philosophical nous, while the other self-consciously applied some heuristic. Should we *withdraw* our judgment that the latter philosopher's idea was creative, while maintaining our judgment that the former philosopher's was? That seems absurd. In that case, we ought to suspend pretty much *all* our judgments of creativity of philosophical ideas. If certain kinds of workings rather than others are essential to an idea's being creative, then we are rarely in a position to make judgments of creativity. Yet we frequently make such judgments. It's as if a version of the Turing test applies to philosophical creativity: We judge philosophical *outputs*, not the thought processes that produced them. If it *looks* creative, we count it *as* creative. How could it be otherwise? We seldom have access to the processes in the case of others, and we often have rather imperfect access to them even in our own case. Again, I am regarding the creativity of philosophical products as a matter of their originality and value, however they were produced. This accords with the definition of "creativity" widely used in psychology—in particular Amabile's *consensual assessment technique*, according to which the best way to measure creativity is by using experts' assessment of the relevant products (see Amabile 1996, especially pp. 33–35.)

Let me summarize. Starting with the philosopher, let's ask: Is she less likely to produce a creative product if she uses heuristics such as I have identified? No—on the contrary, the heuristics make creative breakthroughs easier to achieve by making hard problems easier and by reducing the distance to philosophical targets. Once internalized, they free the mind all the more to exercise the natural light of reason. Starting with the product, let's ask: Is it less creative if someone produced it by following heuristics rather than by a leap of insight? No—insofar as a philosophical product is creative to the extent that it is novel and valuable, it does not matter how it was produced. And if a heuristic that previously was used consciously is internalized and now operates implicitly, then the upshot of its operation may well count as a leap of insight in any case.

But suppose I concede for the sake of the argument that philosophical creativity requires certain mental processes rather than others, *and* that employing my heuristics thwarts those certain processes (two big concessions!). Then I am left wondering why we should care about creativity, so understood. Give me a less creative (so understood) but superior product over a more creative but inferior product, any day. If the heuristics stifle creativity (so understood) but promote first-rate products, more power to them, I say. Whoever thought that creativity was the only thing, or even the main thing, that we value? We should value philosophical understanding and philosophical progress, however they are achieved.

By the way, the answers to the trivia question are Mexico and Luxembourg.

This is just a start. As I have said, I have hundreds more heuristics, of varying degrees of usefulness. I invite you to come up with some of your own; this may prove to be a somewhat creative enterprise in itself! If you care to share them with me, I would be glad to hear about them. Or perhaps you will find a way to use some of my heuristics against me. There—I even managed to finish with a gesture at one of them: self-reference.

Go forth and be creative![12]

References

Adams, Robert Merrihew (1979), "Primitive Thisness and Primitive Identity," *Journal of Philosophy*, 76: pp. 5–26.

Amabile, Teresa M. (1996), *Creativity in Context*. Boulder, CO: Westview Press.

Armstrong, D.M. 1989.*Universals: An Opinionated Introduction*. Boulder, CO: Westview Press.

Baldwin, Thomas. 1996. "There Might Be Nothing," *Analysis*, 56: pp. 231–238.

Baumeister, Roy, Brandon J. Schmeichel, and C. Nathan DeWall (this volume), "Creativity and Consciousness: Evidence from Psychology Experiments."

Bigelow, John, and Robert Pargetter. 1987. "Beyond the Blank Stare," *Theoria*, 53: pp. 97–114.

Block, Ned. 1981. "Psychologism and Behaviorism," *The Philosophical Review*, 90(1): pp. 5–43.

Boden, Margaret. 2004. *The Creative Mind: Myths and Mechanisms*, 2nd ed. London: Routledge.

Chalmers, David. 1996. *The Conscious Mind*. New York: Oxford University Press.

[12] Thanks especially to Elliot Samuel Paul, who gave me incisive and detailed feedback during the writing of this chapter—particularly regarding some of the relevant psychological and philosophical literature on creativity and its bearing on my philosophical heuristics project. I thank him again for inviting me to present a version of this essay to his NYU seminar on philosophy of creativity, and I am grateful to the audience there for further valuable comments. Thanks also to Nick Beckstead, John Bengson, Zoe Drayson, Renée Hájek, Katrina Hutchison, Jeremiah Joven Joaquin, Uriah Kriegel, Dan Korman, Joshua Luczak, Angela Mendelovici, Daniel Nolan, Wolfgang Schwarz, Peter Vranas, and David Wall for many helpful comments and suggestions, and to Ralph Miles for editorial assistance.

Church, Alonzo. 1940. "On the Concept of a Random Sequence," *Bulletin of the American Mathematical Society*, 46: pp. 130–135.

Descartes, René. 1637. *Discourse on Method*; Laurence J. Lafleur (trans.) (1960), *Discourse on Method and Meditations*. New York: The Liberal Arts Press.

Field, Hartry. 1980. *Science Without Numbers*. Princeton, NJ: Princeton University Press.

Fitelson, Branden. 2008. "A Decision Procedure for Probability Calculus with Applications," *Review of Symbolic Logic*, 1: pp. 111–125.

Fitelson, Branden (unpub. ms). "Gibbard's Collapse Theorem for the Indicative Conditional: An Axiomatic Approach."

Frigg, Roman. 2006. "Scientific Representation and the Semantic View of Theories," *Theoria*, 21(1): pp. 49–65.

Gaut, Berys. 2010. "Philosophy of Creativity," *Philosophy Compass*, 5(1): pp. 1–13.

Howson, Colin, and Peter Urbach. 2006. *Scientific Reasoning: A Bayesian Approach*, 3rd ed. Chicago: Open Court.

Jackson, Frank. 1998. *From Metaphysics to Ethics: A Defence of Conceptual Analysis*. Oxford, UK: Clarendon Press.

Jammer, Max. 1974. *The Philosophy of Quantum Mechanics: The Interpretations of Quantum Mechanics in Historical Perspective.*New York: Wiley-Interscience.

Joyce, Richard. 2005. "Moral Fictionalism," in Mark Eli Kalderon (ed.), *Fictionalism in Metaphysics*. Oxford, UK: Clarendon Press: pp. 287–313.

Kim, Jaegwon. 1982. "Psychophysical Supervenience," *Philosophical Studies* 41: pp. 51–70.

Lewis, David. 1972. "Psychophysical and Theoretical Identifications," *Australasian Journal of Philosophy*, 50: pp. 249–258.

Lewis, David. 1973. "Causation," *Journal of Philosophy*, 70: pp. 556–567.

Lewis, David. 1986a. *On the Plurality of Worlds*. Oxford, UK: Blackwell.

Lewis, David. 1986b. *Philosophical Papers*, vol. II. Oxford, UK: Oxford University Press.

Lewis, David. 1993. "Many, but Almost One" in Bacon, John (ed.), *Ontology, Causality and Mind: Essays in Honour of D. M. Armstrong*. New York: Cambridge University Press.

Lewis, David. 1999. *Papers in Metaphysics and Epistemology*. Cambridge, UK: Cambridge University Press.

Lloyd, Elisabeth. 1988. *The Structure and Confirmation of Evolutionary Theory*. Princeton, NJ: Princeton University Press.

Menzies, Peter. 1996. "Probabilistic Causation and the Pre-emption Problem," *Mind*, 104: pp. 85–117.

Norton, John. 2003. "Causation as Folk Science," *Philosophers' Imprint* 3, no. 4 (November), www.philosophersimprint.org/003004/.

Parfit, Derek. 1984. *Reasons and Persons*. Oxford, UK: Oxford University Press.

Pollock, J. 1983. "How Do You Maximize Expectation Value?" *Nous*, 17: pp. 409–421.

Pólya, George. 1957. *How to Solve It*, 2nd ed. Princeton, NJ: Princeton University Press.

Quine, W. V. O. 1951. "Two Dogmas of Empiricism," *The Philosophical Review*, 60: pp. 20–43.

Rosen, Gideon. 1990. "Modal Fictionalism," *Mind*, 99: pp. 327–354.

Sheffer, H. M. 1913. "A Set of Five Independent Postulates for Boolean Algebras, with Application to Logical Constants," *Transactions of the American Mathematical Society*, 14: pp. 481–488.

Shoemaker, Sydney. 1980. "Causality and Properties," in Peter van Inwagen (ed.), *Time and Cause*. Dordrecht, NL: Reidel.

Smith, Michael. 1992. *The Moral Problem*. Oxford, UK: Oxford University Press.

Smullyan, Raymond M. 2000. *Forever Undecided: A Puzzle Guide to Gödel*. Oxford, UK: Oxford University Press.

Sorensen, Roy. 1996. "Modal Bloopers: Why Believable Impossibilities are Necessary," *American Philosophical Quarterly* 33(1): pp. 247–261.

Sorensen, Roy. 2000. "Faking Munchausen's Syndrome," *Analysis* 60(2): pp. 202–209.

Stokes, Patricia. 2005. *Creativity From Constraints*. New York: Springer.

Stove, David. 1991. *The Plato Cult and Other Philosophical Follies*. Oxford, UK: Blackwell.

Thomasson, Amie. 1999. *Fiction and Metaphysics*. Cambridge, UK: Cambridge University Press.

Unger, Peter. 1980. "The Problem of the Many," *Midwest Studies in Philosophy*, 5: pp. 411–468.

van Fraassen, Bas. 1980. *The Scientific Imag*. Oxford, UK: Oxford University Press.

von Mises, Richard. 1957. *Probability, Statistics and Truth*, revised English ed. New York: Macmillan.

Ward, Thomas B., and Yuliya Kolomyts. 2010. "Cognition and Creativity," in James C. Kaufman and Robert J. Sternberg (eds.), *The Cambridge Handbook of Creativity*. Cambridge, UK: Cambridge University Press.

INDEX

abstractions: and metaphors, 165–66
Adams, Robert Merrihew, 305
adaptive originality, 250
Africa, 202, 207
Amabile, Teresa M., 134, 283n16; consensual assessment technique of, 314
Amadeus (Shaffer), 141
American Psychological Association, 4–5
animal kingdom, 200; as agent-neutral, 202; apes, insight behavior among, 204; Australian butcher birds, 202, 205; bower birds, 202, 205; escape behavior, 201; New Caledonian crow, 203; pretense behavior in, 213, 220
Arab Horseman Attacked by a Lion (Delacroix), 81
Archimedes, 151, 235
Aristotle, 3, 142, on virtuous acts, 128
Armstrong, D. M., 293
art: artistic genius, and Kant, 3–4, 6–7, 12, 68, 248, 267; classic art: v. romantic, 94–95; as creative process, 7; creativity, as expression of, 7; philosophy of, 7
artificial grammar learning (AGL), 43
artificial intelligence (AI): autonomy, 236–37, 242; creativity, 11–12, 224, 226; emotions, 240–41; novel sensor, 231; as transformational, 230–32. *See also* computers
The Art of Thought (Wallas), 150
Ashbery, John, 71–72
astronomy, 249
As You Like It (Shakespeare), 105
"Auf dem See" (Schubert), 88–89, 99
autobiography, 106–7

Bacchae, 151
Bach, Johann Sebastian, 159, 162–63, 167
Bach, Kent, 31
Bacon, Francis, 141
Baensch, O., 84
Baer, John, 283n16

Bain, Alexander, 12, 247, 251–52; Bainian tradition, 248
Baker, Alan, 297
Baldwin, Thomas, 306
Bargh, John, 187, 196
Barry Lyndon (Thackeray), 48
Bate, Jonathan, 40
Baumeister, Roy, 10, 216
Beerbohm, Max, 39
Beethoven, Ludwig van, 94, 96, 154, 163, 167
Berlioz, Hector, 92, 97
Bevington, David, 40
Bickerton, D., 205
Bigelow, John, 305
biological evolution, 227, 234
biology, 249, 253
bipolar disorder. *See* mental illness
Blackburn, Simon, 9–10, 48n25
Blake, William, 134
blind-variation and selective-retention (BVSR), 257; blindness, 251–52; creativity, 12–13, 247–48, 251–53, 258–59; developmental experiences, 256, 259; dispositional traits, 256, 259; ideational variations, 251–52, 255; primordial thought (primary process) v. conceptual thought (secondary thought), 255
Bliss, Henry, 249
Block, Ned, 306
Bloom, Harold, 120
Blume, F., 93
Boden, Margaret, 11, 18, 21–23, 126, 127n2; historical and psychological creativity, distinction between, 163, 199, 289
Bono, Edward de, 265n1
Borges, Jorge Luis, 164, 164n13
Bradbury, Malcolm, 280
Brand, Myles, 31
Breton, Andre, 234–35
Brideshead Revisited (Waugh), 76
Bristol, A., 219
Bronowski, Jacob, 28–29

319